Far Eastern Politics
in the Postwar Period

Far Eastern Politics
in the Postwar Period

❈❈❈❈❈❈❈❈❈❈❈❈❈❈❈❈❈❈❈❈❈❈❈❈❈❈

by

HAROLD M. VINACKE
University of Cincinnati

New York: Appleton-Century-Crofts, Inc.

PRINTED IN THE UNITED STATES OF AMERICA

Preface

❋✳❋✳❋✳❋✳❋✳❋✳❋✳❋✳❋✳❋✳❋✳❋✳❋✳❋✳❋✳❋✳❋✳❋✳❋✳❋

THE TITLE of this study is designed to indicate its limitations in both time and space. From the geopolitical point of view, it is limited to the Far Eastern area. During the nineteenth century and the first quarter of the twentieth century the Far East was generally considered to include only the Manchu Empire (China), Korea, and Japan. Russia developed a territorial position in the Far East, as thus delimited, but as a European power moving into Eastern Asia. Similarly, Britain, France, Holland, Portugal, Germany, and the United States came into the area from the West, some establishing extensive interests in the countries referred to, and some also establishing colonies on its periphery in Southeast Asia. Thus the northern area limits were viewed as established at the Amur River and the southern continental limits at the southern frontier of China, where the colonial area of southeast Asia began.

Japan, however, in the second quarter of the twentieth century, came to envisage the Far Eastern area as including also the colonial countries of southeast Asia, Indonesia, and the Philippines. Japanese argued that the enlarged area, including China, could be integrated under Japan's direction and control and could live a largely self-sufficient life, virtually independent of the rest of the world. Thus the attempt was made to bring into being the Greater East Asia Co-prosperity Sphere, at the cost of loss of independence for China and Thailand which, with Japan, were the states which had successfully resisted absorption into Western imperial systems; and at the expense of the Western states which had established themselves as colonial powers. The result of the Japanese attempt at conquest was failure. But in that attempt, and as a conse-

v

quence of its failure, a new set of political relationships was established which necessitated and justified the extension of the conception of the "Far Eastern" area much beyond the original limits. The failure of the attempt brought into being the Republic of Indonesia and started a chain of events in Indochina and Malaya which placed those countries in a different position with respect to Far Eastern politics. The Philippines and Burma also entered the postwar period as independent Far Eastern states.

The widest extension of Japanese power during World War II brought most of Burma within Japan's Co-prosperity Sphere and thus within the Far Eastern area, if it be viewed as co-terminous with the region which the Japanese government thought could be organized and administered as a geopolitical entity. Burma also became independent as a consequence of the war, although this was actually more rapid extension of prior movements toward that end in British policy. Nevertheless, it is questionable whether Burma should be viewed as part of the extended Far East. Its political orientation has been westward, toward India, rather than eastward. Within the prewar British system, this orientation was confirmed with the early oganization of Burma as a part of India. In spite of the separation before the war, and despite Burma's attainment of independence since World War II, the movement has been toward the development politically of a closer working relationship with India, Pakistan, and Ceylon than with the countries which are viewed and which view themselves as within the Far Eastern area. Burma is included in this study, however, as a part of the Far Eastern region, but as distinctly a peripheral country rather than an integral part of the Far East. India, on the other hand, is viewed, as are the United States, the Soviet Union, France, and Britain, as an outside power with an interest in shaping events within the Far Eastern area along lines satisfactory to itself, rather than as a country which because East Asian is Far Eastern.

From the point of view of time, the study is focused on the years since the Japanese surrender. No limited period of history, however, can be properly treated as if it were self-contained unless the primary purpose is the presentation of a sequence of events. Thus for purposes of understanding the politics of the postwar period, it has been found necessary to reach back into the war and the prewar periods, even where the connections had been violently and apparently completely broken. This has been the case, for example, with respect to the establishment of the Communists in power in mainland China, as well as for purposes of understanding the new nationalism that has been a force of primary importance in China as well as in the countries of Southeast Asia. The attempt has been made, however, to deal with the past only as essential to the present.

Since the restriction in time is to the present, another set of limitations has to be recognized. These grow out of the fact that the subject matter is current and much of it controversial. Lacking the perspective and the documentation which time alone can give, dependence for accuracy of treatment has to be placed on objectivity of analysis. The reader will have to judge the success of the author in maintaining this essential objectivity.

The author is deeply indebted to several friends for their kindness in reading, criticizing, and offering suggestions regarding various parts of the manuscript at various stages; Dr. Amry Vandenbosch in connection with the chapter (13) on Indonesia; to Dr. John M. Maki, in connection with the first two chapters; to James J. Dalton, in connection with the chapter (14) on Philippine politics; to John Everett, Jr., and William K. Braun, who had sections of the manuscript tried out on them and who assisted with the preparation of the bibliography; the author is especially grateful to Dr. Stanley K. Hornbeck for his kindness in reading and criticizing the entire manuscript and offering suggestions which led to its improvement in general as well as in many particulars. While gratefully acknowledging this indebtedness, the author well knows, and would emphasize, that he is entirely responsible for the substance and the details of the presentation of postwar politics in the Far East.

H. M. V.

University of Cincinnati

Contents

✳✳✳✳✳✳✳✳✳✳✳✳✳✳✳✳✳✳✳✳✳✳✳✳✳✳✳✳✳✳

ix

Illustrations

❀✻❀✻❀✻❀✻❀✻❀✻❀✻❀✻❀✻❀✻❀✻❀✻❀✻❀✻❀✻

(*between pages* 242-243)

War in the Pacific: U. S. Carrier Force Strikes Wake Island in 1943 (Triangle Photo Service)

Peace Commission at Yenan, 1946. Left to right: Gen. Chou En-lai, Gen. George Marshall, Gen. Chu Teh, Gen. Chang Chi Chung, and Mao Tse-tung (Wide World Photos)

United States 7th Infantry Occupying Seoul, Korea, 1945 (Wide World Photos)

Russian Occupation Troops in Pyongyang, Korea, 1947 (Wide World Photos)

Ho Chi Minh, President of Viet Minh (Eastfoto)

Premier Chou En lai Opening the First People's Congress, 1954 (Eastfoto)

U Nu, Prime Minister of Burma, and Mao Tse-tung (Eastfoto)

Ichiro Hatoyama, Prime Minister of Japan (Japan Public Information and Cultural Affairs Bureau)

President Syngman Rhee of Korea (Wide World Photos)

President Soekarno of 7th Republic of Indonesia (Courtesy of the Embassy of Indonesia)

Chiang Kai-Shek, President of Chinese National Government (Wide World Photos)

Operation "Castor" During the Defense of Dien Bien Phu (French Embassy Press and Information Division)

xi

Defensive Operation in Viet Nam (French Embassy Press and Information Division)

Ceremony Marking the Independence of Indonesia (Courtesy of the Embassy of Indonesia)

Bandung Conference of Asian and African States, 1955 (Eastfoto)

MAPS

Far Eastern Politics
in the Postwar Period

Introduction

❉❈❉❈❉❈❉❈❉❈❉❈❉❈❉❈❉❈❉❈❉❈❉❈❉❈❉❈❉❈❉❈❉

WESTERN IMPERIALISM IN EASTERN ASIA

THE FORCES IN conflict in the Far East during the past century have
been traditionalism and western modernism, imperialism, and nationalism. The purpose of this study is to describe and analyze this conflict
in its contemporary or postwar phase. By the mid-nineteenth century
European states had brought India and all of the countries of Southeast Asia except Siam under their control. As colonies, those countries
represented the Western outlook and interests in the Eastern world and
for a long time had political significance as such rather than as independent factors in Far Eastern politics. This was the case until the
colonies began, at different times and with differing tempos, to seek to
throw off the external imperial control. Thus India, despite its size, had
political importance in the area before 1945 mainly as a factor in the
shaping of British policy. What was true for India was even more true
for Burma and Malaya, in the British imperial system; for the Netherlands' East Indies; and for French Indochina. For decades there was
acquiescence in what had been, in effect, a transfer of power from
native sovereigns to foreign rulers.

It was only as the Western idea of the national state was gradually
introduced that nationalism as a political force began to challenge
imperialism. And, in the countries referred to above, it was only after
World War II that nationalism became strong enough as an organized
force to compel recognition of independence and thus to enable the
countries which gained it to define a relationship with others in terms
of their own purposes and interests. In other words, for the full

1

century before 1941 the active participants in Far Eastern politics were Britain, Holland, and France, based territorially upon their colonies, and the United States, Germany, and Russia rather than India, Burma, Malaya, Indonesia, the Philippines and Indochina. From the end of 1941 until 1945 European imperialism was replaced by that of Japan as the stimulus to nationalism. Thus nationalism developed as reaction against colonialism and imperialism. In this respect it was defensive in nature.

This was also true in the case of those countries in the area which were either wholly or partially successful in maintaining themselves against Western imperialism. In Siam, however, other considerations than defense against Western imperialism were involved in the nationalist emphasis. Siam was enabled to maintain its sovereignty, independence, and integrity not because nationalism gave it strength but because of its buffer position between British and French dependencies. Its nationalism, as it expressed itself in the 1930's, was anti-Chinese in stimulus and expression. The presence of influential Chinese minorities in Siam and in the other countries of Southeast Asia (or of Indians, as in Burma) supplied an incentive for nationalist defensive agitation, in addition to that provided by Western imperialism.

Korea also had its development shaped, although differently, by its relations with China and with Japan. As of the middle of the nineteenth century, Korea viewed itself as being under Chinese suzerainty. Under pressure to end its hermit-like seclusion, it first entered into external relations on the basis of a treaty with Japan which was concluded in 1876 as between two independent states. This led to a struggle within Korea between two factions, one supported by China and the other by Japan. The Chinese-supported faction stood for traditionalism; that supported by Japan for change. The issue was finally joined directly between China and Japan in the war of 1894-95, and was resolved in favor of Korean independence. Severing the bond of Korea to China did not, however, definitively establish Korea as an independent state. Rather, it inaugurated a series of moves designed to transfer the connection from China to Japan.

The principal subsequent challenge to Japanese ascendancy in the Korean peninsula was made by Russia. This threat was decisively dispelled by the terms of the Treaty of Portsmouth which terminated the Russo-Japanese War of 1904-5. As a consequence of victory Japan was enabled to proclaim Korea a protectorate, which it did in preference to assisting it to an effective independence. And finally, in 1910, the very appearance of independence was lost when Korea was made a Japanese colony. Between 1876 and 1905 Korea was a problem country rather than an independent participant in Far Eastern politics. Between 1910 and 1945 it was neither participant nor problem except as it was a factor in the development and application of Japanese policy. But during the years from 1876 to 1945, just as was the case in Southeast Asia, nationalism developed in Korea as a reaction to imperialism. The fact that Korean nationalism came into being as an expression of hostility to the imperialism of an Asian rather than a European state is noteworthy, but not as distinguishing nationalism there from similar manifestations elsewhere.

JAPAN AND WESTERN IMPERIALISM

The rise and fall of the Japanese empire is treated in the first chapter of this study. Here, however, it must be noted that Japan itself entered into relations with the Western states under conditions accepted only under pressure. Those conditions, as embodied in treaties, unilaterally restricted Japan in the exercise of its sovereign powers. Not only were designated ports and special areas within them opened to the trade and residence of foreigners but, through extra territoriality, Japan lost jurisdiction over foreigners. As a result of the imposition of the conventional tariff system the Japanese government lost control of customs' levies on imports and exports. Domestic control of the monetary system was lessened through treaty stipulations for the introduction and free exchange of foreign coins and for the right to export Japanese coins.

The justification for the imposition of treaty limitations lay in the possibility that Japan would use its power over foreigners and over foreign trade so as to restore the pre-treaty condition of seclusion and nonintercourse; and there was the further consideration that the Japanese legal and political order was so different from the European as to raise doubts of the ability or willingness of Japan to establish a reasonable position of security of person or property for foreigners. But, regardless of the justification of these treaty provisions at the time of their imposition, it soon became clear that, in the absence of reciprocity, they debarred Japan from participating in international relations on a footing of equality with the "treaty powers." As Japanese leaders carried through an internal program of political, economic, and military modernization it became apparent that the original justifications had lost their validity. Nevertheless treaty revision was resisted by those Western states which found themselves important beneficiaries of the system until Japanese power had been developed to the point where the views of the Japanese government on such matters could not be disregarded.

JAPANESE INDEPENDENCE

The point of emphasis within Japan in the second half of the nineteenth century was on the creation of economic and military strength sufficient to enable the country to assert its independence and develop its foreign policies on a footing of legal and political equality with other states. Thus its initial preoccupation was with treaty revision. This goal was attained by the end of the century because of internal changes which removed the justification for the restrictions of the early treaties, and because, in the process of reorganization, the country had developed the power of resistance which it had lacked in 1854. Thus actually the Japanese government concerned itself with development of power to enable national policy to be implemented.

The importance of state power did not have to be learned by the Japanese as it did by the Chinese. Japanese traditional conceptions of the nature and purposes of the state and of government were similar to those carried to Japan from the West, while those of China were quite different. The dominant class, the Samurai, originated as men-at-arms. The Shogun, who had displaced the emperor as the secular head of the state, was in the beginning the head of a purely military organization called the Bakufu, which translated literally as "camp office." The authority of the Tokugawa Shogunate was established within Japan by military means. The more than two centuries of internal peace under the Tokugawa was also the period of Japan's seclusion and thus of freedom from external influences and pressures. This long period of internal and external peace resulted from the successful organization of power so that it did not need to be exerted directly by military means. By the middle of the nineteenth century, however, this very situation had made it possible for the feudal lords who had been subordinated to the central authority of the Shogun to find suitable grounds for the overthrow of the Tokugawa. This justification was found in the historic conception of the Imperial Institution as the rightful center of temporal as well as spiritual power.

The conception of the unity of the nation under its traditional Imperial head, was advanced as the proper alternative to a system of division of the country into clans, and of Japanese into men of Satsuma, Choshu, Hizen, Fujiwara, and other clans ruled over by the Tokugawa. Lack of national unity due to clan divisions and to the existence of two centers of power (the Emperor with spiritual functions and the Shogun with temporal power) was revealed as a source of weakness when Japan, the state, was forced to change its policy from that of seclusion to that of intercourse with other states. The external pressure for change was exerted at a time when the basis and nature of the existing organization of power was under question, and it re-enforced the internal argument in favor of a restoration of power to the Emperor.

The new regime, which proclaimed itself to be national as well as imperial, removed the internal barriers which separated groups of Japanese from one another. It then sought out the sources of strength of the Western states and acted (as some say by imitation) to develop those sources for itself. Traditionalism immediately manifested itself in the primary emphasis put on the organization of a national army and a national navy. These were organized, however, in a non-traditional way, since the use of arms was not restricted to the governing class, the Samurai. This made possible the development of the Western-style national army. Nevertheless traditional lines of authority were preserved, since the control of the armed forces remained with an officer class drawn from the former Samurai.

The Restoration of Meiji (1867-68) made possible the creation of a state, in the Western meaning of the term, through the destruction of the traditional feudal order. This was accomplished initially through the transfer to the central government of the clan registers of land and of people. This brought the people, as Japanese, into allegiance to the government of Japan, transferring their loyalty from clan leader to Emperor as head of the state. This transfer, furthermore, made it possible for a system of national taxation to be developed to replace the tradition feudal contributions for support of government. But it was military power, applied against the Tokugawa in the War of the Restoration and against the Samurai when they rebelled in 1877, which effectively established the new national order.

The organization of military power along new lines gave an effective instrument for the suppression of internal dissent. The removal of grounds of dissent, however, was accomplished with the establishment of a concensus among the leaders of the new Japan concerning the political organization of the state under the Emperor. This agreement on an acceptable governmental system was registered with the promulgation of the Meiji constitution of 1889, under which Japan was governed until the fundamental revision of 1947. The Meiji constitution, while it organized authority largely along traditional lines, introduced innovations, such as the House of Representatives, through which the support of the people could be sought and secured. This emphasized the idea of the state as being national and thus gave it greater strength in time of emergency.

The real strength of the new Japan, however, resulted from the development of the national economy along Western, and thus non-traditional, lines. Here again the traditional reasserted itself in one important particular. It was under the auspices of government that economic development occurred. The foundations had to be laid, in any event, through governmental planning of the tax and fiscal system; through action creating a stable currency system; and through creation of a national system of banks. The government also took the initiative, and assumed some of the risks involved, in the introduction into Japan of Western methods of production. As its experiments became successful the government encouraged and assisted private capitalists to assume direction of the national economy, although in close continuing association with the government and governmental institutions. Thus there came into being the modern Zaibatsu—the great family industrial empires—which controlled the national economy in intimate relationship with the government.

The industrial economy which was in process of creation by the end of the nineteenth century was essential to the support of a strong modern military establishment. But meeting the requirements of the new military establishment, especially in time of war, also applied a stimulus, and gave direction, to economic development. The population increase which began to be appreciable after the third quarter of the nineteenth century also stimulated change in economic emphasis from agriculture to industry. By the end of the First World War Japan had established itself as one of the major industrial and military powers of the world.

As a result of military and political reorganization Japan had acquired by 1895 sufficient strength to assert successfully a position of legal equality with Western states. This was signalized with the attainment of the goal of treaty revision. Almost concurrently it was made evident that Japan was militarily more powerful than its continental neighbor, China, against which it waged war successfully over the question of Korean independence. Within a decade it had again demonstrated its military power, this time against Russia in Manchuria. From that time its energies were no longer directed toward the establishment of national independence in the political sense. That had been won. National power continued to be built, however, and it was utilized for purposes of national expansion to secure the resources and markets deemed essential to the national economy. Thus Japan became a competitor with the other builders of territorial and economic empire in the Far East. It entered the competition at a moment when the "other builders," all but Russia, had lost or were losing their zeal for "empire."

CHINA, THE FOCAL POINT OF IMPERIALISM

It was China, however, which was the real focal point of imperialism in the Far East during the late nineteenth and early twentieth centuries. The initial interest of the West was in the opening of China to trade. To bring this about force had had to be employed and treaty terms, which served as the prototype for the early Japanese treaties, were imposed. Thus China as well as Japan had its "unequal treaties" which it sought to disregard in the nineteenth century and to revise and terminate in the twentieth century. Termination was finally accomplished only after nationalism had become a determinative force in China and the Nationalist Party (the Kuomintang) had come into power in 1928.

By the end of the nineteenth century the steps taken to open China to Western intercourse had changed into a competitive movement among the Western states to acquire economic or political control of all or portions of the Manchu Empire. Russia secured boundary adjustments which took from China the territory north of the Amur and east of the Ussuri rivers (1858-60). France added Tongking in 1884-85 to its other Indochinese dependencies; in 1886 China recognized Britain's position in Burma; and in 1895 Formosa was ceded to Japan and Korean independence was acknowledged. Finally, following the first Sino-Japanese War, the Western powers divided much of China into spheres of "interest" or of "influence."

It was only at this point that China began to concern itself seriously with questions of reform. The second half of the nineteenth century, to be sure, had been marked by internal convulsions of which the most significant was the mid-century T'ai P'ing rebellion. But even that major uprising was undertaken in the traditional context of dynastic change. It had the effect of seriously weakening the Manchus but not the traditional Chinese system. The dynasty itself had been preserved partly through Western assistance, partly because of the inner weaknesses of the T'ai P'ings, and only partially because of its ability to bring organized military power to bear against the rebels.

In the traditional Chinese thinking those who concerned themselves primarily with the physical instruments of power were viewed as barbarians. Thus the military were placed at the bottom of the social scale in contrast with traditional Japan where the Samurai constituted the ruling segment of society. As a result the Chinese reaction to the use of superior force by the West differed from that of the Japanese. Until the end of the nineteenth century there was in China no serious concern with the organization of military strength along Western lines. Protection of the country was sought through the playing-off of one Western power against another rather than by reform in the interest of national self-defense.

BEGINNINGS OF NATIONALISM IN CHINA

Trade with the non-Chinese world increased, but through an exchange of China's traditional domestic production against Western manufactured goods rather than as a result of internal changes in the methods of production. As a result of the expanded trade, new wants were developed which could only be satisfied through increased imports. Trade consequently created dependence rather than serving to strengthen the foundations of national independence. The desired safeguarding could be achieved only through modernization of the national economy along Western lines. This was resisted by the Chinese until after 1900, and then was undertaken under a measure of Western pressure, applied first competitively and then co-operatively. Transport began to be modernized with the building of railroads and roads and finally the establishment of air transport. Steam power was introduced for navigation on the Yangtze River and in coastal waters during the late decades of the nineteenth century and its use extended in the first decades of the twentieth. Currency reform was undertaken and the foundations were laid for a modern national banking system. And modern industry began to be developed, first of all in the treaty ports and by foreigners; and then by Chinese, in and beyond the security provided in the International Settlement at Shanghai and the foreign concessions there and elsewhere.

Western ideas had begun to be introduced into China during the late nineteenth century, mainly through missionary educational enterprise. Without sponsorship from the upper Chinese social and political levels, however, "Western learning" penetrated the country slowly until after 1905, when the Manchu government not only undertook educational reform but encouraged and assisted its subjects to go abroad for purposes of study. Even so, in a country the size of China, where life was lived in reasonably self-contained peasant villages not intimately connected with one another through communication facilities, the dissemination of new ideas which went counter to the traditional could not take place overnight. As the new ideas took root, however, and as economic change came to be connected in the public mind with foreign domination, a nationalism which was above all a reaction against Western pressures began to express itself in revolutionary terms.

The first revolutionary expression was anti-Manchu. It conformed to the traditional Chinese view that the ruling dynasty had responsibility for the protection of the country and the welfare of its people, a responsibility which the Manchu rulers no longer were discharging either in the conduct of foreign or domestic affairs. Furthermore, since the dynasty came from outside China proper and thus was non-Chinese, responsibility for the failures of the immediate past could be transferred ideologically from the Chinese themselves to the alien rulers, on the theory that they had proved deficient as rulers because they were alien. With the success of the anti-Manchu movement in 1911, however, the Western idea of a republic and of parliamentary government was seized upon as offering a workable alternative to the alien dynastic rule.

The revolutionaries succeeded in overthrowing the Manchus and in replacing monarchy with a republican system. They failed, however, in their attempt to replace authoritarian with parliamentary government. Within less than three years, the first President elected, Yuan Shih-k'ai, had displaced Parliament and the Cabinet responsible to it, as the center of authority. He was able to do this because the people were accustomed to personalized government, because he was given financial support by the Western powers, and because he had at his command effective political and military forces. After his death in 1916, the only effective national authority disappeared and the country fell apart politically along traditional provincial and local lines. Local and provincial "war lords," supported only by military power, struggled with one another to extend their control over as much of China as possible. In this struggle many of them sought and secured open or covert support from foreign powers, bringing about an association between northern warlordism (militarism) and imperialism.

The second revolutionary upsurge was nationalist in a deeper and broader sense than the antidynastic, anti-Manchu movement which established the republic. Between 1911 and 1924 the idea of China as a territorial state to be defended, as well as a culture to be preserved, had begun to penetrate the country. Events of World War I were significant in this respect. Some of these events were: the Japanese penetration of Shantung, traditionally a province of China, the state, as contrasted with Manchuria, the domain of the Manchus, to which the Chinese provincial system was extended only in 1907; the threat to the independent state in the Japanese Twenty-one Demands of 1915; the nature of China's participation in World War I itself, which gave large numbers of Chinese a greater knowledge of the forces moving in the Western world, and at the same time lessened Chinese fear of Western power because of the revelation of Western division; the dissemination of the Wilsonian principle of the right of self-determination of peoples; the failure of the Allies to support China against Japan at the Paris Conference; and the Russian Revolution, followed by the proclaimed renunciation by the Soviet government of imperialism as a policy. Each of these developments produced a reaction in China which strengthened the cement of nationalism.

Related to this was the forcing of the scholar class out of the country's officialdom as a consequence of warlordism. This stimulated the intellectual "renaissance" movement and a "student" movement broke down the barriers between the educated class and the people, and gave those who were the traditional leaders of the country an opportunity to re-enter politics as leaders of the people rather than as officials speaking for a remote governmental authority.

The debasement of government into a system of ruthless exploitation of power for personal advantage, which northern militarism had brought about in China by 1923-24, gave an internal focus for the nationalist revolution. The refusal of Western capitalistic states to give recognition and support to Sun Yat-sen as a claimant for power, coupled with their apparent determination to maintain the privileged position within China which was symbolized by the treaty-port system of foreign residential areas, gave it an anti-imperialistic focus. Anti-militarism and anti-imperialism thus gave purpose to the revolution. But the nationalist revolution was accomplished by military means and with the employment of nontraditional techniques of organization. In the process of winning the victory, those means came to be accepted by the National Party (the Kuomintang) as ends in themselves. The Nationalist victory, however, was not complete and definitive. The National Government continued to have to use its energies and resources to combat hostile elements both within and outside the Kuomintang in order to attain the objective of complete unification of China under a central government. Of those hostile elements the strongest and most effective in its resistance was the Communist Party in China, a branch of the Comintern.

The struggle of the Kuomintang against the Communists was complicated by the conflict between Chinese nationalism and Japanese imperialism, which entered upon its decisive phase with the Japanese action at the Marco Polo bridge in July of 1937. Thus the conflict between nationalism and imperialism, especially in China, was a major theme of the overture to World War II which in its course and outcome shaped the developments of the postwar years in the new Far East.

The Rise and Fall
of the Japanese Empire

❋❋❋❋❋❋❋❋❋❋❋❋❋❋❋❋❋❋❋❋❋❋❋❋

POSTRESTORATION JAPAN

POSTWAR POLITICS in the Far East have been shaped by the rise and fall of the Japanese Empire. In 1845 Japan was a small feudal state, composed of the four islands of Honshu, Kyushu, Shikoku, and Hokkaido. Those islands were then inhabited by an estimated thirty-three million people. By the end of 1942 the imperial superstructure erected on this national foundation included: Formosa and Korea; Manchuria and Inner Mongolia; the coastal provinces of China; the countries of Southeast Asia; the Netherlands East Indies; the Philippine Archipelago and such Pacific island groups as the Kuriles, the Marshalls and the Marianas. As a consequence of defeat in World War II, however, Japan was reduced to its earlier territorial limits, although its population had more than doubled.

Aside from its territorial aspect, the Japan of 1945 had been moved a long distance from the traditional ways of a century earlier. Forced into a renewal of contact with the world in the 1850's, Japan's rulers undertook a drastic program of political and economic reorganization directed toward the creation of a national polity with the elements of strength essential to self-preservation and to national expansion. The political reorganization undertaken had been substantially completed by the end of the nineteenth century with the erection of a new constitutional structure, the formulation of new law codes, and the creation of a modern army and navy. The modernization of Japan's political, military, and legal systems had been carried so far by 1894 that it became expedient for the dominant Western states to agree to revision of the terms of relationship established in the first treaties of intercourse. Thus Japan entered the twentieth century on a footing of legal equality with the Western states in the conduct of its foreign relations.

During this same half-century the government of Japan undertook to lay the foundations for a modern economy through improvement of communications, currency reform, and the institution of a modern banking system. During the first quarter of the twentieth century an imposing industrial structure was erected on these foundations. In this, as well as in the laying of the foundations, the Japanese governing bureaucracy played a leading role, assuming responsibility for the development of national power sufficient to enable national purposes to be realized.[1]

PRESSURES TOWARD IMPERIALISM

As military, political, and economic power was built up the rulers of Japan showed an intention to use state power for more than purposes of territorial defense. An initial determination was shown to establish title to territory which had been in some sort of relationship to Japan in the historic past, as in the case of the Ryukyu Islands, the Southern Kuriles, and Saghalin. Except for Saghalin, Japanese title to these islands had been successfully asserted by the end of the nineteenth century. As for the exception, the Japanese government had given up its claim to Saghalin in exchange for a clear title, against Russia, to the southern Kuriles. Thus by 1895 Japan, territorially, had been extended beyond the four home islands. It may be argued that Japan's policy toward Korea also expressed this historical interest since the Korean peninsula had been successfully invaded and held for a time by Japan at an earlier period.

Whether or not Korea is so viewed, the initial nineteenth-century expansionism of Japan was in the nature of an outward territorial thrust designed to push the frontiers to be defended, as far as possible, away from the Japanese islands. From this point of view, Korea came to be portrayed as "a dagger pointed at the heart of Japan." Defense of Japan was associated with making sure (1) that no other power held the dagger and could thus use it for purposes of attack on Japan, and

[1] A more detailed summary of internal developments is given in the introductory chapter. See pp. 3-7.

(2) that finally Japan itself should hold the dagger. Since China was accepted as the sovereign power in Korea, its controls first had to be eliminated. This was accomplished when China accepted Korean independence as one of the terms of the Treaty of Shimonoseki (1895) which terminated the first Sino-Japanese War. That treaty also extended the territories of Japan to include the island of Formosa. The attainment of the second objective with respect to Korea, however, had to be postponed until after Japan's victory over Russia, which had become a competitor for power in both Korea and Manchuria in the decade after the termination of the Sino-Japanese War of 1894-95. Victory in the Russo-Japanese War of 1904-5 enabled a protectorate to be proclaimed in 1906. This paved the way for the incorporation of Korea as a colony in the Japanese Empire in 1910.

That Manchuria as well as Korea was envisaged as an area of territorial and political interest to Japan was also clearly indicated as early as 1895, when the Japanese government demanded, as one of the conditions of peace, that China cede the Manchurian Liaotung promontory to Japan. This was conceded by China but Japan was immediately faced with a demand by Russia, France, and Germany that the territory be returned to China. This Japan did because of realistic perception of its inability to maintain the position sought against superior power. But it should be noted that this restraint enforced on Japan came from application of European rather than Chinese or Asian power.

This "Three-Power" intervention and its aftermath marked out the limits within which Japan would have to plan and confine its expansion. Although by the end of the nineteenth century Japan had developed sufficient military strength to overcome the resistance of other Far Eastern states to its contemplated encroachments on their territories, it lacked the power to overcome the resistance of Western states standing in its way in competition for dominion within the Chinese Empire. The rivalries, suspicions, and fears among the European states themselves, however, enabled Japan to advance its own interests with the support of some Western states against others. Thus Japan sought and secured support against Russian imperialism in Manchuria from Britain and the United States, both of whom were seeking means, short of military action on their part, of limiting Russian expansion southward in the Far East. Subsequently, it was the alliance of 1905 with England, and agreement with Russia on mutual support in their respective spheres in Manchuria, which enabled Japan, over objections

from the United States, to consolidate and extend its position in South
Manchuria which had been won through the war against Russia. And it
was the circumstances of World War I, involving a withdrawal of
European power from the Far East, which gave Japan sufficient assurance to begin to move from Manchuria into China south of the Great
Wall. Even so, the Japanese government found it constantly expedient
to move within limits set by the need for the support of some European
states against others which had competitive interests with Japan or with
one another in China. While constantly advancing toward those limits
(or beyond them with a view to determining where they were fixed)
successive Japanese governments consistently showed a retractive ability when confronted with what they concluded was superior power,
provided they were not compelled to move back to the point of departure. In considering forward movement or retraction, the Japanese
government's evaluation of the probability of European resistance,
and not the defensive power of China, actually set the limits of possible
expansion. This probability had to be measured in terms of the circumstances of European or world politics rather than the Far Eastern
interests of the European states. This was the case even after Japan's
own power had been built up to a point where it was unmatched among
the Asian states.

As Japan became seriously concerned with the construction of
empire in Manchuria and China after 1905, and especially after 1914,
the imperialist motivation became increasingly economic, rather than
military and territorial, thus being differently related to the maintenance of national security. Two developments within Japan itself help
to explain this shift in emphasis. One was the increase in population to
the point where it presented a serious problem. The other was the
accelerating industrialization of Japan.

One solution of the population problem, which at best could only
be viewed as a temporary one, was through emigration. But the Western countries which were most attractive to Japanese settlers quickly
erected barriers against the immigrant from Asia. The "Great West"
of the Far East itself was Manchuria. Unfortunately, from the point of
view of Japan, entrance of settlers into Manchuria was controlled by
China, which also determined the conditions under which title to land
could be acquired. Consequently, when Manchuria was opened to
settlement during the twentieth century it was China rather than
Japan which supplied the largest stream of migrants who remained as

settlers. Until the 1930's the Japanese government was unable to overcome the obstacles to Japanese settlement which Chinese policy erected. Actually, however, the first economic interest the Japanese government expressed through the acquisition of rights in Manchuria was not that of settlement of its excess agricultural population. What Japan acquired from Russia in South Manchuria in 1905 by the terms of the Treaty of Portsmouth, aside from the Kwantung leased territory, which had a strategic and commercial-outlet importance, was the South Manchurian Railway, and rights of exploitation of mineral and other resources for purposes of operation of that railway and appurtenant enterprises in the Railway Zone. Exploitation of the resources of Manchuria came to be viewed as of primary importance to an increasingly industrialized Japan. And industrialization of Japan seemed to offer the most effective way of sustaining the increased population.

As Japan shifted its economic base from agriculture to manufacturing, whether to solve the population problem or to add to the country's national strength, there was an increasing awareness of the economic insecurity resulting from dependence on others who determined the conditions of Japan's access to essential raw materials and also to markets for its manufactured goods. Because of its resources in coal and iron and other key raw materials, Manchuria came to be sloganized as Japan's "economic life-line," just as Korea, in geopolitical terms, had been accepted as the "dagger pointed at the heart of Japan." Neither slogan, however, actually set any real or natural limits to Japan's expansionism. The extension of the frontier to Korea gave Japan concern with developments in Manchuria. Since the position which had been established in Manchuria was viewed as essential to the protection of Korea, the same reasonable interest in North China and Mongolia expressed itself in relation to defense in Manchuria, and so on into and beyond the countries of Southeast Asia. Similarly as Japan's industrial needs grew it was realized that they could not be met in Manchuria. The "Manchurian life-line," once it was in Japan's hands, came to be replaced by the conception of a Japan-Manchukuo-North China economic bloc as essential to Japan's economic security. As economic security became more and more postulated in terms of the largest possible economic self-sufficiency, the objective, as world conditions seemed to bring it within reach, grew into the creation of the "Greater East Asia Co-Prosperity Sphere." After 1939 this objective had replaced the reliance on Manchuria or even China as the "economic life-line" in Japanese imperial planning.

The creation of the "Greater East Asia Co-Prosperity Sphere" as the objective of Japan's foreign policy gave an economic content to the slogan of "Asia for the Asiatics." The basis of this idea, even in Japan, was not limited to economic considerations. But one long step would have been taken toward its realization if the regional economy could be detached from the world economy. This Japan attempted on the assumption that, by reorganization of distribution, the several countries in the area defined could attain reasonable self-sufficiency in foodstuffs and raw materials. Japan, as the processing center, in control of access to the essential raw materials produced in the area, could, it was felt, meet area requirements for manufactured goods.

JAPAN'S EXPANSION AND EUROPEAN POLITICS

This gradual enlargement of Japan's imperial objectives to the point of attack on the colonial position of the European powers was intimately related to the circumstances of European politics. As expansion was undertaken, with movement south from Manchuria to North China, from North China to Central and South China, and then to Southeast Asia it was a progression from the countries of least developed interests of the Western states toward those of the greatest importance. Because of the world situation it was possible to time the steps taken so as to encounter the minimum Western resistance as the area of greatest interest was approached.

Western resistance to Japanese expansion into China during the 1930's was, on the whole, only diplomatic and verbal. It was effective in slowing the pace of the Japanese advance to the extent that it suggested the possibility of forcible resistance by Western powers. But the probability of effective military resistance, even when it was threatened, steadily lessened, especially as Britain found itself confronted with the possibility of loss of power in Europe and the Mediterranean. As the conflict in the Far East developed, furthermore, the objective of the Western powers became that of safeguarding their established interests within the extending area of Japanese political control in China rather than that of preventing the extension of such control. By analogy, viewing China as a Japanese sphere of influence, the Western states sought, as had the United States against Europe in the negotiation of the "Open Door" agreements in 1899, to find a formula acceptable to Japan which would keep the door into China open for purposes of trade, while committing Japan to respect already vested rights and interests. The preservation of the "Open Door" had been immediately found by the United States to necessitate respect for the maintenance of the territorial and administrative integrity of China. Thus there had been a shift in emphasis, from that of concern for trade rights to that of respect for the integrity of China. This broader formulation of American policy, made in 1900, became treaty doctrine with its acceptance at the Washington Conference of 1921-22. The return by the United States, Britain and other states to the attempt to have vested interests respected by Japan within its enlarged sphere of interest indicated at least temporary acceptance of the principle of limitation of the concern of the state solely to the protection of its own national interests through the exercise of national power in place of concern for the territorial and administrative integrity of the state threatened with extinction.

SECOND SINO-JAPANESE WAR

Developments of the decade 1931-41 clearly indicated that the limits of Japanese expansion would be set only at the point where Japan met with effective military resistance. During that decade it became increasingly clear that China would continue to exist as an independent sovereign entity, even with restricted territories, only if it was able to preserve itself. The only result of reliance on the system of collective security, organized through the League of Nations, was a commitment of the League states not to recognize the new position in Manchuria which Japan had gained by force after 1931. Even this commitment was established mainly through the initiative of the United States, not a League member but seeking through the League to maintain the Nine-Powers Treaty of Washington and the Pact of Paris. Thus the legality of the Japanese gains in Manchuria remained in question but the three Northeastern provinces were in fact detached from China by Japan.

As North China became the focal point of Japanese activity, the pressures of Chinese nationalism, coupled with a stronger domestic position than had existed in 1931, caused the National Government of

China in 1937 to undertake direct military resistance to Japan. The course of the resulting undeclared war indicated that China did not itself have the power to set the limits to Japanese expansion. Limited direct assistance was received from the outside in the form of credits for the purchase of essential military equipment and other war supplies. Indirect assistance was lent to China's military position as long as Japan felt unable to direct its operations against Western rights, interests, and establishments in China. Thus the International Settlement, and the French Concession at Shanghai, the foreign Concessions at Tientsin, the International Settlement at Amoy, and the British Crown Colony of Hongkong, with the Kowloon leased territory near Canton, were fixed Western positions in China which Japan had to avoid in military operations unless it was prepared to discount the possibility of the intervention of foreign powers. This situation assisted China in maintaining its military position in the Shanghai-Nanking area until December, 1937, when the seat of government was moved inland from Nanking to Hankow. The occupation of Canton, together with the fall of Hankow in October, 1938, did not bring Chinese resistance to an end, but it did entail the transfer of the capital further inland to Chungking. This signalized the reduction of the area of effective authority of the Chinese government to the southwestern provinces of China, since the area marked out as the Northwest Border Region was under the control of the Chinese Communist Party. Thus, in effect, from 1939 until 1945 China was divided into three parts: (1) Japanese-occupied China, extending eastward to the sea from a limit roughly marked on the west by a line dropped from Peiping through Hankow to Canton; (2) "Free China," made up of the southwestern provinces under the (Kuomintang) National Government; and (3) Communist China in the northwest. From the point of view of the war, of course, the Kuomintang and the Communists were in alliance against Japan, both parties theoretically acting within the organizational framework of the National Government. The authority of that government, however, could not be effectively exercised within the Communist-controlled area.

Japan, however, did not have, or did not apply, sufficient power to bring about the capitulation of the National Government. It had not, consequently, been able to re-establish peace with China on conditions satisfactory to itself by 1945.

One reason for the refusal of the Chinese government to accept

Japanese proposals for termination of the war was Chiang Kai-shek's belief that protracted resistance would force Japan into actions which would finally bring about intervention in defense of their interests by Britain, the United States, and other Western states. This finally occurred, but not in direct consequence of the displacement by Japan of Western interests in China. It was as the area of Japanese activity was enlarged, from China into the Greater East Asia area, bringing the future status of the colonial territories of the European states and the United States into question, that the Chinese finally saw Western power brought into play against Japan.

The military situation in China provided a reason for the extension of Japanese operations into the immediately adjacent area of French Indochina and for the initial pressures exerted on Britain in relation to Burma. If the connections between China and the outside world could have been completely severed the capitulation of the Chinese government would ultimately have been brought about with the minimum of military force. Even without formal capitulation, if interior China had been completely cut off from contacts with the non-Japanese world its government would have been forced to act as if it were within the Japanese political and economic orbit. By 1939, except as there was limited smuggling trade and movement of persons between "free" and "occupied" China and beyond, the avenues of movement of goods and persons had been limited to air contact between Hongkong and Chungking; to rail access from Hanoi in Indochina to Kunming in Yunnan province; to road travel from Burma to Kunming, and into the Northwest from the Soviet Union.

The first Japanese moves beyond China to sever communications of other powers with it were taken with the occupation of the island of Hainan and the Spratly islands. This put Japan in a position to cut communications between Singapore and Hongkong, and gave it a strategic position in relation to Hanoi. In 1940, after French power in Europe had collapsed under the German offensive, the Japanese government demanded of France supervisory rights in Indochina to prevent any supplies from reaching Chungking through Indochina; and also air bases in Indochina from which Japan could operate more effectively against the supply route into China from Burma. Earlier in the year, pressure against the British had brought about a temporary closing of the Burma road itself. Subsequently Japan demanded and, secured from the French Indochinese regime the right to move troops against China across Indochina and to use Indochinese airports for war purposes.

JAPAN AND THE WEST: 1937-41

The comparative ease with which Japan was able to move against the French was a direct reflection of the power situation in Europe. Such reflection had previously been shown in the timing of the Japanese attack on Canton in disregard of the British position at Hongkong, followed by pressure on the British position at Shanghai and Tientsin. These moves were made after the demonstration of Britain's weakness in Europe at Munich and immediately thereafter. During 1939 Japan had hesitated to attempt a complete consolidation of its position within "occupied" China at the expense of the Western states, largely because of the measure of solidarity among the Western powers, including the United States, developed for protection of their interests in China against Japan. Where particular European interests could be separated from the complex of Western interests, the Japanese government found that it could threaten attack and bring about acceptance of its demands. For this purpose Japan sought to distinguish between the material interests of Britain and France, on the one side, and those of the United States, on the other. Thus German successes in the war in Europe tempted Japan to act on the assumption that, if it could avoid areas of particular American interest, it could move rapidly and against minimum resistance toward the creation of the Greater East Asia Co-Prosperity Sphere.

In the development and application of its policy of expansion Japan obviously had to consider the effect of its actions on the Soviet Union as well as on the United States, Britain, and France. The Soviet government had reluctantly acquiesced in the loss of its position in North Manchuria with the forced sale to Manchukuo of the Chinese Eastern Railway. It had, however, successfully resisted the further northern and western extension of the Japanese position. And the U.S.S.R. had been an important source of military supply for the Chinese National Government during the years 1937-39, maintaining direct contact with the National Government rather than with the Chinese Communist regime for that purpose.

As early as 1936, however, Japan had entered into an agreement with Germany which gave some assurance against a Russian attack. This agreement, called the Anti-Comintern Pact, while directed in its terms against the activities of the Communist International rather than the Soviet Union, established working political relationships between Berlin and Tokyo of a friendly sort. It also gave Japan a basis of association with Italy, similarly committed subsequently against the Communist International. This collaboration of Japan with two strong European powers on the basis of hostility to communism helped to immobilize the Soviet Union and to weaken the vigor of its opposition to Japan as that country enlarged its continental objectives after 1936. While the agreement fell short of a military alliance it did, nevertheless, present the Soviet Union with the possibility of a two-front war if Russia should carry its support of China to the point of hostilities with Japan.

The Soviet-German Neutrality Pact of September, 1939, however, would have relieved the pressure in the West on the Soviet Union and enabled it to follow a more vigorous policy in the Far East if war had not broken out in Europe in 1939. That war did create an opportunity for the extension of Soviet territory in the Baltic area in eastern Europe. But that, in turn accentuated the underlying German distrust and suspicion of the Soviet Union and had the effect of maintaining the two-front dilemma for the latter.

Japan's military objectives were completely shifted from the north to the south of China in 1940, but not because of fear of Soviet resistance in the north. It was rather because German successes against the Dutch, the French, and the British in 1940 had apparently opened the way to a relatively easy move into Southeast Asia. Soviet strength had been shown to be great enough for vigorous defense, to be sure, but it could be anticipated that Russian power would be used only for defense of Russian territories in eastern Asia as long as relations with Germany remained uncertain. Nevertheless Japan sought to secure itself against attack in the north through an agreement with the Soviet Union similar to that which Germany had made before launching its attack on Poland. Negotiations were begun for an agreement on spheres of interest and for neutrality in case either became involved in war. The resulting Neutrality Pact was signed on April 13, 1941. At that time the Japanese government believed that German military plans involved an all-out attack on Britain, since Germany was then encouraging Japan to apply pressure to Britain in Southeast Asia.

The German attack on the Soviet Union in June, 1941, under these circumstances, inevitably produced a measure of confusion in Japanese thinking. Certainly it made necessary some re-examination of the various factors in the equation of expansion. On the one hand, the initial German successes in the war against Russia gave additional assurance to Japan that the Neutrality Pact would be respected by Russia if Japan became involved in war in the attempt to attain its objectives in Southeast Asia. On the other hand, these same German victories indicated the possibility of success if Japan should make an attempt to drive the Soviet Union out of the Far East, as urged at this time by Germany after the decision had been made by Hitler to attack the Soviet Union.

Another element which had to be weighed even more carefully in relation to action was the attitude and policy of the United States. The Anti-Comintern Pact had been transformed into a military alliance in September, 1940. The new military agreement was designed as insurance against military support of Britain, France, and Holland by the United States. Thus, on the one hand, if the United States should use its fleet in the Pacific to prevent Japanese occupation of the Netherlands' Indies or Malaya, Germany, and Italy would be expected to declare war and wage it in the Atlantic against the United States. Or, on the other hand, if American aid to Britain went beyond that of supply into belligerency, or if its economic assistance threatened to become decisive, Japan would be expected to act against the United States in the Pacific. The signatories nevertheless were left free to determine, each for itself, what constituted an act of war by the United States which would bring into operation the obligations of the alliance. It was clearly the intention, however, by threat of action, to warn the United States away: (1) from taking decisive action in support of England in the European war by threatening the United States with war in the Pacific; and (2) from impeding Japanese progress in the enlarged Far East because that would face the United States with the probability of war in the Atlantic. In the negotiations at Washington immediately preceding the attack at Pearl Harbor, nevertheless, Japan indicated that there was a possibility of trading nonfulfillment of the obligations of this military pact with Germany for assent, either explicit or implicit, by the United States to Japan's further conquest in eastern and southeastern Asia.

The Lend-Lease bill enacted by Congress early in 1941 did not provide for American belligerency in either the Atlantic or the Pacific, but it did forecast an increase of American aid to both Britain and

China. It thus constituted, in effect, a reply of the United States to the threat to it in the Axis military alliance. Since the action taken did not indicate willingness to assume military obligations, however, and since its primary motivation was the support of Britain against Germany rather than the support of colonial regimes against Japan, the question remained unanswered as to the nature and extent of the American reaction to a southward Japanese expansion at the expense of other colonial powers.

To find an answer to that question conversations were initiated by Japan and entered upon by the United States to explore the possibility of defining a basis upon which formal negotiations might be conducted with some prospect of success. These conversations, initiated in April 1941, were being conducted between the American Secretary of State, Cordell Hull, and the Japanese Ambassador, Admiral Kichisaburo Nomura, when the German attack was launched on the Soviet Union on June 22, 1941.

Although they revealed no real willingness on either side to modify the fundamental positions taken up at the outset, the conversations were continued until the outbreak of war between the United States and Japan. During their course the pressures of Japan on Indochina were intensified rather than relaxed, and pressure began to be exerted on the Dutch in Indonesia. Economic counter-pressures on the part of the United States were carried to the point, in July, of freezing Japanese assets within American jurisdiction but not to the point of threat of war if Japan did not reverse its movement toward the creation of the Greater East Asia Co-Prosperity sphere.

The British government sought a statement to that effect and, at the Atlantic conference, President Roosevelt committed himself to the issuance of a stronger statement of warning to Japan than the Secretary of State believed advisable.[2] Military Staff Conferences between the British and Americans had, however, been begun in Washington early in 1941.[3] Reports of these developments caused the Japanese to conclude that they were threatened with "encirclement" through military alliance of the United States with Britain, the Netherlands and China. Japanese propaganda enveighed against this encirclement and used it

[2] Cordell Hull, *The Memoirs of Cordell Hull* (New York: Macmillan, 1948), 2 vols., Vol. II, pp. 1017-20.
[3] Herbert Feis, *The Road to Pearl Harbor* (Princeton: Princeton University Press, 1950), Chap. 21.

to whip up national sentiment for defense of the country against the encircling powers. The United States officially disclaimed any intention on its part to bring about the encirclement of, or otherwise to menace, any nation. This did not, however, prevent continued agitation in Japan against encirclement, although what was actually threatened was the establishment of limits on Japan's expansion to the south.

In view of the unwillingness of Japan to give up its expansionist objectives and of the United States to modify its position an explanation has to be sought of the willingness of both sides to continue the negotiations which had been instituted but which seemed to offer no promise of agreement.

One reason for their continuation was the need felt by the United States for time to complete military preparations before threatening to use or actually using military means to implement political policy. Part of the explanation, however, must be found in the unreadiness of American public opinion to support a clearly defined policy of using military power for other purposes than the defense of national territory. It cannot, of course, now be determined whether the Japanese might not have attained their ultimate objectives without war with the United States if they had confined their military action to the European colonies, even though that would have made certain the ultimate destruction of any political or economic ties between the United States and the Philippines. In any event, gradual extension of the area of imperial control, such as Japan had undertaken before 1940, with effective consolidation of positions established before the next forward movement as a method of avoiding maximum resistance, required time and a greater degree of patience than those who had moved into control of the Japanese government felt should be exercised under existing circumstances. Consequently the decision on war was taken, and an attack was launched on American territory simultaneously with the movement against the British and Dutch territories. The attack at Pearl Harbor, however, was designed to reduce American naval power in the Pacific and thus to lessen the effectiveness of any possible American resistance to the establishment and the consolidation of Greater East Asia rather than to bring the Hawaiian Islands under Japanese control.

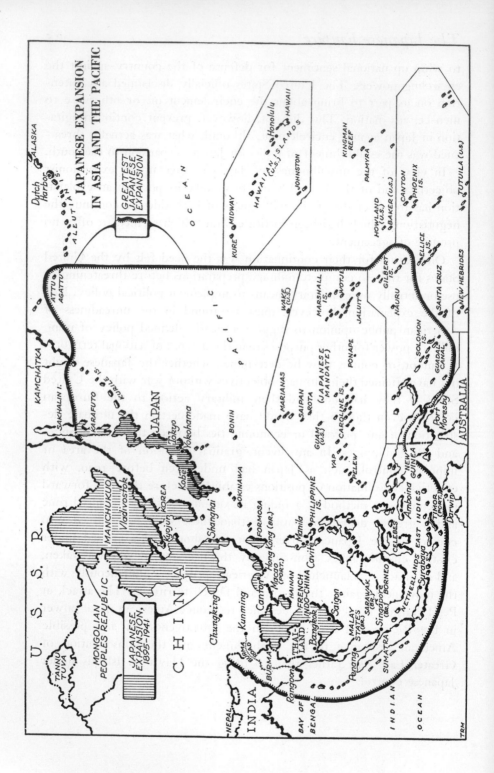

JAPANESE EXPANSION
IN ASIA AND THE PACIFIC

GREATEST
JAPANESE
EXPANSION

JAPANESE EXPANSION,
1895-1941

THE PACIFIC WAR

Between December 7, 1941 and May 6, 1942 (when the American forces in the Philippines were ordered to surrender) the Japanese armies successfully overran the territories initially included in the plans for the Greater East Asia Sphere. The rapidity and ease with which they had attained what had been set as their most advanced objectives, however, encouraged the military elements which controlled Japan to go still further. Consequently time, resources, and energies which might have been devoted to consolidation of the position won in Greater East Asia were spent in the conquest of Burma, which had been completed by June, 1942; in subsequent attempts to move against the British in India; and in the attempt to extend the defensive perimeter in the Pacific to Attu and Kiska in the Aleutian Islands (thus offering a threat to Alaska), to Midway in the Central Pacific, and to the Gilberts, New Guinea, and the Solomon Islands in the Southwest Pacific, with a consequent threat to Australia and New Zealand. These advanced positions, once they had been taken, had to be defended. They could be brought under harassing attack by the United States much more readily and effectively than could territories more remote from American and British bases. Their defense, consequently, committed more and more of the military resources of Japan, thus preventing the effective consolidation and integration of the Co-Prosperity Sphere as originally conceived.

Aside from this, there were two very serious miscalculations both in the original and in the revised war plans of Japan. The first resulted from misreading by the Tojo government of the effect on American opinion of an attack on the United States' fleet within American waters. Instead of paralyzing the national will and giving greater play to existing American pacifistic, isolationist, and antiadministration sentiment, the disaster at Pearl Harbor forged national unity for war purposes and hardened the national determination to make the necessary effort, for reasons of national security, to prevent Japan from maintaining the position won in Greater East Asia. The second was the underestimating of the rapidity with which the United States could translate its resources into ships, planes, tanks and guns, and thus bring them to bear for war purposes.

It was the unforeseen rapidity and power of the immediate counter-attack, transformed into a continuing offensive, which denied to Japan the opportunity to test the validity of the hypothesis that the Greater East Asia area could be organized and administered as a relatively self-contained economy sufficiently strong to maintain itself against external attack. For three full years the countries conquered were under Japanese control. But during this period Japan could not divert the necessary trained manpower and resources from war purposes to that of development of the area and its integration into the industrial economy of Japan. This proved, under the circumstances, to be impossible even to the extent of replacing the British, Americans, Dutch, and French as the source of supply of required manufactured goods. It proved to be equally impossible to restore the production of the area sufficiently to meet Japan's great need for raw materials for war purposes. First the submarine and then the bomber disrupted and finally severed sea communications between Japan and countries in the southern region. Thus the result of the period of Japanese military control was economic disorganization rather than effective organization on an area, rather than a country, basis. To a very considerable extent, each country was compelled to meet its own needs out of its own resources. Consequently each came to be organized on an independent rather than an integrated economic basis. Japan was unable to supply goods to the Philippines in exchange for Philippine sugar, chrome ore, tobacco, and copra, as the United States had previously done. Burma had its rice but no place to turn for goods to exchange for its surplus. Japan could not replace Europe and America in Indonesian commodity exchanges. Nor was Japan in a position to supply the necessary machinery and technicians to enable these southeastern Asian countries to supply their own needs through manufacture. Since they were all countries engaged in staple-crop production for export, self-sufficiency, even in foodstuffs, required considerable shifts in agricultural production. In the attempt to enforce changes in the customary methods of agricultural production on an independent country basis further dislocations were made in the economy of the area. Thus "co-poverty" rather than "co-prosperity" resulted in Greater East Asia from the Japanese "war of liberation." All of this was added to the normal distresses resulting from military operations in the countries fought over.

While war circumstances precluded the effective organization of the area by Japan on an imperial basis, the fact remains that Western power was completely, even though as it proved temporarily, driven out of the area. The economic ties binding the several countries to Europe and America were cut for a three-year period. The one exception was "Free" China which, as an ally, maintained a friendly political contact with the United States and Britain and received limited supplies from the outside by air transport. The supply was, however, essentially military, and it was so limited that southwestern China was, to all intents, forced, as were the southeastern Asian countries, to live on its own inadequate and underdeveloped resources, except as trade was carried on with occupied China, and through it with Japan. The Japanese-occupied provinces of China never had their communications with Japan as completely cut as did the countries of the "southern region."

JAPAN IN THE CO-PROSPERITY SPHERE

During the war period Japanese policy was directed toward two ideological objectives. One was the firm fixing in the occupied countries of an attitude of independence of the West. War operations were advertised in Japanese propaganda as being designed to liberate the Greater East Asia area from "Anglo-American imperialism." The advertised objective was thus liberation from the West, in which sense the war was widely accepted as one of liberation. Set against the background of Japanese expansionism and of initial Japanese military organization of the several occupied countries, liberation from the West, however, had a strong undertone and a clear implication of subjugation to Japan. In spite of this implication, however, Japan's propaganda against the West, coupled with its military successes, stimulated nationalist thinking and activity throughout the area.

A second objective was to replace Western countries as the cultural-exchange-center within the enlarged Japanese sphere. Thus an earnest effort was made to substitute Japanese for English or Dutch as the second language in the various countries. This was attempted through an emphasis on Japanese as a medium of instruction in the schools and in the conduct of public business. Japanese literature of various sorts was introduced and its superior merits were advertised. Japanese movies, plays, and music took the place of Western productions for purposes of entertainment. In the field of religion Christian propaganda was purposefully eliminated and the attempt made to interest the people in Shinto. Exhibits of things Japanese were brought into the several countries to portray Japan's advancement in the arts and sciences. Trips to Japan were arranged for students and intellectuals, and carefully staged conferences of representatives of the various countries were held in Tokyo so that their intellectual leaders could be introduced in Japan itself to Japanese culture, with a view to demonstrating its "Asiatic" nature and its superiority to that of the West and to the local indigenous culture.

Although this was a long-run method of bringing about integration under Japan, cultural assimilation was of fundamental importance in relation to the objective because of the role traditionally played in Asian countries by the intellectual class. The emphasis on cultural exchanges also had the immediate importance of obscuring for that class some of the divergencies of practice in occupation from the theory of "liberation." But while the goal of cultural attachment to Japan was not reached, this double move in the field of cultural reorientation during a three-year period clearly had the effect of complicating the problem of re-entry of the Western states into the occupied countries after the Japanese surrender.

The United Nations also proclaimed their purpose as that of liberation, but liberation from the Japanese and not from colonialism itself. The colonial powers did, during the course of the war, indicate some awareness of the fact that the status quo ante 1941 would have to be modified toward self-government, autonomy, or independence. Too precise or formal commitments as to the direction or the timing of change were, however, studiously avoided, apparently for two principle reasons. The first reason frequently advanced was that no precise commitment could wisely be made in the absence of fairly exact knowledge of the situation which would actually exist at the end of the war. The second was the assumption made that the colonial power would be welcomed back into its colony because of a general acceptance of the beneficence of its rule in contrast with that of Japan. Consequently it was felt that it would have freedom to determine the nature and timing of modifications of prewar relationships. Exceptions to this were: the commitment of the United States to meet, or possibly advance if war circumstances permitted, the schedule set up for Philippine independence; and a broad statement made by the Netherland's

Queen Wilhelmina (December 7, 1942), committing the Netherlands to the establishment of a new form of relationship to Indonesia. Nevertheless even these exceptions were self-imposed commitments designed to be interpreted and applied by the colonial power without prior consultation and agreement with the new nationalism which Japanese policy and actions had stimulated.

Japanese political policy during the war years was shaped for the colonial area first to meet the exigencies of war and then the prospect of defeat. As Western control was eliminated Japanese military occupation was instituted. Under army auspices all available surplus production was appropriated for transfer to Japan or for local military use. Following this initial period of undisguised military exploitation and expropriation of resources, the pattern of rule already developed and in use in Manchuria and occupied China was applied, with the necessary variations to adapt it to the circumstances of the different countries. The range of variation in status at the outbreak of war in the Pacific was: from the existing independence of Thailand, whose government entered the war in alliance with, rather than in subjugation to, Japan; through the virtual political autonomy and self-government, with promised independence, which the Philippines had enjoyed under the Commonwealth Act since 1936, and the self-government initiated by the British in Burma after 1937; to the mixture of indirect and direct colonial rule, with almost no existing basis for self-government, which then existed in Malaya, in Indochina,[4] and in Indonesia.

Where local leadership existed as a result either of an already developed nationalist movement or of the existence of institutions of local self-government, the attempt was made to bring into being a native government which would be responsive to Japanese direction and control. Ultimate Japanese control was ensured because of the dependence of such a government on Japanese military forces operating within the Japanese chain-of-command rather than under the authority of the local regime. Direction was given through an elaborate network of "advisers" whose advice had to be taken because they, rather than the nominal government, could call upon the existing agencies of enforcement or coercion. Advisers, within the Japanese conception, were viewed as agents of the Japanese government in

[4] Here the maintenance until almost the end of the war of French rule was a further modifying factor.

presenting their "advice" to a native government, rather than as individual Japanese nationals employed by a foreign government to assist it in an advisory capacity in the development and application of its own policies. In other words, the Japanese conception of the role of adviser in the twentieth century was quite different from the role which the adviser played in the nineteenth century in Japan itself when foreigners were employed by the Imperial government to assist it in making a transition from the pre-Restoration military, political and economic system to that of modern Japan. Thus, in the Japanese point of view, the governments to which power was transferred by the military in the Philippines and in Burma were designed as instruments of Japanese rule and not as autonomous or independent governments.

While this must be recognized, it must also be understood that many of those who accepted responsibility in these puppet governments did so either in unawareness of the realities or in the unwarranted anticipation that if they secured power as a result of Japanese support they could use Japan to forward the move toward realization of their own aim of establishing national independence rather than being used by Japan in the long-run for the purpose of subjugation of the country to it.

Where such local leaders were not immediately available or were unwilling to collaborate with the Japanese, direct rule was instituted. Power was, however, transferred to Japanese civilian regimes from the military, which remained as the prop for civilian authority. This was the case in Malaya, and also in Indonesia, although in Indonesia the Japanese began immediately to search out and use in government nationalist leaders who had been imprisoned or driven underground by the Dutch. Under the circumstances of war and of military dominance at Tokyo itself, however, in all cases of transfer of authority to civilian regimes the ultimate power of decision locally rested with the military command operating within the Imperial Japanese Army chain-of-command.

As the Allied counteroffensive successfully got under way, and with greater rapidity and power than had been anticipated in Tokyo, Japanese planning for the southern occupied area changed in purpose and method of execution. By 1943 it had become apparent that Allied power could not be successfully contained at the outer limits originally set for the defense of the Greater East Asia sphere, while the sphere itself was being reorganized to serve Japanese purposes. As the outer defense zone was pushed inward it became increasingly necessary to plan the conditions of defense, especially of the Philippines and Burma, so as (1) to enable defense to be undertaken with a minimum expenditure of Japanese manpower and military resources, and (2) to offer the maximum difficulties to the Allies in organizing newly won territories to serve as bases for further operations. Both advantages could be gained to the extent to which the local governments and peoples could be induced to accept responsibility for the defense of their countries against Allied attack. This required the creation of a situation in which the Allied armies would be viewed popularly as invaders, threatening the independence and the liberties of the peoples concerned, rather than coming in as liberators. To fix this idea became the principal task of Japanese propaganda throughout the area.

Action, however, was required to support the propaganda as well as to give it a base. Thus the proclamation of independence of Burma (August 15, 1943) and of the Philippines (August 15) represented tactical moves by Japan in relation to the changed war situation (although obscured as such by Japanese propaganda), rather than the attainment of a strategic objective in Japan's foreign policy. It should be noted that these were the two countries, aside from occupied China, in which Allied attacks were certain and those in which extensive ground operations had to be undertaken before the Japanese military began even to contemplate surrender. These were also the two colonial countries in which a groundwork for self-government and eventual independence had been laid before the war. This, as already noted, had made possible the transfer of authority to a local regime, and had channeled a current of sentiment which set some limits on Japanese policy and action.

The former Federated Malay States were not even promised self-government until 1943, and military rule in Indonesia was modified only in October, 1943, with the establishment of an advisory council headed by an Indonesian, Soekarno. Independence was proclaimed as an ultimate objective only in 1944 when it had become clear that Japan would not be able to maintain any position in the country which the Japanese considered, aside from China and Indochina, most vital to them. The French regime in Indochina, in view of its willingness to collaborate with Japan, was left undisturbed until March, 1945, when it also was displaced. In the months remaining before the end of the war the Japanese transferred authority in Indochina to local nationalist administrators, apparently also in the hope that they would collaborate even more effectively with Japan than the French regime had in defense of Indochina against the Allies.

RISE OF NATIONALIST RESISTANCE
IN THE COLONIAL AREA

The course and the immediate outcome of the war was not seriously affected by this Japanese tactic. A major reason was the antipathy to the Japanese which had already been created among the people in the area by the behavior of the Japanese as conquerors. This prevented the Japanese officials from eliciting warm popular support in what continued to be viewed popularly as Japan's war against the Allies rather than as war in defense of national liberties. The only concrete move made by a puppet government toward transformation of the Pacific war into a war of national defense against Allied attack was the declaration of war on the United States by the Japanese-supported Philippine government headed by José P. Laurel. This was generally viewed, however, either (1) as an action of Japan's taken through the medium of a government under its control, rather than as an act of a genuinely independent government, or (2) as a measure necessary for the protection of the Laurel government itself. That government must have taken the view that it had nothing to lose by the declaration of war since its internal authority was contested by the Commonwealth government-in-exile. Its tenure of power was clearly conditioned by that of Japan because the United States had made it clear that the authority of the Commonwealth government would be re-instituted simultaneously with victory by the United States.

The authority of the Laurel regime, as well as that of Japan, had been continuously disputed by Filipinos through guerrilla warfare and by other means from the time of its establishment. These guerrilla activities had been supported and co-ordinated from Brisbane, head-quarters of General Douglas MacArthur's Southwest Pacific Command. The guerrillas also found considerable internal support among those who outwardly acquiesced in the Japanese conquest and in the rule of the Laurel government. Some of those actively participating in that

government, furthermore, gave such aid and support as they could
to the guerrillas in their anti-Japanese activities. Thus the internal situation had so shaped itself as to make it impossible for Japan to transfer
the burden of defense of the Philippines to the local regime, or for it to
rally the nation for defense against the Americans as invaders.

Somewhat the same situation developed in Burma during the war,
although there the invasion by the Japanese had been actively assisted
by anti-British nationalist extremists, whereas in the Philippines collaborationists were found by the Japanese only after the surrender
of American and Philippine military forces. The "Free Burma administrations" which were initially set up were, however, suppressed by
the Japanese military because of their violent and high-handed behavior.
On August 1, 1942, as previously noted, the power of government was
ostensibly transferred by the Japanese Military Administration to the
Burma Executive, headed by Dr. Ba Maw. This collaborationist government was so obviously dominated by the Japanese that it was not
accepted by Burmese nationalists, who came to be organized into The
Anti-Fascist People's Freedom League which, after the middle of 1944,
carried on guerrilla activities against the Japanese regime. As in the
Philippines, this guerrilla opposition made it impossible for the Japanese
to organize the defense against invasion on a national basis to preserve
the independence which had been granted by Japan.[5]

Similarly, in Indonesia many of the nationalist leaders went underground after the invasion. When belatedly, the Japanese secured the
collaboration in their Advisory Council of such nationalists as Soekarno
and Hatta, and when they finally promised Indonesia ultimate independence, the anti-Japanese and collaborationist nationalists continued
to maintain contact and were able to assume control against the Dutch
as well as the Japanese at the time of Japanese surrender.[6]

The situation in Indochina during the war had been much more confused than in the other colonial countries. After the fall of France
under the weight of the German attack, the Indochinese regime had
accepted the direction of the Vichy government. In addition to the
direct pressures which the Japanese had exerted on the colonial regime,
Tokyo had been able to apply pressure on the Pétain government

[5] For a more detailed summary, Chap. 12.
[6] On the war time situation in Indonesia see Soetan Sjahrir, *Out of Exile* (New
York: John Day, 1949); also *infra.* Chap. 13.

through Germany. In combination these pressures had been sufficient to enable Japan to exercise the authority of government in Indochina through the medium of the French regime. Anti-Vichy Frenchmen, however, as well as those unwilling to accept collaboration with the Japanese, went into opposition, operating either underground or from Free China. They were joined by Indochinese nationalist leaders in the organization of resistance to Japan. The latter were naturally animated by anti-French or anticolonial considerations, while the former were mainly interested in the re-establishment of French authority in the colony. Japanese policy and actions, especially during the months in 1945 before the surrender, had the effect of paving the way for control by native nationalists rather than by the French leadership.[7]

Even in Thailand, an independent state which had entered the war in alliance with Japan, anti-Japanese activity was organized during the war. This resulted from the fact that, although independent, Thailand came under the control of a government which was just as subordinated to Japanese authority as was that of Laurel in the Philippines or that of Ba Maw in Burma. Recognition of this fact led some Thai officials outside the country, notably the Thai Minister in Washington, to repudiate the Japanese-dominated Thai government and to ask for recognition by Allied governments as a government-in-exile. This was accorded by the United States which did not, as Britain did, view itself as being at war with Thailand on the basis of the declaration of war by the Thai government of Pibul Songgram. Thus resistance to Japan and to the government was at first organized from the outside. It also developed subsequently from within the country under the leadership of the head of the People's Party, Luang Pradit, even though he remained a member of the government.[8]

Although Japanese policy did not enlist the whole-hearted co-operation of the people in the area for defense against invasion, it did have the significant consequence of putting an enlarged emphasis in each of the countries on independence. The new policy enhanced the importance and increased the powers of the puppet regimes and gave them more internal prestige. This in turn gave more weight to their assertion that their objectives were nationalist and directed toward independence rather than designed to serve Japanese purposes and inter-

[7] For developments in Indochina, *infra*. Chap. 10.
[8] On the internal situation in Thailand during the war, *infra*. Chap. 11.

ests. In this respect, Japan's policy had the effect of erecting barriers to the ready re-establishment of the colonial status quo ante 1941. The promise of either immediate or ultimate independence, and even the largely fictional transfer of all or some of the authority of government to native leaders put more fuel on the fire of nationalism which even before the war had begun to burn among the people. Furthermore, those who had had a taste of authority were not willing to accept subordination to an outside rule. Liberation from Japan was coupled with the idea of self-government and independence of external control. This objective was intimately related to the determination (1) of those who thought that they were actually exercising power with the support of Japan and (2) of those who had seized power as resistance leaders to retain the power which the circumstances of the war had placed in their hands.

A prewar argument against transfer of authority from the metropolitan country to local leadership had been the lack of training and experience in modern government and administration of the native governing class. The objectives and the nature of colonial rule had, to be sure, worked against the establishment of conditions which would develop experienced native administrators. Nevertheless the absence of such was held to be justification for continued administration by the colonial regimes. As educational opportunities were opened to the native population, a Western educated class of intellectuals began, before World War II, to appear in the several Asian colonial countries. This Western training had the effect of separating the intellectuals from the local community, but without securing for them the status in the European community to which their education entitled them. Certainly it did not bring them into the governmental and administrative heirarchy except in clerical and subordinate roles. In many cases it caused them to identify themselves with the colonial governing class at least to the point of acquiescence in colonialism and of effective administrative service within prescribed and assigned limits. Nevertheless the content of their education in many other cases prevented emotional and intellectual acquiescence in the status given them in colonial society. Those thus affected were inevitably led in the direction of revolt against colonialism. The Western idea of nationalism, to which their education introduced them, gave them a doctrine useful as a *rationale* of revolt, and a basis of appeal to the masses. The poverty of the latter could be attributed to foreign exploitation or, where the colonial structure had been erected on the basis of local rule, to foreign support of an exploitive traditional native rule. This latter consideration, where perceived, gave a Marxist twist to the local nationalist movements in their attempts to gain mass support. Joining the idea of national self-control to that of socioeconomic purpose in the use of power when attained broadened the basis of the nationalists' appeal for mass support.

But all of this was in the realm of ideas which were essentially Western and thus foreign. They could be shrugged off by practical men as the ideas of theorists, or as theory which could only be blueprinted or made effective by those with some practical understanding of the problems of government and administration.

This practical experience in organization and leadership was gained by those who collaborated with the Japanese and by those who organized and led, with a minimum of foreign assistance, the anti-Japanese guerrilla or resistance movements. By the end of the war the nationalist leadership, which had been intellectual and inexperienced, had begun to be hardened in the school of experience. The prewar generalizations as to its incapacity were no longer quite as valid as they had been. And, especially in the guerrilla movements, the native nationalist leaders had been able for the first time to establish a firm contact with the masses of the people who, because of the economic dislocations of the war, had been shaken into active revolt.

An equally important new factor in the equation of colonialism was that by 1945 nationalism had secured arms and the nationalist leaders had armed forces under their control. In addition to the armed anti-Japanese guerrilla forces, there were local "peace preservation" forces which had been organized under Japanese-puppet auspices to protect their authority. These were augmented and given more and better arms by the Japanese toward the end of the war to enable local invasion to be prevented. Additional stocks of arms and ammunition were made available to the local "defense" forces with which authority was shared by the Japanese before the arrival of those with Allied authorization to receive the Japanese surrender. Consequently the colonial powers returned to find themselves confronted with armed resistance to the re-establishment of even a modified colonial status. Even in the Philippines, where liberation had been accomplished and authority turned over to the Commonwealth government, supported by the American army, before V-J Day, it proved impossible immediately to establish a government monopoly of armed power.

CONSEQUENCES OF JAPAN'S SURRENDER

The end of the military operations of World War II, which came with the acceptance of the Allied surrender terms by the Imperial Japanese government, consequently, did not serve automatically to re-establish the normalities of the past. In many instances surrender by the Japanese in advance of invasion created a power vacuum which the Allies attempted to fill but where they immediately found themselves in conflict with local authority more or less hastily set up. The terms of surrender did give the Allied powers the right to act so as to eliminate completely direct Japanese power and influence throughout the area. Those terms also brought Japan itself under Allied control and occupation. The elimination of Japanese power in the occupied areas posed a problem of disarmament and repatriation of the Japanese forces for the Allied commands. It also raised the immediate question, in some instances, of purpose in relation to ultimate authority in the military take-over from the Japanese. The implications of this question were different where the Allied Command, and the forces involved, did not assume a double responsibility: (1) that of receiving the surrender of the Japanese forces, disarming them, and preparing for their quick repatriation; and (2) that of acting as the agent of their own colonial office in re-establishing the authority of the colonial power. Where this second responsibility could be effectively discharged there was no vacuum left as a result of the repatriation of the Japanese armies.

In the case of the Philippines, for example, the avowed purpose of the liberation was the re-establishment of the authority of the Commonwealth government and the restoration to it of the powers of an independent state. At the time of the Japanese surrender the military aspects of the problem, *vis-a-vis* the Japanese armed forces, were already in process of solution in the form of mopping-up military operations. The remaining problem was that of repatriation of prisoners-of-war and the disarmament and repatriation of the Japanese forces under the command of General Yamashita, following his surrender in compliance with Imperial orders. The two major problems, consequently were: (1)

that of re-establishing internal peace and order under the authority
of the recognized government; and (2) that of determining the time
and re-defining the conditions of independence and of relationship
between the United States and the Philippines. At least until the end of
1946, the presence and position of the American military forces in the
Islands gave a decisive importance to the views of the United States as
to the proper solution of both of the above stated problems. Both were,
however, divorced from the problem of the take-over from the
Japanese. Nevertheless the elimination of Japanese power did not present
vacuum conditions because of the established American military
position.

In Malaya and Burma the situation was similar to that in the Philippines in at least one important respect. The prewar metropolitan
country supplied the military forces and had the responsibility of
receiving the Japanese surrender and of re-establishing Allied authority. In Burma there was a further similarity in that the liberation of the
country by military means was already well under way by V-J Day,
so that British power had already returned there. The (British) Southeast Asia Command, in other words, already operating in Burma, had
the double responsibility, which it proceeded expeditiously to discharge, of simultaneously terminating war operations and restoring the
colonial regime.

In Indonesia, on the other hand, military forces of the colonial power,
Holland, were not available, nor was an Allied force of sufficient size
already operating there. It was just on the eve of the Japanese surrender
that Indonesia had been brought, for military purposes, under the
Southeast Asia Command. When the Allies arrived in the country they
found some areas, as in Java, already under control of a native regime.
In that situation, the Allied Command limited itself to effecting the
Japanese surrender and to evacuating Allied prisoners-of-war and civilian internees, refusing to embark on the reconquest of Java against
Indonesian resistance. Here one colonial power (Britain) failed to put
Allied forces at the disposal of another colonial power (The Netherlands) to enable it to re-establish its authority against the opposition of
a revolutionary regime. This attitude delayed entrance of the Dutch
forces into Java. By the time of their arrival reconquest had become
more difficult since time had been afforded the Indonesian Republic to

perfect its organization and to equip its forces from available Japanese military supply dumps. In other words two sets of forces met in competition to fill the vacuum resulting from the enforced Japanese withdrawal. This general situation created the necessity for prior negotiation by the Dutch with the Republican government. Such negotiations gave that government additional *de facto* standing in the international community beyond that previously gained from the initial attitude of the British military authorities.

In Indochina the Southeast Asia Command was deputized to receive the Japanese surrender south of the 16th parallel, and the Chinese National Government forces north of it. The Chinese, like the British in Java, limited their mission to that of dealing with the Japanese military aspects of the problem, except as they sought to bring about a more satisfactory definition of the conditions of relationship between China and Indochina. In this respect they used their position to bring pressure to bear on the French, but in their own interest rather than to assist the newly proclaimed native regime. During the period of their control, however, they allowed the revolutionary government to organize and consolidate its power, leaving it to France to re-establish its own authority in Tongking against the newly proclaimed Viet Nam government after the withdrawal of the Chinese forces. In their zone, the British simultaneously took over from the Japanese, and assisted in re-establishing French authority against the nationalist regime.

The British Command also was authorized to receive the Japanese surrender in Thailand.[9] The independence of Thailand had been maintained in theory but lost in fact to the Japanese for the period of the war. Thailand had been formally accepted as an enemy state by Britain but not by the United States and China during the same period. But there had been reached no agreement between those three allies concerning the treatment of Thailand at the end of the war. When the British Command took over from the Japanese, therefore, it was essentially as a military occupant determined to extract suitable peace terms from an enemy. Chinese and especially American objections to the political and economic use which the British sought to make of their power brought about a modification of British policy. Ultimately, their war mission having been accomplished, the British withdrew

[9] Which called itself for a time by the earlier name, Siam.

under conditions which secured the sovereignty of the country but restored the political and economic position held there by the British in 1932.[10]

As described before, the other independent country which Japan had sought to bring within the Co-prosperity Sphere was China where there was still functioning an independent government which could be authorized to receive the surrender of the Japanese forces. This was a task of considerable magnitude, since it involved establishment of control over approximately a million and a half troops, organized under three separate commands, followed by their disarmament and their repatriation. It also involved the reintroduction of the authority of the Chinese National Government into heavily populated provinces of considerable size which had been under Japanese control, indirectly exercised through Chinese regimes, for better than six years. The problem was complicated by the presence of a competitive authority in the form of the Chinese Communist Party and armies under its direction and control.

Two other factors in the Chinese equation were presented in the form of the position of the United States in "China Proper" and of the Soviet Union in Manchuria. In relation to the implementation of the Japanese surrender, the United States was in a position to put military facilities which the Chinese government lacked at its disposal to enable it to discharge its responsibilities toward the Japanese in the occupied provinces. In the process, Washington found itself in effect supporting one side against the other in what was assumed to be purely an internal struggle for power. It was in fact supporting the recognized government against an armed rebellious faction assumed to be of indigenous origin and animation. The Soviet Union, on its side, as the military occupant of Manchuria, was authorized to receive the Japanese surrender there, and it was also committed to the National Government as the ultimate authority to which its control would be relinquished. The Russians, however, had been conceded the right to retain a position in Manchuria which had been defined under the Yalta "Agreement regarding Japan" and the Soong-Molotov Treaty of August 14, 1945. Existing circumstances put the Soviet authorities in a position either to facilitate or to render more difficult the re-establishment of the authority of the National Government of China in Manchuria. The

[10] For a summary of prewar conditions in Thailand see Chap. 11.

U.S.S.R. used its special position to retard the effective introduction of the authority of the National Government into Manchuria, whereas the United States lent that government its support in the rest of the Japanese-occupied area.[11]

Japan itself, by the surrender terms, came under Allied occupation. One aspect of the problem of occupation was similar to the postsurrender problem in other countries of the area. A primary mission of the Allied Command was to demobilize the Japanese army in Japan, and to demilitarize the country.

Since however, the Japanese Empire was to be reduced to its original territories, surrender had to be received and arrangements for government under re-defined conditions had to be made in Korea, Formosa, the Ryukyu and Kurile Islands, and the Central and Southwest Pacific Islands mandated to or formally a part of the prewar Japanese Empire. Under agreements entered into at the Yalta Conference, the Soviet Union established its authority over the Kuriles. As provided by the Cairo Declaration China displaced Japan in Formosa. Allied forces were already in occupation of the Central and Southwest Pacific islands in question. The Central Pacific mandated islands were subsequently erected into a strategic trusteeship under the United States, while Australia and New Zealand were given trusteeship responsibilities in the Southwest Pacific over former Japanese-administered territories. Some of the Ryukyus, through war operations and before the Japanese surrender, had also been brought under American military control with the conquest of Okinawa.

At the time of the Japanese surrender, consequently, the only part of the prewar Japanese Empire which presented a serious problem was Korea. The United States was in a position quickly to move troops into Korea only by sea, whereas the Soviet Union, as a result of its military operations in Manchuria, which had been extended across the Yalu River into Korea, and the proximity of its own territory to Korea, could move quickly in force into the northern part of the country across the land frontier, to receive the Japanese surrender and rapidly displace Japanese authority. The United States consequently took over from the Japanese south of the 38th parallel while the Russians displaced the Japanese in the part of the peninsula north of that parallel. There had been reached an agreement at Cairo between Britain, the

[11] This situation is described in more detail in Chaps. 4, 5.

United States, and China that Korea should "in due course" be erected into an independent state. This policy was reaffirmed, and was accepted by the Soviet Union, at the Potsdam Conference. Consequently this division at the 38th parallel can only be viewed as having been made for the military purpose of rapid implementation of the surrender terms. The Japanese were thus displaced by two strong military occupants, before a unified Korean government had been established and recognized by the two occupants. This left a serious problem of relationship between the United States, the Soviet Union, and the Koreans which had to be solved by negotiation or otherwise.

It thus becomes apparent that the termination of the military operations of World War II in the Far East and Pacific settled immediately only one question. It made clear the inability of Japan, through its own power, to incorporate in its empire the countries defined by it as the Greater East Asia Co-Prosperity Sphere. It redefined the conditions under which the struggle between nationalism and colonial imperialism would be waged in the area but it did not solve the problem of imperialism. It brought the United States into a new position of both power and responsibility in the Far East, and thus made its policy objectives of major importance to all of the countries concerned. It restored the Russian position as a competitor for power and influence in Korea, Manchuria, and China, and thus posed from the outset the problem of agreement or conflict between the Soviet and the non-Soviet countries.

Because of this last fact, as well as on account of the positions and interests in the area of the British, the Dutch, and the French, it was early made clear that postwar politics in the Far East would be shaped to a considerable extent by the operation of external forces. To serve its own purposes Japan had made a major effort to eliminate intrusive Western nations from the area and to confine the politics of the Far East to the operation of purely internal forces, with Japanese power dominant. In this Japan had failed. Power developed and applied from outside the area rather than resistance to Japan from within it destroyed the Japanese Empire, preventing in the process the creation of the Greater East Asia Co-Prosperity Sphere. This Japanese failure ensured a continuing interaction of European, American, Soviet Russian, and Far Eastern politics. For that reason Far Eastern politics during the postwar period must necessarily be approached within the framework of world politics.

BIBLIOGRAPHICAL REFERENCES

Cressey, G. B., *Asia's Lands and People* (New York: McGraw-Hill, 1950).

Department of State, *Foreign Relations of the United States, Japan, 1931-1941*, 2 vols. (Washington, 1943).

East, W. Gordon, and Spate, V. H. K., *The Changing Map of Asia: A Political Geography* (New York: Dutton, 1950-51).

Elsbree, W. H., *Japan's Role in Southeast Asian Nationalist Movements, 1940-45* (Cambridge: Harvard University Press, 1953).

Emerson, Rupert, Mills, Lennox A., and Thompson, Virginia, *Government and Nationalism in Southeast Asia* (New York: International Secretariat, Institute of Pacific Relations, 1942).

Feis, Herbert, *The Road to Pearl Harbor* (Princeton: Princeton University Press, 1950).

Grew, Joseph C., *Ten Years in Japan* (New York: Simon & Schuster, 1944).

Hishida, Seiji G., *Japan Among the Great Powers: a Survey of Her International Relations* (New York: Longmans, Green, 1940).

Hornbeck, Stanley K., "Eastern Asia," Chap. 29 in Thorsten V. Kalijarvi and Associates, *Modern World Politics*, 3rd ed. (New York: Crowell, 1953).

Jones, F. C., *Japan's New Order in East Asia—Its Rise and Fall, 1937-45* (New York: Oxford University Press, 1954).

Matsuo, Kinoaki, *How Japan Plans to Win*, translated by Kilsoo K. Han (Boston: Little, Brown, 1942).

Mills, Lennox A. (ed.), *Southeast Asia and the Philippines* (Philadelphia: The Annals of the American Academy of Political and Social Science, Vol. 226, 1943).

Mills, Lennox A., and Associates, *The New World of Southeast Asia* (Minneapolis: University of Minnesota Press, 1945).

Purcell, Victor, *The Chinese in Southeast Asia* (New York: Oxford University Press, 1951), esp. Chaps. 4, 31, 32.

Quigley, H. S., *Far Eastern War* (Boston: World Peace Foundation, 1942).

Reischauer, Edwin D., *The United States and Japan* (Cambridge: Harvard University Press, 1950).

Takeuchi, T., *War and Diplomacy in the Japanese Empire* (Chicago: University of Chicago Press, 1935).

Vinacke, Harold M., *History of the Far East in Modern Times*, 5th ed. (New York: Appleton-Century-Crofts, 1950), esp. Chaps., 21-26.

Ward, R. S., *Asia for the Asiatics: The Techniques of Japanese Occupation* (Chicago: University of Chicago Press, 1945).

Yanaga, Chitoshi, *Japan Since Perry* (New York: McGraw-Hill, 1949), esp. Chaps. 17-35.

2

Power Relationships
in the Far East Before 1945

❋❋❋❋❋❋❋❋❋❋❋❋❋❋❋❋❋❋❋❋❋❋❋❋

ANGLO-AMERICAN UNITY FOR WAR PURPOSES

THE SUMMARY VIEW presented in the preceding chapter of the rise and fall of the Japanese Empire demonstrates that forces external to the area were as important as internal ones in the shaping of the politics of eastern Asia. This in turn suggests the necessity of approaching postwar Far Eastern politics within the framework of world relationships. The states with the power of decision at the end of the war were the United States, Britain and the Commonwealth countries, and the Soviet Union. Their interrelationship determined the climate of politics in eastern Asia as well as in Europe. It is, consequently, necessary to appraise those relationships as they were maintained during World War II, recognizing that the war had been brought to a successful conclusion by means of a combination of the power of (1) Britain and the Commonwealth, (2) the U.S.S.R., and (3) the United States.

Joint planning had enabled the United States and Britain to make the most effective wartime use of their combined resources. Joint planning enabled them to resolve most differences of opinion as they arose with the minimum stress and strain because of a realization of the existence of common purposes. The complementary qualities of the heads of the two states, President Franklin D. Roosevelt and Prime Minister Winston Churchill, helped to make this possible; as did the early organization of the Combined Chiefs-of-Staff for the purpose of global planning of military strategy. It was this view of the war as a joint undertaking to realize common purposes which made it possible for British and American troops to serve under American commanders in some cases and under British command in others. The point is not that Anglo-American rivalry and consequently friction at both the individual and governmental levels vanished, but rather that for war purposes the governments concerned were able to function as partners to a degree unusual in the prior relationships of states allied against a common enemy.

RELATIONS WITH THE U.S.S.R.

Intimate co-operation with the Soviet Union in the waging of the war was not developed by either the United States or Britain. No Soviet forces were brought under either American or British command; nor were British or American officers or troops utilized in the Soviet military zones. Allied officers in fact were not permitted, except very occasionally, to enter Soviet combat areas even for observational purposes or to facilitate the mutual exchange of military information. The United States and Britain did give extensive material aid to the Soviet Union, sufficient to enable it first of all to maintain itself against the Nazi onslaught and finally to undertake and sustain a powerful offensive against Germany. The amount and nature of this assistance was, however, negotiated rather than being jointly planned as part of a general war effort as was the case with American assistance to the British after 1941. To a considerable extent, throughout the entire course of the war, Britain and the United States were confronted with Soviet demands, with which they complied as far as their own war exigencies permitted.

The principal lever used by the Russians to secure assistance, even sometimes beyond the apparent capacity of their allies to supply it, was the threat of a separate peace with Germany. The circumstances of negotiation of the Ribbentrop-Molotov Pact of 1939 created and preserved a doubt throughout the war concerning the willingness of the Kremlin to continue to wage war to the point of the unconditional surrender of Germany if Hitler should propose a separate settlement on the basis of evacuation of Russian territory and restoration of the status of June, 1941. Since 199 German divisions were absorbed in operations against Russia at the time of the Normandy landings,[1] there was a real necessity felt by the United States and Britain to stand by

[1] Figure given by W. Averill Harriman, *Military Situation in the Far East, Hearings before the Committee on Armed Services and the Committee on Foreign Relations,* United States Senate, 82nd. Cong., 1st Session, 5 parts (Washington, 1951). Pt. 5, p. 3329. Hereafter cited as *Joint (MacArthur) Committee Hearings.*

Russia, at least to the extent necessary to avoid a separate peace which would have enabled the total German military power to be employed in the west.

Until the Second Front, consistently demanded by the Russians, could be opened by the United Nations, the Kremlin argued with some plausibility that Russia was more indispensable to the Allies than Britain and America were of direct military assistance to it. The terrific human losses which had been incurred by Russia and the material destruction which had accompanied and followed the German invasion had so weakened the Soviet Union that, unless adequate assistance were forthcoming, including the opening of the Second Front as a method of diverting substantial German forces from the east, it was recurrently reported Russia might have to make peace. This situation and threat inevitably caused Britain and the United States to adjust themselves to the Russian demands to the greatest possible extent in order to attain their objective of destruction of German and Japanese military power.

Put more generally, it may be asserted that the British and Americans sought to promote co-operation and to develop friendly relations with the Soviet government for the purpose of winning the war against Germany, but without full reciprocation on the part of Russia. The fact of alliance against a common enemy did not cause Moscow to forget that the Soviet Union was a revolutionary state, comparatively recent in its origins and communist in its forms and aims. It remained distrustful of its capitalist allies, remembering the past attempts on their part to overthrow the Soviet system and their reluctance to recognize it. Past experience supported the view held in Russia that the United States and Britain offered assistance to the Soviet Union to enable the former to realize their own purposes. They might be expected to change their attitude toward the U.S.S.R. when they no longer needed Soviet co-operation. Consequently the Soviet government sought to maintain itself in a position from which it could utilize its allies against Germany but not be utilized by them beyond the immediate requirements of the war situation.

The development of full co-operation during the war, furthermore, was rendered difficult because of Soviet neutrality in the war against Japan. Anglo-American planning had to be on a global basis whereas Soviet planning of use of its manpower and resources could be restricted to the area of eastern and southeastern Europe. This necessarily

led to more constant association of the American and British governments for planning purposes than of either government with that of
the Soviet Union. It had the further effect of introducing into planning
for the postwar world the prewar and war view of Europe as the focal
point of international relations, with Asia in a secondary position. This
was shown, for example, in the method of approach to the construction
of the United Nations Organization. The American proposals for the
creation of a world organization to preserve the peace were first presented to Britain and Russia at the Moscow Conference of Foreign
Ministers of October, 1943. China was associated with the proposal
only after it had been accepted by the three powers. Similarly, the
draft of the charter was negotiated at Dumbarton Oaks by the same
three powers, with the Chinese consulted principally through the
medium of the United States. When the important Security Council
voting formula was agreed upon at Yalta, China was not consulted at
all. It was only after agreement had been reached by the United States
and Russia on the conditions of participation by the Soviet Union in
the war in the Pacific and in eastern Asia that the Russians were willing
or felt able to enter into discussions of even postwar relations with the
Chinese government.

The Russian argument for this position was accepted for some time
as reasonable by the United States and Britain. It was that no excuse
must be given the Japanese for an attack on Soviet territory until the
Soviet government was able to divert forces from the German front
sufficient at least to provide effective defense for the Russian Far East.
This argument had to be accepted as valid in view of the fact that
Anglo-American strategy from the beginning was based upon the
view that priority had to be given to the European theater of the global
war. The conclusion had been reached that it would be more feasible
to establish a firm defensive position against Japan while carrying the
European war to a successful termination than it would be to contain
German power while concentrating the necessary power in the Pacific
to bring Japan to the point of surrender. In other words, it was decided
that it would be easier to defeat Japan after Germany had been defeated
than the reverse. This required acceptance of the view that other
considerations should be subordinated to the development and application of the maximum Russian power against Germany, and thus
acceptance of the Soviet view as to the necessity of preserving Soviet

neutrality in the war against Japan until the defeat of the Germans. It also meant that Europe was the primary focus for the United States and Britain as well as for Russia in political as well as in military planning, at least until early in 1945. After the defeat of Germany, furthermore, and even after the unconditional surrender of Japan in August, 1945, attention continued to be centered on Europe and on the problems of reconstruction and readjustment of relationships which the collapse of Hitler's "new order" and the destruction of governmental authority within Germany itself posed.

WARTIME CO-OPERATION PROJECTED INTO THE POSTWAR PERIOD

The United States, Britain, and the Soviet Union had the power to determine the conditions of peace and reconstruction in Europe if they could agree among themselves on those conditions. They did agree on the charter of the United Nations. This was generally taken as an indication of their willingness and determination to adjust through negotiation any differences of opinion which might arise over the conditions of peace and reconstruction. The making of peace was not, however, made a United Nations function. Major peace treaties were to be negotiated directly by the foreign ministers of the United States, Britain, and the Soviet Union, with the French participating in the German, Austrian, and Italian treaty negotiations and China in the Japanese. By the time the conditions of European peace had been defined in the necessary treaties, it was anticipated that the United Nations would be a going concern as a result of the constitution of its primary organs. To it, then, could be given the responsibility for the maintenance of international peace and security.

Primary responsibility for the maintenance of international peace and security was given to the Security Council of the United Nations. Decisions in the Security Council could be taken, however, only if the United States, Great Britain, the U.S.S.R., France, and Nationalist China (the five states with permanent seats) agreed on the necessary action. Agreement on the provision for voting in the Security Council, together with other decisions taken in 1945, represented an acceptance of the probability that without a measure of understanding and co-operation among the major powers it would be impossible to restore the world order and thereafter to maintain by collective action international peace and security. It was, therefore, considered necessary to project at least the measure of co-operation which had existed for war purposes into the postwar era. The assumption that this would be possible, the validity of which assumption remained to be demonstrated, rested on the belief that the United States, Britain, and the Soviet Union had a great enough common interest in the restoration of order in Europe and in avoiding a third world war to enable them to adjust by negotiation their specific foreign-policy objectives where they were certain to be in conflict.

By 1947 the validity of the above assumption had been brought into serious question. While it is true that the United Nations had been organized and had begun to function, and while the major powers had been in negotiation with a view to defining the conditions of peace and had concluded the less controversial treaties, it had been demonstrated that the Soviet Union was not prepared to negotiate in the customary sense of participating in a process of agreement by compromise. It may be that the Kremlin felt no impulsion to compromise in Europe since, while it had maintained its military strength, other nations, and especially the United States, undertook a demobilization of their military forces on the assumption that they were no longer necessary since both Germany and Japan had capitulated and had been brought under military occupation. This demobilization had the effect of shifting the balance of power in favor of the Soviet Union.

There was, however, another consideration. As one student put the problem of negotiation with the Soviet government:

> There is a deep-seated tradition in western diplomacy that an effective diplomat must be a two-way interpreter. He must present his own government's policy forcefully to the government to which he is accredited and defend the essential interests of his country. If he is to give intelligent advice to his government, he must also develop a keen insight into the policies of the government with which he deals and become skilled in distinguishing basic interests and sentiments which it cannot disregard from secondary ones which it may adjust or limit for the broader purpose of reaching agreement....
>
> No such problem of delicate balance in functions arises to plague the Soviet negotiator. This has been especially true since the great purge of the Commissariat of Foreign Affairs in 1938-39 and the replacement of Litvinov by Molotov in 1939.... The present-day Soviet Representative can hardly be called a "negotiator" in the customary sense. He is rather treated as a mechanical mouthpiece for views and demands formulated centrally in Moscow, and is deliberately isolated from the impact of

views, interests and sentiments which influence foreign governments and peoples.[2]

Possibly this should have been perceived, and the conclusion reached by the United States and Britain earlier that co-operation with the U.S.S.R. was impossible. Certainly, as stated above, war relationships and attitudes suggested the advisability of questioning the possibility of continued co-operation once the stimulus supplied by a powerful common enemy had been removed. Nevertheless, since the apparent alternative to an attempt at Great-Power co-operation was movement directly from World War II into World War III, it was felt by the American and British governments that every effort should be made to maintain the common front and to explore to the limit the possibilities of co-operation.

"CONTAINMENT" REPLACES CO-OPERATION
IN AMERICAN POLICY

By 1947, at least in the thinking of the American government, the possibility of arriving at settlements through negotiation with the Soviet government had been given up. The original assumption was thereupon replaced by the concept of "containment" of Soviet power. Underlying this so-called Truman Doctrine of containment was the conclusion that an important consideration in the invalidation of the original hypothesis had been the decline in effective American power in Europe (and also in Asia) which had occurred during 1946. It consequently came to be argued that it would be possible to negotiate agreements with the Soviet Union only when sufficient power had been developed to make clear to the Kremlin that it could not attain its objectives short of a general war in which power at least equivalent to its own would be brought to bear against it. But while the United States was in process of reviving its own military strength, together with that of its allies, further Soviet expansion had to be prevented.

The first concrete expression of the shift in the base of American policy was the acceptance of responsibilities in relation to Greece and Turkey. President Truman then said of American policy in general:

I am fully aware of the broad implications involved if the United States extends assistance to Greece and Turkey....

[2] Philip E. Mosely, "Techniques of Negotiation," in *Negotiating with the Russians* (Boston: World Peace Foundation, 1951), pp. 271-72. Quoted by permission.

One of the primary objectives of the foreign policy of the United States is the creation of conditions in which we and other nations will be able to work out a way of life free from coercion....

We shall not realize our objectives, however, unless we are willing to help free peoples to maintain their free institutions and their national integrity against aggressive movements that seek to impose upon them totalitarian regimes. This is no more than a frank recognition that totalitarian regimes imposed upon free peoples by direct or indirect aggression, undermine the foundations of international peace and hence the security of the United States.

The peoples of a number of countries in the world have recently had totalitarian regimes forced upon them against their will. The government of the United States has made frequent protests against coercion and intimidation, in violation of the Yalta agreement, in Poland, Roumania, and Bulgaria. I must also state that in a number of other countries there have been similar developments....

I believe that it must be the policy of the United States to support free peoples who are resisting attempted subjugation by armed minorities or by outside pressures.

I believe that we must assist free peoples to work out their own destinies in their own way.

I believe that our help should be primarily through economic and financial aid which is essential to economic stability and orderly political processes.[3]

Experience in Greece revealed, however, that the successful use of economic and financial assistance required the establishment of internal peace and order. Consequently the initial task was shortly perceived as one of military assistance in order to create and safeguard the conditions for economic reconstruction and rehabilitation. The balance between military and economic assistance correspondingly shifted in the application of the Greek-aid program. In the same fashion military revival in western Europe came to be related to economic reconstruction first in a secondary way in the Marshall plan and then, after the signature of the North Atlantic Treaty, in a primary way. Thus through economic revival sufficient strength was regained to enable governments to maintain themselves against internal subversion by national Communist parties acting essentially as instruments of Russian foreign policy. Then through military assistance and re-organization the attempt was made to build up sufficient collective military power to prevent the easy over-running of western Europe by Soviet armies.

[3] Text published in *Recent American Foreign Policy*, F. B. Wilcox and T. V. Kalijarvi, ed. (New York: Appleton-Century-Crofts, 1952), p. 817.

As part of this general movement, which was the direct result of the inability of the free world and the Soviet Union to reach agreement either in general or in the solution of particular European problems, the policies of both sides with respect to Germany underwent fundamental change. Each sought to gain German support. In the face of Russia's attempts to extend its influence from the eastern zone in Germany to the western zones, the United States shifted its view from that of Germany as an enemy state, to be kept weak, divided, and under strict control, to the policy of reconstruction of western Germany and its integration into the western European defense system.

POSTWAR INTERACTION OF EUROPEAN
AND FAR EASTERN POLITICS

It was because of immediately stronger and more direct Soviet expansionist pressures in Europe, as compared with eastern Asia, which violated agreements providing for co-operation in the reconstruction of the new governments in eastern Europe and in control of Germany and Austria, that Europe presented the first postwar battleground in the struggle between the Western powers and the Soviet Union. But in relation to the struggle in Europe it should have been recognized to a far greater extent than it was in the United States that an important element of European strength or weakness was to be found in Asia. For that reason, conditions in China and in Southeast Asia had a distinct relevance to the European aspect of the world struggle for power between the United States and its European allies and the Soviet bloc. This interaction was shown, for example, in the case of Holland. At the same time that it had to undertake reconstruction at home, the Dutch government was faced with the problem of re-establishment of Dutch rule in Indonesia. When that attempt was unsuccessful the Netherlands' government had to find a satisfactory basis of adjustment to the demands of Indonesian nationalism. Thus Dutch recovery in Europe was inevitably retarded by the necessity of diverting resources and energy to the struggle in Indonesia. Except as it proved possible to regain economic assets and to re-establish trade relationships within the framework of acceptable new agreements, the developments in Indonesia can only be viewed as lessening the importance of Holland as a factor in European politics. The point is not that the new relationships were good or bad. It is that there was an interdependence between

Europe and eastern Asia of a nature too infrequently taken into account.

Similarly, while the United Kingdom was seeking, with American assistance, to recover from the ravages of war, it was confronted with a situation of disorder and a problem of economic reconstruction in Burma and Malaya, to say nothing of the fact that it had also to reorganize its relationships with India. Attempts to find a solution of these Far Eastern and Asian problems brought about a diversion of some British resources and manpower from Europe to Asia, making the solution of the problems both of economic recovery at home and of the regaining of its world power position more difficult. In the balancing of its accounts with the United States, furthermore, there was a measure of dependence of Britain on the economic recovery of its colonies or former colonies, especially Malaya, since tin, rubber and tropical products in general found a ready dollar market in the United States.

Still another European colonial power, France, offers an even more striking illustration of the interrelationship of Far Eastern and European conditions. France's strength in postwar Europe was steadily sapped as a result of the demands made on French military resources by the protracted military operations which the Republic carried on in Indochina after 1945 against the Communist-led Vietminh. This was clearly a retarding factor in French recovery and especially in the revival of French military power in Europe.

The conditions of political disorder and instability which prevailed in Southeast Asia after 1945 had the natural result of preventing the revival of full production in the area. And, because of the nature of this production, the effects were felt by the industrial nations of western Europe and by the United States, and would have been so felt even without the complicating factor of conflict involved in the readjustment of political relationships. The postwar conflict between nationalism and colonialism was important in preventing the rapid re-establishment of the peace and order on which production and prosperity depend.

But even where this issue was early resolved in favor of nationalism, as in India, Burma, and the Philippines, it did not automatically bring about peace and order. None of the new states had the resources to carry through the program of reconstruction, rehabilitation, and readjustment necessary to repair the damages of war and occupation and to resolve the confusions incident to the establishment of self-government and independence. Thus the creation of stable political institutions and the establishment of orderly political processes was gradual and dependent on outside assistance, the conditions of which had to be carefully negotiated in each case to ensure that national independence was not compromised. Except to a limited extent by the European powers with particular responsibilities, the necessity for economic, financial, and technical assistance was perceived belatedly and then only as a result of operation of one or both of two sets of considerations. The first came from a renewed perception of the relationship of the production of the area to the world economy, and especially to the problem of western European recovery. The second resulted from a greater appreciation of the extent to which conditions of disorder and economic disorganization and distress provided fertile soil for Communist propaganda, and thus were related to the struggle to limit indirect Soviet expansionism through local Communist parties. This perception became more acute with the rise to power of the Chinese Communist Party concurrently with the re-establishment of Soviet power in the Far East. The relationships of the Russian to the Chinese Communist Party meant that the success of the latter at first carried with it an extension of Soviet Russia's influence into and over China.

RUSSIA IN THE FAR EAST

Before the outbreak of war in Europe in 1939 Russia had withdrawn completely from Manchuria with the forced sale to Manchukuo of the Chinese Eastern Railway. The U.S.S.R. did, however, still have a dominant position in Mongolia and it presented the principal outside threat to China's control of Sinkiang Province. Recurrent border incidents on the not precisely delimited frontier between Manchukuo and Mongolia indicated, nevertheless, that Russia's position in Mongolia was threatened by Japan, and the Soviet government had been forced to build up a defensive position for the protection of its own territories against a threatened Japanese attack. This defensive position had been seriously weakened with the shift of forces necessitated by the German attack in June, 1941. On the eve of that attack, however, Japan had negotiated a neutrality pact with the Soviet Union. Article II of this agreement stipulated that: "Should one of the contracting parties become the object of hostilities on the part of one or several third powers, the other contracting party will observe neutrality throughout the duration of the conflict." This gave Japan some assurance against an attack in the north if it should seek to capitalize in Southeast Asia on German victories against France, Britain, and the Netherlands in Europe. But it also gave Russia some degree of assurance against a Japanese attack on its Far Eastern territories while engaged in a life and death struggle against Germany. As already pointed out, it became Soviet policy to afford Japan no excuse for breaching this neutrality pact until it was absolutely clear that the war in the west had been won.

As the end of the war against Germany approached, however, the Soviet attitude began to change. At the conference at Teheran (November 28–December 1, 1943),

> The question of Soviet participation in the Pacific war was discussed in some detail. Roosevelt proposed to Stalin the basing of American heavy bombers in the Maritime Provinces north of Vladivostok. This was deemed a necessary requirement by our air force in order to cover the Japanese Islands. In addition, Roosevelt suggested the possible use of Soviet ports for our naval forces and requested the immediate exchange of military intelligence concerning Japan. Stalin agreed that these matters should be studied. Shortly thereafter we established exchange of combat intelligence. The other matters continued to be the subject of discussion on my (Harriman's) part with Stalin in Moscow during the ensuing year.[4]

In these conversations carried on after the Teheran Conference, the conditions of Soviet participation in the war against Japan began to be defined. Ambassador Harriman states that in one of his talks (in June, 1944) with Stalin the latter

> minimized the Chinese Communists, and stated that Chiang was the only man who could hold China together and that he should be supported. Molotov reiterated this position when Mr. Donald M. Nelson and Major General Patrick J. Hurley stopped at Moscow enroute to Chungking. Although Stalin had on several occasions mentioned Soviet political objectives in the East, it was not until December, 1944, that he outlined these objectives to me in detail. He said that Russia's position in the East should be generally re-established as it existed before the Russo-Japanese War of 1905. The lower half of Sakhalin should be returned to the Russians, as well as the Kurile Islands, in order to protect Soviet outlets to the Pacific. The Russians wished again to lease the ports of Dairen and Port Arthur and to obtain a lease on those railroads in Manchuria built by the Russians under contract with the Chinese, specifically, the Chinese

---

[4] Harriman Statement, *Joint (McArthur) Committee Hearings*, Pt. 5, p. 3329.

Eastern Railway, which was the direct line from the Trans-Siberian Railroad through to Vladivostok, and the South Manchurian Railroad making a connection to Dairen. He stated that the Soviet Union would not interfere with the sovereignty of China over Manchuria. In addition, Stalin asked for the recognition of the *status quo* in Outer Mongolia. I pointed out to Stalin that the talks at Teheran had envisaged internationalization of the Port of Dairen, rather than a lease. Stalin replied that this could be discussed. I immediately reported Stalin's proposals to President Roosevelt, and they became the basis of the discussions at Yalta ... (At the Yalta Conference). The crucial issue was not whether the Soviet Union would enter the Pacific war, but whether it would do so in time to be of help in the carrying out of the plans of the Joint Chiefs of Staff for an invasion of the Japanese home islands. The great danger existed that the Soviet Union would stand by until we had brought Japan to her knees at great cost in American lives, and then the Red Army could march into Manchuria and large areas of Northern China. It would then have been a simple matter for the Soviets to give expression to "popular demand" by establishing People's Republics of Manchuria and Inner Mongolia. President Roosevelt sought to reduce the general assurances which Stalin had previously given to specific undertakings for the early entrance of Russia in the Pacific War, to limit Soviet expansion in the East and to gain Soviet support for the Nationalist Government of China.[5]

The extent of President Roosevelt's success is shown in the agreement reached at Yalta. The Agreement Regarding Japan reads as follows:

The leaders of the three Great Powers—the Soviet Union, the United States of America and Great Britain—have agreed that in two or three months after Germany has surrendered and the war in Europe has terminated the Soviet Union shall enter into the war against Japan on the side of the Allies on condition that:

(1) The *status quo* in Outer Mongolia (The autonomous People's Republic) shall be preserved.

(2) The former rights of Russia violated by the treacherous attack of Japan in 1904 shall be restored, viz:

(a) the southern part of Sakhalin as well as all the islands adjacent to it shall be returned to the Soviet Union,

(b) the commercial port of Dairen shall be internationalized, the pre-eminent interests of the Soviet Union in this port being safeguarded and the lease of Port Arthur as a naval base of the U.S.S.R. restored,

(c) the Chinese Eastern Railroad and the South Manchurian Railroad which provides an outlet to Dairen shall be jointly operated by the

[5] *Ibid.*, pp. 3330-32.

establishment of a joint Soviet-Chinese Company, it being understood that the pre-eminent interests of the Soviet Union shall be safeguarded and that China shall retain full sovereignty in Manchuria;

(3) The Kurile islands shall be handed over to the Soviet Union.

It is understood that the agreement concerning Outer Mongolia and the ports and railroads referred to above will require concurrence of Generalissimo Chiang Kai-shek. The President will take measures to obtain this concurrence on advice from Marshal Stalin.

The heads of the Three Great Powers have agreed that these claims of the Soviet Union shall be unquestionably fulfilled after Japan has been defeated.

For its part the Soviet Union expresses its readiness to conclude with the National Government of China a pact of friendship and alliance between the U.S.S.R. and China in order to render assistance to China with its armed forces for the purpose of liberating China from the Japanese yoke.[6]

The negotiation of the Sino-Soviet Treaty of Friendship and Alliance, which Stalin expressed willingness at Yalta to conclude with the National government of China, was not undertaken until July of 1945, the reason officially assigned for delay in informing China of the Yalta agreements and in instituting negotiations being fear of premature disclosure to Japan of the Russian intention to enter the Pacific war. This delay made it necessary for negotiations to be pressed to ensure the conclusion and ratification of the treaty before the end of hostilities. The treaty was in fact signed only on August 14, 1945, five days after the Russian declaration of war on Japan and on the actual date of the surrender of Japan, although the formal instrument of surrender was not signed until September 2.

As finally concluded, the treaty and the accompanying exchange of notes [7] went somewhat beyond the Yalta agreement in restoring the Russian position in Manchuria and Mongolia. In place of the stipulation for the preservation of the *status quo* in Outer Mongolia, for

[6] Text as published in *A Decade of American Foreign Policy, Basic Documents, 1941-1949.* 81st Con., 1st Session, Sen. Doc. No. 123, pp. 33-34; also, Wilcox and Kalijarvi, *op. cit.,* as cited.

[7] The following quotations from the treaty are taken from the text printed as Annex 51 in *United States Relations with China,* Department of State Publication 3573 (Washington, 1949), hereafter cited as *China White Paper,* 1949. The exchange of Notes on Outer Mongolia, the Agreement concerning Dairen and the Protocol to it, the Agreement on Port Arthur and the Appendix to it, the Agreement Regarding Relations between the Chinese Administration and the Commander-in-Chief of the Soviet Forces . . ., and the Agreement Concerning the Chinese Changchun Railway, are printed as Annexes 52-59 in the same volume.

example, China agreed to "recognize the independence of Outer Mongolia with the existing boundary as its boundary," if after the defeat of Japan "a plebiscite of the Outer Mongolian people confirm this desire" for independence. This had the practical effect of confirming in advance the transfer of sovereignty over Outer Mongolia from China to a regime which was dominated by Moscow.

As to Manchuria, the stipulated Russian railway and leased-territory rights were to run for a period of thirty years. China was committed to "declare Dairen a free port open to the commerce of all nations" but to grant "the Soviet Union a lease of half of the port facilities, free of charge." This was the formulation given to the Yalta stipulation for safeguarding the "pre-eminent interest of the Soviet Union in this port." It was agreed that Port Arthur, with somewhat restricted boundaries as compared with those of 1904, should be jointly used by Russia and China as a naval base "with a view to strengthening the security of China and the U.S.S.R. against further invasion by Japan." In developing arrangements for joint use of the port as a naval base: "There shall be established a Sino-Soviet Military Commission. . . . The Commission shall consist of two Chinese and three Soviet representatives. The Chairman of the Commision shall be appointed by the Soviet side and the Vice Chairman shall be appointed by the Chinese side." This and other provisions put China in the position of the junior partner in administering the base. Similarly, the agreements on joint administration of the Manchurian railways during the thirty-year period placed Russia in the superior position.

These agreements were a matter of concern to the United States both during their negotiation and subsequently. The American government took the position that China was under no obligation to make concessions to the U.S.S.R. beyond those agreed upon at Yalta:

> Mr. Harriman, acting on instructions, informed Dr. Soong as a matter of record that the United States government considered that the proposals which he had already made fulfilled the Yalta Agreement and that any further concessions would be made with the understanding that they were made by the Chinese Government because of the value it attached to obtaining Soviet support in other directions.[8]

As the details of administration of the leased territory and the railways were worked out, the United States fell back on its policy of

[8] *China White Paper*, p. 117; also, Harriman Statement, *Joint (McArthur) Committee Hearings.*

1899 and sought from Russia and China a statement "affirming respect for the Open-Door policy in connection with the Soong-Stalin agreements." This was promised but "in the end, however, the Chinese Government seemingly took the position that the Sino-Soviet Treaty constituted a sufficient guarantee, since it did not again raise the question. The Soviet Government, which from the beginning had been reluctant, also seems to have allowed the question to lapse." Thus the definition of the re-established Russian position in Manchuria was viewed by the signatories as of concern only to the Soviet Union and China, without commitment to respect the interests of other states.

The "Soviet support in other directions" which the National Government at Chungking felt that it had secured in exchange for concessions beyond those of the Yalta Agreement were in general commitments to friendly collaboration. In Article V of the treaty

The High Contracting Parties, having regard to the interests of the security and economic development of each of them, agree to work together in close and friendly collaboration after the coming of peace and to act according to the principles of mutual respect for their sovereignty and territorial integrity and of non-interference in the internal affairs of the other contracting party. (Beyond this, in Article VI) The High Contracting Parties agree to render each other every possible economic assistance in the post-war period with a view to facilitating and accelerating reconstruction in both countries and to contributing to the cause of world prosperity.

But what was viewed as the real *quid pro quo* for the Manchurian concessions is to be found in the Exchange of Notes Relating to the Treaty of Friendship and Alliance, where it was laid down that:

(1) In accordance with the spirit of the aforementioned Treaty, and in order to put into effect its aims and purposes, the Government of the U.S.S.R. agrees to render to China moral support and aid in military supplies and other material resources, such support and aid to be entirely given to the National Government as the Central government of China.

(2) The Government of the U.S.S.R. regarded the Three Eastern provinces (Manchuria) as part of China and reaffirmed its respect for China's full sovereignty over the Three Eastern Provinces and recognize their territorial and administrative integrity.

(3) As for recent developments in Sinkiang the Soviet Government confirms that, as stated in Article V of the Treaty of Friendship and Alliance, it has no intention of interfering in the internal affairs of China.[9]

[9] From text of treaty and of Exchanges of Notes as published in *China White Paper*, Annex 51, 52, pp. 585-588.

This was designed to commit the U.S.S.R. to the National Government and against the Chinese Communists if the internal struggle should be resumed after the conclusion of hostilities against Japan. As a minimum, it seemed to ensure that the Chinese Communist Party would not have Soviet Russian support or encouragement if it sought either to maintain itself by armed force in its control of a part of China or to overthrow the National Government throughout China. As a maximum, it held out the possibility of direct assistance against the Chinese Communists and even of Russian pressure on them to come to terms with the (Kuomintang) National Government. This commitment was viewed by the National Government as an acceptable *quid pro quo* for the extension of the terms of the Yalta agreements.

THE U.S.S.R. IN THE PACIFIC WAR

The concessions made at Yalta to the Soviet Union were for the purpose of bringing about early Russian entrance into the war against Japan. Russian belligerency also gave the U.S.S.R. the right to participate in the negotiation of the conditions of peace with Japan. At the time of the Yalta Conference the Russians were unquestionably better informed than the Americans and the British concerning the imminence of Japanese surrender. The American military leaders had perhaps been oversold on the "no surrender without a guarantee of preservation of the National (i.e. Imperial) Polity" doctrine proclaimed by the Japanese. Whether or not that was the case, Anglo-American military planning, as of the beginning of 1945, was based on the view that Japan would not surrender without a successful invasion of the Japanese islands. To facilitate invasion and hold the resultant losses of American and Allied life to a minimum, it was thought necessary to bring Russian power to bear in Manchuria concurrently with Allied invasion of Japan. Military action in Manchuria would preclude the transfer of the vaunted Japanese Kwantung Army from Manchuria for the defense of Japan. Since Russia, as a neutral state, was in direct diplomatic and consular relationship with Japan until after the Yalta Conference, the Soviet government knew at first hand the desperate straits to which Japan had been reduced by submarine and air blockade and by air bombardment, before the atomic bomb had been perfected. Since it was the government approached by Japan, the U.S.S.R. also knew that the Japanese were seeking means to bring the war to an end. None of the information at the disposal of the Soviet government was apparently made available to its allies in the war against Germany, since Russia was not yet joined with them against Japan. Instead the Russians took advantage of the situation to secure their own interests at a minimum cost. Even so, the Soviet government delayed almost too long in concluding the necessary treaty with China and thus establishing a legal and, of more immediate importance, military position in Manchuria before the termination of hostilities. The Soviet government declared war on Japan on August 9, 1945. The Imperial order to surrender came on August 14. The Russians did not cease military operations in Manchuria and northern Korea on that date, however, but continued them to the time of the signing of the instruments of surrender on September 2, by which time they were in full military occupation of Manchuria. This gave them a much stronger position from which to deal with China and their other allies than one based only on the Yalta Agreement and the Sino-Soviet Treaty which was finally concluded only on August 14, the day of the Japanese capitulation.

This military position in Manchuria and Korea, together with the proximity of Russian territory to Korea in the northeast, made it possible for the Russians quickly to take over northern Korea from the Japanese. United States forces, moving by sea, could make a similarly quick entry into southern Korea. Since it was viewed as expedient from the military standpoint to execute the surrender terms as expeditiously as possible, the Russians were authorized to take over from the Japanese north of the 38th parallel and the Americans south of it. This purely military decision brought Russia back into Korea where it had sought to establish itself fifty years earlier in competition with the Chinese and the Japanese. The decision also had the consequence of making Korea again a "problem" in Far Eastern and world politics.

PREDOMINANT POSITION OF THE UNITED STATES IN 1945

In spite of this extension of Russian power in the Far East, the circumstances of the war and of its conclusion gave the United States rather than the Soviet Union the predominant position in the area. Until World War II the United States had not developed a substantial power position in the Far East, nor had it attempted to use military means to implement its policies. The occupation of the Philippines during and after the war with Spain represented an initial projection of American power across the Pacific into the Far Eastern area. It was soon made apparent, however, that there was not a settled determination to build up or to use national military power to implement policy in the American reaction to the controversies and conflicts which arose over China. The United States was: (1) prepared to define the policies and procedures which it felt should be followed by itself and others toward China; (2) to make vigorous diplomatic protests in the event of departure by others from those policies or procedures; (3) to give, on occasion, assistance of a financial and economic nature to China or to third states whose interests brought them to take action in apparent support of the defined policies; and (4) to refuse to recognize the consequences of action taken by others in contradiction of the principles of American Far-Eastern policy. But it came to be generally understood in the United States, as well as in the foreign offices of Europe and Asia, that the interest of the United States was not sufficiently great to cause it to use military means to support the policy of the Open Door and maintain the integrity of China. A partial exception to this generalization may be found in the use of force to establish control over the Philippines. But the definition of American policy toward the Philippines as that of ultimate independence, and the view which was widely held in the United States in the 1930's that the retention of the Philippines was a mistake, made this a partial rather than a complete exception. Certainly the United States did not use its possession of the Philippines to build up a power position in the Far East so as to implement its Far-Eastern policies. Its intentions, from that point of view, were revealed when it agreed at the Washington Conference (1921-22) not to further fortify the Islands.

Except where its interests were directly involved in national self-defense or in the protection of the life and property of its nationals abroad, the traditional policy of the United States had been one of neutrality, coupled with an emphasis on the use of pacific procedures, such as arbitration and conciliation, in the settlement of international disputes. This traditional attitude toward war was given extreme expression in the 1920's in the negotiation of such international instruments as the Kellogg Pact; and, in the 1930's, in the revision of the national neutrality law. With this attitude, the United States had consistently underemphasized the importance of power in the conduct of its foreign relations at the level of world politics as well as in the Far Eastern area.

Thus the outbreak of war in the Pacific found the United States without a developed military position in the Far East. It had to transform itself into a dominant military power before it could effectively seek to establish the principles of its Far-Eastern policy. This was accomplished with the Japanese "unconditional" surrender. At that time the United States had the power of decision in the Philippines. Upon liberation, authority was immediately transferred formally to the Commonwealth government, but that government was practically dependent on the American military for the exercise of its authority. The British, the Dutch, and the French, in the colonial area, were not in a position immediately to reestablish themselves in their colonies over strong American objection. It had been largely because of the insistence of the American government that Britain and the Soviet Union accepted China as a principal ally and a Great Power. And in China itself the United States had the facilities which made American assistance essential if the National Government was to re-establish its control over the provinces which had been under Japanese occupation since 1939.

During the war an American had served as the Chief-of-Staff to Chiang Kai-shek, as Commander-in-Chief of American forces in China and of such Chinese forces as were assigned to him, and as allocator of Lend-Lease supplies. Chinese armies had been equipped and trained by Americans in India and in China itself, where military and air-training missions had been constituted. General Chennault's "Flying Tigers" (at first an unofficial, volunteer air group) had been transformed into the United States' Fourteenth Air Force and as such had played an important part in the defense of "Free China" against the Japanese.

Thus, as of V-J Day, the best divisions of the Chinese National Army were American trained and equipped, and the United States had air and other transport facilities within China superior to those of the National Government itself. Without those facilities, which were put at its disposal, the National Government would have been hard put to it to move its armies into liberated China so as to accomplish a rapid transfer of power from the Japanese to itself.

In order to assist the Government in reoccupying Japanese-held areas and opening lines of communication, the United States immediately after V-J Day transported three Nationalist armies by air to key sectors of East and North China, including Shanghai, Nanking, and Peiping, and likewise during the ensuing months provided water transport for an additional large number of troops until, according to Department of the Army figures, between 400,000 and 500,000 Chinese soldiers had been moved to new positions. The plans for these operations and the planes and vessels to carry out the moves were provided through Headquarters, United States Forces, China Theater. In order to assist the Government further in maintaining control of certain key areas of North China and in repatriating the Japanese, and at the request of the National Government, over 50,000 United States Marines were landed in North China and occupied Peiping, Tientsin, and the coal mines to the north, together with the essential railroads in the area. With such American assistance, forces of the Generalissimo, who had been designated by SCAP as the sole agent to receive the surrender of Japanese forces in China proper, were able to effect the surrender of the great majority of the 1,200,000 Japanese troops stationed there, together with their equipment and stocks of military material.

Prior to V-J Day, the American Government had embarked on programs to equip an air force commensurate with the Chinese Government's needs and a 39 division army. Following V-J Day, transfers were continued to provide for an 8-1/3 group air force, and under an authorization to assist in equipping reoccupation forces, transfers of military material for ground troops were continued until, by the end of December, 1945, according to Department of the Army records, sufficient equipment had been transferred to complete by tonnage the requirements of the 39-division program. Other Lend-Lease transfers included quantities of vehicles and quartermaster items which were of major significance in giving the Nationalist armies mobility and in equipping them for operations in North China and Manchuria.[10]

Britain, the third major power, used its military and naval forces in the Far East mainly to re-enter the colonial area, the (British) Southeast Asia Command having been authorized to receive the Japanese surrender and take over from Japan in Burma, Malaya, Indonesia, Siam, and southern Indochina. It also re-established British authority in the Crown Colony of Hongkong. Britain was not, however, able to exercise the political influence in China which it had possessed in the past.

Thus, except for Russia in Manchuria, at the end of the war the United States was the only outside state which had a position of power within China sufficient to enable it to exert strong influence on the Chinese government. Molotov led General Hurley [11] to believe that the Soviet Union would keep its hands off and let the United States play the leading role in China. This view was held to be confirmed by

10 *China White Paper*, pp. 311-12.
11 See *infra.*, Chap. 4.

the commitment of the Soviet government to the National Government under the terms of the Soong-Molotov Treaty.

It was in Japan, however, that the predominance of the United States was most apparent. The surrender of Japan was followed by its occupation. The country occupied had been reduced territorially to the four islands originally constituting the Japanese state (Honshu, Shikoku, Kyushu, Hokkaido), together with the subjacent islands. Formosa, in accordance with the Cairo Declaration, had been allotted to China and was occupied by National Government forces. Korea, which was to become independent "in due course" under the terms of the Cairo Declaration, was in American occupation south of the 38th parallel and in Soviet occupation north of that parallel. The Soviet Union had, under the Yalta Agreement, occupied the Kuriles. But the Ryukyu Islands, with Okinawa, together with the most important Pacific island possessions of Japan, were occupied by United States forces, pending their ultimate disposition. Thus it was the Japanese homeland which was brought under Allied occupation, with General of the Army Douglas MacArthur designated as the Supreme Commander for the Allied Powers and concurrently Commander-in-Chief, United States Forces in the Far East.

While the occupation of Japan was described as Allied, the occupying power was actually the United States. The occupation forces were United States troops, except for token forces from Britain and some of the Commonwealth countries. The basic policy to be followed by the Allied Supreme Commander was embodied in a United States policy paper entitled *U.S. Initial Post-Surrender Policy for Japan*, substantially reaffirmed subsequently by the (Allied) Far Eastern Commission.

It may have been, as Secretary of State James F. Byrnes states in his book *Speaking Frankly*, that the United States "intended that the occupation of Japan should be an Allied responsibility." But what was proposed along that line, according to Secretary Byrnes, was the establishment of a ten-power advisory commission, to which "Great Britain objected because the commission would have only advisory powers. Australia and New Zealand wanted more decisive roles. Consequently, the establishment of a commission was delayed." Subsequently, the Russians proposed the establishment of a four-power *control* council for Japan. This was not acceptable to the United States. The ultimate agreement was on an eleven-member (later increased to thirteen) Far Eastern Commission to meet in Washington and a four-power Council to meet in Tokyo. The Far Eastern Commission, continues Mr. Byrnes, was given

> authority to decide upon the principles which control the administration of Japan, and its decisions are put into directives issued to the Supreme Allied Commander by the United States Government. This means, of course, that no basic policy may be adopted without our concurrence, and, pending agreement in the commission (by majority vote, including the concurring votes of the United Kingdom, the Soviet Union, China, and the United States), we are free to give interim directives on all urgent matters.[12]

Under these conditions, the organization of the Far Eastern Commission did not materially lessen the control of the United States over Japan. This was even more the case with respect to the Council established in Tokyo. It had advisory powers which it could exercise only with respect to such matters as were submitted to it by the Supreme Allied Commander, who, either in person or through a deputy, served as Chairman of the Council. Thus, although labelled "Allied" the occupation of Japan was actually American and represented the major projection of American politico-military power across the Pacific.

LIMITATIONS ON AMERICAN POWER

A false impression will have been created, however, if it is understood from the foregoing that the United States actually had a completely free hand in the Far East even in 1945. This was closest to being the case in Japan where there was general acceptance by the Japanese of the right of the United States, as the victor, to call the tune. The refusal of the United States to share with others the responsibilities of the occupation, especially by permitting other Allied powers to exercise authority over parts of Japan, reduced the area of international competition and rivalry there to a minimum.

In the Philippines, also, the United States had not only power but also a relatively free hand in its exercise. It was completely free (even more so than in Japan) as far as outside influences were concerned. Its freedom of decision was, however, restricted by the self-imposed limitations of its past policy and by its accepted obligations to the Philippine peoples who had been drawn into the war and had suffered

[12] These statements from James F. Byrnes *Speaking Frankly* (New York: Harpers, 1947), pp. 213-18. Quoted with permission from the publisher.

tremendous hardships because of American opposition to Japanese expansionism. Although they could not have maintained themselves as an independent state against Japan, and were in fact occupied by the Japanese as part of their Greater East Asia policy rather than because the Philippines were an American colony, the Philippine people felt that they had been fighting and incurring hardship in behalf of the United States rather than in their own separate cause. This feeling, accepted as a reality by the United States, was an effective restraint on United States' postwar Philippine policy, committing Washington to the implementation of the Commonwealth Act in its original terms.

A conception of legality and also a real sense of obligation to Britain as its principal ally in the Pacific as well as in the European war set limits to the ability of the United States to exercise its power decisively in terms of its own judgment in the remainder of the colonial area. Legality compelled it to proceed on the view that the Dutch, the British, and the French had title and the right to define policy in their colonies. They could be urged to introduce self-government or to en-large its area, but the United States could not with propriety go beyond that point. The American war objective had been to prevent the Japanese from adding those colonies to their empire and not to end empire in that area. The interest of the United States in Southeast Asia and Indonesia was primarily in freedom to trade. That interest had been generally satisfied through the trade policies followed by the European colonial powers. It was threatened by the "closed economy" policy of the Japanese. Thus there had been no policy interest or issue raised between the United States and the metropolitan countries with histori-cally established legal title to the several colonies.

The colonial countries were, furthermore, allies of the United States, with Britain especially playing an indispensable war role against both Germany and Japan. To have acted otherwise than in accordance with the accepted legalities of the situation would have had a seriously dis-ruptive effect on the partnership between Britain and the United States which had been evolved for war purposes and which it was intended should be projected into the postwar period. Thus, although it was the strongest power, the United States was not in a position to assert the right to decide the status and the future of Southeast Asia. It had in effect recognized that fact in the reallocation of commands in prepara-tion for the contemplated invasion of Japan. In that reallocation, United States power was dissociated from the colonial area, except in a supporting and supply role, since those parts of the area which had been within the command responsibilities of the Southwest Pacific (American) Command, except for the liberated Philippines, were transferred to the (British) Southeast Asia Command. While this was a decision taken on military grounds, it unquestionably had political implications and, with the Japanese surrender without further military operations, political consequences.

The implication was that policy for the colonial area would be expressive of interest of the colonial powers instead of one formulated by negotiation between colonial and noncolonial powers. This was clearly the immediate consequence. Britain determined the initial conditions of relationship after liberation from the Japanese not only in its own colonies of Burma and Malaya but also in Indonesia, southern Indochina, and Thailand.

In China also the complications of the situation were such that the United States did not have the unquestioned power of decision. In spite of the Molotov expression of Russian lack of interest in China, the insistence by the U.S.S.R. on its right of re-entry into Manchuria rapidly forced the United States to act with an eye on the possible Soviet reaction. In spite of the commitment of the Soviet Union to develop its relations with China exclusively through the medium of the National Government, the strength and militancy of the Chinese Communist Party and the not-too-well understood relationship which it had with the Soviet government through the Comintern needed to be taken into account in the development of relationships with the National Government itself. And the very commitment of the United States to the National Government as the recognized government of China reduced the actual freedom of action of the United States, in spite of the dependence of Chiang Kai-shek on American assistance. Here again the question of legality as a factor in the development of American policy arose. With it was also presented the question of the development and application of policy on the basis of traditional principles.

In conclusion, then, it must be reiterated that the postwar politics of the Far East cannot reasonably be examined in dissociation from the rest of the world. The projection of American power across the Pacific and the re-entry of the Soviet Union into Manchuria and Korea, together with the Far Eastern position and interests of Britain, in themselves should have prevented this dissociation at least in the development of policy. The politics of the Far East, either on an area or a country basis, could be self-contained only if Far-Eastern countries were the sole important parties interested in the development of relationships and of economic, political, and social activities in the area.

With this constantly in mind, attention can now properly be turned to the internal and external politics of the several countries of the area. Since China, as of 1945, was not only the most important country of the Far East but also the immediate center of the largest-scale disturbance, with the effects of the disturbance reaching far beyond its borders, attention must be first turned to its wartime and postwar politics.

BIBLIOGRAPHICAL REFERENCES

Baldwin, Hanson W., *Great Mistakes of the War* (New York: Harpers, 1950).

Beloff, Max, *The Foreign Policy of Soviet Russia, 1929-1941*, 2 vols. (New York: issued under the auspices of the Royal Institute of International Affairs, Oxford University Press, 1947-49).

Byrnes, James F., *Speaking Frankly* (New York: Harpers, 1947).

Carr, E. H., *The Soviet Impact on the Western World* (New York: Macmillan, 1947).

Chiang Kai-shek, *China's Destiny* (New York: Macmillan, 1947).

Churchill, Winston, *The Grand Alliance* (Boston: Houghton, Mifflin, 1950).

———, *The Hinge of Fate* (Boston: Houghton, Mifflin, 1950).

Dallin, David J., *The Big Three* (New Haven: Yale University Press, 1945).

———, *Soviet Russia and the Far East* (New Haven: Yale University Press, 1948).

———, *The New Soviet Empire* (New Haven: Yale University Press, 1951).

Deane, John R., *The Strange Alliance* (New York: Viking, 1947).

Hornbeck, Stanley K., "Eastern Asia (cont'd)," Chap. 30, in Thorsten V. Kalijarvi and Associates, *Modern World Politics*, 3rd ed. (New York: Crowell, 1953).

Hull, Cordell, *The Memoirs of Cordell Hull*, 2 vols. (New York: Macmillan, 1948), Vol. 2.

Millis, Walter, ed., *The Forrestal Diaries* (New York: Viking, 1951).

Moore, Harriet L., *Soviet Far Eastern Policy, 1931-1945* (Princeton: Princeton University Press, 1945).

Sherwood, Robert E., *Roosevelt and Hopkins: An Intimate History* (New York: Harpers, 1948).

Stimson, Henry L., and Bundy, McGeorge, *On Active Service in Peace and War* (New York: Harpers, 1947).

Welles, Sumner, *The Time for Decision* (New York: Harpers, 1944).

——, *Where Are We Heading?* (New York: Harpers, 1946).

Zinkin, Maurice, *Asia and the West* (London: Chatto and Windus, 1951).

3

The Kuomintang Period
of the Chinese Revolution

✳✳✳✳✳✳✳✳✳✳✳✳✳✳✳✳✳✳✳✳✳✳✳✳✳✳✳✳✳✳✳✳✳✳✳✳

EARLY KUOMINTANG-COMMUNIST PARTY RELATIONS

THE JAPANESE SURRENDER brought to a successful conclusion a war which had involved all of China for the eight-year period from July, 1937 to August, 1945. In actual fact the complication of the problem of government in China as a result of external aggression began even earlier. The external threat to the integrity of the country and to the stability of its government was made initially in 1931 with Japanese military action in Manchuria. This threat was presented at the same time as the domestic challenge which was made by the Chinese Communist Party to the authority of the Kuomintang as the governing party. After an initial period of Communist-Kuomintang co-operation, the Communist members had been purged from the Kuomintang in 1927 as the result of an attempt on their part to displace Chiang Kai-shek as the revolutionary leader and to assume control of the Chinese revolution. The purge disorganized and weakened but did not destroy the Communist Party. It had begun to recover strength by 1931 and thereafter offered the most serious of several internal threats to the power of the Kuomintang, and of the National Government which was established by it in 1928.

Presented in the early 1930's with the double threat (1) of Japanese aggression first in Manchuria and then in North China and (2) of Communist Party resurgence in the Kiangsi-Fukien area, Chiang Kai-shek felt compelled to subordinate the realization of the revolutionary purposes of the Kuomintang (a) to consolidation of the authority of the National Government within China against internal opposition and (b) to defense of the country against the Japanese, in that order. In so doing, he laid himself open to the charge of putting personal power and party interests above defense of the country and maintenance of its territorial integrity. Regardless of the merits of the charges, however, it must be recognized that Chiang did act on the assumption that the first requirement was for the government to bring the country under its exclusive authority. For that purpose such military power as the National Government possessed was utilized mainly against the Communists rather than the Japanese during the years from 1931 to 1937. As a result of these military operations, the Communists were finally dislodged from their base in the mountainous Kiangsi-Fukien region. They were not, however, eliminated as a challenge to the authority of the National Government, being able to break through its encircling forces and move their seat of government to the northwestern part of China. From their new territorial base adjacent to the provinces from which Japan was seeking to dislodge the National Government the Communist leaders began to sloganize the need for a united front to resist the Japanese. This coincided in point of time with a shift in tactics on the part of the Communist International (Comintern) which had always exercised an important influence over such national affiliates as the Chinese Communist Party. The general international situation had made it expedient, in the opinion of the Comintern, for national Communist parties in all countries to join forces with all except the extreme rightist elements in support of existing governments threatened with displacement by non-Communist totalitarian regimes. Thus participation in government was not merely authorized but directed by the Comintern for all Communist parties, where that could be arranged, in place of systematic opposition to all non-Communist governments, regardless of their political complexion.

This shift in the international party line was well adapted to the requirements of the Chinese situation. The problem in China was not, to be sure, that of bringing about co-operation between leftist parties for purposes of defense against an internal threat from the extreme right. It was rather that of establishing internal unity for purposes of defense against the Japanese. The underlying purpose, from the Communist point of view was, nevertheless, the same. It was that of finding an agreed basis for the termination of domestic hostilities at a time of party weakness. Consequently the party slogans were shifted from the earlier demand for the extinction of the Kuomintang to insistence that

Chinese should stop killing one another and unite against Japan as the common enemy.

Early in 1937, following the release of Chiang Kai-shek, who had been seized by non-Communist army leaders seeking to bring about a change in policy in the direction sought by the Communists, the terms of an alliance had been defined by the Kuomintang and accepted by the Communists. The arrangements made can properly be described as terms of alliance in spite of the fact that the Communists theoretically subordinated themselves to the National Government. The Communist area was organized as the Northwest Border Region, but it remained autonomous under the exclusive authority of the Communists, although its officialdom technically exercised authority as National Government officials. It actually remained a proscribed area for the Kuomintang. The Communist military forces, formerly called the Red Armies, were renamed as Route Armies of the National Government, but with their own commands and separately maintained identities, although, again theoretically, brought under the over-all command of Generalissimo Chiang Kai-shek and the Supreme Military Council of the National Government. Thus the Communist Party, with its governmental apparatus and its military forces, remained intact and in control of a portion of China. Throughout the war its relations with the National Government were conducted through negotiations rather than in subordination to Nanking. This United Front, realizing the intent of the Communist slogans, thus was on the road to formal conclusion at the time of the outbreak of the Sino-Japanese "incident" in July, 1937, at the Marco Polo bridge in North China.

One beneficial effect of this alliance, from the point of view of the National Government, was that it enabled the groundwork to be laid for aid from the Soviet Union after the outbreak of hostilities with Japan. The U.S.S.R. had encouraged the Chinese Communists in their moves to form the United Front because Moscow did not want to see Chiang Kai-shek succumb to Japanese pressure and enter the anti-Comintern camp. Consequently the Soviet government had begun to attempt to allay Chinese suspicion of the Soviet Union. This suspicion to some extent was an outgrowth of Russian policy toward Outer Mongolia and in China's Sinkiang Province, but it resulted even more from the party conflict in China. The suspension of that conflict made possible the conclusion of the Sino-Soviet Nonaggression Pact of August 21, 1937.

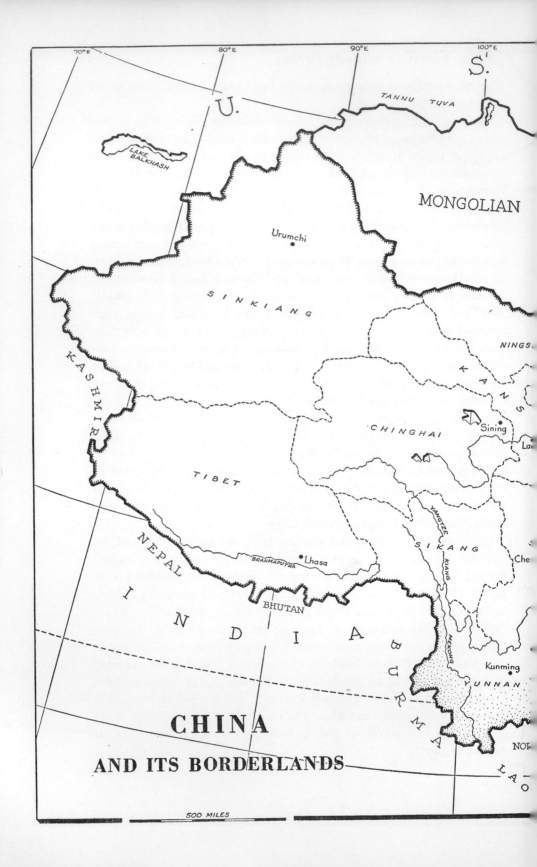

CHINA

AND ITS BORDERLANDS

500 MILES

CHINA AND THE SOVIET UNION: 1937-39

It was the Soviet Union which gave the most extensive material support to China during the first two years (1937-39) of the second Sino-Japanese war.[1] Russia also gave China strong diplomatic support at the Brussels Conference, called to seek a basis of accommodation between China and Japan. During this two-year period, the U.S.S.R. extended total credits of U.S. $250 million to China for the purchase of Russian arms and ammunition at prices fixed in American currency. The loan agreements provided for an interest rate of 3 per cent and for repayment by China, over a period of some thirteen years, in such raw materials as brick tea, wool, and tungsten. During 1937-38 Soviet-supplied ammunition came by sea from Odessa, but after the fall of Canton, the old "silk" route through Sinkiang to Lanchow was mainly utilized. During 1937-39 the Chinese authorities modernized this route sufficiently for it to carry lorries loaded with ammunition and other supplies. Camel caravans carried supplies of petrol to the various fueling stations along the route of over two thousand miles. Of direct military importance, furthermore, the Soviet government sent into China planes and pilots. Such assistance was essential since, after the signature of the Anti-Comintern agreements, Japan finally succeeded in securing the withdrawal of the Italian Air Mission and of the German Military Mission which had been sent to China at the request of the National Government.

This Soviet military assistance was extended to the National Government directly and not through the Chinese Communists. What the latter received from it came to them through the medium of the National Government. In this respect the attitude of the Soviet Union and also that of the Chinese Communists at this time can only be described as correct. For that reason, this period of relationship had importance since it helped to bring about acceptance as reliable of the pledge of the Soviet Union in the 1945 treaty and agreements to deal with China exclusively through the medium of the National Government. This part of the record supported the view, in other words, that the U.S.S.R. would respect its pledged word. Its interest during these years, of course, was served by its correct behavior.

[1] Aitchen K. Wu, *China and the Soviet Union* (New York: John Day, 1950), Chap. 7. See also F. C. Jones, *Japan's New Order in East Asia: Its Rise and Fall, 1937-1945* (New York: Oxford University Press, 1954), Chap. 6.

Russian assistance to China came to an end with the outbreak of the war in Europe in 1939, preceded as it was by the Nazi-Soviet Neutrality Pact, and followed as it was by the protracted negotiations between Russia and Japan which finally resulted in signature of the Japanese-Soviet Neutrality Agreement.

DETERIORATION OF KUOMINTANG-COMMUNIST PARTY RELATIONS AFTER 1941

Almost concurrently with these developments in Sino-Soviet relations, the relations between the Kuomintang and the Chinese Communists began to deteriorate. While the Nationalist armies were engaged against the Japanese at Shanghai, Nanking, and Hankow, the Communists applied against the Japanese the tactics which Mao Tse-tung had exploited successfully in the civil war. The Communists had come to be viewed as masters of the art of guerrilla warfare, and they employed guerrilla tactics against the Japanese with more success than attended the Nationalist armies in their attempts to meet the Japanese in the more conventional positional warfare. Thus the Communists grew stronger through their methods of waging war while the National Government grew weaker as Chiang's best troops were decimated and as the territorial base of the National Government was steadily contracted through enforced retirement into the southwestern provinces. These Communist tactics enabled them to build up centers of power in North China behind the Japanese lines and thus beyond the area in the Northwest into which at the outset they had been constricted. They also received permission from the National Government to organize guerrilla forces to operate against the Japanese in the Yangtze region south of Nanking. The organization and operations of this Communist force, consequently, brought the Communists back into the area from which they had been driven in 1934.

It was out of the activities of this new Communist army (the Fourth Army) that major friction between the Kuomintang and the Communists developed. This friction was revealed in a demand of the National Government's Minister of War in November, 1940, that the Fourth Army withdraw from the south Yangtze region. The Communist leaders, on their side, demanded not only the reconsideration of this order but also action on their earlier requests for legalization of their party, release of imprisoned Communists, cessation of action against

Communists and their families, and resumption of supply of ammunition which they charged had been denied them for some fourteen months. The issue was so sharply joined by 1941 that there was a reasonable possibility of renewal of hostilities between the Kuomintang armies and those of the Communists. If the position of the National Government had been further weakened as a result of renewal of the internal struggle it might well have concluded that its continued existence depended upon acceptance of the terms of peace which were then being proposed by Japan. In that case Japan would have given up the attempt being made to establish in power the government at Nanking headed by Wang Ching-wei which it had sponsored as the alternative to the National Government at Chungking headed by Chiang Kai-shek. To ensure continued resistance to Japan, the Communists made concessions and Chiang also showed a readiness to negotiate a new agreement with the Communists. Consequently the formal split, followed by a renewal of hostilities, was averted, but relations were essentially those of armed truce for the duration of the international war. The Kuomintang sought, with some measure of success, to block off the Communist area from the rest of "Free" China, but the Generalissimo insisted that he would seek a settlement with the Communists by political and not by military means. Without a firm political settlement, however, the internal struggle was merely suspended for the period of the Japanese war and not concluded.

COMMUNIST PARTY ORGANIZATION

For an understanding of the situation which existed after the Japanese surrender, it is essential to examine more closely the political situation in these two relatively separate parts of unoccupied China. In each, from different premises, a single party sought to maintain a monopoly of the power to govern. In spite of appearances, this monopoly of power in the northwest was more complete in the hands of the Communist Party than that exercised by the Kuomintang in southwestern China. The appearance to the contrary, which greatly impressed foreigners when they were able to enter the Communist area shortly before and immediately after V-J day, was to be found in governmental arrangements. The Communist Party on the surface accepted the fact that its membership was a minority in the population of the area. Consequently it avoided a monopoly of governmental positions.

In village and local government representative bodies, for example, it asserted a right to only one-third of the membership, two-thirds representing the non-Communist elements in the community which were not, however, allowed to organize into competitive parties. The same formula was used in the distribution of administrative positions. Those who were suspected of being anti-Communist, of course, were denied any right of participation in government. This would include, by definition, any who had Kuomintang affiliations or sympathies. Only the Communists, however, had the right to organize for political purposes and thus had the right to concert programs of policy or action. In fact, the non-Commmunists were fragmented to the individual since it was prohibited for even two persons to enter into advance agreement on questions at issue. The Communists, on the other hand, were a compact and single-minded group, bringing into the structure of government policies which had already been debated and agreed upon in party meetings. Thus a cohesive minority was in an effective position to chart the course of government in competition with an unorganized majority. Consistent dissent on the part of the individual might readily cause him to be labelled anti-Communist and thus put him outside the area of political participation. And, in the background, was always the fact that the military and police power in the area was exclusively Communist. From the outset the party itself had had the Red armies as its most important supporting agencies. Under these circumstances it was possible for the party to give a semblance of authority to the unorganized people while retaining power exclusively in its own hands. The outward appearance of democracy in the organization of the Communist area was superficially impressive but it did not conform to the inner reality which was that of effective monopolization of power by the Communist Party leadership.

The premise on which the Communist Party organized this monopoly of power may be stated as follows: the party membership was the spearhead of the proletariat, which had the mission of leading the peasantry toward revolutionary objectives. The monopoly of power was to be maintained until the ultimate objective of creating a classless society, assimilated to an urban proletariat, had been attained. Under this premise, consequently, the party dictatorship had no actual terminal point.

The scheme of revolutionary party organization which had been introduced into China by the Russians during the first period of collaboration (1925-27) had as its central feature the principle of democratic centralism. This conception involved the establishment of an hierarchy of party organs, with the higher and smaller organs elected by the lower. Thus the democratic method of elections, starting at the mass base, was theoretically applied within the party. But decisions taken at the higher levels were binding on the party officialdom and organs at the lower levels, even to the point of cancellation or suspension of decisions already put into effect. This was the element of centralism, within the democratic framework provided by elections. The final power, consequently, rested in the hands of the Presidium of the Central Committee of the party. The effective organization of centralism as a principle, furthermore, made readily possible the manipulation of the democratic elements in the system.

The conclusion which has to be reached, then, is that, within the Communist area, in spite of a large degree of participation in government by individuals who were not Communists but were not anti-Communists, there was single-party control, with a few individuals at the apex of the party pyramid actually possessing the effective powers of government. No organized opposition was tolerated nor was the Kuomintang admitted to the Communist area even for purposes of ideological competition through discussion and publication.

ORGANIZATION OF GOVERNMENT
UNDER THE KUOMINTANG

Kuomintang China also was organized on the basis of single-party monopolization of power. This was provided for in the program of Sun Yat-sen for progression from "warlord" government to constitutional democracy through a period of "tutelage" during which the Kuomintang would be the sole legal party, with responsibility for preparation of the people for the exercise of power, starting at the local level and moving by stages to that of the nation. Party dictatorship thus was viewed as a means to the end of successful introduction of constitutional democracy and was designed to be self-liquidating. The termination of party tutelage had not been proclaimed, however, by the end of the war, although it had been promised frequently by Chiang Kai-shek. The reasons for delay were found in the necessity first for concentrating all efforts on the establishment of complete internal unity under the party government and then on the defense of the country against external aggression. Until 1937 the Communist attempt to overthrow the government by military means gave the Kuomintang its most acceptable excuse for maintaining its exclusive position, since the revival of the Communist Party as a military opposition to the new government established at Nanking in 1928, even before its power had been consolidated over remnants of warlord provincialism and against the Canton "reorganizationists," really meant that the military opposition to the Nationalist Party had not been overcome. This continued condition of insurgency supported the tendency toward concentration of power within the Kuomintang and prevented a shift in emphasis from the military to the civil elements within the party. As the Commander-in-Chief of the revolutionary forces, and the accepted head of the new officer corps of the National Government's armies, Chiang Kai-shek was able fairly consistently to dominate the Kuomintang and to utilize it as an instrument of personal rule. The oppositional elements both within and outside the party, however, were sufficiently strong so that he was never able to assert fully a personal dictatorship outside the framework of Sunyatsenism. What did emerge was a strong personal identification of his power with the position of the Kuomintang, and an identification of the welfare of China with the maintenance of control by the Kuomintang.

While organized along lines similar to those of the Chinese Communist Party, leading to a similar flow of power from the top down, the Kuomintang was never a monolithic party to the same extent as the Communist Party. It included elements representative of points of view on policy ranging (after the Communist purge of 1927) from the non-Communist extreme left (led by Wang Ching-wei) to a reactionary right. Chiang Kai-shek was able to maintain a dominant position by utilizing his military power and by playing one group off against another. In the process he showed considerable skill as a politician. But this situation within the Kuomintang made it difficult, to the point of impossibility under civil war conditions, for the party to agree upon and put into effect a vigorous program of internal economic and social reform in competition with the Communists.

One element in the party, as stated above, was the military in the form of a new officer class which constituted a solid core of personal support for Chiang Kai-shek. The old warlord element which had come into the party on the principle of conversion represented by expediency was sometimes competitive with the new military group but tended to support Chiang Kai-shek when his star was clearly in the ascendancy.

A second element in the Kuomintang, also personally loyal to Chiang Kai-shek, was "rightist" in its undeviating hostility to communism. It may also be considered conservative because it sought to promote a revival of Confucian social values rather than emphasizing the new techniques and values which were an importation into China from the West. This element, called the C.C. Clique (from the names of its leaders, Ch'en Li-fu and Ch'en Kuo-fu), interested itself in party organization and indoctrination. The Ch'en brothers sought to develop intraparty discipline in order to maintain the party as an effective instrument of power in the state. Thus they helped to bring into the administrative mechanism people who were conditioned to exercise authority under direction from above, following faithfully the party line thus authoritatively set. There was no particular concern on the part of those thus indoctrinated with the political, economic, or social uses of the power possessed by the Kuomintang. Because they were neo-Confucianist and anti-Communist, however, their leaders were, for example, in general opposed to drastic land reform because of the role played by the landed gentry in the society of traditional (Confucian) China. Since the party indoctrination undertaken under the direction of the Ch'en brothers was carried on under the guise of education, however, it was not rigorous enough to ensure complete and unquestioning ideological conformity to the views of the party leadership.

A third party element, more reformative and modern, in the sense of being interested in the development of a modern economy, came from the new commercial, industrial, and financial interests which had recently come into being in the cities of the coastal area. This element included most of the Western-trained Chinese and many of the students who were influenced by the nationalist-minded faculties of the colleges and universities of China. These people played a most important role in the Kuomintang until they were cut off from their area of economic activity with the enforced retirement of the government to Chungking. They remained influential within the party and the governmental bureaucracy thereafter to the extent that their services were essential: (1) to the organization of the war production of the provinces which remained under the control of the National Government, and (2) in dealing with the United States and Britain, within

China as well as abroad. Otherwise, since the part of the country which remained under the control of the National Government between 1939 and 1945 had remained largely unaffected by the revolutionary tide, territorial contraction of the area of governmental control strengthened the position of those around Chiang who had a backward rather than a forward look. Thus the more progressive elements in the party found their influence lessened after the shift in the seat of government to Chungking.

Furthermore, the effect of World War II inevitably had been to tighten up both the party and the intraparty controls of an essentially authoritarian system. The repressive activities of censorship and of the secret police were magnified in Free China to the point where there was little formal freedom of speech and of the press, and consequently no opportunity for effective criticism of public policy or of individuals protected by them. Much of this tightening was necessary for war purposes. Nevertheless, the net effect of restriction of criticism was to lower public morale, lessen efficiency, and open the way to exploitation of the war for purposes of individual aggrandizement. Even personally honest officials became suspect, as tea-shop gossip about officials was substituted, under these circumstances, for responsible criticism. Unless drastic reform was instituted and public confidence in the disinterested leadership of the Kuomintang restored, the party, and the Kuomintang-controlled National Government would clearly enter the postwar competition for continued power under severe handicaps.

THE PEOPLE'S POLITICAL CONFERENCE (PPC)

Aside from occasional personnel shifts in the top bureaucracy, which were, however, without fundamental significance, the only modification of the system of one-party rule, supported by repression, was that resulting from a continuation of the People's Political Council (PPC),[2] established by a decision of the emergency session of the Kuomintang Party Congress held in Hankow in March, 1938. While this was an appointive body it nevertheless gave some expression to the variety of articulate opinion in the country, giving representation to the opposition parties, including the Communist, through represen-

[2] On the PPC see Ch'ien Tuan-sheng, *The Government and Politics of China* (Cambridge: Harvard University Press, 1950), Chap. 19.

tatives of their own choice. It had the right to advise the government on questions of public policy and the government was expected to consult it, except in emergency cases, before putting important measures into effect. Its role, however, was strictly advisory and consultative. Nevertheless, in the sessions of the first PPC held between 1938 and 1940, and in the sessions of the second Council, which held its first session at Chungking in 1941, the opinions of non-Kuomintang China, and of the more critical elements within the party itself, could be expressed, and their expression served to modify policy. These years were, of course, those of largely unassisted self-defense and of national self-respect maintained in the face of extreme adversity. It was also the period of mutual observance of the conditions of alliance between the Kuomintang and the Communist Party.

The renewed antagonism between the Communists and the Kuomintang in and after 1941 lessened the importance of the PPC as an organ of political unity. Communist Party representation in the Council came virtually to an end, and with it the expression in the Council of a strong, organized minority opinion. The constant increase in the size of the PPC [3] also lessened rather than increased its representational capacity since it resulted in giving more seats to Kuomintang local party members, the great increase being in the category of those representing the provincial organizations of the party. These provincial organizations were frequently dominated by local or personal factions. They consequently selected representatives who, on the whole, might be expected to make an approach to national problems from the point of view of local rather than national interests. Thus the increased Kuomintang representation did not improve the quality of majority party representation in the Council. This was not of the highest in any case since the most important and capable among the party leaders had been legally debarred from membership at the outset since they held office in the government or were members of the party Central Executive or Supervisory Committees.

The non-Kuomintang and non-Communist members of the PPC either represented minor parties or were independent from the point of view of party affiliation. The minor party representatives were primarily concerned with securing tolerance for the party which they represented by avoiding too extreme criticism of Kuomintang (i.e.,

[3] From 200 in the first to 240 in the second and third Councils and 290, later increased to 362, in the fourth. Figures given by Ch'ien, *Ibid.*, pp. 281-82.

National Government) policies. The independents, frequently men of real distinction in private life, were only in a position to express individual opinions. Their views frequently lacked weight because expressed by those previously uninterested, uninstructed, or inexperienced in politics except where questions had previously impinged on such other areas of activity as the educational and cultural, or the social, in which they had been interested.

In spite of its serious weaknesses and the limitations of its members the PPC, nevertheless, had importance as indicating a limited measure of tolerance of non-Kuomintang parties and of "independents." Its mere existence indicated that there was more freedom of organization and expression in Kuomintang China during and after the war than there was in reality in Communist China. In spite of this fact, however, which was underscored by the tolerated maintenance of a Communist mission in Chungking without similar representation of the Kuomintang being permitted at the Communist capital, the Communists came, in and after 1944, to be viewed by many both in China and abroad as the more democratic of the two regimes, and thus preferable to the Kuomintang as an instrument of government.

In this very tolerance, because of its necessarily restricted application, may be found at least a partial explanation of acceptance of a conclusion which was really at variance with the facts. During the war period the China theater and particularly Chungking itself was a peculiarly closed environment for those living in Kuomintang China. Conclusions were reached in general on the basis of experience restricted to wartime China. Comparisons could only be made on the basis of experience with Kuomintang restrictions set over against what such persuasive advocates as Chou En-lai and Madame Sun Yat-sen reported concerning conditions and restrictions in Communist China. Even after the American Military Mission at Yenan had been authorized by Chiang Kai-shek, its members had their contacts with reality in the Northwest Border Region softened and colored by filtration through the persuasive expositions of Mao Tse-tung and other important Communist leaders. The accessibility of these top leaders marked them as "democratic" as contrasted with the "undemocratic" aloofness of Chiang Kai-shek. And, of greater importance, none of the direct contacts in China with the Communist world was marked by the restrictiveness, leading to a feeling of personal frustration, which was a marked feature of life in Chungking.

The minor parties referred to above as having representation in the PPC were not parties in the sense of having a mass following during the war period or thereafter. They did, however, come together and pool their strength after V-J Day in a party confederation known as the Democratic Alliance or League. Through it they sought to assert themselves as a mediatory group between the Communists and the Kuomintang. Because they were articulate and because of their access to the foreign press, they even gained some recognition as a possible alternative to the two competitive systems of party dictatorship. They had, however, little real internal political power in their own right since they lacked, even in coalition, any sort of mass organization and support and had none of the instruments of power at their disposal. Although attempting to play the role of make-weight in the internal struggle for power, actually they were used by one group or the other to give the appearance of a broadening of the effective base of political participation beyond that of the single party.

EFFECTS OF THE WAR IN AND ON CHINA

The political situation between 1941 and 1945, then, was one in which the National Government was accepted for international purposes as the government of China, and that government was in fact as well as in theory the instrument through which a single party, the Kuomintang, ruled China. A line could not be readily drawn between party policy and governmental or state policy. It was this which made for confusion when, during and after the war, the United States sought to extend aid of various sorts to China through the medium of the recognized government but also tried to play a mediatory role between the minority party (the Communists) and the controlling party (the Kuomintang). Criticism of the Kuomintang could not readily be dissociated from criticism of an Allied government. The internal political situation also brought about a decline in morale in Free China after 1941, as might, under the circumstances, have been anticipated.

It was primarily the economic situation, however, which both caused and gave evidence of decline in morale in Free China. The division of the country had disrupted normal economic exchanges; the areas of major industrial productivity had been lost to the Japanese; and, finally, outside sources of supply were largely cut off. Consequently, after 1941, shortages of almost every kind of commodity, already serious as a result of developments from 1937-41, were constantly on the increase. The inevitable result was inflation.

This was not effectively controlled by the government in the interest either of the war effort or of the welfare of the individual. Instead, the existing situation caused many officials to use their positions to advance their own private interests. The profits of the trade in goods smuggled (with the connivance of officials on both sides) from Japanese-occupied China into Free China enriched both officials and traders. It was even more profitable to be able to control the distribution and use of goods brought by the American airlift into China. Even imports made for war purposes by the government itself began to find their way into private trade channels. Since much of the wealth accumulated by profiteering was illicit it escaped taxation and the burden of the war had to be borne to an increasing extent by the peasants. But a fair proportion of the taxes collected in kind was retained by the tax-gatherer to cover the "cost of collection." This further aggravated the National Government's financial problem.

The outbreak of war in the Pacific in December, 1941, coincided in point of time with the virtual breakdown of the alliance between the Kuomintang and the Chinese Communist Party. Consequently the United States,[4] which had an interest not only in keeping China in the war against Japan but also in re-energizing China's war effort for purposes of an ultimate offensive against the Japanese, could not avoid concern with the internal situation in China. The principal American agent in China, General Joseph W. Stilwell, was eminently fitted to undertake the training of Chinese armies and leading Chinese ground forces against the Japanese. He was not so well fitted to perform the delicate diplomatic tasks involved in persuading the head of the Chinese government, for whom he had and continually showed antipathy, to take decisions which were personally distasteful to him, nor to be a balance-wheel among the competitive forces, some of which were American, in play at Chungking. His objective was to utilize American aid so as to bring China's total forces to bear on the Japanese in ground operations, first in Upper Burma and finally in China itself. To accomplish this, General Stilwell came to the conclusion that it was necessary

[4] In relation to China during the war, it seems appropriate to limit reference to the United States, rather than referring to the Allies because on the whole Britain followed the United States in the development of policy and of relationship to the internal situation.

to undertake extensive retraining of the Chinese armies. Since he had little confidence in the military capabilities of the upper levels of the Chinese Command, he felt it essential that Chiang's armies be brought under American direction. The attainment of the war objective, as he saw it, further required: (1) that the national armies, which had been withdrawn from military operations against the Japanese to maintain the Kuomintang position against the Communists, be utilized once more against the Japanese in offensive operations; and (2) that the Communist armies should be similarly utilized and supported for that purpose, and be incorporated in his command. The generalissimo, however, was not willing to permit the transfer of direction of his forces to American officers. Neither was he willing to weaken his position against the Communists either by withdrawal of his own troops from the Communist frontier for use (and probably decimation) against the Japanese, except in an extreme emergency, nor to permit operations by the Communist armies throughout China, even if it were possible to bring them effectively under American command.

Since, however, Chiang Kai-shek was under strong pressure not merely from General Stilwell but also from President Roosevelt [5] to agree to the Stilwell proposals, he did accept them in principle "but suggested that as a preliminary step a high ranking American official, well acquainted with political as well as military matters and having the complete confidence of the President be sent to Chungking to discuss the problem." [6]

In response to this request, General Patrick Hurley was sent as a special representative of the President to Chungking, on the assumption

[5] Who wrote to the Generalissimo on July 7, 1944: "The critical situation which now exists in my opinion calls for the delegation to one individual of the powers to co-ordinate all of the Allied military resources in China, including the Communist forces.... I am promoting General Stilwell to the rank of full General and I recommend for your most urgent consideration that you recall him from Burma and place him directly under you in the command of all Chinese and American forces, and that you charge him with the full responsibility and authority for the co-ordination and direction of the operations required to stem the tide of the enemy's forces. I feel that the case of China is so desperate that if radical and promptly applied remedies are not immediately effected, our common cause will suffer a disastrous setback." (*China White Paper*, p. 66). Other messages to the same effect were sent on July 7 and August 23. It should also be noted that Secretary of War Stimson and General Marshall, Chief of Staff, Stilwell's immediate superiors, consistently supported Stilwell and approved his policies. Their support was, as a matter of fact, more consistent than was that of President Roosevelt.
[6] *Ibid.*, p. 66.

that the Generalissimo would proceed immediately to put into effect that agreement in principle. The latter was not done, however, and the relations of Chiang Kai-shek and General Stilwell became, in consequence, increasingly bad. This meant that General Hurley was unable to carry out successfully that part of his mission which was "to promote harmonious relations between Chiang and General Joseph Stilwell and to facilitate the latter's exercise of command over the Chinese armies placed under his direction." [7] Stilwell was recalled in October at the insistence of Chiang, and his successor, General Albert C. Wedemeyer, was not given the command responsibilities which the American President had viewed as indispensable to relieve the "desperate" situation in China and to which Chiang had earlier agreed in principle.

After his subsequent appointment as Ambassador, General Hurley outlined his understanding of his mission as: (1) to prevent the collapse of the National Government, (2) to sustain Chiang Kai-shek as President of the Republic and Generalissimo of the Armies, (3) to harmonize relations between the Generalissimo and the American Commander, (4) to promote production of war supplies in China and prevent economic collapse, and (5) to unify all the military forces in China for the purpose of defeating Japan. [8]

Thus while Stilwell's aim had been the single-minded one of making more effective China's participation in the war, Hurley added to that the objective in internal politics of supporting the Generalissimo. He thus sought ways and means to bring the Communist armies under the control of the National Government. This made it necessary that he assist in bring about agreement between the Generalissimo and the Communist Party leaders.

THE HURLEY PERIOD

To lay the groundwork for interparty agreement in China, General Hurley felt it essential to secure a definition of Soviet policy toward China. With this in mind, he and Mr. Donald Nelson, head of the War Production Board, went to Chungking [9] from Washington by way

[7] *Ibid.*, p. 71.
[8] *Ibid.*, p. 71.
[9] Mr. Nelson was also en route to Chungking to establish a "little" war production board to organize and stimulate production in Free China.

of Moscow. In conversations with Molotov, the Russian Foreign Minister

> stressed that it (the Soviet Government) would bear no responsibility for internal affairs or developments in China. Molotov then spoke of the very impoverished conditions of the people in parts of China, some of whom called themselves Communists but were related to Communists in no way at all. It was merely a way of expressing dissatisfaction with their economic condition and they would forget this political inclination when their economic condition improved. The Soviet Government should not be associated with these "communist elements" nor could it be blamed in any way for this situation.... Molotov said in conclusion that the Soviets would be glad if the United States aided the Chinese in unifying their country and in improving their military and economic condition and in choosing for this task their best people.... His government would be glad to see the United States taking the lead economically, politically, and militarily in Chinese affairs.[10]

These views, transmitted to Washington as well as to Chiang Kai-shek, had an especially significant effect on American policy. As to Chiang, General Hurley believed that he had been successful in changing his mind concerning the relationship of the Chinese Communist Party and the Soviet Union. Hurley thus informed Washington that:

> He (Chiang) is now convinced that the Russian Government does not recognize the Chinese Communist Party as Communist at all and that (1) Russia does not want dissensions or civil war in China.... He (Chiang) now feels that he can reach a settlement with the Communist Party as a Chinese political party without foreign entanglements.[11]

Undoubtedly Hurley gave Chiang the impression that he need not go so far as the actual sharing of power with the Communists to persuade them to bring their troops under his command, although it was evident that some concessions would have to be made to them. The Communists soon made it clear, however, that they felt strong enough to refuse assent to agreements which would result in a weakening of their military position *vis-à-vis* the Kuomintang except as they were able to make their political position secure.

When General Hurley arrived in Chungking in September, 1944,

---

[10] *China White Paper*, p. 72. This statement, as reported, was made in reply to Mr. Nelson's request "for Soviet opinion" on the American view of the China problem.
[11] *Ibid.*, p. 73.

negotiations designed to bring the Communist forces under the control of the National Government were still under way. In these negotiations and with respect to the American relationship to them, the point of view of Chiang Kai-shek was expressed to the American Ambassador (Gauss) who reported it as follows:

> It is not unfriendly for us (the United States) to suggest that China should improve relations with the Soviet Union. China should receive the entire support and sympathy of the United States Government on the domestic problem of the Chinese Communists. Very serious consequences for China may result from our attitude. In urging that China resolve differences with the Communists, our Government's attitude is serving only to intensify the recalcitrance of the Communists. The request that China meet Communist demands is equivalent to asking China's unconditional surrender to a party known to be under a foreign power's influence (i.e., that of the Soviet Union). The Communists are growing arrogant and refuse to continue negotiations since our (the American) observer group arrived in Yenan. The United States should tell the Communists to reconcile their differences with and submit to the National Government of China.... The need of Communist forces to defeat Japan should not be stressed by us.[12]

The American policy to which Chiang voiced objection at this time was based upon the views being transmitted to the Department of State by foreign service officers in China and others to the effect that the Kuomintang was coming into a steadily weaker internal position, with "morale low and discouragement widespread," and with the governmental and military structure "being permeated and demoralized from top to bottom by corruption, unprecedented in scale and openness." The Kuomintang, in this view, had ceased to be the unifying and progressive force in Chinese society, "the role in which it has made its greatest contribution to modern society." The Communists, in contrast, were held to be increasing in strength and vitality, and that because they enjoyed the support of the masses.[13]

Given this view which, at least as far as the Kuomintang was concerned, conformed fairly closely to the facts, American policy became directed toward strengthening the National Government through stimulating reform of a democratic nature. This policy involved the

[12] Report, August 31, 1944, of the American Ambassador (Gauss) to Secretary Hull of a conversation with Chiang Kai-shek. The United States is meant when "we" or "our" is used in this despatch. *Ibid.*, Annex 45, p. 561.
[13] For extensive excerpts from the Memoranda of the Foreign Service Officers see *Ibid.*, Annex 47.

broadening of the base of participation in the government to include the Communists as well as the representatives of other non-Kuomintang groups. Thus the Generalissimo was urged to agree to conditions for their political participation which were acceptable to the Communists; and the Communists were urged to merge their armies with those of the National Government, all forces to be made more effective for purposes of attack on the Japanese by being brought under American command.

As to Soviet policy, prior to the assurances accepted by General Hurley, there was not too much divergence between the views held by Chiang Kai-shek and those being reported to Washington from China. As one foreign service officer, John Davies, reported to the Department of State in September, 1943:

> It is not perhaps too early to suggest that Soviet policy will probably be directed initially at establishing frontiers which will ensure Russian security and at rehabilitation of the U.S.S.R. There is no reason to cherish optimism regarding a voluntary Soviet contribution to our fight against Japan, whether in the shape of air bases or the early opening of a second front in Northeast Asia. The Russians may be expected to move against the Japanese when it suits their pleasure, which may not be until the final phases of the war—and then only in order to be able to participate in dictating terms to the Japanese and to establish new strategic frontiers.[14]

It was also recognized that the Chinese Communists had "a background of subservience to the U.S.S.R." and so might be expected to serve as instruments of Russian policy. It was, however, suggested in some of the reports and memoranda that wartime nationalism had sufficiently modified communism in the Communist Party outlook so that the Communists might be detachable from the Russians if efforts were made in that direction.

The problem consequently perceived was that of ensuring that any tendencies of the Communists away from Moscow control were supported and strengthened. It was apparently felt that reasonable participation in the government would confirm the nationalist motivation of the Communist Party while at the same time helping to revitalize the National Government. On the other hand, if Chiang was not willing to undertake reform, then, on the assumption of growing Communist strength, it was argued in reports from the Chungking Embassy to Washington that the United States should establish direct relations

[14] *Ibid.*, p. 564.

with the Communist regime with a view to weaning it away from the Russian orientation. The threat of this, it was argued, would in any case probably develop a greater willingness on the part of Chiang to undertake the necessary governmental reforms. The alternative to such a policy was to give full support to Chiang, without qualification as to reform. This, it was argued, would commit the United States to prop up a government which would otherwise fall of its own internal weaknesses in the form of corruption, general inefficiency, and loss of popular support.

General Hurley's report of the Russian lack of interest in the Chinese Communist Party, coupled with the view that Russian support was an essential element of its strength, had a double effect. It made the Generalissimo willing to continue negotiations with the Communist leaders because he felt that he could reach a settlement with the Communist Party as a Chinese political party without foreign entanglements. But this feeling also was joined with the belief that the Communists would ultimately have to accept terms of settlement which they would otherwise have found unacceptable. Thus Chiang did not feel it advisable or necessary to adjust his program to make it acceptable to the Communists, except as the Americans put pressure on him to do so.

But while General Hurley was initially convinced, and felt that he had convinced the Generalissimo, of Russia's lack of interest in the Chinese Communist Party, this conclusion was apparently not reached by the Communists themselves. General Hurley himself reported early in July, 1945, his conviction

> that the influence of the Soviet will control the action of the Chinese Communist Party....I believe the Soviet's attitude toward the Chinese Communists is as I related it to the President in September of last year and have reported many times since. This is also borne out by Stalin's statement to Hopkins and Harriman. Notwithstanding all this the Chinese Communists still believe that they have the support of the Soviet. Nothing will change their opinion on this subject until a treaty has been signed between the Soviet and China in which the Soviet agrees to support the National Government. When the Chinese Communists are convinced that the Soviet is not supporting them, they will settle with the National Government if the National Government is realistic enough to make generous political settlements.[15]

---

[15] *Ibid.*, p. 99.

It was later shown (after the signature of the Soong-Molotov Treaty in 1945), that not even a treaty would convince the Communists of lack of Soviet support. Nor were they ever convinced, as General Hurley and Chiang Kai-shek were, of the internal weakness of their position as compared with that of the Kuomintang. Consequently they entered negotiations, during the Hurley period, completely unwilling to accept terms which would mean an inability to bid for power by military means if they could not acquire a sufficient control in the National Government to exercise real influence by political means.

To carry forward the negotiation of an agreement, upon his arrival at his post General Hurley established direct contact with the head of the Chinese Communist Party, Mao Tse-tung, at Yenan. As a result of two days of conference at Yenan, he brought back to Chungking a "Five-Point Draft Agreement" which he felt offered a practical plan for settlement with the Communists. Since this embodied the terms to which the Communists steadily adhered thereafter, the draft is quoted in full:

(1) The Government of China, the Kuomintang of China and the Communist Party of China will work together for the unification of the military forces in China for the immediate defeat of Japan and the reconstruction of China.

(2) The present National Government is to be reorganized into a coalition National Government embracing representatives of all anti-Japanese parties and non-partisan political bodies. A new democratic policy providing for reform in military, political, economic, and cultural affairs shall be promulgated and made effective. At the same time the National Military Council is to be reorganized into the United Military Council consisting of representatives of all anti-Japanese armies.

(3) The coalition government will support the principles of Sun Yat-sen for the establishment in China of a government of the people, for the people, and by the people. The coalition National Government will pursue policies designed to promote progress and democracy and to establish justice, freedom of conscience, freedom of the press, freedom of speech, freedom of assembly and association, the right to petition the government for the redress of grievances, the right of writ of habeas corpus and the right of residence. The coalition National Government will also pursue policies intended to make effective the two rights defined as freedom from fear and freedom from want.

(4) All anti-Japanese forces will observe and carry out the orders of the coalition National Government and its United Military Council and will be recognized by the Government and the Military Council. The supplies acquired from foreign powers will be equitably distributed.

(5) The Coalition Government of China recognizes the legality of the Kuomintang of China, the Chinese Communist Party and all anti-Japanese parties.[16]

Wrapped up in the verbiage of this "Five Point Program" was the determination of the Communists to secure a guaranteed legal access to all of China for propaganda purposes. If that could be secured, the party leaders felt confident of their ability to displace the Kuomintang as the governing party. Such access, however, could not be viewed as guaranteed and secure merely because promised by the Kuomintang-controlled National Government. Thus the demands for a coalition government, with real policy functions, instead of an advisory position such as that of the PPC; and for a share in the development and implementation of military policy through a reorganization of the National Military Council, with a commitment to an "equitable" distribution of foreign-secured supplies, were more than bargaining points. These changes, it was subsequently made clear, would have to be actually accomplished before the Communists would take steps to integrate their armies into the National army. Thus they put political reconstruction ahead of military integration.

It should be noted further that at the outset the Communists distinguished the National Government from the Kuomintang, a distinction which, when the Americans subsequently attempted implicitly to make it, they viewed as untenable.

Chiang Kai-shek did not agree with General Hurley's judgment that this Five Point Draft Agreement offered a practical plan for settlement. The National Government consequently submitted a "Three-Point" counter-proposal for the consideration of the Yenan government. It read:

(1) The National Government, desirous of securing effective unification and concentration of all military forces in China for the purpose of accomplishing the speedy defeat of Japan, and looking forward to the postwar reconstruction of China, agrees to incorporate, after reorganization, the Chinese Communist forces in the National Army who will then receive equal treatment as the other units in respect of pay, allowance, munitions and other supplies, and to give recognition to the Chinese Communist Party as a legal party.

(2) The Communist Party undertakes to give their full support to the National Government in the prosecution of the war of resistance and in

[16] *Ibid.*, pp. 74-75.

the postwar reconstruction, and give control of all their troops to the National Government through the National Military Council. The National Government will designate some high ranking officers from among the Communist forces to membership in the National Military Council.

(3) The aim of the National Government to which the Communist Party subscribes is to carry out the Three People's Principles of Dr. Sun Yat-sen for the establishment in China of a government of the people, for the people and by the people and it will pursue policies designed to promote the progress and development of democratic processes in government.

In accordance with the provision of the *Program of Armed Resistance and National Reconstruction*, freedom of speech, freedom of the press, freedom of assembly and association and other civil liberties are hereby guaranteed, subject only to the specific needs of security in the effective prosecution of the war against Japan.[17]

The National Government's counter-proposal was in effect a demand that the Communists should transfer their troops to Kuomintang control in exchange for promises with respect to the future; just as the Communist proposal constituted a conditioned promise to give up to the National Government control of their armies after they had achieved a political position from which they could not only determine the use which would be made of the national military power, but could possibly, by political means, either displace or seriously weaken the Kuomintang and the Generalissimo as the governing authority. As the Americans later came to conclude, the fundamental obstacle to agreement thus was the unwillingness of the Communists to place trust in the promises of the Kuomintang leaders and of the latter to trust the former to put their promises into effect in good faith.

Partly because of American insistence that each side view the other's proposals not as final but only as a basis for negotiation, and in part because neither side was prepared to attempt to secure a military decision through open civil war until China had been cleared of the Japanese, negotiations were continued during General Hurley's ambassadorship, which extended to November 26, 1945. At that time no agreement had been reached, although there had been some additions and subtractions from the original proposals.

During the last stages of these negotiations General Hurley had been

[17] *Ibid.*, p. 75.

in Washington, having been asked by "Chiang Kai-shek to go to Washington (together with General Wedemeyer), the better to explain to the President and the chiefs-of-staff his situation, his efforts, and his needs." [18]

The situation had been greatly changed since acceptance by Japan of the Allied surrender terms. The Russians had Manchuria within their military control and were making it difficult for the National Government to introduce its forces into the Northeastern Provinces and to re-establish Chinese administrative control ahead of infiltrating Chinese Communist troops. In North China the Communists were disputing the sole right of the Generalissimo to take over from the Japanese. The efforts of the National Government to discharge its responsibilities under the surrender terms, expecially in North China, were being supported by the United States. General Wedemeyer, however, had to walk the precarious path marked out in the United States' policy of assisting in operations to bring the war to an end by disarming and repatriating the Japanese armies but without American forces becoming involved in the struggle between the National Government and the Communists. Furthermore, the surrender of Japan shifted the emphasis in China from that of military operations against Japan to that of postwar economic and political reconstruction.

AMERICAN POLICY AFTER V-J DAY

In this new situation the Chinese Government perceived the need for assurances of enlarged American support. Assistance for purposes of reconstruction of the national economy was not in question, even though there might be difference of opinion over the necessary totals and the conditions of its use. What was in question at Washington and between Washington and Chungking was (1) the extent and nature of assistance in building up the Chinese military establishment; and (2) the extent to which the United States should commit itself to the National Government as then constituted.

While Ambassador Hurley had sought to bring the Communists and the Kuomintang to an agreement on the conditions of reconstruction of the National Government he had at the same time steadily moved toward support of the contention of the Generalissimo that

[18] Herbert Feis, *The China Tangle* (Princeton: Princeton University Press, 1953), p. 367.

the agreement must fall within limits defined by the National Government. He thus tended to exert less and less pressure on Chiang Kai-shek in the interest of governmental reconstruction. Those, in the State Department and the foreign service, who felt that such pressure should be exerted, even to the point of threat that the United States would give some assistance to the Communists if the National Government was not "democratized," were increasingly felt by Ambassador Hurley to be acting in a manner disloyal to him, if not to the United States. As American policy was brought under review at Washington in the light of the new conditions following the Japanese surrender, and as it began to appear that this policy involved a lessening of affirmative support of the National Government, General Hurley tendered his resignation as ambassador in a manner which ensured its acceptance, as previous proposals to resign had not been.[19]

The new policy, as far as a really new one can be said to have been evolved, had at least one element in common with that followed by General Hurley. This was in the use of American influence to bring about agreement between the two principal contending parties on the conditions of construction of a government for a truly unified China. Thus the United States continued to try to play the part of mediator.

A major obstacle to successful mediation in China was, however, presented in the fact that, if it was to mediate successfully, the United States had to be viewed as impartial between the Kuomintang and the Communists. This was impossible in a situation in which the recognized government was a single-party government, controlled by one of the two contenders for power, as long as it was the settled policy of the mediator to uphold and strengthen that government. Thus General Hurley, and subsequently General Marshall, could, in the last analysis,

---

[19] For the text of the Hurley letter of resignation, *China White Paper*, pp. 581-84. Of it one writer says: "Hurley's letter of resignation so twirls about that it is hard to locate its center. It did not admit failure; it diffused blame. It did not attempt to tell of the existing situation in China and trace its conclusions to formative facts. The dissatisfied Ambassador seems in one twist to attribute American difficulties in China to the activities of the professional diplomats in the Embassy and State Department who opposed our policy as he understood it. In another twist he seems to conclude that this policy was confused and divided, simultaneously supporting imperialism and communism. Some of his comments seem to be a plea for isolation or neutrality, as for example the statement that 'The weakness of American policy has backed us into two world wars ... There is a third world war in the making. In diplomacy we are permitting ourselves to be sucked into a power bloc on the side of colonial imperialism against Communist imperialism. I am opposed to both.'" (Feis, *op. cit.*, pp. 409-10.)

only mediate within limits acceptable to the National Government and thus to the Kuomintang. In other words, Hurley could advise the Generalissimo that he "could afford to make political concessions and shorten the period of transition (to democratic constitutionalism from the party dictatorship of the period of tutelage) in order to obtain control of the Communist forces [20] but he could not properly go beyond the tendering of advice. As suggested above, and as proposed by General Hurley's predecessor, Ambassador Clarence E. Gauss, the only effective way pressure could have been put on the Generalissimo to act on American suggestions would have been to condition any and all American aid to China on his acceptance of and action on those suggestions. This withdrawal of American aid, if Chiang had stood firm, could only have had a weakening effect on the National Government and the position of the Generalissimo. If he had given way to secure American aid, however, the effect would also have been weakening, since he would have "succumbed to foreign pressure" and become a "tool of American imperialism." The same weakening effect on the National Government would have been felt from an allocation by the Americans of supplies to the Communists as well as to the National Government.

If the means had been available pressure might, on the other hand, have been brought to bear on the Communists to compel acceptance of Kuomintang terms. Since the Communists felt themselves immediately to be in a sufficiently strong position within China to make it unnecessary to modify their fundamental demands and accept Kuomintang terms of settlement, outside pressure on them of some sort would have been required to bring them to the point of agreement. The Americans, however, were not at that time in a position to apply effective pressure, which would have had to be military, on the Communists in behalf of the government. Consequently Ambassador Hurley was actually in no position to do more than to start negotiations and keep them going, and thus to prevent the immediate resumption of civil war.

Success in mediation could only have been anticipated if the view expressed by General Hurley in March, 1945 had been correct. This was that the Communists and the Kuomintang alike were "striving for democratic principles," and that the United States, if it were tolerant and patient could help to bring them to their common goal.

[20] *China White Paper*, p. 80.

It was not, in fact, a correct view even at that time. Both parties were struggling for power—the Kuomintang to retain it, and the Communists to secure it throughout the entire country. Nevertheless it was this view of the Communists as "striving for democratic principles," to be applied both in governmental organization and in politics, which helped to shape American policy after V-J Day. The earlier Hurley view that this was Communist policy, as well as its propaganda line, seemed to be confirmed in the reports of American correspondents as well as government officials who later were able to enter Communist-controlled territory. On this assumption emphasis in American policy began to be shifted from that of preventing the collapse of the National Government and sustaining Chiang Kai-shek to that of reform and reconstruction of the National Government on a democratic basis, with an end to party tutelage.

However, after V-J Day limited civil war broke out. This was a result of the conditions under which the occupied areas were taken over from the Japanese. The Soviet Command was designated to receive the Japanese surrender in Manchuria, and Chiang Kai-shek, for the Allies, was given similar responsibility for China proper. The Communist leaders had anticipated that they would at least be able to replace the Japanese in North China, where their administrative apparatus had already been extended in the countryside, and into which their armies could move quickly from the adjacent areas which had been under Communist control since before 1937. American assistance, especially in transport facilities, however, enabled National Government officials and troops to be moved into North China rapidly enough to take over the cities, the railheads, and the arteries of communications, which constituted the extent of effective Japanese occupation; and the United States took care of the repatriation of Japanese troops and civilians. Much of the countryside, however, remained or came under Communist control. In the competition to replace the Japanese, Chinese Nationalist and Communist forces inevitably came into open, although at first only local, conflict.

The relative success of the National Government in extending its authority over Japanese-occupied China was attributed by the Communist Party leaders to the assistance given to it by the United States, which consequently was accused by them of intervention in China against one faction in an internal struggle for power. The American contention that its actions were taken in behalf of China and against Japan, rather than in behalf of Chiang against the Communists, did not serve to lessen the impact of the charge on Chinese opinion. Nor did the fact that American assistance was given to China through the medium of the government then universally recognized as the legitimate government of the country prevent the propagation of the view, both within and outside of China, that American assistance to the National Government was in fact intervention in behalf of one party, the Kuomintang, against the other party, the Communists, arrayed against one another in an undecided struggle for control of the government. This view was strengthened by the previous and subsequent attempts of the United States to play the role of mediator between the Kuomintang-controlled National Government and the Chinese Communist Party and regime. Since the Communists actually governed part of China and the National Government was in fact the Kuomintang, mediation seemed to be either between two governments or between two parties standing on a footing of equality. This had the appearance, if not the effect, of elevating the rebellious faction to a position of parity with the government and thus gave support to the Communist argument that the United States was intervening if it assisted the recognized government. At and after this time, furthermore, the view, more and more emphasized after 1944, of the National Government as being corrupt, weak, and ineffective in contrast with the vigor and high morale of the Communists began to make a real impact on American policy. This contrast between the two regimes was attributed by those propagating the view of lack of efficiency and of public morality in Kuomintang China as much to lack of democracy in the Kuomintang system as to the effects of the war. Thus democratizing the National Government came to be regarded in many circles, both Chinese and American, as the proper solution of China's problems. Guided by this opinion, the American government felt that it was proper for it to insist that the National Government should undertake political reform, while disclaiming any intention to intervene in the domestic situation. Thus there was in fact intervention in support of the National Government and at the same time intervention against it in the form of demands that the Kuomintang should share power with the Communists and by this means democratize, reform, and revitalize the National Government.

EFFECT OF CONDITIONS OF RUSSIAN
PARTICIPATION IN THE WAR

Another element of confusion in the situation in China had been introduced with the definition of the conditions of Soviet participation in the war against Japan. To ensure that participation, apparently viewed by the American chiefs of staff early in 1945 as essential to bring about the unconditional surrender of Japan with the minimum loss of life, it was agreed at the Yalta Conference (February, 1945) that the status quo in Outer Mongolia, represented by the autonomous Mongolian People's Republic, should be preserved, and that the Soviet Union should regain substantially the position in Manchuria held by the Russians before the Russo-Japanese War. President Roosevelt agreed to attempt to gain Chiang Kai-shek's acceptance of this agreement. This was given with the negotiation of the Sino-Soviet Treaty of August 14, 1945, together with the notes exchanged at that time. That treaty, in fact, extended somewhat, in Russia's favor, the position accepted by the United States and Britain at Yalta. From the Chinese point of view, the *quid pro quo* for the re-establishment of the earlier Russian position in Manchuria and the acceptance of the loss of Outer Mongolia was the commitment of the Soviet government to exclusive support of the National Government. In the notes exchanged between the foreign ministers of the two countries it was explicitly stated that:

(1) In accordance with the spirit of the aforementioned treaty, and to put into effect its aims and purposes, the Government of the U.S.S.R. agrees to render to China moral support and aid in military supplies and other material resources, such support and aid to be entirely given to the National Government as the central government of China.

(2) In the course of conversations regarding Dairen and Port Arthur and regarding the joint operation of the Chinese Changchun Railway, the Government of the U.S.S.R. regarded the Three Eastern Provinces (Manchuria) as part of China and reaffirmed its respect for China's full sovereignty over the Three Eastern Provinces and recognize their territorial and administrative integrity.[21]

Under the authorization of General MacArthur as Supreme Commander for the Allied Powers, the Russians received the Japanese

[21] From text as printed in Feis, *op. cit.*, p. 587.

surrender in Manchuria. During the period of their occupation, prolonged beyond the agreed time at the request of the National Government, the Russians reduced the postwar usefulness of Manchuria to China by removing from it, as war booty, much of the industrial plant which the Japanese had constructed there.

The reason for the Chinese Government's request for prolongation of Russian military occupation was its inability to introduce its forces into Manchuria so as to be able to take over as the Russian troops were withdrawn. This inability resulted from obstacles the Soviet authorities placed in the way of entrance of National Government troops into China's Manchurian provinces. By the time these had been admitted in force the Chinese Communist forces, infiltrating into Manchuria as individuals and in appearance as civilians, had formed into armies and were allowed to equip themselves with the arms taken by the Russians from the Japanese Kwantung Army upon its surrender.

It was in this way that the Russians fulfilled their pledge of aid and support "to be entirely given to the National Government." None of their actions, furthermore, could be construed as being designed to give "moral support" to the National Government as the "central government of China." Neither did the removal of "war booty" from Manchuria constitute anything but the reverse of assistance in the postwar reconstruction of China. The best that can be said is that on the surface the U.S.S.R. avoided direct and open intervention in behalf of the Communists. This must be said because it was an important factor in China in placing the onus on the United States of attempting to establish internal peace and order and seeking to re-establish the unity of China through mediation between the Kuomintang and the Chinese Communist Party under circumstances which enabled the interventionist label to be attached to the United States.

THE MARSHALL MISSION

Broadly stated, then, the above were the political circumstances which existed when General of the Army George C. Marshall was sent to China as Special Presidential Representative with the personal rank of ambassador. He was instructed "to bring to bear in an appropriate and practicable manner the influence of the United States" to the end that "the unification of China by peaceful, democratic methods be achieved as soon as possible." [22] As a method of bringing American influence to bear, General Marshall was authorized "to speak with the utmost frankness" to Chiang and other Chinese leaders:

> Particularly, you may state, in connection with the Chinese desire for credits, technical assistance in the economic field, and military assistance (I have in mind the proposed U.S. military advisory group which I have approved in principle), that a China disunited and torn by civil strife could not be considered realistically as a proper place of American assistance along the lines enumerated.

In a publicly released "Statement by President Truman on United States Policy Toward China" of December 15, 1945, which by attachment became a part of General Marshall's instructions, it was laid down in justification of the policy to be followed that it was

> the firm belief of this Government that a strong, united and democratic China is of the utmost importance to the success of the United Nations organization and for world peace. A China disorganized and divided either by foreign aggression, such as that undertaken by the Japanese, or by violent internal strife, is an undermining influence to world stability and peace, now and in the future. The United States Government has long subscribed to the principle that the management of internal affairs is the responsibility of the peoples of the sovereign nations. Events of this century, however, would indicate that a breach of peace anywhere in the world threatens the peace of the entire world. It is thus in the most vital interest of the United States and all of the United Nations that the people of China overlook no opportunity to adjust their internal differences promptly by means of peaceful negotiation.

On the basis of this justification for departure from a policy of strict nonintervention, the statement continued:

> The Government of the United States believes it essential:
>
> (1) That a cessation of hostilities be arranged between the armies of the National Government and the Chinese Communists and other dissident Chinese armed forces for the purpose of completing the return of all China to effective Chinese control, including the immediate evacuation of the Japanese forces.
>
> (2) That a national conference of representatives of major political elements be arranged to develop an early solution to the present internal strife—a solution which will bring about the unification of China.

[22] President Truman to the Special Representative of the President to China (Marshall.) *China White Paper*, Annex 61, pp. 605-6 for the complete text, from which the above and following quotations are taken.

In carrying out his instructions, General Marshall was successful initially in securing an agreement on conditions for the cessation of hostilities. This cease-fire agreement of January 10, 1946, was designed, pending the conclusion of permanent agreements, to "freeze" the existing military positions, with two exceptions. One exception was "to permit the movement of National Government troops into Manchuria" since the United States government was committed to such movement. This was agreed to by Chou En-Lai, for the Communists, because it not only "conformed to American policy" but also to the Sino-Soviet Treaty of August, 1945.[23] The second exception authorized "the movement of National government troops south of the Yangtze River in connection with the Government military reorganization plan."

To supervise the application of the Truce Agreement, an Executive Headquarters was set up in Peiping under three commissioners, one representing the Chinese Communist Party, one the National Government, and one the United States. Truce teams, with a similar composition, were to be sent into the field to observe compliance with the truce terms.

A measure of success in implementing the truce was attained except in Manchuria, where the National Government refused to authorize an Executive Headquarters field team until the end of March, and then under a directive which was not "sufficiently broad to bring about a cessation of the fighting, which meanwhile was developing into a dangerous situation for the National Government forces."[24]

There was also a

justified complaint by the Chinese Communists that the National Government commander at Canton had violated the terms of the cessation of hostilities order by refusing to recognize the authority of the Headquarters in his area of command, and that the Supreme Headquarters of the National Government armies at Nanking had failed to carry out the specific stipulation of the cease-fire order to report all movements of the National Government troops to the Executive Headquarters at Peiping.[25]

The general stability or instability of the truce, except in Manchuria, however, was mainly determined by the ebb and flow in negotiations with respect to the political agreements and those of a more permanent military character.

[23] The quotations are from *Ibid.*, p. 137.
[24] *Ibid.*, p. 146.
[25] *Ibid.*, p. 146.

The release to the press of President Truman's December 15 "State-ment on United States Policy" informed the National Government, if the Generalissimo was not already aware of that fact, that:

> the United States is cognizant that the present National Government of China is a "one-party government" and believe that peace, unity and democratic reform in China will be furthered if the basis of this govern-ment is broadened to include other political elements in the country. Hence the United States strongly advocates that the national conference of representatives of major political elements in the country agree upon arrangements which would give those elements a fair and effective representation in the Chinese National Government. It is recognized that this would require a modification of the one-party "political tutelage" established as an interim arrangement in the progress of the nation toward democracy by the father of the Chinese Republic, Dr. Sun Yat-sen.[26]

Since Chiang Kai-shek, and thus the Kuomintang, had proclaimed earlier the intention to establish constitutionalism within a year of the ending of the war, there was no valid ground for objecting to the anticipated American demand for the termination of the period of tutelage. To avoid the charge that action was taken in response to foreign pressure, however, and with a view to ensuring Kuomintang control of the movement toward constitutional democracy, Chiang proceeded to convene an interparty advisory body which was called the Political Consultative Conference (PCC).[27]

In pursuance of one of the resolutions of the PCC, a Military Re-organization Agreement was signed on February 25, 1946. It defined the conditions (1) for gradual reduction in size of a new national army, and (2) for the integration of the Communist Party Armed Forces into the National Army and the reorganization of all armies in China on a democratic basis.[28]

Partly because of the breakdown of the truce and partly because of the failure or refusal of the Communists to supply essential data on the size and composition of their armed forces, the terms of this Military Reorganization Agreement were never executed. The Communist Party attitude toward fulfillment of the agreement was determined by dissat-

[26] *Ibid.*, p. 608. The full text is given pp. 607-9.
[27] In session from January 10 to January 31, 1946, the PCC was composed of 8 representatives of the Kuomintang, 7 of the Communists, and 21 of the minor parties and of nonparty interests. Its resolutions had to be ratified by the Central Committees of the parties before they could be viewed as governing decisions.
[28] *China White Paper*, Annex 66, for the text of the agreement. For a commentary on it, from which the quotation is made, *Ibid.*, pp. 140-43, 162-72.

isfaction of its leaders with the lack of progress in the political field, and by their previously revealed unwillingness to give up to the National Government control of the Communist armies in advance of gaining the political position which the party sought throughout China.

With respect to immediate as well as ultimate political and governmental reform, the PCC adopted resolutions which provided (1) for the reconstruction of the State Council, which was to be made the supreme organ of government in control of national affairs, and (2) for the convocation on May 5, 1946, of a National Assembly to adopt a permanent constitution. As viewed by the Communists, however, the National Assembly could not be convened until after the State Council had been reconstituted and put in a position to determine the composition and terms of reference of the National Assembly. Otherwise the National Assembly, they held, would be an instrument of the Kuomintang which would thus be able to determine unilaterally the conditions of constitutional democracy. Consequently, since the terms of establishment of the State Council had not been agreed upon, the meeting of the National Assembly had to be postponed and when it did meet on November 15, 1946, the Communist Party refused to participate.

The PCC resolution on the State Council provided for a total membership of forty, including ex officio the presidents of the five Yuan (branches of the government.) The members were to be appointed by the President of the National Government on the nomination of the different parties concerned, half coming from the Kuomintang "and the other half will be members of other political parties and prominent social leaders." A qualified veto over decisions of the State Council was to be given the President. A majority vote of the members was sufficient to enact general resolutions but "if a resolution before the State Council should involve changes in administrative policy, it must be passed by a two-thirds vote of the State Councillors present." [29]

Determined to have the safeguard of a veto on changes in the policy which was defined by the PCC, the Communist Party insisted that it and the Democratic League between them should have a minimum of fourteen seats, which would enable them to exercise a veto in this respect. The Generalissimo ultimately agreed on a representation of

[29] From text of the Resolution on Government Organization adopted by the PCC January, 1946. *Ibid.*, Annex 64, pp. 610-11. The Resolution on Program for Peaceful Reconstruction, which established administrative policy, is published textually as Annex 65.

twelve, with a thirteenth seat to be given an independent to be recommended by the Communist Party, but he was unwilling to meet the demand for fourteen seats. This *impasse* made it impossible to implement the decision of the PCC on the State Council.

The National Assembly, consequently, met on November 15, but without the participation of the Communist Party and the Democratic League, which was equally hostile to the Kuomintang. Their decision not to participate decisively put a period to negotiations since the National Government had already offered its maximum concessions and the Communist Party thus rejected them.

During the year of his residence in China as the President's Special Representative General Marshall had attempted to prevent civil war by making effective the cease-fire and by securing the implementation of the Military Reorganization Agreement. His ultimate lack of success in this effort was largely a consequence of the situation which developed in Manchuria. But while this was his major undertaking, considerable effort was at the same time made to bring the National Government and the Chinese Communist Party to direct agreement on the details of application of the PCC political agreements so that they could be put into effect. After the appointment, at Marshall's suggestion, of Dr. J. Leighton Stuart as United States Ambassador to China on July 11, 1946, however, the latter was given the principal responsibility in this connection, serving as chairman of a five-man committee which had the function of reaching agreement on the constitution of the State Council. As noted above, no such agreement was reached.

A review of the American mediation would seem to warrant the conclusion that both General Marshall and Ambassador Stuart sought to maintain the essential characteristic of the mediator—impartiality— as between the Kuomintang and the Chinese Communist Party. An appearance to the contrary, however, as has been pointed out, was inevitable in view of the fact that one of the two contending parties— the Kuomintang—was in effect the government to which both were accredited and through which such economic and military assistance as China received from the United States was utilized. This circumstance was used by the Communists, as time went on and as they were not able to bring the government to accept their views as to how the PCC resolutions should be implemented, to establish in China the view that American mediation was not in fact impartial and disinterested. On the other hand, when the fortunes of the civil war turned decisively against the Kuomintang, its supporters in the United States as well as in China charged General Marshall with action in support of the Communists. If the test of impartiality is to be found in somewhat equal accusation by each side of partiality to the other, then the conclusion is warranted that the mission headed by General Marshall tried to play a truly mediatory role in China during 1946, even though the mediation was unsuccessful.

Nevertheless the necessity General Marshall was under in fact of mediating between the recognized government of China and a hostile party which had military control of part of the territory of the state can only be viewed as weakening the position of the government *vis-a-vis* the Communists. The truce agreement and its implementation had a similar consequence; as did some of the steps taken to put into effect Marshall's and General Wedemeyer's instructions with respect to military assistance in general and in particular in connection with the movement of troops into North China.

General Marshall's own conclusions as to the situation which he tried unsuccessfully to change were stated in part as follows:

> In the first place, the greatest obstacle to peace has been the complete, almost overwhelming suspicion with which the Chinese Communist Party and the Kuomintang regarded each other.
>
> On the one hand, the leaders of the Government are strongly opposed to the communistic form of government. On the other, the Communists frankly state that they are Marxists and intend to work toward establishing a communistic form of government in China, even though first advancing through the medium of a democratic form of government of the American or British type.
>
> The leaders of the Government are convinced in their minds that the Communist expressed desire to participate in a government of the type endorsed by the Political Consultative Conference last January had for its purpose only a destructive intention. The Communists felt, I believe, that the Government was insincere in its apparent acceptance of the PCC resolutions for the formulation of the new government and intended by coercion of military force and the action of secret police to obliterate the Communist Party. Combined with this mutual deep distrust was the conspicuous error by both parties of ignoring the effect of the fears and suspicions of the other party in estimating the reasons for proposals or opposition regarding the settlement of various matters under negotiation...
>
> I think the most important factors involved in the recent breakdown of negotiations are these; On the side of the National Government, which is in effect the Kuomintang, there is a dominant group of reactionaries who

have been opposed, in my opinion, to almost every effort I have made to influence the formation of a genuine coalition government. This has usually been under the cover of political or party action, but since the Party was the Government, this action, though subtle or indirect, has been devastating in its effect...

On the side of the Chinese Communist Party there are, I believe, liberals as well as radicals, though this view is vigorously opposed by many who believe that the Chinese Communist Party discipline is too rigidly enforced to admit of much difference of viewpoint. Nevertheless, it has appeared to me that there is a definite liberal group among the Communists, especially of young men who have turned to the Communists in disgust at the corruption evident in local governments—men who would put the interest of the Chinese people above ruthless measures to establish a Communist ideology in the immediate future. The dyed-in-the-wool Communists do not hesitate at the most drastic measures to gain their end as, for example, the destruction of communications in order to wreck the economy of China and produce a situation that would facilitate the overthrow or collapse of the Government without any regard to the immediate suffering of the people involved.[30]

General Marshall was correct in his conclusion that the anti-Communists in the Kuomintang, who were also the "dominant group of reactionaries," controlled government policy. He was also correct in his view that there were supporters of the Communists, some of them party members, who sincerely desired a peaceful solution of the internal situation on a democratic basis. Where he was wrong was in believing, if he did, that these were at all able to determine the policy of the Communist Party. That party was controlled by the dyed-in-the-wool Communists and not by the "liberal" Communists.

At any rate the National Assembly, without Communist participation, proceeded to adopt a permanent constitution, which was promulgated on January 1, 1947, and was to become effective December 25, 1947. In the interim steps were taken looking toward the transfer of power from Kuomintang organs to state organs. Thus the Council of State was proclaimed (April, 1947) as the ruling body. Its membership of forty was made up of: the five Yuan presidents, ex officio; twelve from the Kuomintang; four from the China Youth Party; four from the Social Democrats; and four independents. Eleven seats were, even at this late date, reserved for the Communists and the Democratic League. Since, however, this composition did not meet the earlier

[30] Personal Statement by the Special Representative of the President (Marshall), January 7, 1947, *Ibid.*, Annex 113, pp. 686-89.

demands of the Communists, neither they nor the Democratic League were willing to participate. Neither did the Communists come into the Cabinet which was constituted on April 23 with non-Kuomintang as well as Kuomintang representation.

The Communists not only refused to participate in the National Assembly and in the reorganized government but they also refused to take part in the elections which were held (January, 1948) under the new constitutional and election laws, for the legislative Yuan, and in the National Assembly which met at the end of March to inaugurate formally the new system. The principal task of the Assembly was the election of the new President and Vice President. After some maneuvering, Chiang Kai-shek was, as anticipated, elected to the presidency for the constitutional term of six years. General Li Tsung-jen, over the expressed opposition of the Generalissimo, was elected, after a sharp contest, as the Vice President. Li had run on a platform of reform which was, however, not too extreme.

The structure of the constitutional government was erected in 1948 but the circumstances were such that existing power relations in the government, and existing governmental operations, were very little changed. Full-scale civil war had already developed, following acceptance of the failure of the American mediation efforts. Chiang Kai-shek declared the intention of the government to fight the war against the Communists to a victorious conclusion within, first, six months, and later, to the bitter end. Initial Kuomintang successes, including the capture of the Communist capital at Yenan were followed by reverses, and finally in 1949 by the loss of power on mainland China. The National Government from that point on continued the struggle from Formosa, the only Chinese territory remaining under its control.

BIBLIOGRAPHICAL REFERENCES

Chang, Chia-sen, *The Third Force in China* (New York: Bookman Association, 1952).

Ch'ien Tuan-sheng, *The Government and Politics of China* (Cambridge: Harvard University Press, 1950).

Department of State, Far Eastern Series 30, *United States Relations with China* (Washington: 1949).

Fairbank, J. K., *The United States and China* (Cambridge: Harvard University Press, 1948).

Feis, Herbert, *The China Tangle* (Princeton: Princeton University Press, 1953).

Fitzgerald, Charles Patrick, *Revolution in China* (London: Cresset Press, 1952).

Forman, Harrison, *Changing China* (New York: Crown, 1948).

Keeton, George W., *China, The Far East and the Future* (London: Stevens, 1949).

Levenson, Joseph Richmond, *Liang Chi-chao and the Mind of Modern China* (Cambridge: Harvard University Press, 1953).

Linebarger, Paul M. A., Djang Chu, and Burks, Ardeth, *Far East Government and Politics* (New York: Van Nostrand, 1954).

North, Robert and Pool, *Kuomintang and Chinese Communist Elites* (Palo Alto: Stanford University Press, 1953).

Pan Wei-tung, *The Chinese Constitution: A Study of 40 Years of Constitution Making* (Washington: Institute of Chinese Culture, 1946).

Peck, Graham, *Two Kinds of Time* (Boston: Houghton, Mifflin, 1950).

Rosinger, Lawrence Kaelter, *China's Wartime Politics, 1937-1944* (Princeton: Princeton University Press, 1944).

Vinacke, Harold M., *The United States and the Far East, 1945-1951* (Palo Alto: Stanford University Press, for the American Institute of Pacific Relations, 1952).

White, Theodore, H., and Jacoby, Annalee, *Thunder Out of China* (New York: William Sloane, 1946).

Winfield, Gerald F., *China, the Land and the People* (New York: William Sloane, for the American Institute of Pacific Relations, 1948).

4

The Communist Phase
of the Chinese Revolution

❋❋❋❋❋❋❋❋❋❋❋❋❋❋❋❋❋❋❋❋❋❋❋❋❋❋❋❋❋❋

THE COMMUNIST INTERNATIONAL AND THE
CHINESE REVOLUTION

THE COMMUNIST INTERNATIONAL (Comintern) was organized at Moscow in March, 1909 at the first World Congress of national Communist parties. From the outset the Communist International emphasized the revolutionary importance of the non-European world and sought a foothold in such countries as China through an attack on imperialism. Following the Bolshevist revolution, Marxist ideas began to penetrate Chinese intellectual circles by means of Marxist study groups formed initially at Peking University in the spring of 1918. Thus the ground was somewhat prepared for agitation when representatives of the Comintern and Chinese who had become Communists in Europe became active in China. The Chinese Communist Party, however, was not organized until 1921 when, on July 1, with twelve delegates in attendance, the first National Congress of the Chinese Communist Party was held and formally organized the party. The party was organized while the Third Congress of the Communist International was still in session at Moscow. This enabled the Chinese Communist Party at its inception to become affiliated with the International. Such affiliation, under Comintern rules, gave the latter a decisive voice in the development of both the strategy and the tactics of the Chinese Communist Party. Under the conditions existing during the 1920's and 30's, this meant that the Chinese Communist Party in effect took its direction from the Russian Communist Party (Bolshevik) since the Russians had the dominant voice within the Comintern.

The Chinese Communist Party began its activities at a time when the moving forces in China were nationalist. In the early 1920's the Nationalist Party (the Kuomintang) began to show new life. Up to a point its leaders had the same objectives as the Communists. If each party proceeded independently of and competitively with the other in the struggle for power in China neither might be able to attain its objectives. Consequently the Communist Party leaders debated the question of relationship with the Kuomintang at the same congress at which the decision was taken to affiliate with the Comintern. A year later, at the third congress, party members were authorized to join the Kuomintang as individuals. This decision of the Communist Party could only be made effective, however, if the Kuomintang was willing to accept Communists into its membership. Dr. Sun Yat-sen, the then personal leader of the Kuomintang, apparently felt that the decision of this question should be taken on the basis of definite understanding with the Soviet Union as to revolutionary objectives.

Seeking outside support for the nationalist revolution, and having failed to secure it on acceptable terms from the recognized members of the international community, Dr. Sun engaged in conversations with Mr. Adolph Joffe, Soviet emissary to the Far Eastern countries, early in 1923. As a result of these conversations, it was agreed that the problem of the Chinese revolution had two aspects: (1) the attainment of national unity through the overthrow of the provincial militarists then in control of most of the country; and (2) the establishment of complete national independence. In the solution of that double problem, Dr. Sun was assured of the support of Russia. The Joint Manifesto to which both Sun and Joffe subscribed, then went on to reassure Dr. Sun as to Russian intentions with respect to the Chinese Eastern Railway and Outer Mongolia. This included a general reaffirmation of the principles of the Soviet Declaration of 1919, renouncing all treaty privileges secured by the Tzarist government from China. This had been designed to establish Soviet policy as anti-imperialist, in contrast with the imperialism of the Western powers and Japan.

This decision on the part of the Soviet government to support the Kuomintang as the most effective instrument of revolution in China cleared the way for the acceptance as party members of individual Chinese Communists, provided they accepted Kuomintang party principles and discipline; and it also made it proper for Communists to subscribe to those principles. There was, however, no alliance or coalition formed of the two parties. The Communist members of the Kuomintang, consequently, accepted a dual allegiance and discipline the significance of which would not appear unless and until the policy lines of the two parties sharply diverged. At that point, the individual Communist would have to make a choice which would take him out of one party or the other.

The necessity for making this choice came in 1927 with the purge of the Communists from the Kuomintang. This was an immediate result of an internal struggle for control of the Kuomintang itself. This struggle came to a climax when the Communist members of the party attempted to seize control of the dominantly leftist government which had been moved from Canton to Hankow in November, 1926. Their purpose was to remove Chiang Kai-shek from his position of military and political leadership, and to shift the aims of the revolution from the purely political to the economic and social. In this the Chinese Communist leaders apparently acted on the advice and under the direction of the Russian advisers to the Kuomintang. Premature disclosure of this broke the alliance between the Communist members of the Kuomintang and its non-Communist left-wing, and enabled Chiang not only to purge the party of the Communists, thus liquidating many of them, but also to consolidate his leadership in the Kuomintang.

The purge was sufficiently thorough-going for a time so that the Communists could only struggle to survive. "They did not quite know what to do, for the International was also bewildered by the changing Chinese scene. There were sporadic *coups* and *putches* here and there, but there was no correlated or sustained policy."[1]

It was not the changing Chinese scene alone which bewildered the Comintern and its agents in China. There was the further element of confusion which was an expression in China of the struggle in the Soviet Union between Trotsky and Stalin. The emerging Stalin line of concentration on the attainment of socialism in one country initially subordinated the world revolutionary emphasis to that of alliance, where possible, with the political forces which had the best prospect of controlling other governments. This, in China, meant conciliation of the Kuomintang. But Stalin had not yet succeeded in establishing complete dominance within Russia or over the Comintern representatives in China.

[1] Ch'ien Tuan-sheng, *The Government and Politics of China* (Cambridge: Harvard University Press, 1950), p. 364.

The Comintern continued to direct the Communist Party along the lines of the earlier orthodoxy, viewing the party as proletarian in its base, and under the necessity of re-establishing the leadership of the urban working class which had been lost as a result of the purge. It was for this purpose that the "sporadic coups and putches" referred to above were undertaken in China. The line set required that the power available should be used to regain control of urban centers. This, known as the "Li Li-san line," finally had to be given up as it was demonstrated, as at Changsha, that the Communists lacked the power to maintain urban positions even when won.

This so-called Li Li-san line, although announced in 1929 by the then Chinese leader of the Chinese Communist Party, had actually been set by the Comintern. As previously suggested, it represented an attempt to exploit what was assumed to be a continuing revolutionary situation in China along the conventional lines of Marxist-Leninist theory as then interpreted by the Russian Communist Party and the Comintern. In this view the mass base for Communist revolution could only be found in the urban proletariat, with the Communist Party providing the proletariat with leadership and serving as its vanguard or spearhead. The peasantry was viewed essentially as an inert mass rather than as a potential revolutionary force capable of establishing revolutionary purposes and goals.

THE RISE OF MAO TSE-TUNG TO LEADERSHIP: THE KIANGSI PERIOD

The failures of those attempting to re-establish urban bases during the years 1930-32 was set over against the comparative success of those who, escaping the purge, established themselves in the mountainous and nonurban region of southern Kiangsi province where the first attempts were made to organize Chinese Soviet Governments. As their view of the problem was subsequently put: [2]

Because of the peculiarities of China's social and historical development and its backwardness in science, it is a unique and difficult task to apply Marxism systematically to China and to transform it from its European

[2] By Liu Shao-ch'i, at a time when he was Secretary of the Secretariat of the Chinese Communist Party, in *On the Party*. Quoted in Yang Cheng-fang's review of the book in *People's China* (Peking, Vol. III, No. 1, January 1, 1951). This is reprinted in American Consulate General, Hong Kong, *Current Background Series*, No. 81, June 14, 1951, pp. 3-4. Hereafter cited as *Current Background*.

form into a Chinese form, in other words, to solve the many problems of the contemporary Chinese revolution from the standpoint of Marxism and with Marxist methods. Many of these problems have never been solved or even raised before Marxists throughout the world. Here in China the main section of the masses are peasants and not workers; the struggle is directed against foreign imperialist aggression and medieval remnants, and not against native capital.

This can never be accomplished, as some people seem to think, by memorizing and reciting Marxist words or simply by quoting from them.... It requires profound historical and social knowledge, rich experience in directing the revolutionary struggle and skill in employing Marxist-Leninist methods in order to make an accurate and scientific analysis of the social and historical objective conditions and their development.

It was at this stage of the revolution, with the failure of "Li Li-sanism" recognized, that Mao Tse-tung began to emerge as the accepted leader of the Chinese Communist Party.

"Comrade Mao Tse-tung's outstanding contribution to the revolutionary movement in general and to the Chinese revolution in particular," Liu Shao-ch'i continued, "lies in his masterly combination of the universal truth of Marxism-Leninism and the actual practice of the Chinese revolution. Comrade Mao has successfully and brilliantly accomplished the extremely difficult task of adapting the general principles of Marxism-Leninism to the practical conditions in China." [3]

The "practical conditions in China" from the point of view of Marxism were that China was primarily a nation of peasants without an industrial proletariat sufficiently developed or self-conscious to serve as the revolutionary Communist base. With the beginning of industrialization in China there had appeared an urban working class which met the Marxist specifications for the proletariat. It was small indeed in comparison with the peasantry but "it did exist and, for the most part, proved amenable to Communist leadership." [4]

Mao Tse-tung, however, as subordinate party leader, had been assigned to help organize the peasantry during the period of development of Communist activity within the framework of the Kuomintang. Such work was consistent with the then orthodox Marxist-Leninist line because it represented an extension of proletarian class leadership, under the Communist Party, to the peasant mass which was to be used to attain the objectives of the party. Those objectives were formulated

[3] *Ibid.*, p. 3
[4] Benjamin Schwartz, *Chinese Communism and the Rise of Mao* (Cambridge: Harvard University Press, 1951), p. 120.

in terms of the interests of the urban proletariat rather than the peasantry.

The 1927 purge, however, had the effect immediately of destroying the urban working class base. The Comintern line, consequently, as previously stated, was set in terms of the avowed, although theoretical, necessity of re-establishing party ascendancy over the urban proletariat, giving it a proper base from which to resume the revolution. Mao, however, without initially rejecting this line, or seriously attempting its theoretical reformulation, continued to direct his efforts toward the establishment of peasant bases. He disregarded the directions to use such strength as existed to displace the Kuomintang from the cities in order to re-establish the urban mass base for the Party.

As a result, for a time party leadership was in fact, although not in theory, divided; with the Comintern leaders, as the general staff organization, attempting from Shanghai to direct a movement which nevertheless operated under its own command and which maintained itself by interpreting the Shanghai directives in accordance with its own requirements. In order to justify modifications of the party line by interpretation, however, a theoretical argument began to be made which ultimately gave a new party line and, with its acceptance, transferred the theoretical leadership of the party to Mao Tse-tung from the Comintern representatives at Shanghai.

The view that Mao Tse-tung acted upon and that came to be tacitly accepted as that of the party [5] was that the party could exist and function as a truly Communist Party although entirely divorced from any proletarian base. It could move toward Communist goals with purely peasant support and with its power resting on its armies and party apparatus rather than on class. To secure peasant support for the Red armies, and for Soviet governments when they were established, the major emphasis in policy had to be put on the solution of problems

[5] Officially, of course, there was no break whatsoever between the Comintern line and the theoretical line of the Chinese Communist movement during the whole Soviet period. Actually, however, the gravitation of power into the Soviet areas marked almost the total severance of the Chinese Communist Party from its supposedly urban proletarian base. It was the beginning of a heresy in act never made explicit in theory. Chinese Communism in its Maoist development demonstrates in fact that a communist party organized along Leninist lines and imbued with a sincere faith in certain basic Marxist-Leninist tenets can exist quite apart from any organic connection with the proletariat. The experience of Chinese Communism thus casts a doubt on the whole organic conception of the relation of party to class. *Ibid.*, p. 191.

related to peasant livelihood rather than upon creating in China a socialized industry. The party thus came to advertise itself and to be viewed as a party of agrarian reform.

THE PEASANT BASE FOR THE PROLETARIAN PARTY

The initial approach to reform in the period of the Kiangsi Soviets (1930-34) could be viewed essentially as conforming to the Communist doctrine of class war since it involved expropriation of the landlord (feudal) class in the interest of an "agricultural proletariat" of wholly or partially landless peasants. It also won support through an emphasis on disciplined behavior on the part of its armies, which lived on the countryside as its "liberators and defenders" rather than as military occupants and exploiters. Subsequently, when the Red armies had to move their base to the northwest, the policy of expropriation, except as applied against absentee landlords and those who were actively hostile to the regime, was given up for a conciliatory policy of reform of taxes and of the rent and money-lending systems. While this represented an adjustment of policy to a change in conditions in the geographical base, it could be made without a charge of deviation from international orthodoxy because it coincided in point of time with the tactical shift in the international line from that of "revolutionary opposition" to that of the United Front.

This method of approach to the peasantry and peasant problems put the Communist Party in a strong position to compete with the Kuomintang for popular support throughout the country if the latter's monopoly of power should be replaced with a system of constitutional democracy. This was so because the problem of livelihood for the peasant masses was the most obvious and pressing internal problem. The Communists rather than the Kuomintang were able not only to propose but also to carry out a program of agrarian reform which was simple enough to be understandable and which could be viewed as an end in itself rather than as a means to an end. Such a program could be advanced by the Communists without any alienation of support since the landlords and rich peasants who would be adversely affected by it were in any case opposed to them. The reverse, however, was true with the Kuomintang which was, consequently, inhibited from seizing vigorously what was to the masses the popular side of the issue. This was one reason why the Kuomintang did not develop a simplified program of land reform in implementation of Dr. Sun Yat-sen's third of the "People's Principles" which he called the "People's Livelihood," the people involved being in the main peasants.

By basing the Communist Party on the peasantry, even though its leaders continued theoretically to view it as the vanguard of the proletarian class, Mao Tse-tung, furthermore, was able to establish communism as having a national and unifying rather than a class and internally divisive outlook. The threat to national existence presented in Japanese expansionism, together with the United Front conception, assisted in this since the "objective situation" made it possible and politically profitable for the Communists to take the lead in propagating the slogan that the civil war should be adjourned so that all Chinese could unite in defense of the country against the Japanese enemy.

THE YENAN PERIOD

By 1936 when this had become the dominant Communist slogan, the "Long March" of 1934 had been made from the Kiangsi-Fukien area to the Northwest Border Region. This shift in geographic base, as suggested above, brought about a change in tactics from expropriation of land in the interest of the "peasant proletariat" to reform in the general interest of the peasantry. This, in turn, enabled the party to assert its leadership of the peasant masses rather than continuing to proclaim itself as the instrument of class warfare; a shift which made it possible for it to pose as the true advocate of revolutionary "Sunyatsenism" in opposition to the Kuomintang. Communist propaganda insisted that the Kuomintang had forfeited its leadership of the Chinese revolution because of its failure (1) to discharge its responsibilities in preparing the people at the local level for self-government, and (2) to institute a program of reform which would effectively improve the "people's livelihood."

During the years between the rise to supreme leadership of Mao Tse-tung within the party and victory over the Kuomintang in mainland China, a principal party interest was in establishing territorial bases. Thus the "Long March" involved a shift of the territorial base, but not the giving up of the idea of need for one. With that forced shift of the geographical base, however, the attempt was no longer made to organize governments of soviets. In the poor and undeveloped Northwest Border Region, the party established itself and its armies as the instrument of control, but with government organized on a local level along fairly traditional lines.

No organized opposition parties were permitted to function, but in village and other governmental assemblies, as previously pointed out, the Communist Party representation was restricted to one-third, and thus minority, representation. The same restriction was applied to administrative positions. Thus a contrast had been marked out, by 1945, between the Kuomintang failure to develop popular participation in local and provincial government, in order to give the people experience in government as the first step toward ending the period of tutelage, and the Communist practice of organizing nonparty participation in local government. Thus the theory and practice of single-party monopoly both of power and of government positions was apparently placed in contrast with the "people's democracy" which was supported by the Communist Party and the Red armies. The armies were, to be sure, under exclusive party direction and control. And because no other party organization was tolerated, and since the party had at its disposal the available instruments of coercion, popular participation, even to the point of two-thirds majorities, did not serve to lessen the ability of Mao Tse-tung and his associates effectively to determine policy. It did, however, enable the Communist Party to make an appeal, both in and out of China, as being democratic in its objectives, since it presented outwardly the appearance of seeking only the right to function as a minority party in a democratic framework.

As the United Front slogan began to be emphasized, apparently with a view to the formation of a coalition of the Chinese Communist Party and the Kuomintang in support of a truly national government, the purpose was defined by Mao Tse-tung as being: (1) to resist the foreign invader, (2) to grant rights to the masses, and (3) to develop the country's economy . . . there must be relief for the peasantry, but . . . "Agrarian revolution is of bourgeois character. It is beneficial to the development of capitalism. We are not opposed to the development of capitalism now in China, but against imperialism. This principle meets the demands of all democratic elements in the country and we support it wholeheartedly." [6]

There was thus a reaffirmation of the Leninist principle that in colonial countries nationalists and communists had a common enemy

[6] *Survey of International Affairs* (London: Royal Institute of International Affairs, 1936), p. 885, citing an interview of Edgar Snow's with Mao.

in the imperialist powers; and also of his thesis that in an agrarian country such as China a democratic stage of development, involving "capitalist construction," might properly precede movement from agrarian feudalism to socialism and communism.

As the United Front was constructed in 1937 it involved a theoretical but not an actual change of relationship between the two parties and the government. Theoretically, the Communist area and the Red armies were brought under the authority of the National Government. Actually, they remained under control of their Communist commanders who continued to take their direction from the party authority (i.e., Mao Tse-tung, Chou En-lai, Chu Teh, and others) at Yenan. The Communist area itself was assertedly organized within the Chinese Republic as a border region, but it actually remained under the Communist Party authority. In other words, the Communist Party retained control of its territorial base, although theoretically exercising power as the agent of the National Government. Thus in fact the United Front was more in the nature of an alliance of two territorial governments against a common external enemy than a coalition of parties in support of a common government.

In qualification of this conclusion, however, the establishment of the People's Political Council in 1938 must be recalled. The Communist Party, through participation in the PPC, accepted a direct relationship to and within the National Government. Although the members of the PPC were designated by the Government, the Communist appointees were selected by the Communist Party leaders. The body itself, however, had a strictly advisory and consultative position within the government. Thus while the PPC offered an opportunity for the expression of critical judgments as to public policy, representation in it failed to give the Communist Party an effective, even though minority, voice in the direction and control of the government itself. Nevertheless, even this minority advisory position was a step toward political unification and also extension of the area of Communist influence beyond the Northwest Border Region. Another step forward for the Communists was taken with the authorization of Communist guerrilla operations in the Yangtze River basin after the evacuation of Hankow in 1939. This brought the Communists back to an early center of their power. But these moves toward modification of the Kuomintang monopoly of power outside the Northwest Border Region were not paralleled by any opening of the Communist area to Kuomintang organizers or armies. In this respect, such concessions as were made in the interest of unity were in fact made by the National Government and thus by the Kuomintang and not by the Communists.

While in one sense the alliance continued until 1945, in another sense it ceased to exist as the Chinese-Japanese line became stabilized in and after 1941. From that time, alliance, in the sense of positive mutual or joint action against a common enemy, was supplanted by a truce in the civil war while each party, with of course one eye on the actions of the other, carried on its own operations against the Japanese.

By 1941 the coastal area, as far inland roughly as a line dropped from Peiping through Hankow to Canton had been occupied by Japan to the extent of control of the cities and the arteries of communication. The military efforts of the National Government after 1941 were largely confined to defense of the southwestern provinces with a view to preventing further extension of Japanese control. An emphasis on defense was also shown in the deployment of military forces so to prevent an extension of Communist authority into the areas south of the Yangtze. Otherwise, the emphasis was put on an air offensive against the Japanese in and beyond China and on ground activity directed toward the reopening of land communications by way of Upper Burma between China and the United States and Britain.

CHINESE COMMUNIST WAR TACTICS

The Communists, however, using the guerrilla tactics previously employed successfully against the National Government, carried on that type of offensive constantly but sporadically within the Japanese-occupied areas in North China. They organized the countryside against the Japanese, establishing close relations with the villagers through execution of their program of agrarian reform and local self-government, along with "hit-and-run" military operations against the Japanese in the towns. Thus they operated in North China simultaneously as defenders of the peasantry against the exactions of the local gentry, many of whom had acquiesced in the exercise of Japanese authority, and against the exactions of the Japanese military. While the circumstances of the war reduced the area of effective authority of the National Government, the Communists were thus able to extend their authority beyond the Northwest Border Region eastwards toward the sea even though the Kuomintang was able to prevent them from operating freely in the central and lower Yangtze region. As they penetrated North China, harrying the Japanese through guerrilla attacks and thus pinning down substantial Japanese forces, the view was widely expressed that the Communist forces were more actively contributing to the winning of a decision over Japan than was the Chungking regime. The National Government was also pinning down substantial Japanese forces through its continued defense of Free China and its refusal to make peace with Japan, but its critics held that it relied on the United States for victory rather than on the reorganization of its own military power for purposes of an offense. As a result of this those Americans, as well as Chinese, whose attention was concentrated exclusively on the winning of the war began to appreciate Communist Party leadership within China and to depreciate that of the Kuomintang and the National Government.

In spite of this opinion which existed at the time of the Japanese surrender, Chiang Kai-shek, as the Allied Commander-in-Chief in the China Theater and as head of the reorganized government, was designated to receive the Japanese surrender throughout China and in northern Indochina. With the forces at his disposal, even with substantial American assistance, he was able to take over in North China only what the Japanese had in fact occupied, that is, the cities and towns and the lines of communication. The villages, off the main lines of communication, had their own organization, which had been developed and maintained with the support of the Communist armies. They were willing to accept Kuomintang authority only if the National Government was prepared to continue the existing local government regimes and officialdom, and to accept the changes which had been made in landholding arrangements and in the local tax and debt structure. Otherwise it was made evident that the National Government would have to extend its authority from the towns to the countryside by military means, overcoming peasant as well as Communist opposition.

Communist opposition had to be anticipated in any case, whether or not the changed local structure was accepted by the Kuomintang, except where Communist Party participation in the National Government had been arranged. When negotiations for a political settlement were finally terminated in 1947, the major change which had been made in the North China situation from that of the war period was the replacement of Japanese authority by that of the National Government, with the Communists carrying on guerrilla operations against the

National Government rather than the displaced Japanese. The National Government necessarily continued the Japanese tactics of garrisoning towns and cities and policing the intervening lines of communication, seeking to protect them against Communist depredations, while at the same time it attempted to extend its authority from the towns to the countryside.

CONFLICT IN NORTH CHINA AND MANCHURIA

The National Government seemed to have a sufficient preponderance of military power in 1947 to win a decisive victory over the Communists provided it brought its full power to bear in a campaign directed against a concentration of the Communist armies. The Communist guerrilla tactics made impossible such a decisive engagement in North China until 1949. By the end of 1948, the Communist forces in North China had been augmented and supplied from Manchuria, while the National Government's armies had been reduced in size and strength through the loss of the troops and equipment which had been employed in the attempt to re-establish the government's authority in Manchuria.

This attempt had been continued against the advice of the American Military Mission in China. It had been initiated on the assumption that the Soviet government would not obstruct the entry of National Government forces. Without that obstruction Manchuria might have been brought under the effective control of the Chinese government with sufficient rapidity to prevent it from being used as a major supply base for the Communist armies. By September, 1947, however, General Wedemeyer was compelled to report that:

> The situation in Manchuria has deteriorated to such a degree that prompt action is necessary to prevent that area from becoming a Soviet satellite. The Chinese Communists may soon gain military control of Manchuria and announce the establishment of a government. Outer Mongolia, already a Soviet satellite, may then recognize Manchuria and conclude a mutual support agreement with a *de facto* Manchurian government of the Chinese Communists. In that event the Soviet Union might accomplish a mutual support agreement with Communist-dominated Manchuria, because of her current similar agreement with Outer Mongolia. This would create a difficult situation for China, the United States and the United Nations. Ultimately it could lead to a Communist-dominated China.[7]

[7] Report to President Truman by Lieutenant General Albert C. Wedemeyer, U. S. Army, *China White Paper*, p. 767. The Report is published in full, except for references to Korea, pp. 764-814.

The suggestion for action made by General Wedemeyer was the "prompt" initiation by China of a request for United Nations action "to bring about cessation of hostilities in Manchuria as a prelude to the establishment of a Guardianship or Trusteeship," which might "consist of China, Soviet Russia, the United States, Great Britain and France." If one of these nations should not agree to such a Guardianship, "China might then request the General Assembly . . . to establish a Trusteeship, under the provisions of the Charter." [8]

This proposal could not be viewed as within the limits of practicability unless the National Government was prepared to concede its own incapacity as well as its lack of power *vis-a-vis* the Chinese Communists and the Soviet Union; and to give up formally its contention that Manchuria was an integral part of China. That had also been the contention of the United States since the Manchurian question had been raised in 1900. From that point of view, a principal war objective for China, seeking to maintain its territorial integrity, had been the re-establishment of Chinese control in and over Manchuria. Furthermore, Manchuria was designed to play a key role in the National Government's plans for economic recovery. Thus it was politically essential for Chiang to make the utmost possible effort to establish control over Manchuria. Even though he lacked the power immediately to do so he could not have afforded to renounce the objective as explicitly as would have been done through proposal of a United Nations Trusteeship. [9]

The Wedemeyer proposal of international "neutralization" of Manchuria through "guardianship" or "trusteeship" was based upon the assumption that the National Government could not establish its power in Manchuria against the Russians and the Chinese Communists without military assistance beyond that which the United States was prepared to give it. Washington was unwilling to be drawn as a military participant into what it viewed then as a civil war since that would stamp its policy as interventionist. Such intervention, it was feared, might cause

[8] *Ibid.*, p. 767.
[9] The inability of the United States and the Soviet Union to agree on the conditions of institution of a "guardianship" for Korea as of the time of the Wedemeyer Report, and the subsequent history of the Korean question in the United Nations, indicates clearly what would have happened if the United States had attempted to bring about a solution of the Manchurian question along the lines suggested.

the Soviet Union openly to take a position against the National Government.

On the assumption that sufficient American military assistance would not be given to enable the National Government to establish its authority in Manchuria, and in view of the impracticability of urging on the Chinese government the initiation of a proposal for trusteeship, the official military advice given to Chiang was to use his armies to consolidate the position of the National Government in North China. That being done it was argued, North China could be used as a firm base from which to operate against the Communists in Manchuria. Under existing conditions, with the supply lines necessarily extended to bases in Central and South China, the problem of maintenance and re-enforcement of the armies operating in Manchuria was difficult of solution. Whether it was because of faulty military judgment or of military judgment controlled by political circumstances necessarily viewed as of more immediate importance, Chiang disregarded this advice and attempted to win a decision over the Communists in Manchuria. The result was not merely the loss of Manchuria but the loss to the Communists, through surrender, of entire armies together with their equipment.

When the focal point of the struggle was then shifted from Manchuria to North China the Nationalist strategy continued to be developed in terms of defense of cities, where National Government armies were consequently not only immobilized but cut off from one another and from effective supply and re-enforcement from the base of Nationalist power south of the Yangtze River. Kuomintang strength was then still further reduced through the negotiated or enforced capitulation of these garrison forces as they were penned-up in the principal North China cities. The military power of the Communists was increased (as that of the National Government was decreased) through incorporation of large parts of the surrendered troops, together with all of their arms, into the Communist armies. In this fashion, by the end of 1948, the preponderance of military power had come to be with the Communists rather than the Kuomintang and the National Government.

ELEMENTS OF KUOMINTANG WEAKNESS

The rapidity of the Communists' advance during 1948 and 1949, however, cannot be attributed solely to their armies. Their military successes did, to be sure, strengthen the growing popular view of the ineffectiveness of the Kuomintang as an instrument of government. Nevertheless, the fundamental dissatisfactions with the National Government grew out of its apparent unwillingness or inability to bring about a measure of economic recovery. One obvious example of its failure was seen in the astronomical currency inflation which especially weakened the fixed-income group, and thus weakened confidence in the governing capacity of the National Government. Another weakening influence, from the point of view of confidence in the government, was the continued use of political power by high-placed officials to advance their own personal interests, especially through the diversion of foreign (American) economic assistance from the realization of agreed public purposes to serve private ends. The emphasis in government was felt to have shifted from the new national patriotism back to the old realization of individual and group benefit from the holding of public office. This led to the disillusionment with the government on economic-political grounds which was expressed in the middle and lower ranks of the Kuomintang bureaucracy as well as among those outside the government. This feeling was accentuated by the apparent unwillingness of the Kuomintang to undertake a thorough overhauling of the single-party structure of the National Government, in the interest of efficiency and honesty of administration, through democratization. This loss of confidence in the capacity and integrity of the Kuomintang leadership, as much as the increased military power of the Communists, accounts for the rapidity of the Communist conquest of mainland China. The only available alternative to the Kuomintang as a national instrument of government was the Chinese Communist Party, since it was the only other group with an organized relationship to the masses and, of greater importance, the only one with organized military power. Other party groups, such as the Democratic Alliance, were intellectual in composition and support and had influence only as they needed to be courted by one side in its struggle against the other. As long as a negotiated settlement seemed to be a possibility they could assert their independence and exert an influence as a make-weight in a balance-of-power situation. But they lacked the power to present themselves as an effective alternative to the Kuomintang or the Communists.

It was because of their disillusionment with the Kuomintang, then, that large segments of the intellectuals offered the new regime their services. This shift as it occurred among the intellectuals and the governing bureaucracy was comparable in some respects to the shifts in allegiance which had occurred as the Nationalist (Kuomintang) revolution projected itself northward from Canton in 1925. There was the same illusionment with the new regime on the basis of its promises together with disillusionment with its predecessor because of its failure to improve conditions and to give "good government." And there was the same acquiescence in the verdict of power on the part of the professional soldier and the professional administrator. There was also the same problem presented to the Communists as to the Nationalists and to their predecessors in the establishment of the republic. This was the problem of assimilation of those who, without prior real conversion, transferred their allegiance. This needed to be accomplished without a serious watering down of the original purposes of their particular phase of the revolution if it was not to lose momentum.

Nationalism itself, furthermore, was a part of the explanation of the Communist victory over the party which had been created as the instrument of nationalism. It was American assistance which had enabled Chiang's armies to take over from the Japanese in North China. It was the United States which, in its mediatory efforts, failed to put the pressure on the National Government necessary to bring it to accept the minimum Communist terms for participation in the government. American training, arms, and equipment were important factors in the development of the initially superior military power of the National Government. And, as its fortunes declined, the appeals of the National Government to the American government for support made it appear ever more dependent for its existence upon a foreign power. Thus the Communist leaders sought first to lessen American support for the Kuomintang government by denouncing American aid as intervention in the civil war. They then sloganized all American aid to China as imperialism. Since such aid as was given was properly and inescapably channeled through the recognized government (the National, or Kuomintang, Government) that government was readily identified in the public mind as an instrumentality (the popular phrase was "running-dog") of imperialism. The Communist Party, seeking to overthrow the Kuomintang government, identified itself, consequently, as the anti-imperialist and therefore the true nationalist party. It was in this way able to capitalize on the sentiment of national patriotism which the Kuomintang itself had stimulated and diffused.

The immediate verdict in the civil war was won by the Communist Party but not, it must be reiterated, because of a widespread popular understanding and acceptance of Marx-Leninism or Stalinism. Active peasant support was initially gained on the basis of a program of agrarian reform which was actually more in conformity with the principle of the "People's Livelihood" of Dr. Sun than with the principle of collectivization. The allegiance of the scholar class was transferred from the Kuomintang to the Communist Party not as the revolutionary vanguard of the proletariat but as a party with a program of political and economic reform apparently adapted to the requirements of national postwar reconstruction. The intellectuals accepted Mao Tse-tung's "New Democracy" as a valid formulation of objectives for the postwar stage of the continuing Chinese revolution. They did not, however, make the distinctions which the conception of movement by stages requires.

REGIONAL AND LOCAL APPLICATION
OF MAO'S "NEW DEMOCRACY"

The Chinese Communist Party under Mao Tse-tung's ideological leadership, it must be understood, viewed itself as a Marxist-Leninist-Stalinist party in terms of the ultimate use which it would make of power when it had gained control of the state. The problem of winning power was different, however, from that of use of power when secured. Power could be attained in an overwhelmingly agricultural country only by enlisting the support of the peasantry for the Communist armies which, together with the party, were the custodians of party ideology. This could be accomplished only on the basis of a program of reform portrayed in terms of peasant problems and needs.

The territorial bases in which the party established itself, both before and after the war, were peasant rather than urban in composition. If and when the power of the party could be extended from the countryside to the towns and cities, it would be possible to use the position thus gained to reverse the movement and to reorganize the countryside so as to realize the purposes of the dictatorship of the proletariat. The period of the "New Democracy" thus could be considered one of transition rather than one of realization of the purposes of the Chinese Communist Party. The length of the transitory period would be determined by circumstances. A summary way of putting it is that the Communist party, when it assumed power, had a short-run program emphasizing democracy and agrarian reform which was constructed with a view to gaining support in the struggle for power; and a long-run program which was Marxist-Leninist, and which would displace the short-run program when the struggle for power had been definitively won.

During the war, the Chinese Communist Party operated outward geographically from the so-called Northwest Border Region into the Japanese-occupied area of North China where local governments, supported by guerrilla forces under Communist Party direction, were organized. These local governments frequently were separated from one another geographically but were co-ordinated through the medium of Party-Army direction. After V-J day activity was first directed toward the "liberation" (from the Kuomintang) of the same geographical area. Groups of provinces, after this liberation, were initially organized into local governments and then integrated under a regional organization. This improvised regional system was given a measure of permanence following the organization of the Central People's Government in October, 1949.[10]

This regional grouping of provinces and other traditional administrative areas conformed in the main to the military-command positions of the various "liberating" Communist armies as they took over from the Kuomintang. To some extent the regions also conformed to natural economic-political, or geopolitical, subdivisions of the country. In their perpetuation, however, they were designed as agencies of centralization rather than as instrumentalities of regional or local self-government. Furthermore, the artificial nature of some of the regions indicated the desire to weaken the natural political and economic connections of provinces which might be exploited against the Communists during the period of consolidation of their power. The war-lord system of the

[10] With the enactment on December 16, 1949, of the Organic Law of Regional Government Councils. The country was subsequently organized into seven regions: Northeast (Manchuria); North China; Inner Mongolia; East China; Central-South China; Northwest; and Southwest. The regional system is described in some detail in the *Current Background*, No. 170, titled "Pattern of Control: The Regional Organization of Communist China."

past was rooted in localism and in geopolitical regionalism which had not been completely displaced by the Kuomintang regime during its period of control. Thus the new regionalism seemed designed to nationalize through a further detachment of the people's sentiments and loyalties from their historical provincial and local bases. They had served their purpose by 1954 and were abolished when the new constitution was adopted in that year.

ORGANIZING THE CENTRAL PEOPLE'S GOVERNMENT

No attempt was made by the Communist Party to establish a government for China as a state until the summer of 1949, when the power of the National Government had begun to crumble. Until then the Communist Party ostensibly competed with the Kuomintang as a party for control of the existing National Government. The first step taken in the direction of organizing a new national Communist government was the convocation by the Communist Party of its own Chinese People's Political Consultative Conference (CPPCC) in place of the CPPCC at Nanking in which it had been represented. The new body was empowered to establish a "democratic coalition government" for China. The composition of the new CPPCC revealed the elements which would have the right to participate in government during the period of the "New Democracy." In China, and "in present circumstances," said Mao Tse-tung, "the people are the working class, the peasant class, the small capitalists and the national capitalists." To these economic groups Mao added members of the student, or intellectual class, viewing them as "brainworkers" and thus members of the working class itself; provided they were willing openly to dissociate themselves as individuals from the Kuomintang, whether or not they became members of the Chinese Communist Party. This opened the way for participation in the new CPPCC by the parties which had refused to go along with the Kuomintang in adopting the constitution under which the period of party tutelage was theoretically terminated in 1948. Thus in effect the new CPPCC was made up of the Communist Party and individuals or groups sympathetic to it or hostile to the Kuomintang and thus acceptable to the Communist Party leaders. The function of the old CPPCC had been to work out a peaceful solution of the relations of the Kuomintang and the Communist Party. The assignment of the new CPPCC was to associate other, but sympathetic, elements with the Communists in the establishment of a new central government, from which the "Kuomintang reactionaries" would be excluded. By this maneuver the national Communist government was enabled to present the outward appearance of a party coalition rather than a single-party government.

The proposal that a new United Front of anti-Kuomintang elements be formed under the Chinese Communist Party was initially embodied in a May Day slogan in 1948 which advocated that "All democratic parties and groups, people's organizations, and social luminaries, speedily convene a political consultative conference, discuss and carry out convoking a people's representative assembly to establish a demo cratic coalition government." [11]

The idea was again advanced in the final peace proposals made to the National Government by Mao Tse-tung on January 14, 1949. A preparatory committee was thereafter established. It held meetings June 15-20, 1949, at which time subcommittees were appointed "to draft a Common Program and an Organic Law for the Chinese People's Political Consultative Conference (CPPCC) and an Organic Law for the Central People's Government." [12]

The drafts which were prepared during the summer were unanimously approved by the Preparatory Committee on September 17, and then by the CPPCC itself which was convened four days after the Organic Law for its constitution had been adopted. All that was involved was the changing of the name of the Assembly from the Preparatory Committee to the Council. This rapid action enabled the Chinese People's Republic to be proclaimed on October 1, 1949.

The People's Republic was constructed on the basis of organic acts adopted by the CPPCC acting as a constituent Assembly. One of these acts continued the CPPCC itself until the establishment of an "All-China People's Congress." When established, as it was in 1954, "the Congress was to become the supreme organ of the state." [13]

From 1949 until 1954, consequently, the CPPCC functioned under its Organic Law, which provided that it should meet in plenary session

[11] Alan B. Cole, "The United Front in the New China." *The Annals of the American Academy of Political and Social Science*, September, 1951, p. 39, citing *China Digest*, Vol. 4. No. 1.

[12] *Ibid.*, p. 41.

[13] S. B. Thomas, "Structure and Constitutional Basis of the CPR," *Ibid.*, p. 51.

only triennially. Provision was made, however, for it to act between sessions through its National Committee, supposed to meet semiannually to supervise execution of resolutions of the CPPCC. This supervision, if it had been undertaken would, however, have had little practical importance. Many of the committee members were actively engaged in the business of government in other capacities. As members of the Committee their function would consequently have been that of supervising their own work as officials. For that reason the National Committee had little reason for existence.

The Central People's Government, established by the Organic Law enacted by the CPPCC, was headed by the Central People's Government Council of fifty-six members designated by the CPPCC. During its life the Chairman of the Government Council was Mao Tse-tung. Three of the six vice-chairmen were important members of the Communist Party apparatus, and a majority of the Government Council members were drawn from the upper levels of the Communist Party heirarchy.[14] This enabled policy to be developed within the Communist Party and carried over to the government for ratification by the Central People's Government Council. The appearance of a united front government rather than a party monopoly of power was preserved, however, since three of the Government Council's vice-chairmen and a strong minority of its membership were designated from outside the ranks of the Communist Party.

This Government Council was the directive organ within the new governmental structure, playing a supervisory role with respect to the execution of policy as well as having legislative functions. The day to day operations of government, however, were carried on through another organ, the Government Administrative Council, which was also established in the fall of 1949. The Administrative Council was empowered to act within limits set by the Common Program, National laws and decrees and the decisions and orders of the Government Council.[15]

The definitions of powers and functions of the Government Administrative Council, within the limits set, make it apparent that government was planned by the Communists on a centralized basis, with local,

[14] For details of composition of and representation at meetings of the Government Council between 1949 and 1953, see *Current Background*, No. 206, pp. 3-5.
[15] On the Government Administrative Council, *Ibid.*, No. 209.

provincial, and regional government agencies being designed to serve the purposes of the national regime. As rapidly as circumstances permitted, it was expected that power would flow downward and outward from the center rather than upward and inwards from the districts and regions. In this respect the scheme of government was planned to operate in accordance with the principle of "democratic centralism," a fundamental principle in the Communist scheme of government.

THE CONSTITUTION OF 1954

In its formal application, the democracy in the system of democratic centralism is to be found in elective local, provincial, and national congresses, each of which establishes and supervises government within its territorial jurisdiction. Centralism, from the territorial standpoint, lies in the subordination of local to provincial and provincial to regional organs, with the Central People's Government having the right to set aside any decisions taken by any other governmental body below it. Thus the establishment of the new regional pattern did not mean that a decision was taken for federalism in territorial organization nor for decentralization of authority. In another respect, the "democracy" in the formula lay in the right of the National People's Congress (and until its convocation the CPPCC) to elect the members of the Central People's Government Council and to fix the broad lines of policy for the Government Administration Council. But, given the provision for triennial meetings of the Congress (and the appointive character of the CPPCC which exercised its functions until 1954), as well as the effective control which the Communist Party maintained over election laws and their administration; and in view of the fact that members of the government played an important role in the CPPCC and in the People's Government Council, it is apparent that the element of democracy in the system was more formal than actual.

The principle of democratic centralism, in its territorial aspect, was clearly perpetuated in article 65 of the draft constitution which was approved by the First National People's Congress on September 20, 1954. This article provided that decisions of local people's congresses and administrations could be modified or set aside by the congress or administration at the high or provincial level, provincial decisions in turn could be reversed by the National People's Congress and the national People's Government.[16] Since the new constitution registered the consolidation of the victory of the Chinese Communist Party it is understandable that the Leninist principle written into the Communist Party Constitution should be applied systematically in the erection of the Communist government.[17]

The principal changes made by the new constitution in the structure of government as erected in 1949 were in the direction of centralization and concentration of authority. Thus the six regions were abolished and the twenty-six provinces into which the country had previously been divided were brought under the direct control of the State Council, which replaced the Government Administrative Council. A chairman and a vice-chairman of the state replaced the chairman and six vice-chairmen of the People's Government Council. Mao Tse-tung, elected for a four-year term as Chairman of the State, (with Chu Teh, as Vice Chairman, designated to succeed him in case of death or incapacity), was constitutionally invested with the authority which he had in fact exercised under the previous arrangement. As State Chairman, Mao was designated to serve concurrently as the Chairman of the important National Defense Committee and of the Supreme Council on National Affairs (a much smaller body replacing the Government Council). In the latter capacity he was given the right to present proposals to the Congress or to its Standing Committee, and thus virtually to control its agenda. By these decisions two of the three most important leaders of the Communist Party (Mao and Chu) were placed at the head of the state structure. This correspondingly reduced the participation in the government of those not members of the Communist Party. Dr. Chao's conclusion is that the new constitution concentrates administrative, economic, and military powers in the hands of the Chairman of the Central Government, subject only to responsibility to

[16] For a good brief analysis of the 1954 constitution, based upon an examination of the Chinese text, Chao Kuo-chun, "The National Constitution of Communist China," *Far Eastern Survey,* Vol. XXIII, No. 10, pp. 145-151. The references to its provisions in this chapter are based largely on this excellent article. A translation of the text of the constitution is published, Interparliamentary Union, *Constitutional and Parliamentary Information,* 3rd Series, No. 20 (Geneva, Nov. 1, 1945).

[17] Article 14 of the CCP Constitution provides that: "(1) the leading organs of all levels of the Party shall be established through elections; (2) the leading organs of all levels of the Party shall submit periodic reports to the organizations by which they are elected; (3) individual members shall obey the majority; lower organizations shall obey higher organizations; all organizations shall uniformly obey the Central Committee; (4) Party discipline shall be strictly observed and Party decisions shall be enforced unconditionally." *Ibid.,* p. 151.

the National People's Congress and its Standing Committee. As he points out "The chairmanship is made more powerful by the discontinuation of five of the six vice-chairmanships in the pre-Constitution government." Chu Tuh, as the one Vice-Chairman, has a strong position since he is the replacement for the Chairman and because of his leading position in the military heirarchy and in the National Defense Military Committee, in which he serves as Mao's deputy.

The new constitution substituted a State Council for the Administrative Council. The new body was composed of the Premier (Chou En-Lai, the third member of the Yenan triumvirate, was continued as Premier in 1954), ten vice-premiers, thirty ministers, chairmen of committees, and the secretary general. Here again the reorganization was at the expense of the non-Communists in the government since the ten vice-premiers as well as the premier were designated from the top ranks of the Communist Party hierarchy.

The State Council, as the supreme executive organ of the central government, was constitutionally empowered to issue decrees and orders within the limits set by the constitution and laws, and to supervise their application. It, as well as the Chairman of the State had the right to submit proposals to the National People's Congress or its Standing Committee; [18] to direct the work of the ministries and of local governments, overruling, where necessary, their decisions and to carry out the national economic plan. The State Council also was given responsibility for the development of the defense forces of the state.

In its definition of purposes, as well as in changes made in the organization of government, the new constitution registers the forward movement, from the point of view of consolidation of power of the Com-

---

[18] The National People's Congress is constitutionally "the supreme organ of the state power" and "the sole executor of legislative power in the state." As such it has wide powers, including that of amendment of the constitution; enactment of laws; selection of the highest officers of government such as the Chairman and Vice-Chairman of the State, the president of the Supreme People's Court and the Procurator-General; approval of appointments to the premiership and membership on the State Council and the National Defense Committee; decision on amnesties and on questions of war and peace; ultimate control of the national economic plan and of the budget. Between sessions, however, the powers of the Congress are exercised for it by its Standing Committee, which also has additional functions of its own. Because of its size, its limited sessions, and the intervals of time between sessions, it is probable that the Congress will actually find itself a sounding board for the policies of the government and will otherwise exercise its powers under the direction of the Chairman of the People's Republic and its own Standing Committee, thus having essentially a ratifying role rather than one of effective direction and control. On its constitutional powers and functions, *Ibid.*, p. 148.

munist Party, of the first five years of the People's Republic. In the Common Program of 1949 the Chinese Communist Party was listed as one among the "democratic" parties and forces which had achieved the victory. The Preamble of the 1954 constitution, however, puts it that "the Chinese people, after more than 100 years of heroic struggle, at last, under the leadership of the Chinese Communist Party, achieved in 1949 the great victory of the people's revolution against imperialism, feudalism, and bureaucratic capitalism." And, whereas the CPPCC Common Program laid it down that the new republic was established in opposition to "imperialism, feudalism, and bureaucratic capitalism and strives for the independence, democracy, peace, unification, prosperity and strength of China," the Preamble to the Constitution establishes as the objective "socialist transformation." It states that:

> From the founding of the People's Republic of China to the realization of a socialistic society is a transitional period. The overall task of the state during the transitional period is to realize, step by step, national socialization of industry and, step by step, to complete the socialist transformation of agriculture, handicrafts and capitalist industry and commerce.

The idea was maintained, however, of a transitional period as one not yet completed by 1954 during which the United Front would continue. The components of the United Front, on the other hand, were simply described in the constitution as the "various democratic classes, democratic parties, and popular organizations" in contrast with the Common Program which detailed it as being made up of "the working class, the peasantry, revolutionary servicemen, intellectuals, the petty bourgeoisie, national minorities, overseas Chinese, and patriotic democratic elements."

The People's Government of the People's Republic of China as it had developed under the Organic Laws of 1949 into the new constitutional system of 1954 was, as Mao Tse-tung aptly characterized it, a People's Democratic Dictatorship which had been disclosed more openly as one of Communist Party Dictatorship. It continued to contain within itself representation of four classes and of "independent and minor party elements" which, after 1949, had been brought under the leadership of the working class as it was organized through and under the Chinese Communist Party. The "leadership" of the Communist Party meant that that party was actually dominant at the national level. This gave the party, in application of the accepted principle of democratic centralism, complete power to determine policy for the country at all levels. Mao Tse-tung reconciled democracy and dictatorship in the following working terms:

> The democratic system is to be carried out within the ranks of the people, giving them freedom of speech, assembly and association. The right to vote is given only to the people and not to the reactionaries. These two aspects, namely democracy among the people and dictatorship over the reactionaries, combine to form the people's democratic dictatorship....
>
> Don't you want to eliminate state authority? Yes, but we do not want it at present. Why? Because imperialism still exists, the domestic reactionaries still exist, and classes in the country still exist. Our present task is to strengthen the apparatus of the people's state, which refers mainly to the people's army, people's police, and people's courts, for the defense of the country and the protection of the people's interests; and with this as a condition, to enable China to advance steadily, under the leadership of the working class and the CP, from an agricultural to an industrial country, and from a New Democratic to a Socialist and Communist society, to eliminate classes, and to realize the state of universal fraternity. The army, police, and courts of the state are instruments by which classes oppress classes. To the hostile classes the state is an instrument of oppression. It is violent, and not "benevolent." You are not benevolent. Just so. We decidedly will not exercise benevolence towards the reactionary acts of the reactionaries and reactionary classes. Our benevolence applies only to the people, and not to the reactionary acts of the reactionaries and reactionary classes outside the people.[19]

"RE-EDUCATION" AND "BRAIN-WASHING"

The dominant position of the Chinese Communist Party enabled it to determine at any given moment who were reactionaries and members of the reactionary classes, and to apply its definition, as it carried forward the "present task" of strengthening the apparatus of the people's state. But part of the task was that of developing and utilizing techniques which would enable its supporters and allies to acquiesce in the ultimate loss of their separate party or class status. In other words, while strengthening the apparatus of coercion it had, at the same time, to employ the arts of persuasion. The immediate situation, as well as the previous emphasis on the "democratic" side of the accepted formula, whether phrased as the "new democracy" or the "People's Democratic

[19] "On the People's Democratic Dictatorship" (July 1, 1949), as printed in Conrad Brandt, Benjamin Schwartz, John K. Fairbank, *A Documentary History of Chinese Communism* (Cambridge: Harvard University Press, 1952), pp. 465-57.

Dictatorship," necessitated an emphasis in domestic policy on "re-education" of former reactionaries and of instruction of the "allied" classes and parties in the principles of Marx-Lenin-Stalin-Maoism. The new regime could maintain itself more easily if it could win general acquiescence than if it had to put its main reliance for the long-run on the coercion of substantial elements of the population.

In certain respects the problem faced by the Communists was similar to that confronting the Kuomintang in and after 1928. The party had to bring about acceptance of its principles and purposes by those who had come over to it because of disillusionment with the Kuomintang as the instrument of government and not because of understanding and belief in Communist doctrines. This required rapid re-education. This was undertaken both negatively and positively. On the negative side the intellectuals, especially, were persuaded and encouraged (or compelled) to undergo what came to be called "brainwashing." This involved public recantation of all ideas previously held which were inconsistent with those of the new order, and denunciation of the sources of those ideas. This fitted in with the anti-American campaign since for many it involved denunciation of the "capitalist-imperialist" United States, as many of China's intellectuals had been educated in American institutions, whether in China or in the United States. In many cases it also involved denunciation of fathers by sons, the former being held responsible for the wrong ideas held by the latter which had to be purged through confession of error. Notable examples of this were the broadcast made by the son of Dr. Hu Shih and the statement published by the son of Liang Ch'i-ch'ao. Such confessions as these helped to fix responsibility for error on the United States, but they also served to strike a blow at the traditional family system.

For the less prominent intellectuals, as well as for the gentry and rich peasantry, the public meeting was used as the forum for disclosure of perception of the error of the old ways and relationships through "brainwashing." Meetings were organized and held constantly at all levels to bring about public dissociation of as many as possible from traditional beliefs and from the system of ideas imported from the non-Communist West.

At the same time, a premium was put on study of the new "classics" of Marxism-Leninism-Stalinism and the ideas of Mao Tse-tung, the latter embodying the "combined principles derived from the practical experience of the Chinese (Communist) revolution." Thus "unlearning" the old was put side by side with mastering the new truths. The attempt was made to put the people through a rapid course of intensive indoctrination through formal instruction in the schools, "adult education" lectures, and discussion classes and meetings of all sorts.

For the realization of the purposes of nation-wide "re-education" the party utilized the great number of "mass" or "people's" organizations which rapidly came into being throughout the country under leadership furnished by party cadres. Such organizations enabled the party influence to be extended much more widely and much more rapidly than would have been possible if sole reliance had had to be placed on the party membership for the dissemination of the new doctrines.

In this work of indoctrination the Communists carried over into the new period an emphasis developed during the Yenan period. Plays, dances, and in general the arts and literature, were employed as most important means of political indoctrination. As Mao Tse-tung put it in 1942:

> Having established that our literature and art are for the people, we can go on to discuss the problem of their relationship within the Party, that is to say, the relationship between the Party's literary and artistic work and the work of the Party as a whole; also the problem of their relationship outside the Party, that is to say, the relationship between the Party's literary and artistic work and the non-Party literary and artisic work the problem of the united front of literature and art.[20]

He then points out that art does, and should be expected to, express class ideas, and rejects as a basis of judgment of art and literature the intrinsic merit of the work itself, viewed solely as art. Appraisal of art and literature must be made in relation first of all to the political or social purposes served. And ultimately the determinant for the Communist becomes service of the party interest. "Our demand, then," says Mao, "is a unity of politics and art, a unity of content and form, and a unity of revolutionary political content and an artistic form of as high a standard as possible." With the party in power this point of view had to be accepted, and its acceptance enabled the party to use the writers and artists of the country for purposes of indoctrination. It became heresy to express and disseminate any ideas contrary to doctrine as defined by the party and its creature, the Central People's

[20] In a speech made at the Forum of Literature and Art at Yenan, May 2 and 23, 1942, from text in *Ibid.*, p. 414.

Government. Those who did not disavow formerly respectable ideas and simultaneously seek to re-educate themselves in the new tenets were unable to find a place for themselves in the People's Republic. Finding a place meant much more than maintaining status in the political, social or economic hierarchy. Without at least the outward appearance of successful re-education of the individual it meant, particularly for the intellectual, complete loss of ability to earn a living and thus to maintain any sort of position for himself and his family in the new scheme of things.

To convincingly present an outward appearance of the new "inner grace" could be easy only for the person of shallowness of mind or lightness of conviction. For the person of fundamental conviction it required that he maintain a constant guard against penetration of the appearance. The alternative of real, although essentially coerced, ideological conversion to communism, necessitated a painful and difficult substitution of fundamental premises before there could be other than rationalization and acceptance for purposes of survival. An honest effort to believe was not sufficient unless it was apparent that the effort had led to belief. This could be shown only by reiterative positive affirmation since, as Dr. Hu Shih put it, the Chinese Communists not only denied freedom of speech; of as much importance they did not even allow freedom of silence.

AGRARIAN REFORM

The new regime, however, had to justify itself in action as well as through the creation of a doctrinal uniformity in the country. It had charged the Kuomintang with ineffectiveness as an instrument of government because of its unwillingness or inability to deal with the economic problem. This the Communists had posed as the problem of land reform. If the new regime was to win wide acceptance it would have to avoid a similar charge being made against it. Consequently it promulgated an Agrarian Reform Law on June 30, 1950. This law was applied regionally as the authority of the new government was gradually extended and consolidated in one part of the country after another. It was claimed that by the end of the first two years of life of the People's Republic land reform had been completed in areas with a total population of over thirty millions. The territory involved included, in addition to the earliest liberated areas (Manchuria and North China), the administrative areas of East, Central-South, Southwest and Northwest China.[21]

The agrarian reforms undertaken were not directed immediately toward collectivization under state ownership. Reform, instead, took the form of redistribution of land among private owners, with former landlords and rich peasants retaining land sufficient to support them as farmers. "No one is allowed to retain more than this, but no one willing to work the land is denied title to that proportion of his former property. The landlord can 'redeem himself through work' by becoming a peasant." [22]

In this respect the Agrarian Reform Law was an attempt, in the interest of the maintenance of production, to substitute a somewhat conciliatory national policy for the first wave of violent and disorderly local expropriations of land by the landless and poor peasants. Early behavior in the "liberated areas" was patterned on that of the Kiangsi Soviet period. The reform law, however, embodied in modified form the policy followed in the Northwest Border Region during the Yenan period. Private ownership was permitted. The landlords and rich peasants were not liquidated nor were their total holdings redistributed. They were tolerated if and as they acquiesced in their new status as peasants. Where vestiges of landlordism remained, the old "feudal" payments in kind were transmuted into fixed rent. The land tax remained but it was to be paid directly into the national or local treasury, with the peasant relieved of the obligation of paying the tax, in addition to rent, for the landlord. Thus, as far as law could do it, the situation of the mass of the peasantry was materially improved under the new regime.

In order to make understandable the differentiation which had to be made in application of the Agrarian Reform Law, it became necessary for the State Administration Council to promulgate an analysis of "Class Status in the Countryside," on August 4, 1950. This analysis defined the status of the landlord, the rich peasant, the middle peasant, the poor peasant, and the worker. For the landlord and the capitalist, as well as the rich peasant, it laid down the working principle that:

[21] *Current Background,* No. 120, special article on the "First Two Years of the Communist Regime," p. 9.
[22] C. P. Fitzgerald, *Revolution in China* (New York: Frederick A. Praeger, 1952).

The rich peasant who engaged in serious counter-revolutionary activities before and especially after liberation shall be classified as a reactionary rich peasant. The land and other properties of such reactionary rich peasants and of their family members who took part in these counter-revolutionary activities shall be confiscated.[23]

This, of course, opened the way to widespread confiscation on the basis of judgments of local "People's Courts." Too enthusiastic action on the basis of local prejudices, however, had the effect of disrupting production and thus forced some reconsideration of such local decisions as the party found itself faced with the exigencies of famine and the problems resulting from the Korean War.

Indications of intention to move from this base of private ownership in land and toleration of class distinction in the countryside toward socialism as rapidly as circumstances permitted were given in the active promotion of co-operative movements and societies. These were organized under party control and were intended both to stimulate and to guide production in the villages. Through the co-operative the villager secured better seeds and implements. It made available a few good animals for the use of all members. Through it the village produce was marketed. In general the co-operative was designed to secure some of the advantages of a large collective farm in advance of collectivization, thus preparing the ground for the next step away from the individual ownership to which the Chinese peasant was firmly committed. The intention indicated was that of movement toward orthodox Marxist goals along lines which would not immediately alienate the peasants.

SHIFT FROM PEASANT TO URBAN BASE

This intention to develop along orthodox lines was also forecast in the decision [24] to shift the center of gravity of party work from the rural areas to the cities.

The Plenum pointed out that...from the failure of the Great Chinese Revolution in 1927 up till now, the center of gravity of the Chinese People's revolutionary struggle has been in the countryside, gathering force in the countryside and using it to encircle the cities and then to capture the cities....

[23] *Current Background*, No. 52, p. 10.
[24] Second Session of the Seventh Plenum of the Central Executive Committee of the Party (March 25, 1949).

But the period for using this way of working has now ended. The period has now begun for working from the cities to the countryside.... The countryside must certainly not be cast aside and attention paid merely to the cities. Anyone who thinks this way is entirely mistaken. But the center of gravity of Party work must be placed on the cities.[25]

There were two reasons for this "shift in the center of gravity of Party work:" one theoretical and the other practical. From the point of view of theory:

The decision to put more emphasis on urban areas reflects the continuous attempt of the Party hierarchy to reconcile the Marxist theory of leadership by the urban proletariat with the fact that the CP came to power mainly through the support and strength of the peasantry.... Nevertheless, the Party line had always maintained that "the workers shall retain their leadership of the peasantry" (Lenin) and "the peasants could not have defeated the landlords without the leadership of the workers" (Stalin); it was natural that the CCP, now at last about to rule millions of urban workers, should publicly announce its emphasis on urban areas.[26]

The practical reason for the shift was that the imminent establishment of Communist Party control of mainland China brought the party leaders face to face with the real problem of government. This lay in the organization, administration, and development of the national economy in place of one, and the least complicated, segment of it. In other words, if successful, the party would have to solve the multitude of problems with which the Kuomintang had been faced and with which it had not been able to deal successfully. Of these, the land problem was only one; and it was one which could not be solved, from the standpoint of the "people's livelihood," merely by land redistribution and tax reform. The system of town-country exchanges would have to be revived and reorganized. There would have to be, even for this limited purpose, rehabilitation and reconstruction of the communications system and the productive plant which the Communists themselves had largely been instrumental in destroying as part of the guerrilla war attempt to make the position of the National Government untenable. Inflation would have to be controlled. This could only be done through an increase in industrial production or through imports of both capital goods and consumer goods. The increase in agricultural productivity which was necessary to sustain the increased rural and agricultural population required "biotechnical improvements as well

[25] From text in Brandt, *et al.*, *op. cit.*, pp. 443-44.
[26] *Ibid.*, Commentary V, p. 441.

as other long-range programmes such as urban and rural industrialization, population control and the like." [27]

A peasant party did not contain within itself the trained personnel necessary to develop and implement the program necessary if the party was to demonstrate its ability to govern the country. This managerial personnel was to be found in the cities and in the former Kuomintang bureaucracy. That bureaucracy had to be encouraged to put its talents at the disposition of the new regime.

Thus while, as has been pointed out, the Central People's Government maintained its peasant support through the inauguration of agrarian reform, it was under the practical necessity of approaching the complex of economic problems along lines of national industrialization. In these terms, the new government's initial approach to the problem was similar to that which had been charted by the Kuomintang itself. It sought to stabilize the monetary system and to rehabilitate, reconstruct, and extend the modern communications system. Conservation work along waterways was resumed. Plans were announced for the development of hydroelectric and other power projects. Urban production was emphasized.

The ultimate purpose of the Communist regime in planning industrialization after 1950 was complete socialization of the national economy. Operating within the framework of the "New Democracy" during an undefined transitional period, however, the government did not immediately proceed to attempt itself to operate the national economy. On the contrary, it expressly recognized that for a time a large role would have to be given to private capitalism, although the direction in policy would necessarily be toward a reduction of this role. By 1952 the state had come close to a monopoly position in banking and foreign trade and had a dominant position in heavy industry. Trade, as distinguished from production, and light industry, however, remained predominantly capitalistic. The "five-anti campaign" [28] of 1952 was designed to strengthen the controls of the state over private enterprise rather than to bring about nationalization of that part of the economy which remained in private hands. The nation-wide emphasis on some of the "bad" practices of capitalists, however, helped to create the proper climate of opinion for subsequent moves toward socialization.

[27] *Ibid.*, p. 442.
[28] The campaign was against the five evils of bribery, tax evasion, fraud, theft of state assets, and leakage of state economic secrets.

PLANNING THE ECONOMY

By 1953 the internal position of power of the Chinese Communist Party had been sufficiently stabilized so that the real movement toward the ultimate goal could be begun with the institution of the first of a series of five-year plans.[29] If the goals of this plan of economic development covering the years 1953-57 should be measurably attained it would be possible for the transitional period of the "New Democracy" to be terminated since the state would have extended its sector of the national economy to include most if not all of those now predominantly capitalistic.

Aside from this the plan was significant because of the revelation of the emphases put by Peiping on different forms of productive enterprise. The major emphasis was placed on the production of capital goods, as had fairly consistently been true also in the planning of production in the Soviet Union, the prototype for Communist China. Emphasis was placed on an increase in agricultural production, to be sure, but to give a surplus to be used by the state in the implementing of the plan rather than for domestic and private use. For this purpose state control of grain distribution was also instituted. Similarly wages were to be kept consistently below the level of increases in industrial productivity so that the resulting surplus could be used for state purposes such as meeting the commitment to give large-scale aid to North Korea.

For purposes of the implementation of the plan the Peiping regime turned to the Soviet Union for the assistance which it was impolitic for it to attempt to secure elsewhere. This resulted in the introduction into China of large numbers of Russian technicians as well as in the conclusion of trade agreements establishing the conditions of supply of goods essential to the operation of the plan in its initial stages and the methods of repayment.

In evaluating its successes and failures it must be remembered that the Communist Party, as had been true for the Kuomintang, found itself unable to concentrate its energies wholly on finding ways and means of solving internal problems because of both internal and external attack. Although it was able to assert that it had driven the Kuomintang armies from mainland China by 1950, the People's Government was confronted with the same type of continued resistance as

[29] For a discussion of the first plan, Ronald Hsia "The Chinese Economy Under Communist Planning," *Pacific Affairs*, Vol. XXXVII, No. 2, pp. 112-23.

that which the Communists themselves had offered to the National Government after 1928. The Kuomintang maintained a government on Formosa which stimulated guerrilla resistance on the mainland and gave a rallying point for non-Communist overseas Chinese. And, although the claims of the Nationalists with respect to their co-ordinating and directive role in relation to guerrilla activities might need to be discounted, the fact of armed resistance, whether by guerrillas or by bandits (the term applied to their armed opponents by the Communists in their turn), had to be recognized. Mao himself called attention to the continuing problem of re-establishment of order, which necessitated constant reliance on military and police action. This necessity was as available to the Communists as it had been earlier to the Kuomintang as an excuse for failure to make more rapid progress in the execution of long-range programs of development.

REACTION ON CHINA OF THE KOREAN WAR

To an even greater extent, the situation which developed in Korea enabled the new regime to focus public attention on the requirements of military power. It was thus able to explain away shifts in internal emphases and failures in reconstruction. The fact that the Korean situation, as it affected China, was the consequence of Chinese intervention and thus differed fundamentally from an attack on China such as that launched by Japan in the 1930's, did not interfere with use of the Korean War by the People's Government for purposes of whipping up patriotic sentiment. It had ridden into power partly through cultivation of anti-Americanism. The circumstance of American leadership in Korea enabled Peiping to continue and intensify its campaign of anti-Americanism, shifting responsibility for its failures on the domestic front to the "war-mongering" of the imperialist United States.

The difficulties of establishing its internal control, together with the problem of foreign relations, furthermore, gave the new regime its justification, as well as the need, for tightening controls over all aspects of Chinese life. Foreigners, except for the Russians, were ever more closely confined in their contacts with the Chinese community, even where there was no reason to suspect them of anticommunism. Suspicion of them, especially Americans, was sedulously cultivated so as to prevent normal contacts from being maintained. This suspicion laid the groundwork for charges of improper behavior; of spying and sabotage, leading to imprisonment; and to interrogations designed to produced forced confessions, and, where expedient, to expulsion from the country.

The atmosphere of suspicion extended from the foreigners to the Chinese themselves, poisoning their relations with one another as well as with foreigners. To this end the Chinese Communist Party utilized the same techniques as those which had been found useful for purposes of control in the Soviet Union. The propaganda methods used for purposes of re-education were not confined to the exercise of the arts of persuasion. Control of the press, radio, public meetings, and in fact of all the media of mass communication, was utilized to enforce uniformity of belief as well as conformity in action. The attempt was made to heighten emotional reactions by the staging of "hate" campaigns. All of this created a climate of opinion within which ordinary people found it impossible to behave in the customary ways even in individual relations. If they did they might find themselves in serious difficulty since propaganda was re-enforced through the operations of the secret police, assisted by those seeking security or power at the expense of their neighbors.

In all of this the emphasis was placed on the state and on its security, with of course an identification of the interest of the state with that of the Communist regime. To maintain the emphasis it was necessary to capitalize external threats to state security in order to maintain the essential emotional internal condition of fear and distrust. Where the threat could be perceived as real the problem was not difficult to solve. Whenever it began to lose its reality new reasons for fear had to be found. The general circumstances of international politics and particular developments in the politics of the Far East were of major importance in maintaining this emotional support for action advertised as necessary for security of the state and domestic tranquility in the form of united support of the People's Government.

5

The People's Republic of China: Foreign Relations

✳✳✳✳✳✳✳✳✳✳✳✳✳✳✳✳✳✳✳✳✳✳✳✳✳✳✳✳✳

THE QUESTION OF RECOGNITION OF THE CENTRAL PEOPLE'S GOVERNMENT

THE CENTRAL PEOPLE'S GOVERNMENT of the People's Republic of China, proclaimed on October 1, 1949, was recognized by the Soviet Union as the government of China on October 2. Shortly thereafter (between October 3 and 9) it was accorded recognition by all of the other states with Communist regimes. By the end of December it had been recognized by Burma and India. Britain, Denmark, Israel, Finland, and Sweden extended recognition in January, 1950, and the Netherlands and Indonesia in March. Subsequently Switzerland, of the European states, and Afghanistan, Ceylon, and Pakistan, among the Asian states, recognized the People's Government. Thus altogether seven non-Communist European states and six Asian states, in addition to the members of the Russian bloc, quickly recognized the new regime. France and the United States, of the major powers, the Latin-American states, the Arab states, Canada, Australia, New Zealand and the South African Union, of the British Commonwealth community, and the European states unlisted above, refused initially to recognize the new regime as the government of China.

It is obvious that considerations of national policy determined the decision to recognize or not in each case. The recognition extended by the U.S.S.R. and its satellites was quite clearly premature since it occurred in advance of the consolidation even in mainland China of the position of the government recognized. As late as May 1950, eight months after Soviet recognition, Mao Tse-tung took official cognizance of the existence of widespread continued opposition in the form of Nationalist guerrilla warfare in south and southwest China. At that time, furthermore, the Peiping government was actively planning invasion operations against Formosa as a step toward bringing the internal struggle to an end. The Soviet recognition thus can properly be viewed as an action designed to strengthen the internal position of the Central People's Government. Until recognition, Soviet assistance had been covert. The U.S.S.R. was pledged in the treaty and exchange of notes of 1945 to give postwar assistance to China only through the medium of the National Government. It had respected this pledge only to the extent of giving China no assistance for purposes of postwar reconstruction, and by disguising its intervention until it had a basis for prejudging the outcome. It then recognized the Communist regime and formally withdrew recognition from the National Government, thus terminating all relations with it. Concurrently, the People's Government repudiated the 1945 treaty. These actions enabled the Soviet government to assist China, if it saw fit, through the medium of a government which it recognized and with which it could form a common front in Far Eastern politics. From that time, the Soviet Government joined the People's Government in denouncing the United States as following a policy of intervention in support of those who were attempting to overthrow the recognized government of China. Russia's policy of recognition, consequently, was determined in part by the struggle which it was carrying on throughout the world against the United States.

In a similar fashion, although not quite so clearly, the recognition extended by Britain, India, and other non-Communist states was premature and thus was an act of intervention. It was clearer by January, 1950 than it had been the day after the proclamation of the new regime that the People's Government would probably be able to establish itself in power throughout China. Nevertheless, the internal struggle was still going on, and it was not until June, 1950 that the ease with which the Communists occupied the island of Hainan indicated the then probable inability of the National Government to maintain itself even on Formosa. Thus British recognition was not extended on a purely *de facto* basis from the point of view of successful Communist subjugation of the country through complete overthrow of the Kuomintang government. It was extended: (1) with a view to the protection of the large British interests in China, including the Crown colony of Hong-

kong which had become vulnerable to Communist attack with the occupation of Canton; (2) in the hope of safeguarding the British trade
and economic position in China; and (3) to maintain diplomatic, consular, and other contacts with and in China in the hope that the British
government might be in a position to exercise a restraining influence
on the new regime through lessening its dependence on the Soviet
Union. Because of its greater material interests in China, it was more
essential for Britain than for other Western powers to establish a satisfactory basis of relationships with whatever government had control
of the Yangtze basin and southeastern China.

To some extent however, Britain and some other recognizing states
were cultivating India through following the policy initiated by the
Indian government with respect to China and the Far East. That policy
was premised on nationalism and anti-imperialism and was expressive of
the view that Western states should adjust themselves to the "realities"
of the changing situation in the several Far Eastern countries. In relation to China, the judgment of the Indian government was that the
Communists had the power and, certainly as against the Kuomintang,
had the support of the people. Nehru held that this should be recognized. He argued that those who refused to recognize it were denying
the right of an Asian people to decide for themselves, without outside
intervention, on their own form of government.

The American approach to the problem helped to fix the Indian contention that nonrecognition was due to the unwillingness of the United
States, a Western capitalistic state, to accept a Communist regime, however popular, because it was Communist. The initial tendency in American policy was to extend recognition in accordance with the *de facto*
principle, but only when the outcome of the internal struggle was beyond doubt and the permanence of the new regime reasonably assured;
and only when it was clear that the new government would be willing
and able to accept and discharge its international responsibilities. This,
however, was not clearly defined as the policy to be followed. Such a
positive definition of policy seemed inexpedient because of the circumstances of domestic politics in the United States.

Supporters of the National Government, both in and out of the
American Congress, had already begun to propagate the view that the
Kuomintang debacle on the mainland was due to the failure of the
American government to give the Chinese National Government ade-
quate support rather than, as was indicated in the documents which

were officially published at this time, because of the inherent weaknesses of that government. This led to the charge that the Truman Administration, while proclaiming the doctrine of "containment of communism" had, even if only negatively, assisted in the imposition of a Communist regime on China. Thus it was insisted that that administration had either (1) encountered a major defeat in the "cold war" operations directed toward the containment of communism because of its failure to make an adequate estimate of the situation in China and undertake the necessary action to produce a satisfactory outcome, or (2) its actions had been based upon a "softness" indicative of an underlying sympathy with communism. These conclusions were accepted and disseminated by those who were anti-Administration and by those who were anti-Communist, as well as by those who were primarily animated by sympathy with the Kuomintang. All of this created a climate of opinion in the United States which made it necessary to approach the question of recognition of the People's Government as one involving support of or hostility to communism as a system. This made it difficult to evaluate the immediate situation for purposes of recognition or nonrecognition on a *de facto* basis, dissociated from approval or disapproval of the nature and internal purposes of those who had come into power in China. The attitude taken helped to confirm Mr. Nehru in his prior conclusion that the United States would attempt to use its power to compel the Chinese to repudiate a regime acceptable to them in favor of one acceptable to the United States.

This emphasis in the discussion of the question in the United States actually served to obscure, for other governments as well as for Americans, the realities of the situation as it was presented to the American government. These realities, which supported a policy of nonrecognition without regard to the Communist or non-Communist nature of the Central People's Government, or its Asian or non-Asian geographic location, were to be found in: (1) the continuation of organized opposition to the People's Government, both on the mainland and from Formosa; and (2) the expressed hostility of the Chinese Communist Party and the People's Government to the United States; and consequently its unwillingness to enter into normal relations with the United States, with the normalities defined in established principles of international law.

The first justification for nonrecognition, as stated above, could be viewed as somewhat tenuous in view of the collapse of the Kuomintang armies on the mainland, especially if one accepted the prevalent view that Formosa itself could not be successfully defended by the Kuomintang against the invasion which the Communists in the late spring of 1950 were apparently preparing to stage from the mainland. This view was supported by the low morale of the defeated remnant forces which had been evacuated to Formosa, and by the initial hostility of the Formosans to the National Government. This hostility was an inevitable result of the misrule of the island by the officials of the National Government first sent to rule it after China had displaced Japan as the controlling power. The ease with which the Communists occupied the island of Hainan in June, 1950, in the face of Chiang Kai-shek's assertion that it, as well as Formosa, was defensible and would be defended to the bitter end, rendered questionable the ability of the National Government to maintain itself even on Formosa. In spite of this estimate of probable developments in the civil war situation, however, the fact remained that the internal struggle had not been brought to a decisive end by the time of the outbreak of war in Korea. The continuation of organized resistance gave some grounds for questioning the permanence of the new regime. It consequently supported a policy of postponement of recognition until such time as the consolidation of Communist authority gave assurance of reasonable permanence.

The justification for nonrecognition because of the attitude of the Communist regime toward the United States was less questionable. After the failure of the Marshall Mission, the Chinese Communist Party had steadily embroidered the theme in its propaganda that support by the United States of the then universally recognized National Government was intervention in the internal politics of China to realize American purposes. The United States, consequently, had come to be labelled as the imperialist power in a country where nationalism had become the strongest single force and where nationalism derived its strength from opposition to imperialism. The fact that the United States was supporting the recognized government against those attempting to overthrow it by force, and that it was giving aid to China through the only generally accepted agency available, and thus was behaving with complete legal propriety, had come to be viewed as irrelevant in relation to the charge of intervention and imperialism among those who blamed China's ills and their own on the deficiencies of the Kuomintang as the instrument of government.

The American government, as well as many articulate Americans, apparently viewed the National Government as corrupt, inefficient, and undemocratic. Projected back into China this view confirmed, where it did not initiate, a similar opinion held by a growing number of Chinese. Among these Chinese the question was raised as to the reasons for continued American support of such a government against the Communist Party and the third parties supporting it. The Communists gave their answer in the form of the charge of imperialism. Popular reaction to this slogan helped to weaken the internal position of the National Government. Its demand for, or even the acceptance of, additional American aid, viewed as essential to enable it to remain in power, opened the Kuomintang to the charge that it had been transformed from a nationalist, anti-imperialist, party into an instrument of Western imperialism. The covert nature of Soviet assistance to the Communist enabled the latter to avoid the same charge against the Soviet Union. Consequently, the Communists were able to direct effectively against the Kuomintang the national hostility to imperialism, posing as a national party seeking to save the country from American imperialism. Having cultivated anti-Americanism as a method of weakening the Kuomintang, the Communists found it effective after 1949 as a bridge across which the non-Communist intellectuals could move to their support. Consequently, the Communist regime maintained an attitude of studied hostility to the United States which precluded the establishment of normal relations through reciprocal friendly attitudes and relationships.

Had this been confined to propaganda it might have been disregarded or even viewed as an attitude assumed with a view to impressing on the United States the desirability of extending immediate recognition in order to bring about a change in attitude. But when it was accompanied by actions directed against American officials in China, as well as by discriminatory action taken against legitimately vested American interests in China, it could not properly be disregarded. In some cases it could be argued that the action had been taken under unavoidable Russian pressure and was thus not a true measure of the attitude of the Peiping government toward the United States. And throughout the early months after the proclamation of the People's Government it could be argued that the attitude was a temporary one, cultivated for revolutionary purposes, and was expressive in its several manifestations of the adolescence of Chinese nationalism which would disappear with its maturation. It thus might properly be disregarded.

Nevertheless, it was an attitude which had to be seriously considered in determining policy. While sedulously cultivated as a popular attitude, anti-Americanism came to be expressed officially in terms of unwillingness to accept, with respect to the United States, the normal international responsibilities. There was, consequently, little reason for the United States to recognize the new regime. This was particularly the case as, even before the outbreak of the Korean War, the relations of China and the Soviet Union were cemented through alliance directed obviously at the United States; and as it became clear that it was important in the consolidation of the internal position of the People's Government that it stand before the country as the protector of China against an imperialist enemy. If it had not been possible readily to cast the United States in that role, it would have been more difficult to prevent consideration of the anomaly of alliance between anti-imperialist China and the Soviet Union which had demanded material concessions at the expense of China before it entered the war against Japan. In this respect, apart from the circumstances of the cold war, it was to the interest of both the Soviet Union and the Chinese Communist Party, viewing the latter as an instrument of international communism, to focus attention on the United States as an imperialist power and as China's "enemy number one."

In view of the existing situation, the sole advantage to the United States which could have been anticipated from recognition would have been the access to Chinese opinion which would have resulted from the diplomatic and consular representation normally established reciprocally after recognition. This, if secured, would have put the United States in a position to attempt to dissociate its policies and actions from the charge of imperialism, and thus to remove the barrier to more friendly relations. As a consequence, the dependence of China on the Soviet Union might have been lessened and its independence have ultimately been established; provided always that American policy had continued to be directed toward independence rather than toward a choice between dependence on the United States or on the Soviet Union. Any attempt to win this advantage through recognition was, however, precluded because of the reaction in the United States to the treatment accorded in China to American consular and diplomatic representatives, to American Marines in Peiping, and to American missionaries and businessmen throughout the country. Public opinion in the United States became sufficiently aroused so that it was politically dangerous for the Truman Administration even to contemplate recognition, in advance of clear evidence of a changed attitude on the part of the People's Government, and, in turn, of Chinese opinion.

That recognition would not have won this advantage in any event was shown in the reaction of the People's Government to British recognition and to that of Yugoslavia. Neither found it possible to establish normal conditions of relationship with Communist China after recognition because of a lack of reciprocity on the part of the People's Government. The reasons were different but the consequences were the same. The response of China to recognition was in terms of national policy as clearly as recognition was extended or withheld because of policy considerations. The Communist nature of the regime and its relations with the Soviet Union as a Communist state, to be sure, set the direction of its policies; but it was China rather than the United States which willed it so. There would have been no recognition by the latter, given the policies followed by China as they affected the United States, even had the People's Government not been in fact a government controlled by a Communist Party. This however, was obscured because of the fact that the active hostility to the United States expressed by the People's Government was fundamentally an expression of the Chinese Communist Party. Consequently, nonrecognition by Washington was construed in India and elsewhere to mean unwillingness to deal with a government which in its forms and in its social and economic program was unacceptable to the United States. This view was widely disseminated throughout Asia. It made new governments in Asia suspicious of American purposes in dealing with them. It was given substance by the reaction in the United States to the double problem of "recognition" and the "containment of Soviet power" in terms of domestic politics and the ideological issues posed by the spread of communism.

INTERNATIONAL ROLE OF NATIONAL COMMUNIST PARTIES

What was involved in the development of the situation in China, from the point of view of the United States, was the same issue which had been posed in and after 1947 throughout the world, and which gave rise to the Truman Doctrine of "containment." This question was whether or not there was in the changing internal situation in China an independent development which called itself Communist, or whether there was present the added element of the expansion of the power of the U.S.S.R. into a new area. In these terms, as long as it could reasonably be anticipated that China under the Communist Party could be expected to pursue an independent foreign policy, it could be argued that the United States had no vital concern with the outcome of the internal struggle beyond that of discharging its established obligations to China through the medium of the recognized government. It could well have been perceived, and might have been if more attention had been paid earlier both to Communist doctrine and to the international relationships of national Communist parties, that the accepted national Communist Party functioned as an instrument of Russian foreign policy. This was obscured, as far as the initial postwar period was concerned, by the formal abolition of the Comintern in 1943, when Russia was dependent on the United States and Britain for assistance against Nazi Germany. Subsequently it was obscured for a time by the break between the Yugoslav Communist Party and the Cominform and the Soviet Union. This led to the expression of the view that Mao Tsetung, as a Chinese Nationalist as well as a Communist, could be expected to show a similar independence of the Soviet Union if and as the interests of the two states diverged. This expectation was supported by the apparent fact that the Chinese Communist Party had maintained itself against the Kuomintang as a nationally confined movement, and by its apparent divorce from Communist orthodoxy because it based itself on the peasantry rather than on the proletariat.

A more careful examination would have revealed the continuing connection of the Chinese Communist Party with the Comintern during the 1930's and thereafter, and the acceptance finally by the latter of the point of view expressed by Mao with respect to the peasantry. The reaction of Mao to Titoism, furthermore, as well as his consistent references to the Chinese Communist Party, in terms of its long-run objectives, as Marxist-Leninist-Stalinist, should have brought an earlier understanding of the determination of the party to work within the framework of international communism, and thus its acceptance of the principle of world revolution. This understanding, in view of the organizational relationships of national Communist parties to the Russian Communist Party (Bolshevik) would have brought about an earlier acceptance of the probability that China under the Communist Party would not show early signs of Titoism (i.e., of national independence in the development of its foreign relations), but rather would tie itself closely into the Soviet power system in the Kremlin's contest against the United States and the non-Communist West. This probability became a certainty, however only with the continued cultivation of national hostility to the United States after the proclamation of the People's Republic and Government. From the American side, nonrecognition together with the continued support given by the United States to the National Government on Formosa, even though the reasons were drawn from the Korean War, ensured an intensification of the "Hate America" campaign in China. Chinese intervention in Korea, which brought the People's Government in fact, if not in theory, into armed conflict with the United States, supported and gained support from the campaign, and showed a determination to consolidate the Russian orientation in China's foreign policy.

RELATIONS OF COMMUNIST CHINA WITH THE U.S.S.R.

Extended negotiations resulted in the signature on February 14, 1950 of a treaty and agreements which formalized the relations of Communist China and the Soviet Union. The treaty became effective with the exchange of ratifications on September 30, 1950.

This Treaty of Friendship, Alliance and Mutual Assistance, of six articles, was to be valid for thirty years, and thereafter, unless denounced by either party a year in advance, for additional periods of five years (Art. 6). Like the first treaty of alliance between China and Russia, concluded in 1896, it was ostensibly directed against only one state, Japan, providing in Article 1 that:

> Both contracting parties undertake jointly to adopt all necessary measures at their disposal for the purpose of preventing the resumption of aggression and violation of peace on the part of Japan or any other state that may collaborate with Japan directly or indirectly in acts of aggression. In the event of one of the contracting parties being attacked by Japan or any state allied with it and thus being involved in a state of war, the other contracting party shall immediately render military and other assistance by all means at its disposal.

Since the United States played the dominant role in the military occupation of Japan, and since Japan had been completely disarmed and was incapable of attack, this article necessarily must be viewed as being actually directed against the United States rather than against

Japan. That fact, however, was put in the indirect language of diplomacy. The article goes on to declare the readiness of the two signatories "to participate in the spirit of sincere cooperation in all international actions aimed at ensuring peace and security throughout the world and to contribute their full share to the earliest implementation of these tasks." Read against the established Soviet vocabulary of double-talk, this must be taken to mean that the two states would jointly act against the United States, as that country was viewed as the principal barrier to the establishment of "peace and security throughout the world" on terms acceptable to Moscow. This unwillingness to participate in the making of peace, except as the conditions could be prescribed by Moscow, had been revealed in the response to the attempt made in 1947 by the United States to bring about the negotiation of a peace treaty with and for Japan, as well as in the negotiations over a German and an Austrian treaty. Nevertheless, the second article of the Sino-Soviet Treaty of 1950 provided: "Both contracting parties undertake in the spirit of mutual agreement to bring about the earliest conclusion of the peace treaty with Japan jointly or with other powers which were Allies during the Second World War." Neither Russia nor China, however, accepted the Japanese treaty which was finally signed and ratified by most of the other wartime Allies.

Beyond this, Communist China and Soviet Russia agreed to consult with one another: "in regard to all important international problems affecting the common interests of China and the Soviet Union" (Art. 4). This co-operation and the terms of the alliance were pointed up negatively in the provisions of article 3 that: "Each contracting party undertakes not to conclude any alliance directed against the other contracting party and not to take part in any coalition or in any actions or measures directed against the other contracting party."

All of these provisions were designed to fix the position of China as one of the group of states supporting the Soviet position in international politics. Under existing circumstances the alliance could only have the consequence of preventing China from looking to the United States for the economic assistance which it was apparent would be needed to repair the ravages of war. For that reason, as well as to consolidate the affirmed mutuality of interest:

> Each contracting party undertakes, in the spirit of friendship and cooperation and in conformity with the principles of equality, mutual benefit and mutual respect for the national sovereignty and territorial integrity

and non-interference in the internal affairs of the other contracting party, to develop and consolidate economic and cultural ties between China and the Soviet Union, to render all possible economic assistance and to carry out necessary economic cooperation. (Art. 5) [1]

In execution of this provision it was possible for the Soviet Union to send into China numbers of advisers to assist in the cultural consolidation of the new regime, and technicians to help plan economic reconstruction along Communist lines. At that time, however, the Soviet Union was not able or was unwilling to give much direct economic assistance to China. The principle of mutuality of benefit in any case made it possible for the Soviet Union to serve its own interests in setting the conditions of exchange for such assistance as it was able to give.

An initial agreement on assistance, concluded at the same time as the treaty, did establish a credit for China of U. S. $300 million, with interest of only one per cent per annum because of the "extraordinary devastation of China as a result of prolonged hostilities on its territory." [2]

This credit was to be made available over a five-year period in equal annual installments. It was to be used to pay for "deliveries from the U.S.S.R. of equipment and materials. These were "to include equipment for electric power stations, metallurgical and engineering plants, mining equipment for the extraction of coal and ores, railway and other transport equipment, rails and other materials necessary for the restoration or development of the national economy of China." (Art. 2) Repayment was to be made in "ten annual installments to begin not later than December 31, 1954." Payment was to be made by "deliveries of raw materials, tea, gold and American dollars." Subsequently (April 21, 1950), supplementary trade and barter agreements were announced. Under the barter agreements, mutuality of interest was defined in much the same terms, of supply by China to the Soviet Union of raw materials in exchange for industrial equipment. "At the same time there was signed a protocol for the supplying by the Soviet Union to the People's Republic of China of industrial equipment and materials for the period 1950-1952 against the credit granted under the Sino-Soviet Agreement of February 14, 1950." [3]

[1] The quotations are from the text of the treaty as published in *Current Background*, No. 62, March 5, 1951, "Sino-Soviet Treaty and Agreements," pp. 4-5.
[2] *Ibid.*, p. 8.
[3] *Current Background*, No. 62, p. 11. From text of New China News Agency (NCNA) press release of April 21, 1950. The preceding quotations are from the same issue.

The general lines to be followed in the co-operative development of China were indicated in an agreement announced on March 29, 1950 providing for the formation of Joint Stock Petroleum and Non-Ferrous and Rare Metals Companies to operate in China but not in the Soviet Union. Since such joint enterprises had already been employed elsewhere by the Soviet Union as instrumentalities of economic control, there is no reason to conclude that they were designed to serve a different purpose in China.

ATTITUDE OF THE CHINESE COMMUNISTS
TOWARD THE UNITED STATES

At the time when Communist ascendancy was established in China in and after 1949 there was a widely expressed view that the People's Government would not maintain its anti-American attitude because it could bring about economic change in China, essential to the attainment of its objectives, only with American economic assistance. Russia, it was held, could not, even with the best of intentions, meet China's requirements for outside aid to bring about economic rehabilitation and carry forward with sufficient rapidity the process of industrialization which was essential to solve the problem of the "people's livelihood." It was argued that as this was perceived China would be forced to turn to the United States as the only country in a position to give it the large-scale assistance required. This conclusion was correct as far as it went. But it failed to take into account: (1) the willingness of the nationalist-minded Chinese to sacrifice rapid economic progress on the altar of anti-imperialism, and (2) the determination and ability of the Chinese Communist Party to move toward its objectives only as rapidly as it could do so in complete independence of the "capitalist" and thus by Leninist definition "imperialist" West.

The Party's initial emphasis on agrarian reform enabled it immediately to retain its vigor as a revolutionary party without rapid movement toward industrialization. The allegiance of its peasant supporters could thus be retained without American assistance. The association which it had made of the Kuomintang with American imperialism and of American aid with the promotion of American "imperialist" political and economic interests at the expense of China, gave it internal support for a policy of internal economic development within limits set by China's own resources, supplemented by such assistance as the "friendly" and "anti-imperialistic" Soviet Union could render. The meagerness of Soviet aid was explainable in China on the ground of the problems, both internal and external, which Russia had to solve by utilization in the U.S.S.R. of Russia's limited or underdeveloped resources. Ultimately the issue was posed in terms of intentions. The intentions of the United States were labelled imperialistic and thus bad; therefore acceptance of American aid, although the aid might be necessary and great in amount, would be bad. The intentions of the Soviet Union were good; therefore bad or limited performance could and should be excused.

To the American this charge of imperialism directed against the United States was absurd and the making of it in extremely bad taste. Traditionally, as well as specifically since 1944, United States policy had been directed toward the establishment of unity in China, and postwar American aid had not been made conditional on special favors or rights to be granted to the United States. Any political conditions proposed had been designed to persuade Chiang Kai-shek to end single-party monopoly of control through the establishment of party coalition and the introduction of democracy, to the benefit, it was expected, of the Chinese people and the world in general.[4]

The benefit to the United States if its objective had been attained would have been real, on the assumption that China would, as a result, have become stable and thus a stabilizing influence in the Far East; and that a democratic China would have been friendly rather than hostile to the United States. None of the benefits sought involved the establishment of the special position for the United States within China which is the end-product of a policy of imperialism. Nevertheless, although the charge was inconsistent with the facts, its reiteration and the manipulation of fact to conform to the charge caused the allegation to be accepted as true and made it possible for this alleged "American imperialism" to serve as a strong support for the Chinese Communist Party, both internally and in its foreign relations. This reading of the relationship of the United States to the situation in China, furthermore, had an effect on the relations of the United States with India, Burma, and Indonesia. But this attitude, among other considerations, also made it impossible reasonably to expect that Communist China would follow an independent national policy toward the Soviet Union

[4] An accurate statement of United States aims was made by President Truman on December 15, 1945, as cited, quoted, and discussed *supra*, Chap. 3.

which would lead to a break with the Kremlin over Soviet policy as it affected the territorial position of China.

SOVIET IMPERIALISM IN POSTWAR CHINA

Except for that of Japan, Russian imperialism had, during the late nineteenth and early twentieth century, presented the greatest threat to the territorial integrity of China. It was because of Russian as well as Japanese pressure that Manchuria had become the "cockpit of Asia." Mongolia had been detached from China as a result of Russian actions and policy. And it was Russia alone which offered a threat to continued Chinese control of the vast area of Sinkiang province.

In theory, this threat from Russian imperialism to China's integrity had been removed in 1919, when the Soviet government renounced all rights and interests in China gained by the Tsarist government at the expense of China's sovereignty and integrity. At the same time, the Soviet government expressed the sympathy of the struggling Russian people for the Chinese suffering under the oppression of Western imperialism. In fact, however, the Soviet government took advantage of every opportunity presented to maintain or to regain the rights renounced in those peripheral areas where there was a territorial contact with the Soviet Union. This was certainly true as long as, and to the extent that, China was "Nationalist" and not "Communist" in its organization and purposes. Thus the Soviet government stipulated, as a condition of its belligerency against Japan, and thus in support of China, that the status quo in Outer Mongolia should be preserved. This meant acceptance of the Mongolian People's Republic which had been established with the assistance of the U.S.S.R. Although Mongolia's status was then viewed by the Chinese as that of autonomy within the Chinese state rather than that of independence, the Chinese agreed, in an exchange of notes in connection with the negotiation of the Treaty of Friendship and Alliance of 1945, to recognize the independence of Mongolia if a plebiscite should confirm the desire of the people of Mongolia for independence. This concession, as the American Ambassador at Moscow pointed out, went beyond the stipulations of the Yalta agreements. Soviet dominance in Mongolia at the time of the plebiscite assured a vote in favor of independence, and independence had the effect of confirming Soviet dominance in and over Mongolia. Thus the National Government, against American advice, accepted in advance the loss of this part of the territory of the former Chinese Empire as a method of ensuring Russian aid to China exclusively through the medium of the National Government after the termination of the military operations of World War II. This was considered in 1945 an advantageous bargain since Mongolia was not then viewed as an integral part of China, and since Chinese control there had previously been reduced to the vanishing point as a result of the application first of Tsarist policy after 1911 and then, after 1919, of Soviet policy.

While Sinkiang province did not figure expressly in the agreements entered into in 1945, it had also been an area of Soviet pressure on China before as well as after 1945. The territory involved extends to Russian Turkestan on the west, Kashmir on the south-west, Tibet in the south, Kansu in the east, and Mongolia in the north. Because of its remoteness from the center of Chinese authority, increased on account of the difficulties of communications, Sinkiang had always enjoyed considerable autonomy. It was only under effective Chinese control during the periods of strong and effective government in China proper. At other times it became a center of revolt, sometimes fomented by its neighbor, sometimes due to local reactions against Chinese officialdom. One of these periods of revolt occurred in the third quarter of the nineteenth century. At that time Russian activities in Sinkiang brought that country and China almost to the point of war. The negotiated settlement embodied in the (unratified) treaty of Livadia of 1879 temporarily lost much of the territory for China. Subsequently Russia restored most of the ceded territory, but retained extensive privileges of trade and secured an indemnity of 9 million rubles. After this time the expression of Tsarist Russian interest was mainly economic. This interest was maintained and increased after the Russian revolution, the natural outlet for the trade of Sinkiang being through adjacent Russian territories.

In 1931, the Governor of Sinkiang entered into a trade agreement with the Soviet by which Soviet institutions and nationals were placed upon a footing of equality with the Chinese in respect of customs duties and other taxation. It was also provided that the Soviet should send technical experts, and should give financial assistance for the development of agriculture and industries, and for the improvement of communications. In the following years, Soviet influence increased steadily and in 1934 Soviet troops entered Sinkiang, for the purpose of aiding the Governor to suppress disorder. It was not until 1942 and 1943, when the Soviet was exerting her utmost efforts to resist the Nazi conquest of European Russia that the Chinese Nationalists were able to bring Sinkiang under their control once more, and that Soviet influence waned, until the end of the war brought renewed Soviet pressure.[5]

By the end of the war, however, the Soviet government had stated to China that: "As for the recent developments in Sinkiang the Soviet Government confirms that, as stated in Article V of the Treaty of Friendship and Alliance, it has no intention of interfering in the internal affairs of China." [6]

Despite this pledge, however, the disturbed conditions in China due to the Communist attempt to gain power brought about renewed Soviet interference in Sinkiang. Since, however, Sinkiang's autonomy or independence had not been conceded by the National Government, as had been that of Mongolia, the situation remained open, and presented a possible source of friction between Communist China and the U.S.S.R. at the time of establishment of the Central People's Government.

In the readjustment of relations necessitated by the denunciation of the Soong-Molotov Treaty and the notes concurrently exchanged in 1945, a clue to the future development of Sino-Soviet relations in Sinkiang was offered with the negotiation and ratification of an agreement reached in 1950 which provided for the establishment of a Sino-Soviet Joint Stock Oil Company and a Joint Stock Non-ferrous and Rare Metals Company in Sinkiang.[7]

This would seem to indicate a willingness on the part of the People's Government to permit economic exploitation of the province within forms apparently maintaining Chinese sovereignty and giving the appearance of Chinese participation in control and direction but in fact giving control to the Russians.

RUSSIA'S RE-ENTRY INTO MANCHURIA

It was, however, the perennial question of Manchuria (China's Northeastern Provinces) which seemed to offer the most serious ob-

[5] George W. Keeton, *China, the East and the Future* (London: Stevens, 1949), p. 385.
[6] Exchange of Notes relating to the Treaty of Friendship and Alliance, August 14, 1945, *China White Paper*, p. 587.
[7] *Current Background*, No. 62, March 5, 1951, "Sino-Soviet Treaty and Agreement," p. 10, giving text as reported in the NCNA (New China News Agency) release at Peking on March 29.

stacle to friendly relations between Communist China, playing the tune of nationalism, and the Soviet Union. One reservation to the 1919 renunciation of Tsarist Russian imperialist rights and privileges in China had been with respect to the Chinese Eastern Railway which connects Soviet territories in the west and east across northern Manchuria. The Chinese Nationalists' attempt to dispossess Russia in 1929 had been prevented by force. The Japanese had, however, developed sufficient power in Manchuria to compel the sale of the Chinese Eastern to Manchukuo, thus liquidating Russian rights and interests first acquired by the "imperialist" Tsarist government, but clung to by the "anti-imperialist" Soviet government.

As the Soviet Union bargained its way into the Pacific War at the Yalta Conference, its price was the transfer to it of substantially the Russian rights and interests lost to Japan as a result of the Russo-Japanese war. This was justified theoretically as an application of the Cairo Conference formula under which Japan was to lose all that it had gained by military aggression. Thus Article 2 of the Yalta Agreement read:

> The former rights of Russia violated by the treacherous attack of Japan in 1904 shall be restored, viz:
> (a) the southern part of Saghalin as well as all of the islands adjacent to it shall be restored to the Soviet Union,
> (b) the commercial port of Dairen shall be internationalized, the preeminent interests of the Soviet Union in this port being safeguarded and the lease of Port Arthur as a naval base of the U.S.S.R. restored.
> (c) The Chinese-Eastern Railroad and the South Manchurian Railroad, which provides an outlet to Dairen, shall be jointly operated by the establishment of a joint Soviet-Chinese Company, it being understood that the preeminent interest of the Soviet Union shall be safeguarded and that China shall retain full sovereignty in Manchuria.[8]

This re-entry of Russia into Manchuria, agreed to in general terms by the United States, Britain, and the Soviet Union at Yalta, was accepted by China and the terms given more specific meaning in the notes of August 14, 1945, exchanged in connection with the Soong-Molotov treaty. The railway and port concessions were to run for thirty years and were to be administered under arrangements which made China distinctly the junior partner.

As already noted, the circumstances of the war enabled the Soviet

[8] *China White Paper*, pp. 113-14.

armies to occupy all of Manchuria in very short order, and with a minimum expenditure of manpower and matériel. This put the Russian command in a position to remove from Manchuria, as war booty, and without any accounting for reparations purposes, virtually all of the capital plant constructed by Japan which could conceivably have use in Russia for purposes of rehabilitation and reconstruction. Thus the principal Chinese industrial base relied upon by the National Government for China's own economic rehabilitation was virtually eliminated for immediate use.

By the time of proclamation and recognition by the U.S.S.R. of the People's Republic in October, 1949, Manchuria had been brought under control of the Chinese Communist Party. That control was qualified, however, in two ways. The first was the continued maintenance of the Russian position in Manchuria as given legal definition by agreement with the National Government of China. The second was to be found in the fact that many of the Chinese Communists brought into positions of administrative authority in Manchuria had a history of closer relationship to the Russian Communist Party, and thus to the Soviet Government, than of party service within China during the Yenan period. Thus it was initially questionable as to whether they would be more readily utilizable by Stalin or by Mao Tse-tung for purposes of rule in Manchuria and within the party in China itself.

The total situation in relation to Manchuria, consequently, made it the touchstone of relationship between the U.S.S.R. and the People's Republic of China. For that reason the Manchurian question was taken up in connection with the negotiation of the Treaty of Friendship, Alliance and Mutual Assistance of February 14, 1950, which replaced the Soong-Molotov treaty of 1945, previously denounced by the Chinese Communists. The Manchurian agreements of the same date were premised on the view that the situation as of 1945 had been fundamentally changed: first by the defeat of "imperialist" Japan; and second by the substitution for the "reactionary Kuomintang Government" of a Communist regime which had not only unified China but also "has carried out a policy of friendship and co-operation with the Soviet Union and has proved its ability to defend the national independence and territorial integrity of China and the national honor and dignity of the Chinese people." In view of this change in the situation, the Soviet Union agreed to the transfer to China, without compensation, of Soviet interests in the "Changchun" (formerly Chinese Eastern) Railway and in Port Arthur "immediately on the conclusion of the peace treaty with Japan, but not later than the end of 1952." [9]

As to Dairen, Article 3 of the 1950 agreement provided:

> Both contracting powers agree that the question of Dairen harbor be further considered on the conclusion of a peace treaty with Japan. As regards the administration of Dairen, it fully belongs to the Government of the People's Republic of China. All the property in Dairen now provisionally administered by or leased to the Soviet Union shall be taken over by the Government of the People's Republic of China. To carry out the transfer of the aforementioned property, the Governments of China and the Soviet Union will appoint three representatives each to form a joint commission which, within three months after the present agreement comes into effect, shall draw up concrete measures for the transfer of the property; and these measures shall be fully carried out in the course of 1950 after their approval by the Governments of both countries upon the proposal of the joint commission.

Only the effective execution of these agreements, not merely their signature, would indicate an intention on the part of the Soviet Union to treat China in reality as an ally. The inability of the Chinese to secure representation at the San Francisco Conference on the Japanese Peace Treaty, and the refusal of the Soviet Government to accept the treaty there opened to signature, immediately raised a question as to Soviet intentions with respect to Manchuria. This question was answered in the arrangements negotiated in Moscow in 1952 by Chou En-lai, Communist China's Premier and Foreign Minister for the execution of the 1950 agreements at the end of 1952.

CHINA, NORTH KOREA, AND THE U.S.S.R.

The alliance of Communist China and the U.S.S.R. in the Far East was cemented by the military struggle resulting from the North Korean invasion of South Korea six months after its conclusion. The cement further hardened as a consequence of China's intervention in the Korean War. That intervention did not, to be sure, have the consequence of drawing the Soviet Union into military operations in Korea in support of China. This was made unnecessary because China initially claimed that its forces in Korea were "volunteers" who were

[9] For text of the Agreement on the railway and concerning the future of Port Arthur and Dairen, *Current Background*, No. 62.

assisting the North Koreans to defend themselves against South Korean and United Nations aggression. Thus, as the situation was fictionalized by the Chinese, it was North Korea, whether aided only by Chinese Communists or by the People's Government, which was involved in war with the United States and the United Nations.

In any case, as long as the war was localized to Korea, the terms of the alliance made unnecessary Soviet intervention in support of China. Strictly, or even reasonably construed, it would take an attack on Chinese territory to make automatically operative for Russia the stipulation of the treaty that it should "immediately render military and other assistance by all means at its disposal." Even in that event, the Soviet government would be free to decide whether or not the terms of the United States-Japan Security Agreement constituted an alliance, and thus required it to give military support to China, since the Sino-Soviet Treaty of Alliance stipulated for immediate military assistance only "in the event of one of the parties being attacked by Japan or any state allied with it and thus being involved in a state of war." The last proviso must be viewed as further enlarging Russia's freedom of decision, since attacks on China might be of such a nature as not to be held to create a "state of war." What might happen, however, is purely speculative. The fact is that the alliance was not, by its terms, made operative in a war localized to territories beyond the limits of the signatory states. Without its application, nevertheless, there was undertaken the supply of arms, ammunition, and implements of war by the Soviet Government to a friendly China which found itself engaged in military operations beyond its borders.

Peiping's intervention in the Korean war was a major development in Communist China's foreign relations. The intervention had a number of important consequences. One of these was the enhancement of the position of China within the alliance with the Soviet Union in relation to Asian affairs. Another was the erection of a further barrier to entrance into the family of nations through recognition and through replacement of the National Government in the United Nations because of the formal acceptance of Communist China's intervention as aggression. This made possible the establishment of enforceable limitations on trade with the states which had recognized the Peiping government, and thus made it appreciably more difficult for China to improve its position with such states as Japan, in need of access to the

China market, by negotiating suitable trade agreements. On the other hand, the desire for trade with China produced as much difficulty for the United States in its relations with its associates as it did for China itself.

After the fighting in Korea came to an end with the institution of truce negotiations, China undertook actively to enlarge its trade relations outside the Communist bloc. In 1953 it was able to negotiate an agreement with British private traders for a two-way exchange of goods to the value of about £15 million sterling, and an essentially barter agreement with France for an exchange of commodities to the value of some 12 billion francs on each side. In 1954 (April 22) Burma and China signed a trade agreement providing for the exchange of specified commodities, with payments to be made in sterling. And in the last months of 1954 and during 1955 serious efforts were made to use the possibility of extended trade as an enticement to Japan to re-establish friendly relations on terms satisfactory to China.

Finally, since it raised questions of foreign relations, reference must be made to the re-establishment of Chinese authority over Tibet. This led to exchanges with the Indian government which initially questioned Peiping's right to view Tibet as a part of China. Negotiations were carried on between the two governments over the question until agreement was reached on April 29, 1954. By this agreement India agreed: (1) to view Tibet as a "region of China"; (2) to withdraw its troops stationed at Yatung and Gyuntse (Indian-held points on the trade routes) within six months; and (3) to sell to China all communications installations and rest-houses which it operated in Tibet. The agreement also stipulated the right of China to establish trade agencies in New Delhi, Calcutta, and Kalimpong and of India to establish similar agencies in the Tibetan towns of Yatung, Gyuntse and Gartok. It further provided that shrines in India and Tibet should be opened to pilgrims who would, however, have to follow specified travel routes to reach them and conform to the travel regulations agreed upon. This agreement which had the effect of resolving the major questions at issue in favor of China was to remain in force for eight years. While generally favorable to China it had the advantage to India of defining the Tibet frontier so as to exclude Chinese claims on Nepal and it was accompanied by assurances against the use of Tibetan territory for aggressive purposes.

BIBLIOGRAPHICAL REFERENCES

American Consulate General, Hongkong
  1. *Survey of the China Mainland Press*, 1950–.
  2. *Current Background Series*, 1950–.
  3. *Review of the Hongkong Chinese Press*, 1950–.

Brandt, Conrad, Schwartz, Benjamin and Fairbank, John K., *Documentary History of Chinese Communism* (Cambridge: Harvard University Press, 1953).

China Treaties, etc., 1950, Sino-Soviet Treaty and Agreements, signed in Moscow on Feb. 14, 1950 (Peking: Foreign Language Press, 1950).

Hsia, Ronald, *Price Control in Communist China* (New York: Institute of Pacific Relations, 1953).

Hutheesing, Gunottam Purushottam, *The Great Peace* (New York: Harper, 1953).

Isaacs, Harold, *No Peace for Asia* (New York: Macmillan, 1947).

———, *The Tragedy of the Chinese Revolution* (Palo Alto: Stanford University Press, 1948).

Lattimore, Owen, *Pivot of Asia, Sinkiang and the Inner Asian Frontiers of China and Russia* (Boston: Little Brown and Company, 1950).

Levi, Werner, *Modern China's Foreign Policy* (Minneapolis: Minnesota University Press, 1953).

Liu, Shaw-tong, *Out of Red China* (New York: Duell, Sloan and Pearce, 1953).

Manchester Guardian Weekly, "Communist China: Land Reform and Industry," June 4, 1951.

Mao Tse-tung, *China's New Democracy* (1945, New York: New Century Publish.)

Mao Tse-tung, and others, *Mao's China: Party Reform Documents, 1942-1944*, by Boyd Compton (ed. and translator) (Seattle: University of Washington, 1952).

Mao Tse-tung, *A Single Spark Can Start a Prairie Fire* (Peking: Foreign Language Press, 1953).

Mao Tse-tung, *Selected Works* (New York: International Publishers, 1954).

Moraes, Francis Robert, *Report on Mao's China* (New York: Macmillan, 1953).

North, Robert C., *Moscow and Chinese Communists* (Palo Alto: Stanford University Press, 1953).

Payne, P.S.R., *Mao Tse-tung, Ruler of Red China* (New York: Schuman, 1950).

Rostow, W. W., *The Prospects for Communist China* (New York: Technology Press of the Massachusetts Institute of Technology and John Wiley and Sons, 1954).

Riggs, Fred Warren, *The Economics of Red China* (New York: Foreign Policy Association, 1951).

Schwartz, B., *Chinese Communism and the Rise of Mao* (Cambridge: Harvard University Press, 1951).

Stein, Gunther, *The Challenge of Red China* (New York: McGraw Hill, 1945).

Steiner, H. Arthur (ed.), *Report on China* (Philadelphia: American Academy of Political and Social Science, November, 1951).

Sun, Ching-ling (Sung), *The Struggle for New China* (Peking: Foreign Language Press, 1952).

Thomas, S. B., *Government and Administration in Communist China* (New York: Institute of Pacific Relations, 1953).

————, *Recent Political and Economic Developments in China* (New York: International Secretariat, Institute of Pacific Relations, 1950).

6

Korea between Wars

✽✽✽✽✽✽✽✽✽✽✽✽✽✽✽✽✽✽✽✽✽✽✽✽✽✽✽✽

CHINA, JAPAN, RUSSIA, AND KOREA: 1876-1910

THE KOREAN QUESTION in its contemporary aspect is not a new one in the politics of the Far East. The country emerged from its long seclusion as the result of the negotiation of a treaty with Japan (1876) premised on Korean independence. This treaty was concluded despite China's claim to suzerainty over the Kingdom of Korea—a relationship which China asserted to be one of Korean dependence on China but not one carrying any Chinese responsibility for the behavior of the Korean government. The Japanese treaty was followed (1882) by one between the United States and Korea which, although negotiated under Chinese auspices, had the effect of re-enforcing the conception of Korean independence. The treaty had also the consequence of suggesting what proved to be an undue reliance by the Korean government on the United States, since the first article not only charted a course of perpetual peace between the President of the United States and the King of Korea and between American citizens and Korean subjects, but went on to state that: "If other powers deal unjustly or oppressively with either Government, the other will exert their good offices, on being informed of the case, to bring about an amicable arrangement, thus showing their friendly feelings." [1]

The Chinese claim to suzerainty was terminated as a principal consequence of the defeat of China by Japan in the first Sino-Japanese war (1894-95). One of the stipulations of the Treaty of Shimonoseki was that China conceded formally the independence of Korea. The war itself was the climax of a contest carried on for two decades between China and Japan over the issue of independence. During the

[1] W. M. Malloy, *Treaties*, etc., *Between the United States and Other Powers, 1776-1909* (Washington, 1910), Vol. 1, p. 334.

course of the contest a third party—Russia—had attempted to take advantage of the situation to introduce its own influence into the peninsula. Russia continued to offer opposition to Japan after 1895 as Japan sought to translate Korean independence of China into dependence on Japan. Sino-Japanese rivalry was consequently initially replaced with Russo-Japanese rivalry; with other states, including the United States, unwilling or unable to support the Korean government against either or both.

The interest of the European states was centered on China after 1895, and Korea came within their purview largely incidentally in relation to their China policies. Thus the Anglo-Japanese agreement of 1902 coupled Korea with China in describing the purpose of the signatories as being that of maintaining the "independence and territorial integrity" of those two states. But at the same time it recognized the "special interests" of Japan in Korea.

Russia's primary interest also was in China and its Manchurian provinces. Consequently the Tsarist government was led to agree, in the Nishi-Rosen Convention (1898), not to impede the development of Japanese commercial and industrial interests in Korea, thus implicitly recognizing Korea as within the Japanese sphere of interest. Failure of Russia fully to respect this commitment, as well as the fears engendered in Japan by the projection of Russian military power southward into Manchuria, caused the Japanese government to prepare for the war with Russia which was entered upon in 1904. To avoid that war Japan had sought to reach agreement with Russia on the basis of asserted respect for the independence and territorial integrity of both China and Korea, and on acceptance of the "Open-Door" principle in both those countries. On this basis, Russia was to recognize Japan's special interests in Korea and concede Japan's right (1) to develop those interests further, and (2) to give advice to the Korean government in the interest of reform. In return for this recognition of Japan's freedom of action in Korea, Japan proposed to recognize Russia's special railway rights in Manchuria and to concede to Russia the same right of future development there as that conceded to Japan in Korea.

The Russian counterproposals left China out of the stipulation with respect to independence and territorial integrity. They left out all references designed to restrict the Russian position in Manchuria. And, while conceding the right of Japan to develop its economic interests in Korea, the Russian proposals stipulated against fortification on the coasts of Korea so as to remove any menace to freedom of navigation in the Korean Straits and to ensure against any use of Korean territory for strategic purposes. The Japanese were asked, furthermore, to agree to the erection of Korea north of the 39th parallel into a neutral zone.

The Russians refused to recede from the position defined in these counterproposals until too late, with the result that the Japanese undertook military operations to settle the question. The result of the war, as far as Korea was concerned, was the acceptance by Russia of Japan's "paramount political, military, and economic interests" in Korea. This "paramount" position of Japan in Korea had also been accepted by Britain in the revision made in 1905 of the Anglo-Japanese Agreement of 1902 which extended it into an alliance. The United States, preoccupied with the immigration problem, with the situation in the Philippines, and with Manchuria rather than with Korea, also approved Japan's "suzerainty" over Korea in an "agreed memorandum" negotiated between Secretary of War William Howard Taft and Prime Minister Katsura and signed on July 29, 1905.

> This executive agreement—it was not a treaty and bound only the Roosevelt administration—was enthusiastically approved by the President. He had concluded that since America could not prevent Japanese absorption of Korea, the next best thing was to recognize the inevitable and secure something in return.[2]

What was secured in return was a disavowal by Japan of "aggressive designs on the Philippines." The withdrawal of the American diplomatic mission at Seoul, on November 24, 1905, then closed the books for some time on any attempt at fulfillment of the pledge of 1882 to exert good offices in behalf of Korea against other powers dealing "unjustly or oppressively" with that country. The proclamation of a "protectorate" over Korea after Japan had secured a free hand was followed by formal annexation and the organization of the country as a Japanese colony in 1910. This effectively removed Korea from international rivalry until the Japanese empire was liquidated in and after 1945.

THE PROBLEM POSED BY KOREA

Two considerations determined that Korea would be an international storm center as it sought to emerge into the modern world as

[2] T. A. Bailey, *Diplomatic History of the American People* (New York: Appleton-Century-Crofts, 1950) p. 568.

an independent state. These same considerations, somewhat modified to be sure, must be borne in mind in the consideration of the position of Korea in postwar international and Far Eastern politics. The first is its geopolitical position. The Korean peninsula points toward Japan, and is separated from the Japanese main islands only by the upwards of one hundred miles of the Korean Straits. Thus it represents the readiest invasion route to Japan from the Asian continent and of the continent from Japan. It is separated from China in Manchuria by the river boundary of the Yalu and from China proper by the Yellow Sea. The extension of Russia's Far Eastern territories through the acquisition from China of the Maritime Province (the area to the northeast, above the Sea of Japan) in 1860, brought Russia into territorial contact with Korea. Thus these three states each had an inevitable interest in Korea because of geographical relationship. From this point of view, nevertheless, Korea would have been in a strong position to assert the right to an independent development as a buffer state between the three if it had not been for the second consideration, which came from the internal situation in the country.

What must be kept in mind is that Korean politics during the period of "independence" was marked by bitter factional struggles for power. This, coupled with bad economic conditions which brought about local riots, created the conditions of internal disorder and weakness most readily exploitable by external forces. Thus before 1895 Japan both stimulated and gave its support to one faction and China to another; while Russia and Japan aligned themselves against each other in support of contending internal factions after 1895. If there had been complete internal political unity, and general satisfaction with the uses made of power by those in control of the machinery of government, there would have been less excuse offered for foreign intervention and greater ability to withstand it. While this must be recognized, it may also be conceded that an intervening state may act without an excuse.

Acquiescence by all other states in the control of Korea by Japan after 1910 withdrew the country from international rivalry. At the same time the controlling power was enabled, without external interference, to prevent internal dissatisfaction with economic conditions from effectively expressing itself or being given factional organization. Thus internal unity was imposed in Korea by Japan from 1910 to 1945, and during the same period the country ceased to be a problem in international relations.

JAPANESE RULE OF KOREA: 1910-45

It did not follow from this that general satisfaction with Japanese rule existed. While Japan unquestionably developed the country economically, the development was planned to serve the interests of Japan and the Japanese rather than the needs of the Korean people, who were exploited economically and kept in a condition of political subjection. The people were denied the experience and advantage which might have been gained through participation in either administration in government or in management of the economy of the country. They were not only denied this association with political and economic management but were also subjected to a policy designed to bring about a loss of their cultural identity. This took the form of forcible introduction of the Japanese language at the expense of the Korean; the suppression of Korean literature and of Korean cultural institutions; the expropriation and sale, mostly to Japanese settlers, of a large part of the public lands which had been of common use to the people; the forced sale of much of the best privately owned property, with the consequent migration, especially into Manchuria, of the people whose lands had been taken; the repression of speech and suppression of Korean publications; and the exhibition of much actual brutality in dealing with the people. Funds made available for elementary education were almost equally divided between the 2 per cent Japanese and the 98 per cent Korean parts of the population. The schools established for Koreans, furthermore, were designed to make them good subjects of Japan at the expense of continued awareness of their separate Korean culture.

This policy, as much as the exploitation of the country in Japan's interest, produced an attitude of revolt which took the form of passive resistance and an appeal to the Paris Conference in 1919. Although this revolt was ruthlessly suppressed by Japan, it had two consequences. One was a modification of Japanese policy. The second was the enlargement of the number of Koreans in exile who kept alive the idea of Korean independence among the Koreans who had emigrated for economic reasons. These groups were to be found in Manchuria and China, in the Russian Far East, and in the United States.

As Japan's policy became geared to unlimited continental expansion, the unified Korean economy was planned more and more by Japan in supplementary terms to its own war economy and as a link between Japan and Manchuria as that area was utilized under Japanese military auspices. Thus it was in the 1930's that a primary emphasis was put on the development of hydroelectric power, on mineral exploitation, and on the creation of plant capacity in Korea itself for the processing of the mineral resources of the country. This development occurred in northern rather than southern Korea, which remained essentially agricultural and commercial. In this respect, the two parts of the country were completely interdependent, each being economically dependent on the other. But the nature of the war developmnt of the Korean economy also established a measure of interdependence of Manchuria and northern Korea, most marked in terms of power for industrial purposes.

KOREAN NATIONALISM DURING WORLD WAR II

On the political side, the Second World War stimulated Korean nationalism by holding out the prospect, if Japan should be defeated, of the re-establishment of independence. This prospect gave importance to the "overseas" Koreans; to the relationships to one another of various groups of leaders; and to the relationship of each of these groups to the governments at war with Japan and Germany. The peculiarities of the Soviet relationship to the Far Eastern and Pacific side of World War II put the Koreans in the U.S.S.R. beyond the possibility of negotiation and agreement with those in China and the United States. There is not available sufficient evidence to warrant final conclusions as to the precise relationship of the Koreans in the Russian Far East with the Soviet Government. That the Soviet government was aware of their existence and potential usefulness, however, was shown in its ability quickly to introduce Korean Communists into its zone of occupation in Korea and put them in a position to assume control in place of the Japanese after V-J Day.

The Korean exiles in China and the United States had maintained a form of relationship after 1919. In connection with the passive resistance movement of that year, there had been proclaimed a Korean Provisional Government which, when the internal resistance movement had been suppressed, transferred itself to the International Settlement at Shanghai. There it

had maintained its precarious existence until it made arrangements with the Chinese Government to remove itself to Nanking and later to Chungking, where it received sanctuary and eventually considerable support. The Chinese Government never granted official recognition of any sort to the Korean Provisional Government, but by indirect means the Korean group was aided financially and given other means of encouragement.[3]

When Dr. Syngman Rhee, the leader of the 1919 movement against Japan, established himself in the United States with a view to seeking American support for Korean independence, he sought to carry with him the authority of the Provisional Government. But the effect of this move was to create two separate overseas groups seeking recognition.

The Koreans in the United States had not been able to secure even unofficial encouragement from the United States, beyond expressions of sympathy from a few officials. On the whole, the United States government, again aside from a very few individual officials, failed to concern itself seriously with the Korean question until the end of 1943. Even after the commitment had been made at the Cairo Conference (November 22-26, 1943) to establish "in due course" an independent Korea, there was revealed no intention to assume responsibilities in the implementation of the commitment beyond that of ending Japanese control. There were factional rivalries among the Koreans in the United States which needed adjustment if there was to be unity at the end of the war. It was also essential that the relationships between the Korean Provisional Government at Chungking and the Korean leadership in the United States should be clearly defined in anticipation of the return of both groups of exiles to positions of authority in Korea if and as it became independent. None of this had been carried very far by the time of the Japanese surrender. Nor had any clear-cut and organized relationship been established between the overseas Koreans and the American, Chinese, and British governments. The closest approximation of this was the unofficial connection existing at Chungking between the Chinese government and the Koreans calling themselves a Provisional Government.

None of these exiled leaders had had any except a purely theoretical connection with government and administration, except as they had practically experienced, at the receiving end, the strong-arm Japanese methods of police administration of public order. They might, however, have been somewhat better prepared for the exercise of respon-

[3] George M. McCune and Arthur L. Grey, *Korea Today* (Cambridge: Harvard Univ. Press, 1950), p. 41.

sibility and power, if it was to be given them, if the governments allied in the war against Japan had, even as late as the period after the Cairo Declaration, required them to adjust their differences and aided them in organizing a Government-in-Exile. Such a government might thereupon have been assisted in planning and preparing for the government of Korea in place of the Japanese. This would have been possible only if the United States had exerted a strong leadership in that direction. Such positive leadership was not exerted.

One argument against the institution of such a positive program by the United States was that it would not be democratic and would be interventionist, since it might readily have necessitated choice among those Koreans contending for leadership and even the imposition of American views as to the qualities of leadership and as to planning for Korea's future. Another objection to such action was that it might necessitate a premature commitment to immediate independence and thus carry the definition of Allied policy beyond the area of agreement reached at Cairo. The Korean exiles did institute such pressures as they could to get a definition of the meaning of the phrase "in due course." They naturally wanted to commit the Allied powers to unqualified independence at the end of the war rather than to an indeterminate period of tutelage through some form of mandatory or trustee administration. Conclusions reached as to the experience, or inexperience, of the Koreans in self-government, as well as uncertainty over the conditions which would exist at the end of the war, apparently caused the United States and Britain to avoid commitment beyond the phraseology of the Cairo Declaration.

One thing which made for uncertainty in Washington was lack of adequate information as to conditions within Korea and the attitude of the Korean people toward the groups of exiles. Under the circumstances of Japanese rule the contacts between the exiled leadership and the people in Korea had been limited. It was possible that there was an internal leadership which would contest the claims of right to exercise authority by those who had long been divorced from intimate contact with the people in the country which was to become independent "in due course." As Acting Secretary of State Grew put it in a press release of June 8, 1945, commitment to the Korean Provisional Government might "tend to compromise the right of the Korean people to choose the ultimate form and personnel of the government which they may wish to establish."

One clarifying step had been taken before the Japanese surrender.

At Yalta, President Roosevelt and Generalissimo Stalin had agreed informally that Korea should win its independence and that if a transition period were necessary, a trusteeship should be established. For forty years Korea had been exploited by Japan. The Japanese had permitted few Koreans to secure an education and had made it difficult for them to obtain important positions in trade and industry that would have given them administrative experience. As a result, there was some question whether the people were sufficiently trained to assume the responsibilities of government immediately.[4]

This associated the U.S.S.R. indirectly with the commitment to ultimate independence of the Cairo Declaration. It also revealed, although not publicly, the unwillingness of the American government to commit itself to immediate independence. And it at least developed a line of reasoning supporting that conclusion. The conclusion itself set up an obstacle to the prior preparation, outside of Korea, of the exiles to enable them to assume responsibility for the immediate inauguration of self-government at the end of the war.

ZONAL DIVISION FOR SURRENDER PURPOSES

The formal and public adherence of Russia to the Cairo Declaration came early in 1945 at the Potsdam Conference. Preoccupation at Potsdam with the German problem and with arrangements for the early termination of the war with Japan, however, precluded any serious consideration of the question of Korea beyond the Russian acceptance of previously defined Allied policy. Further consideration of the political aspects of the problem was postponed until the Moscow Conference of December, 1945. By that time the situation had been complicated by the division of Korea at the 38th parallel into two occupation zones, the northern one under Russian military control and the southern under American. The line of demarcation was intended to be temporary and only to fix responsibility between the U. S. and the U.S.S.R. for carrying out the Japanese surrender. Thus the division of Korea was initially made in terms of the military situation and to expedite the elimination of Japanese power from the peninsula. The then existing situation has been summarized as follows:[5]

[4] James F. Byrnes, *Speaking Frankly* (New York: Harpers, 1947) p. 221.
[5] McCune and Grey, *op. cit.*, pp. 44-45.

When Japan surrendered on August 14, 1945, Russian forces had already landed in northeast Korea and were rapidly moving southward. By agreement with the United States, however, the Soviet Union consented to the terms of surrender, which called for a division of Korea at the 38th parallel for the purpose of accepting the surrender of Japanese forces in Korea. On September 8, American forces landed in Korea. By that time, Soviet forces had already spread over most of their northern zone.... The Russians had overrun much of Korea by force of arms. The Japanese sabotaged mines and factories in the path of the approaching enemy. They fled to the south in large numbers, much preferring to await the arrival of the forces of their military foe of the past four years to living in the shadow of the stern authority of a traditional enemy for two generations. The atmosphere between the Japanese and the occupying forces in the north was one of enmity. In the south the Japanese assumed an attitude of guileless cooperation toward the occupying authorities.

By the time of the arrival of American forces in Korea the Koreans themselves had begun to assume governmental power in place of the Japanese. Local committees had been set up throughout the country to preserve order. These committees were formed with the sanction of the Russian forces of occupation in the northern zone. The Soviet Command also established, on August 25, 1945, what was called The Executive Committee of the Korean People to which it transferred the administrative powers of the Japanese government, thus installing the Korean revolutionists in nominal control. The committee thereupon immediately expropriated and nationalized Japanese property. The anti-Japanese revolutionary leaders at Seoul had initiated the establishment of these local committees throughout the entire country. They also took steps to bring into being a congress of a national representative character. This congress, on September 6, proclaimed the establishment of The People's Republic of Korea. The People's Republic was thus in being when the American forces arrived. It was not, however, accepted by the American commander as a government to be supported and utilized in the accomplishment of his primary mission of replacement of Japanese authority and power in the southern zone.

In the absence of American personnel qualified to administer the country in place of the Japanese, the immediate alternative to operation through the People's Republic seemed to be the retention of Japanese in government positions in Korea while the occupants investigated the qualifications of Koreans for administrative work. To the Koreans this presented no change from the status quo ante the Japanese surrender in the American zone, and seemed unnecessary since Koreans had been permitted to replace Japanese in the Russian zone. The widespread objection to the retention of the Japanese brought about a fairly rapid change of American policy in this respect. A system of military government was instituted, with Koreans, where available and technically qualified, and American military government personnel, replacing Japanese in administrative posts. By the end of January, 1946, consequently, some 60 Japanese remained of the 70,000 holding government positions when the American occupation forces arrived. Nevertheless the government in southern Korea was American rather than Korean in outward appearance as well as in the reality of power, while government in the northern zone was Korean in outward appearance, although Russian from the point of view of effective power.

The difference in political development in the two zones may properly be ascribed to the fact that the first internal development of government was revolutionary and thus amenable to Russian direction through Korean Communist Party leaders who, from exile, had been able to maintain some contact with the internal anti-Japanese leadership. In the American zone the internal leadership was suspect until greater familiarity could be gained with its personnel, and until distinctions could be made between those who were revolutionary in social and economic terms and those who were nationalist revolutionaries. Those upon whom reliance was immediately placed by the American Command were the wealthier Koreans, and especially those who could speak English, and thus those with whom there could be direct communication. In this group were included, as time went on, those who, in exile, had professed to speak in the name of the Korean people, and who were brought back from China and the United States to play leading roles in the ultimate establishment of an independent Korea. A well-known leader of the "overseas Koreans," Dr. Syngman Rhee, when he was repatriated from the United States, came to be viewed as the leader of the rightist elements in southern Korea, although the overseas Provisional Government was refused even temporary acceptance. The leaders of the People's Republic consolidated the parties of the left. And the differences in political complexion between the northern and the southern zones served to give political solidity to a division originally instituted solely for military purposes.

THE 1945 MOSCOW AGREEMENTS

Since power in Korea rested with the Soviet Union and the United States, the future course of Korean development needed to be charted by agreement between those two powers, even though they were themselves agents of the wartime United Nations. The future was forecast in the initial inability of the Soviet and American commands in Korea to reach agreement on the conditions of purely local intercourse between the two zones. This, coupled with the general situation, caused the question of Korea, to be placed on the agenda of the Moscow Conference of December, 1945. At this conference the United States delegation proposed

> the establishment of a Joint Soviet-American Commission to unify the administration of such matters as currency, trade and transportation, tele-communications, electric power distribution, coastal shipping, and so on. It also proposed that a four-power trusteeship be established which would endure for no longer period than necessary to allow the Koreans to form an independent, representative, and effective government. The United States, however, accepted a Soviet proposal for a Joint Commission on urgent problems of economic unification, the establishment of a provisional government and a four-power trusteeship to last for five years.[6]

It was left to the two commands in Korea to agree on the conditions of application of this decision.

A joint conference of the two commands failed to agree on the administrative and economic unification of the two zones through a modification of the barriers which had been erected. Similarly, attempts made during 1946 by the Joint Commission, which was established in March, to reach agreement on the conditions of consultation with Korean parties, and on the method of constituting a provisional government for all of Korea, were a failure. Since the general Korean demand was for independence, there had been a widespread unfavorable reaction by all of the Korean parties, except the Communist, to the idea of trusteeship as formulated at Moscow. The Soviet members of the Joint Commission held that only those parties should be consulted which had shown a willingness to accept freely and fully the Moscow decisions. The American members were not willing to accept this view, which would have restricted consultation to a minority of the Korean people.

[6] Byrnes, *op. cit.*, p. 222.

The same *impasse* was reached when the Joint Commission resumed its sessions in May, 1947. After the Soviet government had rejected an American proposal of August 27, 1947, (which was accepted by Britain and China) that "the four powers adhering to the Moscow Agreement meet to consider how that agreement may be speedily carried out," the United States took the question of Korean independence to the United Nations, bringing it before the second regular session of the General Assembly. At that time, through its representatives on the Joint Commission, the Soviet government proposed the simultaneous withdrawal of the military forces of the occupying powers, ostensibly to permit the Koreans to organize their own government without outside assistance. This proposal was not acceptable to the United States, which apparently felt that such action would lead to an extension of Communist, and thus Soviet, control over the southern zone from the northern. It was also rejected by the General Assembly at its 1947 session. The reasons for such rejection must be sought in conditions as they had developed in the two zones.

ORGANIZATION OF THE NORTHERN ZONE

By 1947 the Soviet Korean Command had organized the northern zone under a Korean regime which it had every reason to believe was firmly attached to the Soviet system and which would consequently respond to Russian policy direction in both internal and external relations. Taking over the local committees which sprang up after the Japanese surrender and co-ordinating them under the Provisional People's Committee for North Korea, the Russians gave political positions to Koreans who were oriented toward the Soviet Union. The regime set up by the Russians was designed to create the impression that the Korean leaders had more than nominal control in the North Korean government. This contrasted with the American policy of exercising control directly and of selecting Korean personnel to fill in below. The Russian military control of the zone as well as the Russian selection of personnel, ensured that this interim government would exercise power acceptably to the Soviet government.

The northern regime was put on an elective basis during 1946, when members of provincial, municipal and village committees were voted into office. For election purposes the authorized parties were amalgamated into the Korean National Democratic Front, participated in and led by the Labor Party, which had previously called itself the Communist Party. This party coalition polled 97 per cent of the 99.6 per cent of the registered voters who cast ballots in the election. One-fifth of the membership of these provincial, municipal, and country committees were then elected by the committees to serve in a Convention of People's Committees, which met at the northern capital, Pyong-yang, February 17-22, 1947. Serving as a constituent assembly, the convention ratified all legislation previously enacted by the Interim Committee, adopted a national economic plan, and established a system of government for North Korea.

The government was topped by a People's Assembly, which continued to be based upon the elected committees. It was to meet every two years, its first meeting being held February 21-22, 1947, immediately after the adjournment of the convention. The Assembly then elected the members of the Presidium of eleven which exercised power between its sessions. At that time it also selected the members of the Supreme Court and of the People's Committee which was to exercise the executive power. The chairman of the Presidium and sixteen of the twenty-two members of the People's Committee, including the chairman, Kim Il-sung, came from the labor (Communist) Party.

The system as organized conformed closely to the method of organization of The People's Democratic Dictatorship advocated by Mao Tse-tung and established in China two years later. The other parties were drawn together in a coalition with the Communist Party under conditions which ensured Communist Party dominance. When, in northern Korea, the other parties expressed dissatisfaction, dissatisfied leaders were liable to the purge. Thus the "dominant Labor (Communist) Party exercised almost complete control of the political scene, guided with care by Soviet advisers." [7]

This development enabled the Soviet Foreign Minister, Molotov, to make the following defense of Soviet policy:

As regards northern Korea, considerable progress had been achieved in the field of democratization as well as in restoring the national economy and culture since Japan's surrender. Broad democratic reforms assuring political liberties and raising the living standard of the population have been carried through. I am referring primarily to the inauguration of general suffrage; the law on equal rights of women; the establishment of local bodies of power and of the People's Committee of northern Korea

[7] McCune and Grey, *op. cit.*, p. 178.

on the basis of free democratic elections; the land reform, as a result of which 725,000 landless farmers and small holders were given more than 1,000,000 hectares of land free of charge which had previously been the property of Japanese colonizers and their accomplices in Korea; the nationalization of former Japanese industry; the law on the eight-hour working day, safety of labor and social insurance; the reform of national education, as a result of which the Korean language has been reinstated in the schools, the school network extended and the enrollment of students enlarged, etc.[8]

With the northern zone controlled by a party and government which could be relied upon to take its direction from Moscow, Russian troops could be withdrawn without fear of loss of control, provided this government could support its authority in North Korea against possible internal opposition or external attack.

In this respect the withdrawal of Russian troops could be proposed safely in 1947 because of the early organization of a military police force—the Korean People's militia—which by the end of March, 1947, had been developed into an army with an estimated strength of at least 120,000 to 150,000 men, and which some estimates put as high as 500,000. This force had been supplied with military equipment taken over from the Japanese upon their surrender; it had been thoroughly indoctrinated by the Russians; and it had been given systematic military training. It was, consequently, as reliable, from the Communist point of view, as was the government. In contrast, the constabulary organized in the American zone was reported to total 26,000 men. This contrast is significant because a primary interest of the Koreans, both north and south of the 38th parallel, was in unification as well as in independence, while, from the international point of view, as well as from that of internal politics, unification raised a question of advancement or contraction of Soviet as against American power and influence. Under the circumstances there was reason to believe that if American troops were withdrawn from South Korea, even though Russian troops were simultaneously evacuated from the northern zone, the withdrawal would be followed by a unification imposed by the North Korean government by force or the threat of force. This would mean extension of Russian authority over the entire peninsula because of Soviet dominance over the North Korean government.

[8] *Ibid.*, p. 197. The full text is in Appendix A, pp. 284-87. There are slight verbal discrepancies between the text in the Appendix and the quotations from it by Professor McCune.

Apart from this disparity of organized Korean power between the two zones, there was a difference in the pace and nature of development of government in the two zones which had to be taken into account. In any negotiation of conditions of unification, a monolithic single-party regime would have the advantage of dealing with one in which the government, and the parties supporting it, had to face serious opposition and probable differences of opinion as to the conditions of political and economic unification. It could be anticipated that a Communist Party victory would be the result, even though it might be concealed initially behind the façade of an interparty "united-front" coalition of other parties with the Communist Party.

DEVELOPMENTS IN THE SOUTHERN ZONE

The institution of military government in the American zone, coupled with the concentration of attention on the problem of agreement on the conditions of unification of the two zones, had caused the United States to move less decisively and less rapidly than had the Russians in North Korea toward the institution of self-government in the American zone. Movement by the United States in the political field was also slower because of the desire to enable the Koreans to construct a system of democratic government. This desire was, to be sure, modified by an unwillingness to transfer power to a democratic government which might use its authority in a manner unacceptable to the United States. Nevertheless, the American authorities permitted the activities and agitation of parties ranging from the extreme left to the extreme right, many of which were not so much parties as personal followings. At the same time, American influence was exercised in behalf of the more conservative parties and the leaders, who were also moderate to conservative in economic and social philosophy, with whom they were familiar and with whom they could readily communicate. As relations with the Russians deteriorated, American support of the rightist elements against the extreme left correspondingly increased. Thus when the elections were held in South Korea for the members of the Interim Legislative Assembly (one half of whose members were selected by a system of indirect elections and one half appointed by the Military Government):

leftist parties accused the military government of suppressing all but conservative activity in a reign of terror, while the American command

announced that the agitation was a communist plot. A sweeping conservative victory took place at the polls in the midst of this confusion, but
even the middle-of-the road Korean leaders declared the elections to
have been fraudulent.[9]

The confusion referred to, and also the terroristic or strong-arm
methods of campaigning used by the leaders of the right as well as the
left, were partly the result of inexperience with democratic methods
and partly a carry-over from past experience with the repressive methods used by the Japanese in the government of the country. The
rapidity with which the way had been opened to the organization of
many political parties, and the freedom of expression and of organization which the Americans introduced into a country accustomed to
repression, could only lead to initial confusion. The smoother running
of the regime of "self-government" established in North Korea was
possible because of the extent to which the Soviet Command built on
the adjustment which the people had already made to police methods
of administration and to political repression and lack of freedom.

Despite this confusion and the articulately expressed dissatisfaction
with conditions in the American zone in contrast with the apparent
adjustment to conditions in the Russian zone, such movement of people
as could take place was from the northern into the southern zone. This
began as soon as the significance of one-party rule, with a controlled
press and a denial of freedom of expression, became apparent. Antagonism had first been created by the behavior of the Soviet occupation force of a quarter of a million men. This force had done
considerable looting in addition to its requisitioning of food and other
supplies so that it might live off the country. Under the rigors of one-
party rule that antagonism shifted from the Russians to the North
Korean regime. Since the attempt was made to prevent people from
moving out of the Russian zone except for purposes of political infiltration, the movement of population can only be viewed as indicative of a growing belief among the people that in the long run the
realization of American purposes would develop more satisfactory
conditions of life for the Koreans than would the extension and solidification of the Soviet system throughout the peninsula.

From the economic standpoint, the zonal division created difficulties
for both sets of authorities. The development of industry in Korea had

[9] George M. McCune, "Korea: The First Year of Liberation," *Pacific Affairs*
(March, 1947), p. 8.

been planned by Japan in relation to its own needs rather than to serve the interests of the Koreans.

> Korea had been developed as a part of the Japanese economy, not as a self-sustaining unit. Japanese technicians and managers held the key positions in industry and trade; Japanese industrial corporations exploited Korean mines and were owners of Korean factories; Japanese landlords and agricultural corporations acquired the best Korean farm lands; and Japanese traders controlled Korea's foreign trade. Korean agricultural products went to the Japanese market, and industrial plants were developed to support the Japanese economy. Economic separation from Japan, removal of Japanese controls, and wholesale repatriation of Japanese technicians therefore brought about a complete collapse of the Korean economy, disorganization of production, loss of technical and managerial skills, and an interruption of trade.[10]

Independence consequently posed a series of economic problems, including training of Koreans to replace Japanese managers and replanning on the basis of economic independence of Japan. These problems could only be solved over a period of time.

The division of Korea made it impossible to bring about economic recovery rapidly on an independent basis. Heavy industry was concentrated in the Russian zone, where the mineral wealth of Korea was found. The hydroelectric power of the country had also been developed in the north, serving not only Korean industry but that of South Manchuria which, during the war had also been integrated with that of Japan. South Korea, on the other hand, was the agricultural area, although with a light-industries development. South Korean agriculture was, however, dependent on chemical fertilizer produced in the north and its light-industries were dependent on northern coal and power. Separation at the 38th parallel, consequently, cut off the agricultural south from the industrial north. The consequences were more serious for the American than for the Russian zone, since two-thirds of the population (of about 29 million) came to be located in the American zone as a result of movement both from the northern to the southern zone and also of repatriation after 1945 from other Asian countries. In the face of a larger population to feed, agricultural production in southern Korea declined so that from a food-exporting area it became a food-deficit area. Starvation in the cities, mainly located in the southern zone, was prevented only as a result of the institution

[10] *Korea, 1945-1948*, Dept. of State, Publication 3305, Far Eastern Series, 28, p. 25.

of a grain collection and distribution program similar to that maintained in Japan, and by the importation, by the American Military Government, of foodstuffs. Agricultural rehabilitation required that sources of supply of fertilizer be found outside the country since the northern source was no longer available. By 1948 a land-reform program had been agreed upon for the southern zone, based upon distribution to landless tenants of former Japanese holdings.

Fundamentally, however, economic recovery and prosperity in Korea remained dependent upon the re-establishment of unity so that the needs of the north for foodstuffs and for consumers goods could be met, as previously, from the south, and the needs of the south for fertilizer, power, minerals, and capital goods could be supplied as far as possible from within the country rather than be either denied altogether or acquired through foreign exchanges. This was the case because neither the southern nor the northern government could plan recovery on the basis of acceptance of permanent division of the country into two states since each government hoped to establish its control over the entire country and, of more importance, the Korean people continued to assume, and to insist, that it was historic Korea which was to become an independent state. The attainment of unity depended, however, not on the desires of either government or of the people but on the willingness and ability of the United States and the Soviet Union to agree on the conditions of union of the two zones.

THE KOREAN QUESTION AND THE UNITED NATIONS

Since direct negotiations failed to produce an agreement, the United States took the question to the United Nations' General Assembly in the hope that agreement there on conditions of union, and international pressures directed toward its acceptance, would develop a solution. As their alternative to international consideration of the problem in place of bilateral negotiation, the Russians, as previously stated, proposed withdrawal of troops by both powers. That would give free play to internal power relations in working out a solution of form of state and nature of government.

The Russian proposals were rejected and the General Assembly assumed jurisdiction. Its conclusions were embodied in a resolution adopted, over the opposition of the Soviet Union and those member-states whose votes it controlled, on November 14, 1947. This conclusion was that freely elected representatives of the Korean people should determine the form of government and establish the conditions of unification. To ensure that those representatives should be "in fact duly elected by the Korean people and not mere appointees by military authorities in Korea" a United Nations Temporary Commission on Korea (UNTCOK) was to be established "to be present in Korea, with right to travel, observe and consult throughout Korea."

Because of the Soviet attitude of opposition to United Nations action on the question, the Temporary Commission was not admitted to the northern zone. It was decided, however, to go ahead with the elections in those parts of Korea where the Commission could observe them. Elections consequently were held in the American zone on May 10, 1948, to fill 200 seats in the constituent assembly. One hundred seats were reserved for North Korea, pending the holding of free elections there. The commission, "Having satisfied itself that the electoral procedures which it recommended had on the whole been correctly applied," in its Resolution of June 25 recorded "its opinion that the results of the ballot of 10 May 1948 are a valid expression of the will of the electorate in those parts of Korea which were accessible to the Commission and in which the inhabitants constituted approximately two-thirds of the people of all Korea." Those thus elected made up the first Congress of the Republic of Korea, with which the Temporary Commission then carried on consultations with a view to bringing into being a Korean government to which authority could be transferred by the military regimes of the occupying powers.

ORGANIZING THE REPUBLIC OF KOREA

Serving as a constituent assembly, this Congress adopted a constitution for Korea on July 12, 1948. The new constitution provided for a division of the powers of government among: a president, with wide executive powers, in the exercise of which in policy matters he had the advice of a Council of State; a prime minister who controlled and supervised the work of the administrative departments, each of which was headed by a minister appointed by and responsible to the president, who appointed the ministers as well as the prime minister; a national assembly, to exercise the legislative power, subject to a suspensive presidential veto; and a Supreme Court, together with lower courts to be constituted by law, to exercise the judicial power and review administrative regulations to determine their consistency with the constitution and laws. In addition, the constitution contained a chapter setting forth the rights and duties of citizens, a chapter on economy, one on finance, and one on local autonomous organizations. Provision was made for amendment of the constitution by a two-thirds majority of the National Assembly, on proposal of either the president or one-third of the members of the Assembly. In addition to its legislative powers the Assembly, whose members were to serve for four-year terms, (except that the first, essentially constituent, National Assembly was to continue for a period of two years before new elections were to be held), exercised a measure of power over the president by virtue of its constitutional right to elect the president and vice-president for four-year terms, and to remove them by impeachment.

The National Assembly elected Dr. Syngman Rhee as the first President and, under his guidance, set up the new government. Negotiations were instituted in August, 1948, between that government and the American military authorities, to transfer governmental functions to the former. This was possible because the American government on August 12 found that the new Korean government was "entitled to be regarded as the Government of Korea envisaged by the General Assembly Resolutions of November 14, 1947," and thus, "pending consideration by the General Assembly at its forthcoming Third Session of the report of the United Nations Temporary Commission on Korea," it could properly negotiate with it concerning the conditions of transfer of authority.[11]

The General Assembly, on December 12, 1948, following consideration of the Report of the Temporary Commission, approved its conclusions. This led the Assembly in the Resolution adopted at that time, to declare

that there has been established a lawful government (the Government of the Republic of Korea), having effective control and jurisdiction over that part of Korea where the Temporary Commission was able to observe and consult and in which the great majority of the people of all Korea reside; that this government is based on elections which were a valid expression of the free will of the electorate of that part of Korea and

[11] For a statement of U.S. policy toward the new Korean government, see Department of State, Press Release 647, August 12, 1948.

which were observed by the Temporary Mixed Commission; and that this is the only such Government in Korea. This resolution also provided for the establishment of a Commission on Korea (UNCOK) to:

(a) Lend its good offices to bring about the unification of Korea and the integration of all Korean security forces...

(b) Seek to facilitate the removal of barriers to economic, social, and other friendly intercourse caused by the division of Korea;

(c) Be available for observation and consultation in the further development of representative government based on the freely expressed will of the people;

(d) Observe the actual withdrawal of the occupying forces and verify the fact of such withdrawal when such has occurred...[12]

Following this action, the United States, China, the Philippines, Britain and other countries supporting the United States' position in the United Nations extended recognition to the new government as that of the Republic of Korea. The authority of its government was derived from a constitution which was designed not to freeze the division of the country, since it described the territories of the democratic republic as the Korean peninsula and its accessory islands, and since it made provision for representation in the National Assembly from North Korea when representatives could be chosen through free elections.

It had already been made clear, however, that North Korea would neither accept the new regime nor permit any United Nations' observation within its territories. The North Korean regime held its own elections to a Supreme People's Assembly for all Korea in August, 1948. It claimed that 8,681,745 persons voted in South Korea, 77.6 per cent endorsing candidates offering themselves for the 360 delegates allotted to that part of the country. In fact, however, the 360 delegates to represent South Korea in the Assembly were selected by a convention of 1,002 "delegates" assertedly representing the people of South Korea. This convention met in Haeju, north of the 38th parallel, August 22-24.[13]

This Supreme People's Assembly ratified a constitution (September 3) which had been announced by the People's Committee on May 1. Following the adoption of the constitution, the Supreme People's Assembly set up a government which was advertised as one of party

[12] General Assembly, *Official Records*: 4th Session, *Supplement* No. 9. *U.N. Doc.* A/936, p. 3.
[13] McCune and Grey, *op. cit.*, p. 247.

coalition, and included South Koreans in the ministry. All of these developments were reported from North Korea but had no independent confirmation. The circumstances were such, however, that, as one competent student put it:

> It seems reasonable to suppose that the coalition regime was a convenient fiction which involved no real sharing of power by the Labor (Communist) Party with other political groups and that its main importance was as a device for giving the government a national rather than purely partisan appearance. The other groups in the Korean National Democratic Front were probably entirely tractable to the Labor Party.[14]

The actions taken did not change the existing internal situation and were designed as the Soviet answer to the American attempt to produce a solution through the United Nations.

The government established for Korea, which was approved by the United Nations and which was given recognition by some thirty states, did not command universal support in South Korea. The newly elected President, the Premier, and the Foreign Minister, had previously been criticized for the political methods which they had employed to secure their ends. Additional criticism was encountered because of the political inexperience of the Cabinet as a whole and because of its complete composition of "southerners," in disregard of the "Northern" Koreans who were then living in South Korea and who might have been used to give a "national" complexion to a government which claimed authority over the entire country. Under these circumstances the first years of the new republic were marked by internal controversy, increased rather than lessened by the attempt of the President to establish himself in a position of personal power, and the attempts of members of his Cabinet to enlarge their own personal followings.

These internal conflicts, growing out of personal rivalries for power, had an unfortunate effect on the attitude of the American government toward the regime which it had sponsored. It was recognized that the South Korean government could not survive without economic assistance. Nevertheless, on January 19, 1950, the Congress of the United States rejected the proposal for the second installment of E.C.A. (Economic Co-operation Administration) aid for Korea; although in February it did approve a $60 million aid bill. This was $30 million less

[14] *Ibid.,* p. 249.

than had been expected. Altogether, in the period 1945-50, some $376 millions were furnished Korea by the United States for civilian relief, together with an additional $120 million of E.C.A. aid.[15]

American economic assistance under the ECA program was utilized to increase the coal production necessary both for manufacturing (lessening the need to drastically deplete the timber resources of the country for fuel purposes), and for the production of electric power. It was also used to finance power projects necessary to reduce the power deficiency of South Korea. With this assistance it had been possible to bring about improvement in South Korean industrial activity in and after 1949. Similar improvement was also the case in agricultural production, South Korea having been brought by 1949 to the point of self-sufficiency in food supply. As a result of the North Korean attack in 1950, however, emphasis in American aid necessarily had to be shifted from developmental projects back to relief and rehabilitation, for which it had first been used.

American interest in supporting the new Korean government was determined less by concern for the welfare of the Koreans than by an interest in preventing the further spread of Soviet influence. This interest, however, was qualified by Washington's desire not to find itself automatically committed to the support of anti-Communist governments incapable of developing popular support sufficient to enable them ultimately to maintain themselves without American aid. The defeat of the National Government in China was attributed by Washington to its inherent weaknesses rather than to any failure on the part of the United States to lend it adequate economic aid. These weaknesses were held to have resulted in the misuse of such assistance as had been given.

Thus, after the Communist victory in China, in comparable situations elsewhere, such as that in Korea, the belief came to be held by the Truman Administration that American economic assistance would be useful only if extended to a government operating democratically and willing to use such assistance to promote economic recovery rather than for the purpose of maintaining itself in power or to enrich the individuals composing it. In other words, the American attitude had come to be that the recipient government should assume responsibility

[15] Arthur L. Grey, Jr., *New International Year Book, 1952* (New York: Funk and Wagnalls Co., 1952) "Korea," p. 317.

for the maintenance of satisfactory political conditions so that there could be assurance of the use of the aid received to promote the general interest.

On the political side, Syngman Rhee's government seemed to be showing similar weaknesses to those which were at this time being found objectionable in the Chinese National Government. On the economic side, complete recovery did not seem to be in immediate prospect because of the preoccupation of the members of the government with the enhancement of their political fortunes.

In the general reorientation of policy put under way after the establishment of the ascendency of the Chinese Communist Party in mainland China, these American reactions to the situation in Korea led to a definition, on January 12, 1950, of the outer perimeter of American defense in terms excluding Korea. No public objection was raised to the extension of the security zone westward across the Pacific to a line anchored in the occupied Japanese islands in the north and in the Philippine Islands in the south. Such objections as were raised on strategic grounds were with respect to Formosa rather than because of the exclusion of Korea. The new republic thus seemed to be left to its own military resources and capabilities in the event of an attempt by the North Korean government to unify the country by resort to war, except as the South Koreans were able to rely on United Nations action to maintain international peace and security and to prevent aggression.

From the military standpoint, the Soviet government had announced on September 20, 1948, that the withdrawal of Soviet troops from Korea would be completed by January 1, 1949. This was interpreted by the Americans as meaning that Russia believed that the North Korean regime now had become strong enough to support itself. Since the South Korean government, in comparison with that of the North, had not reached that point of strength, the American withdrawal was delayed; it too was, however, completed on June 29, 1949. Thereafter the United States maintained in Korea, aside from Air Force personnel sufficient to operate the airport in Seoul, a Military Advisory Group with an authorized strength of 500 officers and men which had the mission of training a Korean constabulary and army. The army brought into being between the end of the occupation and the attack on South Korea from the north in June, 1950, was described at that time by the head of the American Military Mission as being capable of the defense of South Korea. Thus the assumption was made by the United

States, at the time of the redefinition of the American security zone just referred to, that in the event of civil war South Korea could maintain itself. If not, the United States would apparently not be prepared to give it military support as part of the American defense system.

BIBLIOGRAPHICAL REFERENCES

Caldwell, John, and Frost, Lesley, *The Korean Story* (Chicago: Regnery, 1952).

Department of State, Pub. 2933, Far Eastern Series, 8, *Korea's Independence* (with Annex of Documents to 1948); pub. 3305, Far Eastern Series, 28, *Korea, 1945-1948* (with 32 selected documents).

Grajdanzev, Andrew J., *Modern Korea* (New York: John Day for the International Secretariat, Institute of Pacific Relations, 1944).

Korean Affairs Institute, *Voice of Korea* (Washington, 1946-) Vol. 5, No. 112, August 14, 1948, contains the text of the Constitution of the Republic.

Korean-American Relations: Documents pertaining to the Far Eastern Diplomacy of the United States (Berkeley: University of California Press, 1951).

Korean Pacific Press, *Korean Report, 1948-1952* (Washington, 1952).

McCune, George McAfee, and Grey, Arthur L., Jr., *Korea Today* (Cambridge: Harvard University Press, 1950).

McCune, George M., "Korea: the First Year of Liberation," *Pacific Affairs*, Vol. 20, No. 1.

McCune, Shannon, "Korea," in L. K. Rosinger and Associates, *The State of Asia* (New York: Knopf, for the Institute of Pacific Relations, 1951).

Meade, E. Grant, *American Military Government in Korea* (New York: King's Crown, 1951).

Oliver, Robert T. (ed.), *Korea's Fight For Freedom* (Washington: Korean Pacific Press), Vol. I, 1951, Vol. II, 1952.

Republic of Korea, Office of Public Information, *The Republic of Korea: Its Constitution and Government Organization Law.*

Tewksbury, Donald G., *Source Materials on Korean Politics and ideologies*, Vol. II of the Series, *Source Books on Far Eastern political ideologies* (New York: Institute of Pacific Relations, 1950).

Vinacke, Harold M., *United States and the Far East, 1945-1951* (Palo Alto: Stanford University Press, 1952).

Washburn, John N., "Russia Looks at Northern Korea," *Pacific Affairs*, Vol. 20, No. 22.

7

War, Stalemate, and Truce in Korea

✳✳✳✳✳✳✳✳✳✳✳✳✳✳✳✳✳✳✳✳✳✳✳✳✳✳✳✳✳✳✳✳

ON THE EVE OF WAR

THE NORTH KOREAN regime apparently felt that it had the power to unify the country by military means since it launched a full-scale attack across the 38th parallel on June 25, 1950. The invasion had been preceded by minor border incidents along the parallel during 1948 and 1949, and by invasion of the territory of the republic on Gngjin peninsula. In these local border actions the North Korean troops "showed themselves well-trained and well-equipped. Their direction and equipment were mainly derived from the Soviet Union, and Soviet officers were reported in 1948 and 1949 to be in control down into the lowest echelons." [1]

The intensification of these border pressures in the spring of 1950 had raised fears in the South Korean government. These fears led to requests for further American military assistance. At the time these requests were made, however, the Seoul government was itself indulging in somewhat bellicose expressions of intention on its part with respect to unification. Consequently its requests were construed, incorrectly as it turned out, as being designed to add to the power of that government so that it could overcome internal opposition and possibly itself undertake extension of its authority into the northern zone by military means.

Divergent views as to ultimate objectives among the Korean gov-

[1] Shannon McCune, "Korea," in L. K. Rosinger and Associates, *The State of Asia* (New York: Knopf, 1951), p. 151.

ernment, the United Nations, and the United States were expressed only three months before the emergency arose.

> Independence Day in Korea is March 1, the anniversary of the Mansei movement of 1919. At a mass ceremony on March 1, 1950, three divergent points of view were expressed which epitomized to some extent the political tenor of the times in south Korea. President Rhee broadly hinted that, in answers to the cries of "our brothers in distress" in the north, he would strive to reunite the country by force if peaceful means were not found. The chairman of the United Nations Commission stressed that the United Nations stood for settlement of differences by peaceful means. The American Ambassador, John J. Muccio, warned that the United States would be deeply concerned if democratic processes were ignored in fighting communism, or if economic problems were not attacked. Thus was summed up in the dilemma of south Korea in the spring of 1950: could the nation unify itself without war, maintain democracy, and remedy its economic ills, all at the same time? [2]

Such statements as that made by President Rhee were exploited in Soviet and North Korean propaganda as evidence of aggressive intentions on the part of the South Korean government. In this respect they were fitted into the general lines of Soviet anti-American propaganda which portrayed all actions or proposals of the United States and states or governments assisted by it as aggressive and imperialistic. Where contradictions in American policy appeared, as in the desire and apparent intention to withdraw from Korea, these were distorted to fit the propaganda line although, as it developed, serving also to shape Soviet policy.

When the final attack against the Republic of Korea was launched from the north, the Soviet Union and North Korea acted upon two assumptions. The first was that the United States would not give military support to the government of the republic, since Washington had seen fit to exclude Korea from the American security zone in the Pacific.[3] The modifying statement of Secretary Acheson, that the United Nations would have the responsibility of preserving the republic against external aggression, and that the United States, as a member of the United Nations, would discharge its obligations under the Charter, was apparently not taken too seriously. This was because the available evidence seemed to indicate that action could not or

[2] *Ibid.*, p. 149.
[3] See Secretary of State Acheson's National Press Conference Speech, Jan. 12, 1950. Dept. of State *Bulletin*, Vol. 22, #551 (Jan. 28, 1950), pp. 111, 118.

would not be taken through the United Nations with sufficient rapidity and decision to determine the outcome if North Korea had the estimated preponderance of military power over South Korea. Action by the United Nations could not be taken, it was thought, because of the ability of the Soviet Union to prevent it through the exercise of the veto in the Security Council. It could be assumed that it would not be taken in time, in any case, because of the necessity of working toward decision through prolonged debate over the question of responsibility for aggression; with many states inclined to reach conclusions in disregard of the evidence because of unwillingness to commit their forces in a somewhat remote area where they did not have interests of their own to protect.

The assumption as to United States unwillingness to act vigorously in behalf of Korea through the discharge of its obligations as a member of the United Nations proved incorrect. The second assumption might have proved to have greater validity if the Soviet Union, when the aggression occurred, had not been boycotting the meetings of the Security Council in the expectation that that body could not function without Soviet representation. The unexpected rapidity with which the United States acted may possibly have caught the Russians by surprise, as may have the willingness of the Security Council to exercise its powers in the absence of one of the major powers. The association of the United Nations with the establishment of the Korean Republic, together with the presence on the spot of a United Nations Commission so that it could report immediately on the question of responsibility, of course, removed the excuse for prolonged consideration of that fundamental question.

REACTION TO AGGRESSION

The report from the American ambassador at Seoul of the invasion of South Korea reached Washington early in the evening of June 24, 1950. Early the next morning the United States requested the Secretary General of the United Nations to call the Security Council into immediate session. At this meeting the Security Council, on the proposal of the United States, adopted (9-0, with the U.S.S.R. absent and Yugoslavia abstaining) a "cease-fire" resolution. This resolution—"Noting with grave concern the armed invasion of the Republic of Korea by armed forces from North Korea," declared this action to be a breach of the peace. The Security Council, therefore, "called upon" the authorities in North Korea (1) to cease hostilities forthwith; and (2) to withdraw their armed forces to the 38th parallel. The United Nations Commission on Korea was requested (1) to observe the withdrawal of the North Korea forces to the 38th parallel; and (2) to keep the Security Council informed on the execution of this resolution. At the same time the Security Council called upon all members of the United Nations "to render every assistance to the United Nations in the execution of this resolution and to refrain from giving assistance to the North Korean authorities."

On the evening of June 25,

> following a conference ... attended by the President, the Secretaries of State and Defense, their senior advisers, and the Joint Chiefs-of-Staff, General Douglas MacArthur was authorized to furnish to the Korean Government additional military supplies and assistance of the type furnished under the Mutual Defense Assistance Program.

Following a direct appeal from the Korean National Assembly for increasing support, on June 27 President Truman announced that he had "ordered United States air and sea forces to give the Korean government troops cover and support." On June 30, when it was obvious that Korean resistance was collapsing, the use of American ground forces was authorized. At the same time the air force was authorized to bomb North Korean targets. All of these actions were taken in implementation of the Security Council Resolution of June 25.[4]

American policy, however, was based upon the view, as stated by President Truman, that "The attack upon Korea makes it plain beyond all doubt that communism has passed beyond the use of subversion to conquer independent nations and will now use armed invasion and war."

NEUTRALIZATION OF FORMOSA

The presidential statement of June 27 also declared unilaterally the neutralization of Formosa for the period of the military operations in Korea. It was laid down that the Nationalists on Formosa must refrain from air and sea operations against mainland China. The Communists were debarred from attempting an invasion of Formosa, the Seventh

[4] The above quotations and summary are from *United States Policy in the Korean Crisis*, U. S. Dept. of State, Office of Public Affairs (1950), Publication 3922, Far Eastern Series 34.

Fleet being ordered to patrol the Formosan straits to enforce the prohibition. This action, announced as designed to localize military operations to Korea, resolved, for the time at least, a conflict as to policy between the Department of State and the military advisers to the President. The latter generally supported the view which had been advanced by General MacArthur that American security requirements could not be met if Formosa was allowed to fall into the hands of a hostile or potentially hostile power. The President and the Secretary of State, had, however, as recently as January, 1950, accepted the Chinese Communist view that Formosa had become part of China. Its status would be, in this view, determined by the outcome of the struggle between the Kuomintang and the Communists for control of China, including Formosa. Thus American policy was then apparently defined in terms of acquiescence in the outcome of the struggle even though the Communists should be successful in an invasion of Formosa and thus succeed in the completion of the destruction of the National Government. As stated above, this policy was changed by the outbreak of war in Korea even though at the time of the announcement of the neutralization of Formosa the Chinese Communists had not intervened in the Korean war. "The determination of the future status of Formosa," the President then stated, "must await the restoration of security in the Pacific, a peace settlement with Japan, or consideration by the United Nations." [5]

As time passed, this action had the effect of joining the Formosan question more and more intimately with that of Korea instead of realizing the announced purpose of keeping them separate. This relationship of the two questions, however, can best be considered, as it must be in some detail, in the light of developments in the war in Korea.

SECURITY COUNCIL RESOLUTIONS

While the United States acted unilaterally in relation to Formosa its military participation in the war in Korea was, as stated above, undertaken in fulfillment of its obligations as a member of the United Nations, even though it took the initiative in the establishment of those obligations to Korea and played the leading part in their execution. The initial military assistance furnished South Korea was authorized

[5] Statement by the President, June 27, 1950, *Ibid.*, Doc. 9, p. 10.

in the June 26th resolution of the Security Council, which called upon the several members of the United Nations to give "every assistance in its execution." By the next day, when the Security Council held a second meeting, the United Nations Commission in Korea had submitted a "Summary Report on Background Events" preceding the outbreak of hostilities which concluded with the statement that "All the evidence continues to point to a calculated co-ordinated attack" from the North on South Korea "prepared and launched with secrecy." [6]

In another communication of June 26, the Commission reported:

> First, that judging from actual progress of operations Northern regime is carrying out well-planned, concerted, and full-scale invasion of South Korea, second, that South Korean forces were deployed on wholly defensive basis in all sectors of the parallel, and, third, that they were taken completely by surprise as they had no reason to believe from intelligence sources that invasion was imminent.[7]

An appeal for United Nations aid, addressed to the General Assembly via the United Nations Commission, had also been received from the Korean government. These and other reports from the United Nations Commission assisted in bringing about the passage, by the required seven votes, of a second resolution introduced by the United States into the Security Council. Yugoslavia voted against the resolution, the Soviet Union was again absent, and India and Egypt abstained from voting because their delegates had not received instructions from home. On June 29, however, the resolution was accepted by India in a communication from the Prime Minister and Minister for Foreign Affairs to the Secretary General which stated:

> The Government of India has given the most careful consideration to this resolution of the Security Council in the context of the events in Korea and also of the general foreign policy of the Government of India. It is opposed to any attempt to settle international disputes by resort to aggression. For this reason Sir Benegal N. Rau, on behalf of the Government of India, voted in favor of the first resolution of the Security Council. The halting of aggression and the quick restoration of peaceful conditions are essential preludes to a satisfactory settlement. The Government of India, therefore, also accepts the second resolution of the Security Council. This decision of the Government of India does not, however, involve any modification of its foreign policy. This policy is based on the

---

[6] Text of the report, UN Doc. S/1505, published also *Ibid.*, Doc. 10, pp. 18-20.
[7] UN Doc. S/1507; *U.S. Policy in the Korean Crisis*, Doc. 13.

promotion of world peace and the development of friendly relations with all countries; it remains an independent policy which will continue to be determined solely by India's ideals and objectives.[8]

This second resolution of the Security Council, although adopted a few hours after the United States had acted to give armed aid to South Korea, put the authority of the United Nations squarely behind that action since:

> *Having noted* from the report of the United Nations Commission for Korea that the authorities in North Korea have neither ceased hostilities nor withdrawn their armed forces to the 38th parallel and that urgent military measures are required to restore international peace and security.
> The Security Council
> *Recommends* that the Members of the United Nations furnish such assistance to the Republic of Korea as may be necessary to repel the armed attack and to restore international peace and security in the area.

A third resolution adopted by the Security Council on July 7:

> 3. *Recommends* that all Members providing military forces and other assistance pursuant to the aforesaid Security Council resolutions make such forces and other assistance available to the unified command under the United States;
> 4. *Requests* the United States to designate the commander of such forces;
> 5. *Authorizes* the unified command at its discretion to use the United Nations flag in the course of operations against North Korean forces concurrently with the flags of the various nations participating;
> 6. *Requests* the United States to provide the Security Council with reports as appropriate on the course of action taken under the unified command.[9]

The following day President Truman designated General of the Army Douglas MacArthur to be Commanding General of the United Nations forces in Korea, leaving him concurrently Supreme Commander for the Allied Powers in Japan and Commander-in-Chief of the United States Forces in the Far East.

THE POSITION OF THE U.S.S.R.

These decisions had all been taken by the Security Council during the period of abstention of the Soviet Union from attendance at its

[8] UN Doc. S/1520, pp. 31-32.
[9] UN Doc. S/1588; *U.S. Policy in the Korean Crisis*, Doc. 99

meetings. That they would have encountered a Soviet veto if a Soviet representative had been present was made clear in the inability of the Security Council to take any further decisions after the Soviet representative resumed his seat on August 1, to preside over the deliberations of the Security Council. Because of the intimacy of relationship between the Soviet Union and the North Korean regime, it seems reasonable to conclude that the former was not ignorant of the intention of the latter to launch the attack, and of its timing. On that assumption it might well be concluded that the explanation of the failure of the Soviet representative to resume his seat on the Security Council in time to veto the first and subsequent resolutions, and thus prevent United Nations action, is to be found in the rapidity with which both the United States and the Security Council acted. The Soviet representative did not have the freedom to act upon his own initiative, and the time element did not permit the Soviet government to prepare a suitable justification of a change in policy, and instruct its representative to resume his seat. It is, on the other hand, conceivable that the Russian absence had been deliberately planned in the hope of creating difficulties for the United Nations from which the latter might find it difficult to extricate itself except on terms satisfactory to the Soviet Union.

In building up its justification, in reply to a note from the United States

> which called attention to "the universally known fact of the close relations between the Union of Soviet Socialist Republics and the North Korean regime," and in which the United States Government "asks assurance that the Union of Soviet Socialist Republics disavows responsibility for this unprovoked and unwarranted attack, and that it will use its influence with the North Korean authorities to withdraw their invading forces immediately." [10]

the Kremlin asserted that:

> 1. In accordance with facts verified by the Soviet Government, the events taking place in Korea were provoked by an attack by forces of the South Korean authorities on border regions of North Korea. Therefore the responsibility for these events rests upon the South Korean authorities and upon those who stand behind their back.
> 2. As is known, the Soviet Government withdrew its troops from Korea earlier than the Government of the United States and thereby

[10] *U.S. Policy in the Korean Crisis,* Doc. 94, pp. 63-64.

confirmed its traditional principle of noninterference in the internal affairs of other states. And now as well the Soviet Government adheres to the principle of the impermissibility of interference by foreign powers in the internal affairs of Korea.[11]

In taking this position the Russians contradicted not only the physical evidence but also the prior findings of the United Nations Commission functioning on the spot in Korea. The commission, to be sure, had no standing in Soviet eyes since the Soviet Union had not accepted the validity of the series of United Nations actions which had brought the Korean Republic into existence.

To further establish its base of action, the Soviet Union took the position that the resolution of June 27th (and also that of July 7th)

> was adopted by six votes, the seventh being that of the Kuomintang representative Dr. Tingfu F. Tsiang who has no legal right to represent China, whereas the United Nations Charter requires that a Security Council resolution must be adopted by seven votes including those of the five permanent members of the Council ... As is known, moreover, the above resolution was passed in the absence of two permanent members of the Security Council, the Union of Soviet Socialist Republics and China, whereas under the United Nations Charter, a decision of the Security Council on an important matter can only be made with concurring votes of all five permanent members of the Council, viz. the United States, the United Kingdom, France, the Union of Soviet Socialist Republics and China. In view of the foregoing it is quite clear that the said resolution(s) of the Security Council on the Korean question has no legal force.[12]

The position taken by the United States on this charge of illegality was that abstention from voting in the past had not been construed, even by the Russians, as a veto. Voluntary absence was held to be equivalent to abstention. At the same time, the United States made the countercharge that since the Security Council had the responsibility under the Charter of maintaining itself in continuous being in order to exercise its functions, Russian absence, designed to prevent the Council from considering threats to international peace and security, was itself a violation of the terms of the Charter. The United States, and the majority of the members of the Security Council, obviously could not accept the Soviet contention as to China.

Regardless of the merits of these charges of illegality the United

[11] *Ibid.*, Doc. 95, p. 64.
[12] Notes to Secretary General Trygve Lie of June 29 and July 11, Texts, UN Doc. S/1517, 1596.

Nations members, other than the minority who took their direction from Moscow, acted on the basis of the two resolutions adopted by the Security Council. After their adoption, however, the Russian representative resumed his seat on the Security Council. Because of the veto, this made impossible further action by that body. Consequently, when the General Assembly met in its annual session on September 19, 1950 it became the forum for further international consideration of the war in Korea.

GENERAL ASSEMBLY ACTIONS

By that time the war seemed about to enter upon a decisive phase. The North Korean attack had come close to meeting with success in overcoming South Korean resistance and in driving the United Nations forces from the peninsula. A firm defensive position had, however, been successfully established by United Nations forces. Following the Inchon landings on September 15, the military position had begun to be reversed when the United Nations General Assembly met. The General Assembly, consequently, felt sufficiently confident to adopt a resolution on October 7, 1950 which, after a recapitulation of the previous actions which had brought into being the Republic of Korea, recommended:

(A). That all appropriate steps be taken to ensure conditions of stability throughout Korea.

(B). That all constituent acts be taken, including the holding of elections, under the auspices of the United Nations, for the establishment of a unified, independent and democratic government in the sovereign state of Korea.

(C). That all sections and representative bodies of the population of Korea, South and North, be invited to cooperate with the organs of the United Nations in the restoration of peace, in the holding of elections and in the establishment of a unified government....

(D). That United Nations forces should not remain in any part of Korea otherwise than so far as necessary for achieving the objectives specified at (A) and (B) above;

(E). That all necessary measures be taken to accomplish the economic rehabilitation of Korea.[13]

---

[13] UN Doc. A/1435, for full text; also *U.S. Policy in the Korean Conflict*, July, 1950-Feb., 1951. Dept. of State, Pub. 4263, Far Eastern Series 44 (1951), Doc. 9, pp. 17-18. The vote on this resolution was 47-5. It should be noted, in view of subsequent developments, that India abstained from voting, warning the General

It will be noted that this General Assembly resolution enlarged the objective from that of bringing about a cessation of hostilities and the retirement of the North Korean forces to the 38th parallel to that of establishment of a "unified, independent and democratic government in the sovereign state of Korea." This seemed to authorize the United Nations (unified) Command in Korea to press military operations to the northern frontier of Korea at the Yalu river if that proved necessary to the accomplishment of its mission as defined in the October 7 resolution. At the time of the passage of the resolution South Korean troops had reached and crossed the parallel although other United Nations forces remained below it while awaiting response to General MacArthur's demand that the North Korean forces surrender. This demand was repeated on October 9, when notice was given of the terms of the General Assembly's resolution. The United States forces then crossed the parallel, with the apparent power to eliminate North Korean resistance in the northern part of the peninsula.

The possibility of unification required immediate decisions on the policies to be followed in the construction of government and the economic reconstruction of the country. Since the South Korean government had been recognized as the government of the Republic of Korea its plan was to extend its administrative and governmental authority north of the 38th parallel in the wake of the advancing armies. However, the United Nations Interim Committee on Korea,[14] took the position (in a resolution of October 12) that the government of the Republic of Korea could exercise civil authority only in the territory south of the 38th parallel and delegated civil authority to General MacArthur in the north. This position was supported by the United States. It was accepted at the time under pressure and reluctantly by the government of South Korea.

Assembly, apparently on the basis of its reports from Peiping, that the authorization of troop movements north of the parallel might stiffen north Korean resistance or draw Communist China directly into the struggle. This warning with respect to Chinese intervention had also previously been given over the radio by Chou En-lai, who had declared on October 1 that "China will not stand idly by and see North Korea invaded."

[14] Created by the General Assembly to act pending the arrival in Korea of the United Nations Commission for the Unification and Rehabilitation of Korea (UNCURK).

THE INTERVENTION OF COMMUNIST CHINA

Political action, however, was conditioned by the military situation. On October 1, General MacArthur felt in a strong enough position to demand the unconditional surrender of the North Korean forces. This demand was reiterated on October 9. It was this military situation which, as suggested above, caused the General Assembly to adopt the resolution of October 7, and to turn its attention to questions of reconstruction and rehabilitation. As the United Nations forces moved north of the parallel, however, with Republic of Korea troops approaching the Yalu on October 26, there were recurrent reports of Chinese participants among the North Korean forces. By the end of October Chinese Communist units had been formally identified in combat. They were, however, alleged to be Chinese who had "volunteered" for purposes of defense of the Yalu region.

A special report from the Commanding General MacArthur, United Nations Command, summarizing the facts of Chinese action in Korea from August 22 to November 4, concluded with the statement that:

> The continued employment of Chinese Communist forces in Korea and the hostile attitude assumed by such forces, either inside or outside Korea, are matters which it is incumbent upon me to bring at once to the attention of the United Nations.

On the basis of this report, the Security Council considered a resolution of November 10, jointly sponsored by Cuba, Equador, France, Norway, the United Kingdom, and the United States. While it was vetoed by the Soviet Union on November 30, and thus not adopted, it is significant as indicating the reaction within the United Nations to Chinese intervention. It reads, in part, as follows:

> *Affirming* that United Nations forces should not remain in any part of Korea otherwise than so far as necessary for achieving the objectives of stability throughout Korea and the establishment of a unified independent and democratic government in the sovereign state of Korea, as set forth in the resolution of the General Assembly dated October 7, 1950,
>
> *Insistent* that no action be taken which might lead to the spread of the Korean conflict to other areas and thereby further endanger international peace and security,
>
> *Calls* upon all states and authorities, and in particular those responsible for the actions noted above to refrain from assisting or encouraging the

North Korean authorities, to prevent their nationals or individuals or units of their armed forces from giving assistance to North Korean forces and to cause the immediate withdrawal of any such nationals, individuals, or units which may presently be in Korea;

Affirms that it is the policy of the United Nations to hold the Chinese frontier with Korea inviolate and fully to protect legitimate Chinese and Korean interests in the frontier zone;

Calls attention to the grave danger which continued intervention by Chinese forces in Korea would entail for the maintenance of such a policy.[15]

This affirmation of policy was designed to meet the demand of the Peiping regime for the withdrawal of foreign troops from Korea and to reassure it with respect to its legitimate interests in Korea, such as the Yalu River electric power system which supplied power to parts of Manchuria.

During this period of limited Chinese intervention, there was a lull in the fighting. This lull was terminated when General MacArthur, on November 24, launched an offensive in northern Korea designed to bring about an early decision by the destruction of the North Korean forces or their elimination from the peninsula. To prevent this, the Chinese People's Government intervened in force, creating what General MacArthur called an "entirely new war" and one which necessitated new definitions of policy. As of December 7, the United Nations Commission for the unification and rehabilitation of Korea (UNCURK) reported to the Secretary General of the United Nations that:

(1). Chinese units were first identified in Korea on October 25.

(2). 48,000 Chinese troops are identified as having been in Eighth Army area by November 25. These troops belonged to the 12th, 13th and 16th Army Groups of the Chinese Fourth Field Army. By November 30 the total number identified had increased to 165,000.

(3). Thus Chinese forces definitely identified total 231,000 men drawn from eight armies and comprising twenty-six divisions.

(4). It is probable that many more Chinese troops are present in Korea. One responsible estimate places the total number of Chinese troops in Korea as high as 400,000 men.

(5). At present the troops fighting the forces of the United Nations consist almost entirely of Chinese. Very few North Korean troops are in action.

---

[15] UN Doc. S/1894; also reproduced textually in *United States Policy in the Korean Conflict*, Doc. 13, pp. 22-23.

On the basis of prisoner interrogations it was found that:

the prisoners interrogated were all members of regular army units acting under normal military discipline and were *not* volunteers in any possible meaning of the term.[16]

Thus, while the Chinese intervention created what General MacArthur called an "entirely new war," the United Nations offensive of November 24 was launched when at least 48,000 Chinese troops were known to have crossed the Yalu and when it was known that there had been heavy concentrations of Chinese Communist troops along the Yalu in Manchuria which, within five days, enabled the force in North Korea to be increased to 165,000 men. "We had knowledge," as General MacArthur subsequently testified later, "that the Chinese Communists had collected large forces along the Yalu River. My own reconnaissance, you understand, was limited entirely to Korea; but the general information which was available, from China and other places, indicated large accumulations of troops." [17]

The offensive, consequently, was apparently launched on the assumptions: (1) that the United Nations forces had the capacity to reach the Yalu against Chinese "volunteer" opposition supplementing the North Korean, and (2) that the Peiping regime would not officially commit itself to the war but rather would negotiate a settlement designed to protect the legitimate interests of China in North Korea. Support for this view was presented in the arrival at Lake Success on November 25 of a nine-member delegation from Peiping in response to an invitation to the Chinese People's Government to participate in general discussions of the Korean problem, "including United States aggression" in Asia.

The United Nations offensive was contained by the Chinese forces by November 27 and the United Nations forces were driven back to the 38th parallel. Negotiations were continued, however, and under their cover the Chinese forces continued to be built up to the point where, on January 1, 1951 the Chinese Communists, having crossed the parallel on December 26, were in a position themselves to launch a major offensive.

[16] For the full text of the report, UN Doc. A/C/1/1638; also *U.S. Policy in the Korean Conflict*, Doc. 16.

[17] *Military Situation in the Far East*, Hearings before the Committee on Armed Services and the Committee on Foreign Relations, U.S. Senate, 82nd Congress., 1st Session, pt. 1, p. 18. Hereafter cited as *Joint Committee, Hearings*.

The negotiations mentioned above were instituted under the pressure of an Asian-Arab bloc, led by India. They were approved shortly before the Soviet veto, November 30, of the Security Council resolution calling upon the Chinese Communists to withdraw their forces from Korea and offering assurances of protection to Chinese interests in North Korea and on the frontier. Concurrently with the Soviet veto, the Communist Party press in China demanded the withdrawal of UN forces from Korea and of the United States 7th Fleet from Formosan waters, and the admission of the Central People's Government to the United Nations, as essential to the restoration of peace in Korea. In the face of this, the thirteen nations of the Asian-Arab bloc appealed to the Chinese Communists and North Koreans to issue a statement committing their forces not to cross the 38th parallel (December 5) and secured (December 13) over Soviet opposition, the creation of a three-member commission "to determine the basis on which a satisfactory cease-fire in Korea can be arranged." This three-member commission was unable even to discuss its proposals for a cease-fire with the Chinese representative in New York. He denounced it as a "trap" and reiterated the Chinese position that peace could only follow United States withdrawal from Korea and the end of American "aggression" in that country. Two days later he left for Peiping.

The proposals which the United States accepted as a basis of negotiations but which the Central People's Government refused to consider involved: (1) the ordering of an immediate "cessation of all acts of armed force in Korea"; (2) the establishment of a "demilitarized area across Korea of approximately twenty miles in depth with the southern limit following generally the line of the 38th parallel"; (3) supervision of the cease-fire by a United Nations commission to ensure withdrawal of forces along lines indicated and to ensure against re-enforcement designed to change the military situation; (4) exchange of prisoners of war "on a one for one basis, pending final settlement of the Korean question"; and (5) "It is our clear understanding and also that of the twelve Asian sponsors, that once a cease-fire arrangement had been achieved, the negotiations visualized in the second resolution should be proceeded with at once.[18]

The initial American as well as European reaction to Chinese successes, especially after they launched their major offensive in January,

[18] Summary from *Report of the Group on Cease-Fire . . .* UN Doc. A/C.1/643; also in *U.S. Policy in Korean Conflict*, Doc. 20.

1951, was toward either an immediate or an ultimate writing-off of the Korean War as an unsuccessful experiment in the attempt to establish international peace and security through international action and by military means. The relatively rapid containment of the Chinese offensive, however, and the subsequent success of the limited but continuous counteroffensive of the United Nations forces which, by April 1951, had brought those forces again beyond the 38th parallel, had the effect of shifting away from the idea of either forced or voluntary retirement from the peninsula.

While the military tide thus ebbed and flowed, attempts, as has already been suggested, were concurrently made to find a political solution to the problems posed by the Chinese intervention in Korea. In general it may be said that the United States showed itself ready and willing to discuss proposals for a political settlement, after suitable arrangements for a cease-fire had been made. The Chinese and Russians, however, were unwilling to discuss proposals even for a cease-fire except in connection with prior acceptance of their terms for settlement of other Far Eastern political issues. Thus prior to negotiation of the conditions for terminating Korean hostilities, Communist China and the Soviet government insisted upon: (1) the withdrawal of all foreign troops (initially apparently not including as "foreign" Chinese troops which were labelled "volunteers"); (2) the seating of representatives of the Central People's Government in the United Nations; (3) the ending of the American "intervention" in support of the Chinese National Government in Formosa; and (4) a conference to bring about a general Far Eastern settlement, including a treaty with Japan acceptable to Peiping and Moscow. Since the United States was not willing to accept conditions for a cease-fire in Korea which represented a prejudgment in favor of the Soviet Union and Communist China of all of the questions at issue between itself and China, it refused to accept the Chinese alternative proposals to those of the Committee of Three, which it had been willing to consider.

THE CHARGE OF AGGRESSION AGAINST CHINA

With the failure of the attempt to bring about an immediate cease-fire in the "new" war in Korea, the United States urged the adoption by the General Assembly of a resolution formally finding the Peiping regime guilty of aggression. Such a step was finally taken on February

1, 1951. In addition to the finding of aggression, the resolution called upon the People's Government to cease hostilities in Korea and re-affirmed "the determination of the United Nations to continue its action in Korea to meet the aggression." A special committee of the General Assembly was formed to examine the problem and report on what additional measures might be necessary to solve it, besides those already authorized and taken by the member states.

The groundwork for this action had been laid in proposals made by the United States to the General Assembly in September, 1950 with a view to preparing the way for action by the Assembly in other situations where the Security Council, because of the veto, was unable to function. These proposals, somewhat modified, were embodied in what came to be called the "Uniting for Peace" resolution which was adopted on November 3, with the states in the Soviet bloc voting against it and India and the Argentine abstaining. It was under the terms of this resolution that the Assembly proceeded to deal with the Chinese intervention in Korea, finally adopting the resolution labelling China an aggressor.

The hesitation of the United Nations in reaching that conclusion was apparently due to fear on the part of India and other states that such action would cut off what they perceived as a possibility of ending the war in Korea by negotiation; and also to fear that the United States would press for action which would enlarge the theater of military operations to include China itself, thus possibly precipitating a third world war. In addition, those states which had previously recognized the People's Government, notably India, apparently believed that no action should be taken with respect to China unless and until the Peiping regime had been given China's seat in the United Nations so that it could participate in all discussions which involved it. This position was not completely changed even after the adoption of the finding that the Chinese Communists were guilty of aggression. That would, however, seem to have precluded recognition of the People's Government, even for purposes of representation in the United Nations, until the aggression was ended either by the enforced retirement of Chinese troops from Korea or by the establishment of a cease-fire negotiated on the basis of their retirement north of the 38th parallel.

NEGOTIATIONS FOR A CEASE-FIRE

Influenced by adverse changes in the military situation in the spring of 1951, and also to give some apparent substance to their propaganda advocacy of peace, the Russian representative on the Security Council proposed that negotiations be instituted between the two commands in Korea to bring about a cease-fire and to determine the conditions of armistice in the Korean War. In retrospect, it appears that the immediate Russian purpose, and that of China, in proposing negotiations was to prevent a decisive victory from being won in Korea by means of a slow-down of the limited offensive then underway. If successful, this would gain the time necessary to re-establish at least a firm defensive position in North Korea. This was a different purpose than that of bringing military operations to an end through agreement on the conditions of an armistice, to be followed by the negotiated settlement of the political issues involved in the Korean question.

The Russian proposal was accepted by the United States for several reasons. One was fear that military victory in Korea might readily be the prelude to the general war which Washington had steadily sought to avoid. A second was a real desire in the United States to explore to their limits all possibilities of restoring peace in the Far East. A third was the desire to conciliate the opinion of such Asian and European states as had been reluctant to follow American leadership against the Soviet Union because of fear of alleged American "warmongering" and "imperialism." Thus negotiations designed to bring about agreement on the conditions of an armistice were instituted without a cease-fire. The negotiations were continued in spite of indications that the Chinese were less interested in agreement than in re-establishing their military position, and with it a stronger influence over the North Korean regime than they had originally possessed. Neither side, however, was apparently willing to break off negotiations and thus assume clear responsibility for their decisive termination.

EFFECT OF THE KOREAN WAR ON
INTERNATIONAL RELATIONS

Except for Berlin and in Austria, Korea was the one place where the United States and the Soviet Union had their power arrayed on opposite sides of a common frontier. Consequently the postwar Korean problem was inevitably cast in the mold of United States-Soviet relations. Under the circumstances, however, attitudes with respect to the solution of the problem were finally determined in part by the issues posed by the outcome of the struggle between the National Government and the Chinese Communist Party for control in China. These attitudes, however, were themselves largely determined by relationships with the United States or the Soviet Union at the time of outbreak of the war in Korea.

In the background of the North Korean aggression was the Soviet Union and a China whose Communist government not only had an ideological affinity with the Soviet Union but also was its declared ally. The position taken by the U.S.S.R. and the People's Government was consistently supported without question only by those states which were within the area of Russian influence and dominance. The anti-Soviet leadership of the United States was accepted by many more states. Since, however, the United States exercised leadership of a coalition of independent states rather than controlling the policy of satellites, its policies had to be formulated, both in and out of the United Nations, in consultation with other governments holding different views from that of the United States on certain aspects of the Far Eastern problem. Some states, Britain being the most powerful of them, for example, had extended recognition to the Peiping government before the outbreak of the war in Korea, whereas the United States had not. This did not necessarily signify approval by Britain of the Communist regime. Recognition was designed (1) to attach the necessary juristic consequences to a *de facto* situation, and (2) by that means to establish a basis for the protection of British interests in China and at Hongkong. Regardless of its justification, nevertheless, this recognition had an especially complicating effect on relationships because of the continued existence of the National Government of China in control of a territorial base on Formosa. The United States continued to recognize that government and support it as the government of China. It was consequently for some time the Formosa question, rather than that, strictly speaking, of recognition or non-recognition of the Peiping regime, in connection with which serious differences of opinion arose.

The "neutralist" position, as between the United States and the U.S.S.R., which such Asian nations as India and Indonesia sought to maintain also complicated for the United States the problem of leadership both within and outside of the United Nations. "Neutralism," it was made clear by Mr. Nehru, did not involve passivity in foreign policy in relation even to situations with which India was not directly concerned. Rather it meant active participation in the search for a solution, but in terms of independent Indian judgment as to the proper solution for each particular problem or issue. This precluded any sort of commitment in advance to the views of the United States. Beyond this, in relation to the Far East the Indian government tended to view the United States, as a non-Asian state, as unduly intrusive in its assertion of Far Eastern leadership. Asian questions, Mr. Nehru felt, should be dealt with primarily by Asian states. With this view, India apparently acted on the assumption that the United States should accept Indian leadership rather than itself attempt to exercise leadership in the Far East.

After the Chinese intervention in the Korean war a new set of considerations became operative in the development of military policy. The European states were alarmed at any tendencies in American policy which indicated an intention to give the Far East priority over Europe in the allocation of American economic and military assistance. If the choice had to be made between (1) acquiescence in the extension of Chinese and thus Communist control over Korea or (2) the serious lessening of the ability of the United States to contribute fully to the defense of western Europe against Russia, generally speaking it was evident that Britain and the peoples and governments in western Europe preferred the former alternative. This was the underlying basis of their reaction against any proposals which might involve the United States and the United Nations in war against China in which military operations were not localized to Korea. To this was joined the fear that such action against China would bring about direct Russian military intervention. This intervention, it was argued, would take the form of an attack in Europe rather than in Asia. This point of view was expressed in Washington as well, although it was not as widely held there as in the European capitals. As General Omar Bradley, Chairman of the United States Joint Chiefs-of-Staff, put the official view:

> "Red China is not the powerful nation seeking to dominate the world. Frankly, in the opinion of the Joint Chiefs-of-Staff, this strategy would involve us in the wrong war, at the wrong place, at the wrong time and with the wrong enemy." [19]

[19] *Joint Committee, Hearings,* pt. 2, p. 732.

PROPOSALS FOR ACTION AGAINST CHINA

The proposals in question were those made by General MacArthur with respect to military operations against China designed to bring about a decisive victory in Korea. They were:

(1). The intensification of our economic blockade against China.

(2). The imposition of a naval blockade against the China coast.

(3). Removal of restrictions on air reconnaissance of China's coastal area and of Manchuria.

(4). Removal of restrictions on the forces of the Republic of China on Formosa, with logistical support to contribute to their effective operation against the common enemy.[20]

For some time there had been recurrent requests from United Nations Headquarters in Tokyo that authority should be given to bomb Chinese bases in Manchuria. The American government, however, did not press for such an authorization from the United Nations. This was possibly because it did not anticipate sufficient support readily to command the necessary two-thirds majority. More probably it was because Washington thought in terms of a chain of events which might precipitate the war with the Soviet Union which it sought, as did its allies and associates, to postpone or avoid. "Removal of restrictions on air reconnaissance of China's coastal area and of Manchuria," in the light of the background of controversy, was viewed as an indirect proposal for authorization which would lead to bombing. It thus carried the same disturbing ultimate implication of probable war with the Soviet Union.

The proposals for the intensification of the economic blockade against China and the imposition of a naval blockade against the China coast were in effect proposals of full economic sanctions against China which might so weaken Peiping as to bring about military capitulation in Korea. This proposal of economic sanctions to be applied by the United States and other active participants in the war raised immediately two principal questions: (1) of effectiveness in relation to the objective; and (2) of reaction of other states to them immediately and during the course of their application. Their effectiveness seemed ques-

[20] Address before the Congress, from text as reported in the *New York Times*, April 20, 1951. In this original press report, item 4 reads "Operation against the Chinese Mainland." This was an error in recording, according to General MacArthur, as reported in the *New York Times*, May 5, 1951.

tionable at the time for two principal reasons. The first related to the nature of the Chinese economy. China had not yet been sufficiently developed in its economic processes to be as seriously and as immediately affected by boycott and blockade measures as would have been the case if it had been transformed from an agricultural to an industrialized state. The second reason was that the economic blockade would necessarily be incomplete, and might consequently lose much of its effectiveness, since trade with the Soviet Union across its long land frontier with China could not be materially affected. In other words, if participation were complete except for the Soviet bloc, it would be effective only with respect to essential commodities which could not be supplied by, or by way of, the Soviet Union. Without full and effective co-operation by all states outside the Soviet orbit, furthermore, economic sanctions would have to be enforced through naval and other measures directed against shipping and other transportation facilities. Such measures of enforcement would be certain to impose serious strains on the relations of the United States with some of its anti-Soviet allies as well as on such neutralist states as India and Indonesia.

In any case, no matter how complete and adequately enforced, economic sanctions could yield results only gradually over an extended period of time. Thus if primary reliance were put on them to end the war in Korea, it would have to be accepted as a probability that there would be no quick and decisive verdict. This would have to be anticipated to avoid immediate demands for action of a more far-reaching military character designed to produce such immediate results. Otherwise economic sanctions would have to be evaluated not merely from the standpoint of their effectiveness, but also as part of a possible chain of events culminating ultimately in World War III.

By themselves, nevertheless, because of their lack of maximum effectiveness against a country at China's stage of economic development, and with its geopolitical relationship to the Soviet Union, and on account of their inability to produce immediately decisive results, boycott and blockade could certainly be viewed as measures which would not necessarily bring into play the alliance between Communist China and the Soviet Union, and thus lead to World War III. For that reason they had been most emphasized among the "additional measures" proposed for consideration even before General MacArthur was relieved of his command responsibilities. The American hesitancy in pressing for their adoption by the United Nations would seem to have been (1) because of the view that, for the reasons suggested above, they could not readily be dissociated from the question of additional military measures necessary to produce the desired result of capitulation in Korea; and (2) because of British reluctance to cut off all trade with China via Hongkong. One such "additional measure" was, nevertheless, approved by the United Nations General Assembly on May 18, 1951 when it adopted by a vote of 47-0 a United States proposal for an embargo on shipment of arms and certain strategic materials to Communist China and North Korea. Subsequently, while truce negotiations were being carried on, the lists of embargoed materials were extended and pressures instituted by the United States to make the embargo more effective.

Increasing military and economic pressure during the spring of 1951 was paralleled by moves designed to bring about a cessation of hostilities. On March 23 General MacArthur declared himself ready to discuss armistice negotiations with the Chinese commander. This offer was rejected by the Chinese Communists on March 29. At the time United Nations diplomatic negotiations to bring about a cease-fire were also being attempted. The MacArthur move, it was charged, was an attempt to bring these negotiations to an end by eliciting a negative reply from the Chinese commander to his proposals. Such a rejection, it was argued, would give him grounds for a more general attack against China. General MacArthur's move was repudiated by the United States Department of State, which took the position that truce negotiations were a responsibility of the United Nations General Assembly and not of the commander-in-chief. The United Nations move toward a cease-fire, if successful, would have been designed to stabilize the military position at the 38th parallel, thus accomplishing the original purpose of repelling aggression against South Korea, but not accomplishing the purpose of unifying Korea nor of terminating Chinese intervention south of the Yalu, and thus beyond the Manchurian frontier. MacArthur clearly did not regard this as a satisfactory termination of the military effort. Before making his armistice proposal he was reported on March 16 to have said that the 38th parallel had no natural defense features, and that any force large enough to hold that line would be capable of advancing to the Manchurian frontier. He called for high-level decisions permitting him to have more troops and also to bomb military targets in Manchuria.

This alleged interference from the field with the exercise of political judgment by the responsible United Nations agencies added to the existing pressures on and in Washington to bring about a change in the United Nations Command in Korea and in the Supreme Allied Command in Tokyo. The issue was brought to a head with the publication of General MacArthur's letter to Congressman Joseph Martin criticizing established policies, with the result that MacArthur was relieved of all of his command responsibilities by President Truman on April 11 and ordered to return to the United States.

The movement toward a truce, however, was resumed in April while the United States was undergoing the ensuing "great debate" on its Far Eastern policies. On April 1, 1951, the British Foreign Secretary, Mr. Morrison, declared that, since most of the area south of the parallel had been recovered, the psychological moment had arrived to cease fighting. The possibility of truce negotiations continued to be discussed during May, and on June 1 the Secretary General of the United Nations, Mr. Trygve Lie, expressed the opinion that the time was ripe for renewed armistice efforts. On June 24 Mr. Malik, the Soviet Foreign Minister, said that the U.S.S.R. felt that a cease-fire could be negotiated. Immediately thereafter, on June 27, the new United Nations Commander-in-Chief, General Ridgway, addressed a radio message to the Chinese and North Korean leaders inviting them to discuss an armistice. On July 8 United Nations delegates, headed by Vice Admiral C. Turner Joy, and Communist delegates, headed by North Korean General Nam Il, met at Kaesong to discuss armistice terms. Prolonged negotiations finally produced July 26, agreement on a five-point agenda for further discussions.

The site of the truce talks was transferred by agreement of October 24 to Panmunjom. The agenda included: the fixing of a military demarcation line between the two sides and the establishment of a demilitarized zone between them; the making of concrete arrangements for the composition, authority, and functions of a supervisory organization for the carrying out of the terms of an armistice; arrangements relating to the disposition of prisoners of war; and recommendations on nonmilitary issues to be made to the governments concerned on both sides.

The resulting negotiations looking toward an armistice were intermittently carried on from 1951 through much of 1953 without agreement. During this period the war itself continued but without operations being extended much beyond the 38th parallel, and with reduced pressure to undertake air and naval operations beyond the Korean theater of war.

This same period witnessed a sharpening of internal political controversy within the Korean Republic. From the outset there had been a struggle for power between the Assembly and President Syngman Rhee. Under the constitution a presidential election was scheduled for 1952. Since it was apparent that the incumbent president would find it difficult to secure re-election by the existing Assembly, whose members remained in office until 1954, President Rhee demanded revision of the constitution so as to provide for direct election of the president. The Assembly, on January 18, 1952, rejected this proposal by an overwhelming majority. On February 29 a resolution was proposed in the Assembly which condemned the president for his "dictatorial tendencies." In April a bill, sponsored by a majority of the members of the Assembly, which called for the surrender of all presidential administrative powers to the premier, was introduced.

The Assembly could propose but the president has the power to dispose. He imposed martial law and instituted a censorship of the press and radio. Since his constitutional term expired on June 23, by which time the opposition in the Assembly had not been brought to accept his proposals for change in the constitution, President Rhee brought a quorum of the Assembly together under police escort and secured from it an extension of his term of office to August 15. Thereafter (in a forty-eight hour session of the Assembly during which no member was permitted to leave the building) the constitution was amended so as to provide for direct election of the President and Vice-President.

The election thus provided for was held on August 5, with four candidates for the office of president and nine for vice-president. President Rhee was continued in the office, polling 5,238,769 votes as against 1,781,915 votes cast for other three candidates. In the temporary capital of Pusan, however, where there was a greater awareness of the methods by which he had overcome the opposition of the Assembly than there was elsewhere, President Rhee failed to secure a majority of the votes cast.

BIBLIOGRAPHICAL REFERENCES

Acheson, Dean G., *Problem of Peace in Korea* (Washington: Department of State, 1952).

Bureau of International Relations, Indian Press Digests, Vol. 3, *Indian Proposals for a Korean Truce* (Berkeley: Department of Political Science, University of California, March, 1954).

Department of State, *United States Policy in the Korean Crisis* (Washington, 1950).

Dille, John, *Substitute for Victory* (New York: Doubleday, 1954).

Dulles, John Foster, *Korean Problems:* An Address by the Secretary of State Delivered before the American Legion in Convention at St. Louis, September 2, 1953 (Washington, 1953).

Farley, Miriam, "The Korean Crisis and the United Nations," in L. K. Rosinger and Associates, *The State of Asia* (New York: Knopf, for the Institute of Pacific Relations, 1951).

Goodrich, Leland M., *Korea: Collective Measures Against Aggression* (New York: Carnegie Endowment for International Peace, 1953).

Great Britain, Foreign Office, *Korea, 1953*, No. 2. Special Report of the Unified Command on Korean Armistice Agreement signed at Panmunjom on July 27, 1953 (London: H. M. Stationery Office, 1953).

Keesing's Contemporary Archives, Vols. 7, 8, 9, (London: Keesing's Publications, Ltd., 1943–).

Oliver, Robert T., *Why War Came to Korea* (New York: Fordham University Press, 1950).

———, ed., *Korean Report, 1948-52; Review of Governmental Procedures During Two Years of Peace and Two of War* (Washington: Korean Pacific Press, 1952).

United Nations, Department of Public Information, *Korea and the United Nations* (New York, 1950).

United States Senate, 82nd Cong., 1st session, 5 Vols., *Military Situation in the Far East: Hearings before the Committee on Armed Services and the Committee on Foreign Relations* (Washington, 1951).

8

Formosa, the United Nations, and the Korean Question

✳✳✳✳✳✳✳✳✳✳✳✳✳✳✳✳✳✳✳✳✳✳✳✳✳✳✳✳✳✳✳✳✳✳✳

THE FORMOSAN QUESTION AND THE KOREAN WAR

THE FORMOSAN QUESTION was joined to the Korean question and thus given concrete international significance from the time of the North Korean attack on the Republic of Korea. The two questions had been joined in the initial definition of American policy toward the Korean War.[1] Attitudes of a number of states within the United Nations toward Korea had been determined to a considerable extent by the Formosan question, and in the national debate over Far Eastern policy in the United States, following the return of General MacArthur, Formosa assumed a central importance. The difference of opinion which was of fundamental importance between General MacArthur, on the one side, and his superiors in Washington and at the United Nations, on the other, related to the steps which he believed must be undertaken to bring about decisive victory in Korea. These were four in number.[2] The fourth action proposed was "Removal of restrictions on the forces of the Republic of China on Formosa, with logistical support to contribute to their effective operation against the common enemy." This proposal raised a series of questions involving attitudes toward and relations with the National Government on Formosa, cutting to the heart of conflicts in American opinion concerning Far Eastern policy.

Critics of the Truman administration, inhibited by the conception of "bipartisanship" in foreign affairs from a full-scale attack on Euro-

---

[1] As indicated above, p. 222. It should be noted that the correct name for Formosa is Taiwan. Formosa has been consistently used here, however, because of its common use in the United States.

[2] All but the fourth are discussed above, pp. 222-224.

pean policy, had centered their opposition on the China policy of the administration as its most vulnerable point. It was vulnerable because of the failure of the United States to prevent the Communists from assuming power in mainland China. It could be attacked without violation of the principles of bipartisanship because it was held that there had been no consultation with the Republican Party in the formulation of the China policy which had proved to be a failure. After 1947, with the proclamation of the Truman Doctrine, the containment of communism had become a primary world emphasis in United States foreign policy. Failure to contain communism in the Far East was held by the critics of the Truman Administration to be a major failure. This failure was alleged to be due either to a misreading of the international affiliation and the nature and aims of the Chinese Communist Party, or to sympathy with it on account of dissatisfaction with the Kuomintang, or to both. Having failed to prevent Communist victory in mainland China, it was argued by critics that the Truman Administration was prepared to acquiesce in control of Formosa by the Chinese Communists if they had the power to take over the island. This asserted acquiescence was in the face of warnings by General MacArthur and others that the strategic position of the United States in the Far East would be seriously weakened if Formosa were to come under the control of any power hostile to the United States. Thus the question of Formosa came to be entangled in the threads of domestic American politics. Beyond noting this fact, however, it is unnecessary here to examine further this aspect of the question.

STATUS OF FORMOSA

The most important side of the problem of Formosa undeniably involved the status of the island in relation to China. Formosa had been transferred from China to Japan under the terms of the Treaty of Shimonoseki which terminated the Sino-Japanese war of 1894-95. Its restoration to China was proclaimed as an Allied objective in World War II in the Cairo Declaration which stated as Allied purpose

> that Japan shall be stripped of all of the islands in the Pacific which she has seized or occupied since the beginning of the first World War in 1914, and that all the territories Japan has stolen from the Chinese, such as Manchuria, Formosa, and the Pescadores, shall be restored to the Republic of China.

Chinese provincial administration under the National Government was instituted on Formosa following V-J Day. After the Kuomintang military collapse on the mainland, the seat of the National Government was transferred to Formosa and the remnants of Chiang's armies were evacuated to the island. Neither at that time nor subsequently was a separate government of Formosa established. Both the Communists and the Nationalists insisted that the island had been made a part of China in 1945. The Communists viewed the struggle for control of China as uncompleted until they had extended their power to Formosa and thus destroyed the remnants of power of the National Government. The Kuomintang maintained a provincial government on Formosa even after the National Government had been transferred to the island. It was the declared intention of that government to use Formosa as a provincial territorial base from which to move to overthrow the Communists in the mainland provinces of China.

If this Chinese view of the status of Formosa is accepted, then Formosa must be approached as an unsolved part of the problem posed in the struggle between the Kuomintang and the Chinese Communist Party for control of China. Action by other states in support of either of the contending parties would be properly viewable as intervention in that conflict. Such interventions have been frequent in international relations, and they have been undertaken on the basis of the interests of the intervening state. From that point of view, the justification of the intervention would be found in its success or failure in attaining the purposes of the intervening state. One of those purposes might be to assist a recognized and friendly government to maintain itself against a rebellious faction. When, however, the rebellious faction has established itself in control of most of the territories of the state and has itself received recognition by some states as its *de jure* government, a question is raised as to whether or not it can properly continue to be viewed merely as a rebellious faction. A much more serious question of policy is raised thereby for the state contemplating intervention since action in support of the still-recognized government may readily result in failure or lead to war. On occasion a question may also arise, however, as to the means by which the successful faction has attained power. Its assumption of control may have been the result of intervention on its behalf. Its recognition may thus have been a measure in support of that intervention at the time when it was extended. This was the situation with respect of Formosa in the first months of 1950.

At that time the Chinese Communists, recognized by Moscow and assisted by the U.S.S.R. to power on the mainland, were apparently preparing an attack from the mainland on Formosa. Had such an attack been launched then it was questionable whether the National Government would have had the power to maintain a successful defense on Formosa. The defense would have had to be prepared and conducted by the same government which, in the view of the then American Secretary of State, Mr. Dean Acheson, had thoroughly discredited itself in China because of its inefficiency, corruption, and military ineptitude. It would have had to be maintained by what was left of armies which had been defeated on the mainland by the Communists partly because of their low morale and apparent lack of will to fight, and partly because of the incompetence of their leadership. Their fighting qualities had not been enhanced by the conditions of their evacuation to Formosa. If anything, those qualities had been lessened. The misrule of the Kuomintang on Formosa in the immediate postwar years, furthermore, had lessened the ability of the island and its people to supply the needs of these forces, and had paved the way for active subversion on the part of those who had suffered from Kuomintang misrule. A forecast of what would probably have happened in the event of invasion, with the defense of Formosa carried on only by National Government forces, had apparently been given in the ease with which Hainan Island had been conquered by the Communists.

THE UNITED STATES AND THE DEFENSE OF FORMOSA

Under these conditions it appeared that the successful defense of Formosa was impossible unless the United States assumed military responsibility for it. Military judgment was apparently against the assumption of this responsibility, although, as has been noted, General MacArthur had earlier indicated his view as to the strategic importance of Formosa as an indispensable link in the outer zone of American security. This zone had come to be placed in the island chain extending from Japan in the north to the Philippines in the south. The political view was expressed by President Truman, January, 1950, as follows:

> Traditional United States policy toward China ... called for international respect for the integrity of China. This principle was recently reaffirmed in the UN General Assembly resolution of December 8, 1949, which, in part, calls on all states to refrain from

(a). seeking to acquire spheres of influence or to create foreign controlled regimes within the territory of China;

(b). seeking to obtain special rights or privileges within the territory
of China.

A specific application of the foregoing principles is seen in the present
situation with respect to Formosa . . .

The United States has no predatory designs on Formosa or on any other
Chinese territory. The United States has no desire to obtain special rights
or privileges or to establish military bases on Formosa at this time. Nor
does it have any intention of utilizing its armed forces to interfere in the
present situation. The United States will not pursue a course which will
lead to involvement in the civil conflict in China.

Similarly, the United States Government will not provide military aid
or advice to Chinese forces on Formosa. In the view of the United States
Government, the resources on Formosa are adequate to enable them to
obtain the items which they might consider necessary for the defense of
the Island. The United States Government proposes to continue under
existing legislative authority the present ECA program of economic assistance.[3]

At the beginning of 1950, consequently, the official American view
was that operations against Formosa from the mainland would be in
pursuance of civil war objectives; that the United States would not
intervene in China's civil war by military means. Consequently, the
United States would not undertake military action, if that should be
necessary, to prevent the conquest of Formosa by the Chinese Communists, as it had not in that of Hainan, if that should prove to be
the outcome of civil war operations, as was anticipated by many observers. If the anticipation had been realized, furthermore, the question
of recognition of the Peiping regime would have been put in a different context. The definitions given of attitude toward a successful invasion of Formosa must, consequently, be viewed as an indication at
that time of willingness to recognize the Chinese Communist regime if
and when the People's Government, having driven it from the mainland,
had completed the process of overthrowing and destroying the National
Government on Formosa.

A counter tendency in American policy, however, showed itself at
the outset of the Korean war. As previously stated, when the North
Korean attack was launched in June, 1950, the United States unilaterally declared the neutralization of Formosa for the period of military operations in Korea. The Nationalists were requested to refrain

[3] White House Press Release, January 5, 1950.

from air and sea operations against the mainland, and the Communists were debarred from an invasion of Formosa. The Seventh Fleet was ordered to enforce this request and prohibition. This action, although announced as designed to localize military operations to Korea, also settled the conflict in American policy by acceptance for the period of hostilities in Korea of the MacArthur thesis that considerations of national security required that Formosa should be kept out of the hands of the strongly anti-American Communist government of China. Similarly, the question of recognition of the Peiping government was answered, for the time being at least, in the negative.

Under the new set of conditions the United States thus committed itself to action to prevent an invasion of Formosa by the Chinese Communists. At the same time it committed itself to the support of the National Government as far as the maintenance of its position on Formosa was concerned. This represented a reversal of the January, 1950, White House statement that the United States would provide no further military aid or advice to the National Government of China. In application of the earlier policy, military aid had been suspended beyond that already given under the authorization of the China Aid Act of 1948 and that provided under the Mutual Defense Assistance Act of 1949. This suspended aid totalled $75 million. This policy was reviewed in July, 1950, by the Joint Chiefs-of-Staff, at the request of the Department of State. The Joint Chiefs, on review, held that Formosa was of strategic value to the United States, and that the continuance of Chinese Nationalist resistance was important to the United States. They recommended, consequently, a revival of military aid to the Nationalists and the making of a survey of their forces on the island by General MacArthur and his staff.

In implementation of the new policy of military assistance, a Military Assistance Advisory Group was constituted and entered upon its duties early in 1951. Under its advice and with assistance in the form of equipment from the United States, the National Government made steady progress in transforming its forces on Formosa from the ill-disciplined horde evacuated from the mainland into a military force capable of defending the island from Communist attack. The odds which had been strongly in favor of Communist success if an invasion had been attempted in January of 1950 had been reversed by 1953 when it could be reasonably concluded that the Nationalists were capable of a successful defense of Formosa. In this reversal the shift in

American policy brought about by the North Korean attack on the Republic of Korea played a large part.

The time necessarily spent by the Communists in preparing an assault on Formosa to ensure its success, to be sure, gave the National Government a breathing space which it used to strengthen its defensive position. Politically and economically it had to recover the position lost in Formosa during the initial years of misrule under the governor, Chen Yi, sent from the mainland to exercise National Government authority in 1945. Chen Yi, a former warlord who had come over to Chiang during the Northern Expedition in 1927, had viewed his Formosan assignment as giving him a new and fruitful field of financial exploitation. Chiang did nothing about Chen's misrule of the island until the situation was dramatized and gained outside notoriety when the people rose in revolt in 1947. In spite of the massacre of the revolters and the consequent suppression of the revolt, the conditions which produced it could no longer be disregarded by the National Government. Consequently Chen was replaced as Governor by Wei Tao-ming, former ambassador to the United States.[4]

NATIONAL GOVERNMENT RULE ON FORMOSA

The new governor found his efforts to reform the administration handicapped by a carry-over of important officials from the Chen regime. Increased attention was, however, paid to Formosa by the Nanking government as, by the latter part of 1948, deteriorated conditions in China caused Chiang Kai-shek to give it his personal attention as the place from which Nationalist resistance might have to be continued against the Communists. With this in mind, Chiang, on January 5, 1949, replaced Wei Tao-ming as Governor of Formosa with General Ch'en Ch'eng, who could be expected to exercise his authority more vigorously. Martial law was immediately instituted by the new governor. On the charge of being Communist sympathizers there were numerous arrests and executions. Economic conditions, however, became worse instead of better and the new administration

[4] Chen was, however, "given a face-saving job and ultimately the governorship of Chekiang province. In January, 1948, however, this opportunistic war-lord secretly connived with Communist agents to surrender his province. Learning of the plot, Nationalist police arrested Chen and on June 18, 1950 a firing squad in Formosa brought to an end his career of duplicity and personal profiteering." Fred W. Riggs, *Formosa under Chinese Nationalist Rule* (New York: Macmillan, 1952), p. 44. Quoted by permission of the publishers.

was less successful than its predecessor in gaining the good will and the confidence of the Formosans. With the transfer of the seat of the National Government to Formosa, however, General Ch'en was made the head of its Executive Yuan and Mr. K. C. Wu became head of the provincial government. Mr. Wu, as Mayor of Chungking and then of Shanghai, had an established reputation as a progressive and efficient administrator. Both he and General Ch'en, with the removal of the National Government to Taipei, were brought under the direct supervision of Chiang Kai-shek, who came to perceive the necessity of instituting reforms in provincial as well as national administration for two purposes. These were: (1) to develop sufficient strength in Formosa for purposes of defense and to enable the island to function as the base of operations in an invasion of the mainland; and (2) to enable the National Government, by example, to re-establish itself in non-Communist mainland and overseas Chinese thinking as an acceptable and preferable alternative to the Chinese Communist Party.

ECONOMIC AND POLITICAL REFORM

All of the reports from Formosa indicated that the situation had been greatly changed by 1953. As an informed writer put it:

> There is general concurrence among postwar American visitors to Formosa in the view that, on the whole, substantial progress has been made there since the Chinese re-occupation. Those who differentiate between the parts played respectively by the National Government and by the Provincial Government speak more enthusiastically of the latter. Nevertheless, since the National Government has jurisdiction over some of the enterprises and exercises jointly with the Provincial Government jurisdiction over other enterprises that have contributed to economic recovery, the former must share with the latter the credit for what has been accomplished.[5]

In this differentiation between the work of the provincial and that of the National Government in connection with economic recovery, the National Government's major achievement, as well as its major effort, had been to transform the troops evacuated from the mainland into a disciplined and effective fighting force. Its actual success in this could not be definitively determined until military operations of either an offensive or a defensive nature had been undertaken. In the absence

[5] Joseph W. Ballantine, *Formosa: A Problem for United States Foreign Policy* (Washington: The Brookings Institution, 1952), p. 181. Quoted by permission.

of such a definitive basis of judgment, however, it could only be concluded from current reports that the military position on Formosa
had undergone real improvement. General MacArthur's testimony to
this in 1951 reads:

> The generalissimo has probably in the neighborhood of a half million
> troops. The personnel is excellent. . . . They have good morale. Their
> material is spotty. They lack artillery. They lack trucks. They lack a good
> many of the modern refinements. They are capable of being made into
> a very excellent force. . . . My own estimate would be, after the material
> was there, that those troops would be in very good shape, probably as
> good as they ever could be made outside of combat, within four months.[6]

After 1951, military assistance from the United States was increased. At the same time the Military Assistance Advisory Group from
the United States was enlarged so as to give the maximum assistance
in training the Chinese in the proper care and use of the new equipment. In this way many of the weaknesses noted by General Mac-
Arthur in 1951 had been materially lessened by 1955. This gave non-
Kuomintang observers, as well as overseas Chinese, a totally different
impression of the strength of the Nationalist position from that which
had been warranted four years earlier.

A comparable achievement had taken place in the development of
the Formosan economy to the point where exports were sufficient in
amount and in value to provide a surplus over imports, except for the
military supplies and economic aid furnished by the United States.
The increase in production was sufficient not only to yield an export
surplus but also to sustain over a million refugees from mainland China
and the military and civilian personnel of the National Government
in addition to providing the upkeep of the provincial government.
Refugee and evacuated personnel represented a substantial increment
to the Formosan population which was estimated in 1946 at slightly
more than six million persons.

This improved economic position was made possible in part because
of American economic assistance. The operation of this factor in recovery has been summarized as follows:

> Roughly speaking the American aid program falls into three stages. The
> first stage can be identified as the period during which Formosa was a
> residuary legatee of the then operating China aid program. The second

6 *Joint Committee Hearings*, Pt. I, pp. 23-24.

stage corresponded approximately with the period when public discussion in the United States of American policy in the Far East was most intense. During this period, the continuation and expansion of economic aid served as a partial compensation for a suspension of military aid and for an unwillingness to make drastic policy commitments respecting Formosa. It could also be regarded as a hedge against the possible immediate consequences of failure to adopt a positive course, since it was calculated to enable the National Government to deal with the internal problems of Formosa and to stabilize its position. The third stage, marked by the resumption of military assistance, was prompted by the outbreak of the conflict in Korea.[7]

During the third stage, it must be emphasized, the United States affirmatively committed itself to the National Government on Formosa as the government of China. As Dean Rusk, the Assistant Secretary of State for Far Eastern Affairs, put it in an address on May 18, 1951, shortly before the outbreak of war in Korea:

We recognize the National Government of the Republic of China even though the territory under its control is severely restricted. We believe it more authentically represents the views of the great body of the people of China, particularly their historic demand for independence from foreign control. That government will continue to receive important aid and assistance from the United States. Under the circumstances, however, such aid cannot be decisive to the future of China. The decision and the effort are for the Chinese people, pooling their efforts, wherever they are, in behalf of China.[8]

This commitment became firmer under the double pressure of domestic debate and the continuation of the war against the Chinese Communists in Korea. The result was not only the resumption of military assistance but also the increasing of the American economic assistance which had continued after military aid had been withdrawn. The end-product was a change in attitude toward the military potentialities of the Formosan regime.

American aid was an undeniable factor in bringing about economic recovery in Formosa but the institution of reform, which was essential to its successful utilization, was even more important. Without reform it would have been impossible to enlist the energies of the Formosan people in the increase of production since otherwise the

[7] Ballantine, *op. cit.*, p. 132.
[8] Full text, in U.S. Department of State, *Bulletin*, Vol. 24 (May 28, 1951), pp. 746, 848 ff.

beneficiaries would have been only those supported by the National Government. Political reform, which had the effect of associating the Formosans with the operation of provincial and local government, helped to bring about a change of attitude, as did the increasing opening of educational opportunities at all levels to the Formosans. In relation to economic development, however, the land reforms instituted in and after 1949 had the greatest significance. These took the form initially of rent reduction from the custom-fixed level of 50 per cent or more of the crop produced to 37.5 per cent. This gave the tenant farmers an immediate increase in income, thus improving their standard of living and at the same time giving them a great incentive to increase production. The enforced reduction of rentals also brought about a drop in land values which enabled the tenants to use their new surplus to acquire land through purchase. Twenty-four thousand tenants, during 1951-52 took advantage of the new opportunity to acquire land of their own. In 1952 almost a third of the public lands was distributed among some 100,000 farming families. Under legislation then proposed, furthermore, landlords would have been required to sell lands which they were not themselves cultivating at a reasonable price, and with payment to be made on a long-term basis.

The falling-off of production after 1945 was not, of course, solely or even primarily due to tenant-landlord relations. Thus reform along the lines taken was not in itself sufficient to bring about increase in agricultural production. This required, among other measures, the resumption of fertilization of the fields. "In 1938 a total of 389,300 tons of fertilizer had been used on rice fields. In 1945 the amount had fallen to 1,960 tons. In 1950 a total of 235,000 tons of fertilizer was used, making a major contribution to increased productivity." Here was one place where American assistance was important since the "ECA played a large role in this program, providing 140,000 tons as of October, 1950. By the end of 1951 ECA had paid for more than $40 million worth of fertilizer. As a result about 280,000 tons of fertilizer were distributed during 1951, and the goal for 1952 is 375,000." [9]

The result of the new program, using rice production for purposes of illustration, was a restoration of and slight increase over, prewar production. The 1938 production was 1.4 million metric tons. This had fallen in 1945 to 0.64 million tons. The rice production figure for

[9] Riggs, op. cit., p. 71.

1952 was 1.6 million metric tons, an increase of 200,000 tons over 1951. A similar recovery in the production of other food crops occurred. There was not, however, restoration of production of the prewar export crops—sugar, pineapples, tea, camphor—to the prewar level. This was partly the result of conditions in the former market countries. Nevertheless, as noted above, there had been sufficient recovery to enable the necessary imports to be somewhat more than paid for by exports. Thus Formosa provided a more solid economic base for the National Government in 1954 than had appeared probable in 1950.

USE OF NATIONAL GOVERNMENT FORCES ON THE MAINLAND

At the outset of the Korean War the National Government had offered a contingent of 33,000 troops to serve as part of the United Nations force in Korea. This offer was rejected. The rejection was put on the ground of the necessity of not diverting any Nationalist troops from the defense of Formosa. An undeclared reason for declining the offer, however, was lack of confidence in the military capabilities of the troops on Formosa. It was also apparent that their use in Korea would complicate an already difficult situation. The South Koreans made it clear throughout that they were opposed to the introduction of Chinese Nationalist troops into the peninsula. This was especially the case after the Chinese Communist intervention, when the extensive use of Nationalist troops might have transformed Korea into the battleground on which the Kuomintang-Communist struggle would be continued. Britain, India, and other members of the United Nations which had broken off relations with the National Government and had recognized Peiping, furthermore, were opposed to action in Korea by the National Government since that would have further embarrassed their relations with Communist China.

As the conclusion was reached in the United States that the Formosan government had an effective army at its command which might be utilized against the Chinese Communists, but not in Korea, the ground was shifted to one of the ideas advanced by General MacArthur. This was that there should be a "removal of restrictions on the forces of the Republic of China on Formosa, with (American) logistical support to contribute to their effective operation against the common enemy" in South China and elsewhere, as a diversionary operation which would relieve pressure on the United Nations forces in Korea. This view was rejected by the Truman Administration when it was initially advanced in the spring of 1951. Such action might have had the diversionary effects anticipated. But the action and the commitment would not have been, from the National Government's point of view, restricted to effects on military operations in Korea. That government's objectives were the restoration of its power in mainland China, something which could be accomplished only through the overthrow of the People's Government. If the United States had lent Formosa the air and naval support necessary to effect and enlarge landings on the mainland, it might readily have found itself committed to the attainment of Nationalist purposes and thus to operations directed toward the complete restoration of the authority of the National Government throughout China. From the use of limited naval and air power in support of landing operations with a purely diversionary purpose in relation to Communist Chinese pressures in Korea, the United States might have had to extend its assistance to include the use of American ground forces, as had occurred in Korea. This would have put the United States in a state of war with China.

Engaged in war in China, it would have been difficult for the United States to extricate its forces if that were necessary to meet Soviet threats elsewhere. Under the circumstances, furthermore, United States support of the National Government in war on the mainland might have created the conditions for application of the alliance which had been made in 1950 between the U.S.S.R. and the People's government. If Russia intervened in behalf of China, its military action would not be necessarily or even probably undertaken in the Far East. So, at least, the argument ran. Such proposals as those made by General MacArthur raised fears among the Western European states concerning the ultimate willingness and ability of the United States to fulfill its obligations with respect to the defense of Western Europe against a possible Soviet attack. These fears had to be taken into account by Washington in formulating its policy since it was seeking to weld together and lead a coalition of independent states acting together in resistance to any aggression which might be undertaken by states in the Soviet bloc acting under the direction of the Kremlin. Consequently the United States continued to follow the policy of confining military operations to the Korean theater.

The policy of the Truman Administration, described by its critics as negative and as not being designed to bring either victory or a quick cessation of hostilities in Korea, was vigorously attacked by the Republicans in the presidential campaign of 1952 in the United States. The Republican promise of a positive policy leading toward an early end of the Korean War was an important factor in bringing about the election of the Republican candidate, General Dwight D. Eisenhower. In implementation of his campaign promises the President-elect made a trip of inspection to Korea to familiarize himself at first hand with conditions there. After his inauguration, however, he immediately changed policy in only one respect. He removed the American prohibition on Nationalist operations against mainland China. Such operations, of a guerrilla or commando-raid variety, had previously been undertaken by National Government forces and tolerated by the Americans. Consequently the change announced merely gave approval to what had previously been officially disregarded. Beyond that, it gave assent to an invasion of the continent by Nationalist troops if and when they had the power to attempt the renewal of the struggle for control of mainland China, but without commitment to assist in an attempted invasion. The position taken by the National Government itself that it lacked the power to undertake an invasion of the mainland without further preparation, further clarified the situation, by leading to the conclusion that the Formosan government had the power, which it had lacked in 1950, to defend its position on Formosa but not to resume war on the continent. Even this conclusion, however, had to be qualified since American naval power continued to be committed to the patrol of the Formosan Straits to prevent a Communist attack on Formosa during the period of United Nations military operations in Korea.

This continued relationship in American policy of Formosa and the Korean War gave Chiang Kai-shek and his supporters a very real interest in the negotiations leading to an armistice and in any political agreements reached with respect to Korea. American interest in the Indochina situation as it developed following the conclusion of an armistice in Korea, because of Peiping's support of Ho Chi-Minh, however, gave Chiang more assurance of continued American support against the Central People's Government than might otherwise have been the case.

BIBLIOGRAPHICAL REFERENCES

Bate, H. Maclear, *Report from Formosa* (New York: Dutton, 1952).

Ballantine, Joseph W., *Formosa: A Problem for United States Foreign Policy* (Washington: The Brookings Institute, 1952).

Chinese Weekly News Service (New York: Information Agency of Republic of China).

Economic Co-operation Administration, *U.S. Economic Assistance to Formosa, January 1 to 31* (Washington, December, 1950).

Grinsburg, Norton Sydney, *The Economic Resources and Development of Formosa* (New York: Institute of Pacific Relations, 1953).

Han, Lih-wu, *Taiwan Today* (Taipei, 1951).

Ravenholt, A., "Formosa Today" in *Foreign Affairs* (July, 1952).

Riggs, Fred W., *Formosa Under Chinese Nationalist Rule* (New York: Macmillan, for the Institute of Pacific Relations, 1952).

Smith, Robert Aura, *The Rebirth of Formosa* (New York: Foreign Policy Association, 1953).

Steiner, H. Arthur, "United States and the Two Chinas," *Far Eastern Survey*, May, 1953.

U.S. Department of State, *Bulletin*, March 23, 1953.

War in the Pacific: U.S. Carrier Force Strikes Wake Island in 1943

Peace Commission at Yenan, 1946. Left to right: Gen. Chou En-lai, Gen. George Marshall, Gen. Chu Teh, Gen.

United States 7th Infantry Occupying Seoul, Korea, 1945

Russian Occupation Troops in Pyongyang, Korea, 1947

Ho Chi Minh, President of Viet Minh

Premier Chou En-lai Opening the First [...]
Congress, 1954

U Nu, Prime Minister of Burma, and Mao Tse-tung

biro Hatoyama, Prime Minister of Japan

President Syngman Rhee of Korea

President Soekarno of 7th Republic
of Indonesia

Chiang Kai-shek, President of Chinese
National Government

Operation "Castor" During the Defense of Dien Bien Phu

Defensive Operation in Viet Nam

Ceremony Marking the Independence of Indonesia

Bandung Conference of Asian and African States, 1955

9

From Panmunjom to Geneva

❋❋❋❋❋❋❋❋❋❋❋❋❋❋❋❋❋❋❋❋❋❋❋❋❋❋❋

INSTITUTION OF ARMISTICE NEGOTIATIONS

A CHANGE in the situation of the Far East, especially as it turned on the question of Korea, came in the spring of 1953, following the death of Stalin. As pointed out above [1] the negotiations looking toward a truce in the Korean war had been intermittently carried on through 1952 without any agreement being reached. Following Stalin's death the Soviet government began to give indications of a willingness to negotiate seriously to bring about peace. With respect to the Far East, this took the form of a proposal for the resumption of negotiations looking toward an armistice in the Korean War. The first step in this direction was taken with the conclusion of an agreement to exchange sick and disabled prisoners of war. This was followed by negotiations on the general question, which still remained unanswered from the suspended truce talks, of the conditions for exchange of all prisoners of war.

It was over this question of repatriation of prisoners of war that truce negotiations had broken down during 1952 and early 1953. An early stumbling block to agreement had been presented in the Communist demand for agreement on a "high-level" political conference to be convened within ninety days from the conclusion of an armistice agreement. Following United Nations' acceptance of this proposal on February 19, 1952, the Communist delegation made an unacceptable additional proposal that such a conference, rather than being confined to consideration of the Korean question, should be authorized to discuss the complex of Far Eastern questions at issue between the United States and its allies, on the one side, and China, the U.S.S.R. and their allies, on the other. This disagreement, however, was resolved in favor

[1] Chap. 7.

of letting the governments concerned determine the agenda of the conference. Another point of disagreement was over the rights of the two sides to take actions, following the truce, which would affect the military *status quo* in the event of the resumption of hostilities. The specific point at issue was that of the postarmistice right to reconstruct or build airfields. The United Nations delegates, on April 28, proposed a formula under which they would have accepted the Communist requirement of the right to reconstruct or build airfields in north Korea, and thus to strengthen their military position for the future, in exchange for a Communist agreement that there should be no forcible repatriation of prisoners of war; and that a commission composed of representatives of Poland and Czechoslovakia for the Communists, and Sweden and Switzerland for the United Nations, should be established with powers of supervision of execution of the truce terms. The United Nations' proposal with respect to the supervisory commission, which both sides agreed should be constituted, was designed to avoid acceptance of Russia as a neutral in relation to the Korean War.

It was on the question of repatriation of prisoners of war that both sides took a firm stand on the ground of principle. The Communist position was based upon the Geneva Convention which provided for the automatic and obligatory repatriation of all prisoners of war after the conclusion of hostilities and the establishment of peace. The principle underlying United Nation opposition to involuntary repatriation was given forcible statement by President Truman when he said (on May 7, 1952): "We will not buy an armistice by turning over human beings for slaughter or slavery."

THE UNITED NATIONS SEEKS A FORMULA
FOR AN ARMISTICE

Following the breakdown of negotiations at Panmunjom on October 8 over this issue of forcible repatriation of prisoners of war, the General Assembly, through its Political and Security Committee, undertook to find a way out of the *impasse*. At the outset the positions of the two sides were reaffirmed. The United States and twenty other member states submitted a resolution the operative provision of which

Calls upon the Central People's Government of the People's Republic of China and upon the North Korean authorities to avert further bloodshed by having their negotiators agree to an armistice which recognizes the

POST-ARMISTICE KOREA

right of all prisoners of war to an unresticted opportunity to be repatriated and avoids the use of force in their repatriation.[2]

The Soviet Union, on October 29, proposed a resolution which was as significant for its omissions as for its definition of a basis of settlement. As originally offered, it proposed

> To establish a Commission for the peaceful settlement of the Korean question with provision for the participation of the parties directly concerned and of other States, including States which have not taken part in the Korean war.
>
> To instruct the said Commission to take immediate steps for the settlement of the Korean question on the basis of the unification of Korea, such unification to be effected by the Koreans themselves under the supervision of the above-mentioned Commission.[3]

Between the times of these definitions of position by the two principal protagonists in the Korean War, informal negotiations had been carried on with both sides by the Indian delegation to the United Nations' General Assembly.[4] As a result, and because, as Mr. Nehru subsequently put it,

> It seemed to our delegation, who kept in constant touch with us, that none of these resolutions offered any hope of a peaceful settlement, the Indian delegation tried to evolve a formula which might prove acceptable to the principal parties concerned as well as to others.

The Indian formula was submitted to the Political and Security Committee on November 17.[5] It was immediately forwarded by the

[2] UN Doc. A/C. 1/725. October 24, 1952.

[3] UN Doc. A/C. 1/729. A new paragraph was added November 23 recommending an "immediate and complete cease-fire ... the question of the complete repatriation of prisoners of war to be referred for its solution to the Commission for the peaceful settlement of the Korean question provided for in the U.S.S.R. draft resolution, in which Commission questions shall be decided by two-thirds majority vote of its members." The proposed resolution had also been changed on November 10 by the insertion of the states to compose the proposed commission: the U.S.A., the United Kingdom, France, the U.S.S.R., the People's Republic of China, India, Burma, Switzerland, Czechoslovakia, the People's Democratic Republic of Korea and South Korea. Another addition was the insertion of a statement that: "The steps to be taken (by the Commission) shall include comprehensive action to promote the repatriation of all prisoners of war by both sides." These changes were made in the light of discussion of the Indian resolution and for purposes of consistency. *Indian Press Digests* (Bureau of International Relations of the Political Science Department, University of California, Berkeley), Vol. 2, No. 3. p. 64.

[4] The quotations are from Nehru's Statement to Parliament on the Indian Resolution, December 15, 1952, as transcribed from *Indian Parliamentary Debates*, Part I, 15 December, 1952, and published in *Ibid*.

[5] The text of the Indian Resolution is in, General Assembly Resolution 610 (VII).

Indian government to Peiping which did not immediately express disapproval of the proposal but which informed the Indian government on November 24 that it was unacceptable. From that time the Soviet Union took the same position although earlier (November 19) the Soviet delegation,

> letting it be understood that they were also speaking for the Chinese, indicated to V. K. Krishna Menon, Deputy Leader of the Indian delegation, that the Indian plan was suitable as a "serious basis for discussion." They approved the proposal to refer prisoners who could not be sent home to a Political Commission, but objected to some clauses and opposed the provisional internment of unwilling prisoners under the control of an International Committee.[6]

The United States initially took the position that the Indian plan was not acceptable "in its present terms," but agreed (1) to its careful examination by an eight-nation drafting committee of the twenty-one nation group which had sponsored the original American resolution, and (2) finally to its being given priority over other resolutions, including its own, in Assembly discussions.

With some modifications made by India itself in the light of the discussions in the Political and Security Committee, the Indian Resolution was adopted (December 3) by a vote of 54-5 in a plenary session of the General Assembly. It remained inoperative, however, because of Soviet opposition and because of its formal rejection by Communist China on December 14. Thus the General Assembly's consideration of the terms of a Korean armistice failed to resolve the issues and left the problem unsolved. Nevertheless it helped to clear the way for agreement when, after the death of Stalin, Soviet Russia indicated a desire to reopen the negotiations.

A positive step toward an armistice was taken when an agreement was signed at Panmunjom on April 11, 1953, providing for the repatriation of sick and wounded prisoners of war "in accordance with provisions of article 109 of the 1949 Geneva Convention relative to prisoners of war." The execution of this agreement was followed by the conclusion on June 8 of an agreement on other prisoners of war. This followed the general lines of the Indian Resolution in working out the detailed arrangements for handling the repatriation of prisoners of war in the event of conclusion of an armistice. It provided that:

[6] *Ibid.*, p.9.

Within two months after the armistice agreement becomes effective, both sides shall, without offering any hindrance, directly repatriate and hand over in groups all of those prisoners in its custody who insist on repatriation to the side to which they belonged at the time of capture....

Both sides agree to hand over all those remaining prisoners of war who are not directly repatriated to the Neutral Nations Repatriation Commission for disposition.[7]

The Neutral Nations Repatriation Commission was to be constituted by appointment of members by Sweden, Switzerland, Poland, Czechoslovakia and India. Disposition of those prisoners who, "while in the custody of the detaining powers," had not "exercised their right to be repatriated" was to be made by the Commission in accordance with certain provisions controlling its action. Among these conditions was a stipulation that

No force or threat of force shall be used against the prisoners of war specified in paragraph 1 above to prevent or effect their repatriation and no violence to their persons or affront to their dignity or self-respect shall be permitted in any manner for any purpose whatsoever....

Provision was made, however, for an attempt by both sides to persuade those who were unwilling to be repatriated, and who were consequently to be transferred to the custody of the commission, to change their minds. These "explanations and interviews" were to be arranged "within ninety days after the Neutral Nations Repatriation Commission takes over the custody" and were to be "conducted in the presence of a representative of each member nation of the Neutral Nations Repatriation Commission and a representative from the detaining side."

POSITION OF THE GOVERNMENT OF THE
REPUBLIC OF KOREA

With this question of treatment of prisoners of war out of the way, the Communists on July 8, two years after the beginning of negotiations, expressed a qualified willingness to resume negotiations for an armistice. The qualification was with respect to the behavior of the South

---

[7] For text of the "Geneva Convention Relative to the Treatment of Prisoners of War" (1949), *Amer. Journal of International Law*, Vol. 47, No. 4, *Supplement, Documents*, pp. 119-71; text of "Agreement on Repatriation of Sick and Wounded Prisoners," *Ibid.*, pp. 178-80; text of "Agreement on Prisoners of War," *Ibid.*, pp. 180-86; Armistice Agreement, *Ibid.*, pp. 186-205.

Korean government, which had unilaterally released North Korean prisoners of war in its custody, without repatriating them. This enabled the Communists to raise a question of good faith in relation to the execution of agreements on prisoners of war and the willingness and ability of the United Nations Command to exercise control over the actions of the Koreans. Prompt protests of the South Korean government's action by the United States, in addition to protests of Britain, France, and Australia, as well as by Mr. Lester Pearson as President of the United Nations General Assembly, and an assurance by General Clark that efforts would be made to recover the released prisoners, enabled negotiations to be resumed.

This action of the government of the Republic of Korea and the resulting reaction to it pointed up dramatically one of the continuing anomalies in the Korean war situation. All of the agreements made were with respect to a war fought on Korean territory and with respect to the future of Korea. The government of Korea, however, was not in a position to define the attitude of its United Nations' allies as to the solution of the Korean question or the termination of the war. Although recognized as the government of the country, it found itself in effect the ward of the recognizing states, some of whom were not in sympathy with it. Even in the United States there was an adverse reaction to any attempt on the part of the South Korean government to act as if it were what it had been officially recognized as being—the government of an independent state. Thus President Syngman Rhee's attitude was viewed as presumptuous and obstructive when he indicated his government's willingness to renew armistice negotiations only if it were understood that a time limit of three months would be set within which negotiations would have to be concluded, with the war to be resumed if a satisfactory armistice had not been concluded. An armistice satisfactory to President Rhee would have provided for the immediate withdrawal of all United Nations and Chinese forces, with military security provided by a United States guarantee of the Republic of Korea. The criticism of his attitude was even more severe when, on June 24, he declared that existing armistice proposals were unsatisfactory to his government, and that if they were embodied in an agreement he would withdraw all R.O.K. forces from the United Nations Command.

The attitude of President Rhee at this time, as well as after the conclusion of the armistice, was fixed by a determination to commit the

United States and the United Nations not to accept a settlement which
would preclude or make impossible of early attainment the objective
of unification of Korea under his government. The United Nations
primary objective in relation to the war had been set as that of preventing successful aggression, even though it had accepted the South
Korean government as the government of the Republic of Korea, and
had, in the General Assembly Resolution of October 7, 1950, set up
unification as a war objective, although not necessarily under the Rhee
government. While the United States was further committed than was
the United Nations to unification and to the Rhee government, the
primary campaign commitment of the Eisenhower administration was
to bring military action in Korea to an end if that could be accomplished without further extension of the Communist position south of
the 38th parallel. This could be realized on the basis of an armistice the
terms of which might put South Korea in the position of the aggressor
if its government should seek subsequently to accomplish unification
by military means. Thus Syngman Rhee's government had to use all
of the resources at its command to prevent the conclusion of an armistice advantageous to its principal supporters but disadvantageous to it
in relation to the attainment of its objective of establishment of control
over the territories of the Republic of Korea. In doing so, however, it
had to reckon with the possibility that too extreme attitudes might
have the reverse effect from that sought.

The initial pressure had the effect of bringing Assistant Secretary of
State Robertson to Seoul and Tokyo to discuss the situation with
President Rhee. These discussions resulted in an agreement on June 25
on collaboration between the two governments in the carrying on of
armistice negotiations, together with a promise on the part of President Rhee not to obstruct further in the move toward an armistice or
in the postarmistice period. On the eve of conclusion of the armistice
agreement, Secretary Dulles said that President Rhee had given written
assurances that he would not obstruct the implementation of the armistice agreement. But two days later (July 24) Rhee raised objections
to the entry of Indian troops into Korea; to some of the provisions in
the agreement on the prisoner of war question; and to the time limit
for the holding of the postarmistice political conference. In the same
statement he stipulated that it would have to be understood that South
Korea would have the right to resume hostilities if the political conference failed to reach a satisfactory agreement on the Korean question.

THE TERMS OF THE ARMISTICE

The armistice agreement was finally signed on July 27, 1953, but without its formal acceptance by the representative of the South Korean government. Its first article established a military demarkation line and a demilitarized zone between the opposing armies. The second article, divided into three sections, laid down arrangements for a cease-fire and armistice, created a Military Armistice Commission to carry out the armistice, and set up the Neutral Nations' Supervisory Commission to supervise the armistice. Article three dealt with the question of repatriation of prisoners of war. It provided: (1) that all prisoners of war wishing repatriation would be exchanged at Panmunjom (or at additional points if necessary) within two months of the conclusion of the armistice; (2) that prisoners of war refusing repatriation during the two-months period would be placed in the custody of a Commission consisting of Sweden and Switzerland, for the United Nations side, and Poland and Czechoslovakia for the Communist side, with India serving as the chairman. The prisoners of war refusing repatriation were to be in the custody of the Commission for a three months' period, during which time political representatives of their home countries would be permitted to interview them (in the presence of representatives of the Supervisory Commission) with a view to persuading them to return home; (3) that the disposition of prisoners of war who still refused repatriation after the end of the three months' period would be referred to the political conference which it was recommended should be held within three months of the conclusion of the armistice; (4) that if the political conference failed to reach agreement on this matter within thirty days, the remaining North Korean prisoners would be released in Korea or sent to a neutral country, as they might choose, while Chinese prisoners refusing repatriation would be sent to a neutral country; and (5) that all Korean and foreign civilians desiring to return home would be assisted to do so; that joint Red Cross teams would assist in all repatriation processes and inspect prisoner-of-war camps; and that both sides would be required to furnish information about prisoners who had died or escaped during captivity. The fourth article stated (in the form of a recommendation by the opposing commanders to the governments concerned) that a high-level political conference would be convened within three months of the armistice to settle through negotiation the withdrawal of all foreign troops from Korea and the peaceful settlement of the Korean question.

The armistice agreement brought military operations to an end but Korea remained in the international spotlight for two principal reasons. The first was the continuing interest in the prisoner-of-war question during the period of repatriation and then of "explanations." The second was because of the protracted discussions concerning the composition and agenda of the recommended political conference.

The repatriation of prisoners of war wishing to return home had been completed by September 6 and without much controversy since the operation fell within the normal pattern of such action at the end of a war. The complications in connection with repatriation grew out of the opportunity given the individual to "choose between repatriation and/or release, thus conforming to the ethical and humanitarian view of the situation rather than following the traditional and more rigid pattern of universal repatriation," [8] coupled with the right to try to persuade the individual refusing repatriation to change his mind. The complications of applying a new point of view and a new procedure were increased because of the administration of the new procedure by a commission which was called neutral but which was so constituted as to include states whose political relationships were such as to preclude really neutral behavior. Under the circumstances ultimate responsibility for the taking of decisions on controversial questions fell upon the Indian member of the Neutral Nations Repatriation Commission since Poland and Czechoslovakia invariably took the same position on the Chinese side of all questions. This responsibility had a somewhat tempering effect on the Indian government's point of view, although it cannot be said to have changed it.

The greatest number of prisoners refusing repatriation were North Koreans and Chinese. Consequently the quantitative burden of interviewing within the agreed time rested on the Communists rather than the United Nations. As they met with little success in persuading their reluctant nationals to accept repatriation they began to place obstacles in the way of completion of the process of interviewing within the stipulated time. They were encouraged to procrastinate because of failure to agree on the composition of the political conference. It was assumed apparently that the ultimate disposition of the prisoners of

[8] Pitman B. Potter, Editorial Comment, *American Journal of International Law*, Vol. 47, p. 661.

war remaining in the custody of the Commission could not be made until a conference had been held.

When, however, the stipulated period of three months had passed without agreement on the conditions of establishment of a political conference, the prisoners refusing repatriation were released and the question of their disposition closed.

The recommendation in the Armistice Agreement for the holding of a political conference brought the Korean question back into United Nations discussions. On the day the armistice was signed the sixteen nations contributing forces to the United Nations Command in Korea declared themselves to be willing to support United Nations efforts to bring about an equitable settlement in Korea based upon United Nations principles. These were declared to call for a united, independent and democratic Korea. The sixteen nations further declared, with an eye on the South Korean government as well as the Communists, that they would support fulfillment of the armistice terms and resist any breach of the armistice.[9]

The reference above to the South Korean government recalls earlier statements concerning the attitude of that government toward the armistice, which it did not formally accept. Syngman Rhee's general point of view was reiterated on August 15 when he expressed the belief that the United Nations had "deliberately decided against victory as the goal." He expressed again the view that unification would be the only test of the success or failure of the recommended political conference. His government's "wish and determination" he said was "to march north at the earliest possible time to save our North Korean brethren."

Knowing this attitude of the South Korean government, immediately after the signature of the Armistice Agreement the American Secretary of State, Mr. John Foster Dulles, went to Korea to reassure President Rhee as to the attitude of the American government with respect to the political conference. This reassurance was given through the conclusion of a Mutual Security Treaty. The treaty provided: (1) for the peaceful settlement of international disputes, both parties committing themselves to refrain from the threat or use of force in any way inconsistent with United Nations obligations; (2) for consultation in case either was threatened with external armed attack when,

[9] This agreement was signed on the day of the armistice but not officially released until August 17.

separately and jointly, by self-help and mutual aid, the parties were to maintain and develop appropriate means to deter armed attack, and take suitable measures in consultation and agreement to implement the treaty and its purposes; (3) for the recognition of armed attack on either as dangerous to the other, with the attack to be met by each in accordance with its constitutional processes; (4) that the Republic of Korea grant and the United States accept the right to dispose United States' land, air, and sea forces in and about the territory of the Republic of Korea, as determined by mutual agreement; (5) for ratification in accordance with the constitutional processes of the two signatories; and (6) for its indefinite continuation, although it was made terminable one year after notice of termination by either party.[10]

On the same day a statement was jointly released by President Rhee and Secretary Dulles stating the meaning of the treaty in relation to the immediate situation. The first paragraph of this statement defined the agreement as providing for automatic reaction of the two states in joint defense in the event of a breach of the armistice terms. The second paragraph stated that

> The armistice contemplates that a political conference will be convened within three months—that is, prior to October 27, 1953. At that conference the United States delegation, in cooperation with the ROK delegation and other delegations from the United Nations side, will seek to achieve the peaceful unification of Korea as a free and independent nation . . . If, after the political conference has been in session for ninety days, it becomes clear to each of our governments that all attempts to achieve these objectives have been fruitless, and that the conference is being exploited by the Communist delegates to infiltrate, propagandize, or otherwise embarrass the Republic of Korea, we shall be prepared to make a concurrent withdrawal from the conference. We will then consult further regarding the attainment of a unified, free, and independent Korea. . . .

The Joint statement then reads:

> We recognize that the Republic of Korea possesses the inherent right of sovereignty to deal with its problems, but it has agreed to take no unilateral action to unite Korea by military means for the agreed duration of the conference.

While designed by the United States to maintain a measure of control over South Korean policy and in the process assure its allies in the

---

[10] The treaty initialed by Secretary Dulles was formally signed in Washington on October 1, and subsequently ratified by both states.

Korea War that the Rhee government would neither violate the armistice nor prevent an attempt at peaceful settlement, the treaty, together with the joint statement, also had the effect of establishing a measure of ROK control over the policy of the United States. It thus rendered it more difficult for the United States to use Korea for bargaining purposes in relation to other problems if it had been inclined to do so. In the move to bring the political conference into being and in the actual consideration of the question of Korea at the Geneva conference this double reaction was repeatedly revealed.

THE QUESTION OF COMPOSITION OF A POLITICAL CONFERENCE

A special session of the United Nations General Assembly debated the question of composition and terms of reference of the recommended political conference from August 18 until August 27, 1953. Before debate was opened in the Political Committee, the attempt was again made by the Soviet delegation to have an invitation to participate extended to North Korea and to Communist China. This raised anew the question of seating the Central People's Government in the United Nations in place of the National Government as a central issue in Far Eastern politics, and one of major importance in the settlement of the Korea question. The Vishinsky motion on China was defeated by a vote of 34-14 and that on North Korea by 34-18. In both cases India and a number of Arab-Asian countries voted with the Soviet bloc or abstained from voting. In this way India, at least, sought to indicate the importance it attached to the recognition of the Chinese Communist regime, and its belief that Asian questions should be settled principally by Asian nations.

On the substantive question of the composition of the political conference, the difference of opinion developed in the debate in the General Assembly was between the United States' view that the conference should be restricted to the belligerent nations and the view that it should be extended into a round-table conference participated in by the U.S.S.R., India, and other states. Thus the resolution first presented by the United States and fourteen other members of the sixteen nations contributing forces to the Unified Command in Korea provided that the United Nations participants in the political conference should be the states contributing armed forces to the United Nations

Command. Under the terms of this resolution India and the U.S.S.R., among others, would not have been invited to participate. China and North Korea, and possibly such other states as they were willing to invite to sit on their side of the table would have constituted the opposing delegation. Against this, the U.S.S.R. proposed an eleven-nation conference, the participants to be the United States, Britain, France, the U.S.S.R., the Chinese People's Republic, India, Poland, Sweden, Burma, North Korea, and South Korea. This would have denied representation to a number of states which had made military contributions to the United Nations' effort to repel aggression in Korea, while weighting the representation against the United Nations itself, from that point of view, as well as against the United States and South Korea. The Russian resolution stipulated that decisions should be taken at the conference when consented to by the states which had signed the Armistice Agreement, thus excluding South Korea, as a nonsignatory, from a decisive voice in the conference.

The united front of the sixteen nations was breached to a limited extent when Britain and France took the position that the conference should not be confined to the military participants in the Korean war but should be made into a round-table, rather than an across-the-table, conference through the inclusion of India and the U.S.S.R. This the United States refused to accept, since it implied (1) Russian neutrality in the struggle, and (2) that the states, such as India, which had refused to accept equal responsibilities with others for the support of the United Nations should have an equal voice with those who had accepted responsibility in the settlement of the issues involved. The United States maintained that the U.S.S.R. had throughout actively supported North Korea and thus could only be viewed as one of the belligerents. Consequently Washington took the position that it would accept Russia as a participant in the proposed conference if Russia was invited to participate by China and North Korea, thus in effect making the U.S.S.R. a co-belligerent with them. As a method of conciliating India and of recognizing India's efforts in behalf of peace, the United States suggested that the settlement of the Korean War, to which the proposed conference should be confined, might properly be followed by a general Far Eastern conference in which India might be expected to play a leading role.

The fifteen-nation resolution was adopted by the General Assembly by vote of 42-7 (with 10 abstentions). The Soviet resolution was separately voted upon, being rejected by a vote of 41 against to 7 in favor, with 13 abstentions. On the other hand, when the question of Soviet participation, "provided the other side desires it" was put it was answered decisively in favor (55-2, with 2 abstentions). On the question of Indian participation, the vote was 27 for, 21 against, and 11 abstentions. Except for Greece, Pakistan, and Nationalist China, all the votes against Indian participation came from Western hemisphere states, and thus from those who were accustomed to follow American leadership on such matters. In spite of the favorable vote, because of its closeness, India withdrew its name as a possible participant, on grounds which the American representative called "statesmanlike."

The adopted resolution left it to the United States to arrange with North Korea and China for a conference to be held not later than October 28 at a place satisfactory to both sides. The adoption of this resolution, of course, did not commit the Communist Chinese or North Korea to its terms which were described, September 13, by the Chinese Premier and Foreign Minister, Chou En-lai, as not completely satisfactory. His counterproposals were: the addition, by invitation, of the Soviet Union, India, Indonesia, Pakistan and Burma; a round-table discussion, but with all decisions to be unanimously accepted by both belligerent sides; China and North Korea to be invited to the General Assembly meeting to discuss the composition of the political conference; and the belligerents to arrange the time and place of meeting after agreement on the composition of the conference. Subsequently (October 11) the Chinese suggested further discussions between the belligerents to determine the time and place of the proposed conference. The United States took up this suggestion and direct negotiations were resumed at Panmunjom, Mr. Arthur Dean being sent to Korea from the United States for that purpose.

The negotiations, which extended from October 26 to December 12, again failed to produce an agreement because of the question of composition of the conference. The United States refused to accept the Chinese list of states to be invited since it included, beyond the belligerent states, the U.S.S.R., India, Indonesia, Pakistan, and Burma as neutrals. As an alternative the United States proposed that the Soviet Union be invited by China and North Korea not as a neutral but as a participant on their side; and that India, Sweden, Switzerland, Poland, Czechoslovakia, Pakistan and Chile be invited to attend as nonvoting members but otherwise with full rights. With no agreement in sight,

Mr. Dean made a final proposal on December 8 that (1) Geneva be the place of meeting, the conference to be held within a period of twenty-eight to forty-two days from the time of conclusion of an agreement at Panmunjom; (2) participants with voting powers be limited to the sixteen United Nations countries with forces in Korea, South Korea, North Korea, China and the U.S.S.R.; and (3) neutrals be invited to participate in the discussions but without the right to propose resolutions or to vote in the taking of decisions. This "final proposal" was characterized by the Chinese as absurd, ridiculous, and meaningless. It was consequently rejected. At the same time the Chinese delegate reiterated charges of perfidy against the United States. This led Mr. Dean summarily to break off negotiations in protest against the constant repetition of such unwarranted charges.

They were merely the last, not the worst, charges which had been constantly levelled against the United States during the course of the war and during the periods of negotiation. The Communists had utilized every opportunity to wage a propaganda campaign of defamation against the United States. With respect to the charges made which were susceptible of proof, such as that of engaging in germ warfare, the United States had, with exemplary self-restraint, invited objective investigation into the truth or falsity of the charges. In every case the charges had been reiterated but opportunity for their serious investigation had been refused by the Communist states, including the Soviet Union. The Chinese had, to be sure, rigged evidence in Peiping on the germ warfare charge and presented it to their friends, but without an opportunity for careful examination of the evidence. To the extent to which the evidence was made available and was subjected to scientific examination it was found to be fraudulent. This, however, did not prevent the widespread dissemination of the charges in the countries of eastern Asia and their acceptance as true because reiterated where there was a will to believe the worst of the United States. It was this utilization of negotiation for purposes of psychological warfare rather than agreement which caused Secretary Dulles and President Rhee, in their Joint Statement, to stipulate a determination to make a "concurrent withdrawal from the conference" when it again became clear that it was designed for exploitation "by the Communist delegates to infiltrate, propagandize, or otherwise embarrass the Republic of Korea." Experience had given even more justification for termination of conference when that point had been reached in terms of the position of the United States.

Since the United States sought to avoid the solution of the Korean question by military means, the breakdown of the negotiations at Panmunjom was not followed by military action to "attain a unified, free, and independent Korea," although that would apparently have been welcomed by the Rhee government which had technically regained its freedom to act unilaterally since no conference had been convoked during the agreed period, and none seemed immediately in prospect. In fact, however, it lacked the power to proceed without the support of the United States.

It was, consequently, during a conference held at Berlin on the German and Austrian questions, January 25-February 18, 1954, among the Foreign Ministers of the United States, Britain, France, and the U.S.S.R., that a conference on Korea was finally agreed on. At the Berlin Conference Mr. Molotov suggested a five-power conference on the Korean question and on that of Indochina. His initial suggestion was rejected on the double ground that: (1) there was no reason to believe that the five powers could solve world problems among themselves, an idea which Mr. Dulles pointed out had been rejected at the San Francisco Conference on the United Nations Charter; and (2) that channels already existed, in the United Nations, for settling both the Korea and Indochina questions. In connection with the Russian proposal Secretary Dulles put his finger on another principal objection to a five-power conference when he said:

> It seems to us that the proposal for a five-power conference to include the Chinese Communist regime is primarily a device to attempt to secure for that regime a position in the councils of the world which it has not earned and which it has not had accorded to it by the international community generally.[11]

Nevertheless a conference was finally agreed upon. The communiqué issued on February 18, at the end of the Berlin Conference, read on this matter that:

> (1) The Foreign Ministers of the United States, France, the United Kingdom, and the Soviet Union, meeting in Berlin, considering that the establishment, by peaceful means, of a united and independent Korea

---

[11] *Keesing's Contemporary Archives, 1952-54*, p. 13439.

would be an important factor in reducing international tension and restoring peace in other parts of Asia:

(a) Propose that a conference of representatives of the U.S.A., the United Kingdom, France, the U.S.S.R., the Chinese People's Republic, the Republic of Korea, the People's Democratic Republic of Korea, and other countries whose armed forces participated in the hostilities in Korea, and which desire to attend, shall meet in Geneva on April 26 for the purpose of reaching a peaceful settlement of the Korean question;

(b) Agree that the problem of restoring peace in Indo-China will also be discussed at the Conference, to which representatives of the U.S.A., France, the United Kingdom, and the Chinese People's Republic and other interested states will be invited.

It is understood that neither the invitation to, nor the holding of, the above mentioned conference shall be deemed to imply diplomatic recognition in any case where it has not already been accorded.[12]

THE KOREAN QUESTION AT THE GENEVA CONFERENCE

In accordance with the understanding reached at Berlin, the United States, on February 26, issued invitations to South Korea and to the thirteen nations contributing forces to the United Nations Korean Command.[13] The Soviet Union, on its side, invited the Chinese People's Republic and North Korea.

This agreement met with considerable criticism in the United States because it meant negotiations with the Communist Chinese at the political level and thus was held to be the first step in a chain of events which would lead to the seating of the representatives of the People's Republic in the United Nations and to recognition. It could have been defended, entirely apart from the formal *caveat* in the communiqué with respect to recognition, by reference to the continued postarmistice negotiations, which had produced, by agreement, the recommendation that a political conference should be held. Because of the domestic political situation, however, Secretary Dulles was unable to rely on this line of defense, and so added to it the view that China would be a participant, but not on a level of equality with the others. It would be brought before the bar of public opinion rather than participating in judgment on its own cause. This, of course, went beyond the fact of

[12] *Ibid.*, pp. 13439-40.
[13] *Ibid.*, 13440. The United States, Britain, and France, of the sixteen nations, were not "invited" because they were sponsoring powers. The thirteen were: Australia, Belgium, Canada, Colombia, Ethiopia, Greece, Luxemburg, the Netherlands, New Zealand, the Philippines, Siam, South Africa, and Turkey.

the matter, as was revealed in the external reaction to Secretary Dulles' explanation of the Berlin agreement. It was even more clearly revealed at the Geneva Conference itself, where the chief Chinese delegate, Foreign Minister Chou En-lai, behaved as a principal in the negotiations, refusing the role both of culprit and that of Russian protegé. The discussion revealed, however, the central importance of China and of the question of recognition of the People's Government, in any attempt to find a pacific solution of Far Eastern political questions.[14]

By the time of convocation of the Geneva Conference the Indochina question had begun to assume even greater importance than that of Korea. It was in Indochina that the area of military action had been enlarged following the conclusion of the armistice in the Korean War. The development of the problem of Indochina is, however, treated elsewhere and need not be allowed to confuse the present discussion of the Geneva Conference in relation to the Korean question. Neverthless, it should be noted at this point that Mr. Nehru, on the eve of the conference, expressed the Indian point of view with respect to Indochina in much the same way as he had in connection with the termination of the Korean hostilities. On April 24 he issued an appeal for a cease-fire in Indochina and proposed a six-point plan for its accomplishment. He urged: (1) that all should desist from making threats or proposing action which would make it more difficult to bring about agreement on a cease-fire; (2) that the negotiation of a cease-fire be given priority on the conference agenda, and that cease-fire group be constituted to be restricted to France, the three Associated States of Indochina, and Vietminh; (3) that the complete independence of Indochina be proclaimed, since that was essential to a settlement; (4) that direct negotiations looking toward a settlement be instituted between the parties concerned; (5) that a nonintervention agreement be entered into, the agreement to be guaranteed by the United States, Britain, the Soviet Union, and Communist China; and (6) that the United Nations be kept informed on the matter.

[14] The situation as to recognition at the time of the Geneva Conference was that 25 countries had recognized. Eleven of these had Communist governments; seven more were Western European and Scandinavian (the United Kingdom, Denmark, Norway, Sweden, Finland, the Netherlands and Switzerland); seven were Asian countries (Afghanistan, Burma, Ceylon, India, Indonesia, Israel, Pakistan). The countries not recognizing were all of the Western hemisphere states (including Canada) Australia, New Zealand, South Africa, France, Belgium, Italy, West Germany, Austria, Spain, Portugal, Greece, Turkey, the Arab States, Persia, Siam, and the Philippines (43 in all).

It was not anticipated by either the United States or South Korea that the Geneva Conference would produce a satisfactory agreement on Korea since they had no reason to believe that the Communists had become willing to accept a settlement except on their own terms. It was, however, viewed as essential to make an earnest effort to reach agreement in order to demonstrate to the satisfaction of Britain and others, as well as India, that it was not the inflexibility of American policy, nor the bellicosity and unreasonableness of the Rhee government which presented the obstacle to peaceful settlement, but rather the lack of interest of the Communists in the establishment of international peace and security.

A general area of agreement on objectives would seem to have been marked out by the four sponsoring powers in the joint view expressed at Berlin that "the establishment, by peaceful means, of a united and independent Korea would be an important factor in reducing international tension...." Thus the search at the Geneva Conference was for an agreed method of bringing about unity in and establishing independence for Korea.

The South Korean formula for bringing about unity under one government was the complete implementation of the original United Nations resolution for the holding, under supervision, of free elections throughout Korea. All that remained to be accomplished, in President Rhee's view, was to hold United Nations' supervised elections in North Korea so that the seats in the Korean Parliament reserved for the people north of the parallel since 1947 could be filled. Since elections had just been held in South Korea, as prescribed by the terms of the constitution of the Republic, it was held to be unnecessary immediately to repeat the process there.

The Communist proposal for unity was that new elections be held throughout the entire country, as a result of which a new government representing all of Korea could be constituted. If supervision was necessary, this supervision should be provided jointly by the North and South Korean governments. This would, of course, put the two governments on a footing of equality in the move toward unification, in spite of the fact that a much larger proportion of the territory and the total population of Korea was within the jurisdiction of the government of the Republic of Korea than of the People's Democratic Republic of Korea.

As an adjustment between these two positions, and as one viewed as equitable, the United States came to support the proposal that elections should be held throughout Korea, but that they should be held under the supervision of the United Nations to ensure freedom of expression of opinion on the part of Koreans both north and south of the parallel.

With respect to independence, the South Korean government took the position that, prior to the holding of elections, which it came to accept for its own part of the country as well as for the northern zone, all Chinese forces must be withdrawn from Korea, while only the beginning might be made of withdrawal of United Nations' forces from the southern zone. In this respect, as well as on the question of method of supervision of elections, the Rhee government was firmly against any proposal which might have the effect of giving, even temporarily, political rather than military significance to the division of the country. For that reason it opposed proposals involving a move toward an ultimate solution of the problem of government through a postconference committee, with the status quo established by the armistice terms being maintained, but with arrangements being made administratively between the two governments for trade and communications between the two zones until a final agreement had been reached by the committee on complete governmental unification.

The decisive issue proved to be that of willingness or unwillingness of the Communist side to accept the United Nations as the responsible agency of supervision in any moves toward unification or independence through the withdrawal of "intervening" military forces. Since the Chinese, supported by the Soviet Union and North Korea, remained unwilling to accept United Nations supervision in Korea, the Geneva Conference failed to produce an acceptable solution to the Korean problem.

BIBLIOGRAPHICAL REFERENCES

Aspaturian, V., "What Should We Learn from Panmunjom?" *The Reporter*, January 19, 1954.

Keesing's Contemporary Archives (weekly) (London: Keesing's Publications, Ltd.), Vol. 9.

New York Times, Index.

Readers Guide to Periodical Literature, for further titles.

U. S. News and World Report, "Armistice in Korea: Text of Official Documents," August 7, 1953.

10

Imperialism and Nationalism
in Indochina

EFFECTS OF THE WAR ON COLONIAL POLICY

THE JAPANESE FOUND it impossible in the four-year period of the Pacific war to implant and organize the conception of regionalism in Greater East Asia. On the contrary, the net effect of the Japanese occupation of the European colonies in southeast Asia, and also in the Philippines and Indonesia, was to deepen and widen the channels of nationalism and anticolonialism on a country, rather than an area, basis. The colonies were, to be sure, actually liberated from the Japanese by those who had previously controlled them rather than by the efforts of an indigenous nationalist leadership. But the fact that the colonial power had been driven from the colony by Japan coupled with the circumstances of the war and of internal resistance in each country, conditioned the ability of the colonial power to re-establish the prewar status. The Dutch had shown an awareness of the need to make readjustments in their imperial arrangements in the declaration of policy made by Queen Wilhelmina at the end of 1942. They had assumed, however, that they would be able to plan the nature of the readjustments in Indonesia and would be able to execute the plan themselves. The British and the French, especially the former, had indicated a similar wartime awareness of the fact that the relationships of 1941 would need to be modified toward self-government, autonomy, or independence. Formal commitments as to change, however, were avoided, apparently for two principal reasons: (1) on the ground that no precise commitment could wisely be made in the absence of fairly exact knowledge of the situation and of the problem which would actually

SOUTHEAST ASIA

exist at the end of the war; and (2) on the assumption that the colonial power would be welcomed back into its colony because of a general acceptance of the beneficence of its rule in contrast with that of Japan. It was, therefore, assumed that the colonial power would be able to determine the nature and the rate of modification of prewar relationships.

The United States alone had previously established a commitment to independence for its former colony and had reached an agreement with Philippine Commonwealth leaders on a time-table for its progressive attainment. The United States, consequently, was able to offer its Philippine policy as an example to the colonial powers with whom it was allied in the war against Japan. Washington also made clear its sympathy with any policy of others directed toward extension of the area of self-government. Under war circumstances, however, Washington could only take the view that it necessarily conceded to others the right which the United States reserved to itself to determine the relationship of the imperial power to its colony. To have taken a different position would have been to weaken rather than strengthen the war effort against Japan. Consequently, each colonial power followed the course which seemed to it appropriate and within the limits set by its power; but each found itself compelled, either in the same or in a different fashion, to find a basis of agreement with native nationalist leaders on the postwar conditions of government. The countries involved presented a sufficiently different set of circumstances, from the point of view of their prior development, their situation during the war, and the conditions of their liberation from the Japanese, to warrant a separate examination of postwar developments in each colony in Southeast Asia, as well as in Thailand, Indonesia and the Philippines. This account can well begin with the country immediately south of coastal China, and the one which, with Korea, came to be most directly affected by the postwar situation in China itself.

In certain respects the war situation in Indochina was more complicated and confused than in other countries of the area. Upon the destruction of French power in Europe by Germany in 1940, the French Governor of Indochina accepted the authority of the Vichy government in France, and attempted to maintain the French position in Indochina by the adaptation of French policy to Japanese requirements. The immediate 1940-41 interest of Japan was in the establishment in Indochina of a base from which to conduct operations against the Chungking government. This was conceded as a result of German pressure exerted at the instigation of Japan on the Vichy government and through direct Japanese pressure on the colonial regime. But in the process of securing rights which would facilitate operations in the China war, Japan also moved to the point where, by the outbreak of the Pacific war, the entire colony was under its influence, with the Indochinese French government committed to work closely with Japan and to recognize "the predominant interest of Japan in the Far East in both the economic and the political domain." [1]

This collaboration of the French authorities with the Japanese, while it enabled the fiction of French rule to be maintained until shortly before V-J Day, had the effect of lowering French prestige in their colony as much as the ease of Japanese conquest at Singapore lessened that of Britain. The fact that a European colonial regime actually took its direction from Tokyo, even to the point of acquiescing in the military occupation of the colony, pointed up the new relations of Asia with Europe, even though they should prove to be temporary. Its significance was not obscured by the fact that anti-Vichy Frenchmen were assisted by a native underground in reaching Chungking, nor by the fact that an underground anti-Japanese movement of some proportions developed in Indochina.

This underground movement represented in effect the direction given by the war to the Indochinese nationalist movement. Resistance was directed, consequently, against colonialism itself rather than being exclusively an anti-Japanese and an anti-Vichy movement. This was obscured to some extent because of participation in the resistance by Frenchmen who were opposed to the Vichy regime and thus acted in opposition to the French colonial authorities. But it was revealed to be a fact at the time of the Japanese surrender.

NATIONALISM IN INDOCHINA

Nationalism in Indochina had its initial growth as a reaction against the early French policy of political, economic, and cultural "assimilation" to France of the colony of Cochin China and the protectorates of Cambodia, Annam, Tongking, and Laos. In the protectorates, to be sure, the native regimes continued to exercise nominal governmental

[1] Cordell Hull, *The Memoirs of Cordell Hull* (New York: Macmillan, 1948) Vol. I, pp. 903-4.

authority, and to some extent they were strengthened. Internal government was also based on respect for local custom and tradition where it did not come into conflict with the needs and interests of the colonial power. Nevertheless the whole administration was centralized in fact under the authority of the governor-general, whose seat of government was at Hanoi.

As it developed, nationalism was essentially Annamite, thus expressing itself particularly in Annam and Tongking. It was initially stimulated by the Japanese victory over Russia in 1904-5, then by the use of Annamites by France both as laborers and soldiers in World War I, and finally by the development and course of the nationalist revolution in China. Its leadership was found among the intellectuals who were educated in the French liberal tradition.

> Though France naturally never wanted an indigenous nationalist movement to destroy her sovereignty, French institutions were so impregnated with the liberal ideas of 1789 that they unconsciously fostered patriotism and a love of political liberty in subject people.[2]

Those who had the advantage of education under French auspices, consequently, were introduced to ideas which were given only very limited application in Indochina, and they themselves, while permitted a measure of social equality, were not used by the French in the higher administrative posts in their own country. Thus the introduction to French ideals which were strongly at variance with the practices of colonial government caused the intellectuals to become nationalists, agitating for self-government and independence, rather than supporters of the French regime and of cultural assimilation.

That the nationalist movement, before World War II, had not developed more strength may be explained in several ways. One important reason for its lack of strength is to be found in the demography of Indochina. The Annamites, the most vigorous single element, comprising 21,000,000 of the total population estimated in 1949 at some 27,000,000, occupied a land

> laid out in a uniquely strange pattern. It extends from the Tonkin (Red River) delta in the north to the southern tip of Cochin China, a distance of 750 miles. At its northern extremity it embraces 5,800 square miles and at its southern extremity, some 20,000 square miles, but between these two

[2] Rupert R. Emerson, Lennox A. Mills, and Virginia Thompson, *Government and Nationalism in Southeast Asia* (New York: International Secretariat, Institute of Pacific Relations, 1942), p. 198.

termini it is extremely narrow. In some parts of Annam the territory that is truly Annamite is only a few kilometers wide, and consists of coastal fishing villages, some distance behind which lie, first, former lagoons, now filled in and occupied by villages and rice fields, and then mountains which the Annamites have not approached and in which, at a short distance, the first Moi hamlets appear. In some sections Annamite territory is only a narrow corridor; elsewhere, as in certain mountain passes, no Annamites at all are to be found.[3]

But even this peculiar configuration was administratively broken up. French authority was first established in Cochin China. It was erected into a colony and brought much more effectively under French cultural and political influence than were the protectorates of Annam and Tongking. The other two protectorates, Cambodia and Laos, which completed French Indochina, were non-Annamite in population, being closer to the Thai; and they had been more affected by Indian than by Chinese culture, whereas the Annamite traditional system, social and political, was Chinese in origin. Both Cambodia and Laos had looked to France for support against encroachments from Siam, as well as against Annamite expansionism, which considerations lessened the anti-French appeal of the nationalists. Thus Annamite nationalism had not penetrated Cambodia or Laos, and it was less firmly rooted in Cochin China than in either Annam or Tongking.

Another weakening factor was the division, before 1941, of the nationalist movement into several parties with different aims. One (the Pham-puynhau Tongking Party)

> did not aim at separation from France, but struggled only to obtain constitutional reforms. There was also the revolutionary party of the young Annamites, which united nationalists and Communists until 1928, when the latter broke away. In addition, there was the nationalist Annamite Party, terrorists in close alliance with Cantonese groups.... Finally and most important, there was the Annamite party headed by Nguyen-Ai-Quoc (Ho Chi Minh) which was well organized and also relied on Canton and Moscow.[4]

A third element of weakness lay in the fact that none of these parties had mass support, except in times of economic distress. "The Annamite masses are, of course," says one writer, "not affected by ideological

[3] Pierre Gourou, "For a French Indo-Chinese Federation," *Pacific Affairs*, Vol. XX, No. 1, p. 24.
[4] Joseph Handler, "Indo-China: Eighty Years of French Rule," *Annals of the American Academy of Political and Social Science*, Vol. CXXVI, pp. 135-36.

considerations, but the hardness of their lives makes them susceptible
to any propaganda leading toward a change in which they would have
nothing to lose and everything to gain." [5] This was true in most of
the Asian countries. But in Indochina, where the nationalists could
blame the French for popular ills, the Chinese, as in Thailand, were
also available as a nationalist target. This was especially the case in
Cochin China and Cambodia, where about 85 per cent of the approximately 400,000 Chinese were to be found. Their position as economic
middlemen and as intermediaries between the ruling Europeans and the
native peasants and workers identified them as supporters of the rulers
and lessened the possibility of development, before the war, of a close
relationship between Indochinese nationalism and that of China.

Despite the failure of the parties to attain significant mass support,
and in spite of the differences which appeared among their leaders
resulting in division into separate parties, the fact remained that the
French had been confronted by a nationalist development in Indochina
before the outbreak of World War II, as had the Dutch in Indonesia,
the British in Burma, and the Americans in the Philippines. While
weak, it had still been able to force the belated introduction of limited
reform in 1928 and again in 1938. The anti-Japanese resistance movement drew together the divergent nationalist elements, who were assisted in forming an underground by those French opposed to Japanese
control of a French colony but not to the restoration of French rule
in Indochina. Consequently the Indochinese resistance movement, as
far as one developed much before the end of the war, presented a
mixture of motives and attitudes with respect to France but had a unified purpose with respect to Japan.

FRANCE AND THE REPUBLIC OF VIET NAM

When defeat was accepted as a certainty by Japan, that country
withdrew its support on March 9, 1945 from the (Decoux) French
regime and gave it to a government, which the Japanese authorities
assisted into being, headed by Bao Dai, Emperor of Annam. The authority of this government, however, was immediately disputed by
the nationalists who had been waging underground war against both
Japan and the Vichy-controlled colonial regime. The nationalists successfully displaced the Japanese-sponsored government in August, 1945.

[5] *Emerson* and Others, *op. cit.*, p. 204.

At that time they were organized as the Viet Nam Independence League, better known subsequently as the Viet Minh, a party acting under the leadership of the veteran nationalist as well as Communist, Ho Chi-minh. It was this party which caused Bao Dai to abdicate on August 25 in favor of the "Republic of Viet Nam" whose independence was declared formally by the nationalists on September 2, 1945. The Republic of Viet Nam was designed to include the French colony of Cochin-China and the protectorates of Annam and Tongking. The proclamation by the Viet Minh government of independence of these territories making up the Republic of Viet Nam, it was hoped, would settle the issue of colonialism.

The French, however, had no intention of withdrawing completely from Indochina, although the French Committee of National Union (the "Free French") promised extensive reform. General de Gaulle, on December 8, 1943, had declared that Indochina would be given "a new political status within the French community" after the war. This was to be accomplished through the extension and re-affirmation of liberty within the framework of a federal organization, and with Indochinese given access to all public offices and positions within the state. Customs and fiscal autonomy, he stated, would replace the prewar position of Indochina within the French economic system. Subsequently (March 24, 1945) the Liberation government in Paris announced a plan for an autonomous Indochinese federation within a French federal union. The new system was worked out in the provisions of the Constitution of the Fourth Republic. On March 6, 1946 France recognized the Republic of Viet Nam as a Free State, having its government, its Parliament, its army, and its finances, and forming part of the Indo-Chinese Federation and the French Union.[6]

The struggle which subsequently developed in Indochina was over the position of the states federated in Indochina to one another, and over the amount of freedom of France which each should have as a state in the French Union. An overly optimistic view of the effects of the new French policy was that:

Neither race, religion nor national origin would bar Indo-Chinese from any federal office in the Federation, the higher echelons of which had hitherto been all-French, while many of the lower ranks had been inadequately manned by a "white proletariat" that also came from France. A

[6] For the text of the Hanoi Agreement of March 6, Isaacs, *New Cycle in Asia* (New York: Macmillan, 1947) p. 169.

dual citizenship of the Indo-Chinese Federation and the French Union would open jobs to Indo-Chinese throughout the empire. Although foreign affairs and defense were to remain a French preserve, the Federation would have its own armed forces which would be open equally to Indo-Chinese and to nationals from elsewhere in the Union. On every front the Indo-Chinese were to receive encouragement to develop socially, culturally and economically.... Hitherto linked economically to France, to the detriment of its more natural ties with the Far East, the country was to develop closer relations with China and other non-French territories. For the first time under France, Indo-China was to enjoy freedom of thought, press, religion and assembly.[7]

The skeptical nationalist, however, gave a different interpretation to the conception of the French Union. In the absence of implementing action, he viewed it as a new formula designed to produce acquiescence in the restoration of a modified colonial order, and not as granting complete self-control with an enlargement of the field of opportunity for the Indochinese. Lack of clarity in the formulation of the exact status of the former colony in relation to France raised a question as to whether the nationalist demand for self-control could be met within the French Union.

Since the new program had not been co-operatively developed, and since it apparently fell short of independence or even, actually, of complete autonomy, its realization as a French program required that France should establish a reasonably firm control of the situation in Indochina at the end of the war. The possibility of French control was, however, initially reduced by the transfer by Japan of the power of government to the Indochinese. It was still further lessened on account of the fact that sufficient time elapsed between the Japanese surrender and the arrival of Allied forces to enable the proclaimed Viet Nam Republic to establish itself in Tongking, Annam, and Cochin China.

The Allied forces which initially arrived to receive the Japanese surrender were British south of the 16th parallel and Chinese north of it. Up to this point developments in Indochina were similar to those in Indonesia.[8] Subsequently an important difference was revealed. The British at Saigon released French troops from internment, armed them, and transferred control of the city to the French. In the process the

---

[7] Ellen J. Hammer, "Blueprinting a New Indo-China," *Pacific Affairs*, Vol. 21, No. 3, pp. 252-53.
[8] On this contrast, Chap. 13.

Viet Nam was forcibly driven from Saigon. There was nothing in the nature of *de facto* recognition of the local regime by the British, as there was in Indonesia. Nor did the timing of the French offer to negotiate, or its recognition of the Viet Nam Republic in the north present the same appearance of *de facto* recognition in Cochin China as did the Dutch action in dealing with the Indonesian Republic. Thus full French control was established by force in Saigon by the end of 1945, when the British forces were withdrawn, the Japanese having been disarmed and the British war mission having been thus accomplished. This withdrawal was possible because of the arrival of well-equipped French troops apparently in sufficient strength adequately to support French authority.

A somewhat different situation developed north of the 16th parallel, where the Chinese had the function of receiving the Japanese surrender. There the Viet Nam government was not impeded by the Chinese in the exercise of such of its functions as the holding of elections and the establishment of a parliament.

The Chinese rather used their position to persuade the French to agree to a revision of the conditions of relationship between Indochina and China. In the agreement signed February 28, 1946 Chinese nationals were promised a continuation of

> the rights, privileges, and exemptions which they traditionally possessed in Indo-China; most-favored-nation treatment for Chinese nationals with respect to the right to travel, reside, conduct commercial, industrial, and mining enterprises, to acquire and possess real property; equality of taxation with Indo-Chinese nationals; and the same treatment as French nationals

in matters of legal procedure and administration of justice. It was further agreed that a special zone, under Chinese customs control, with the necessary facilities, should be established at Haiphong for the service of imports into and exports from China, and that commercial exchanges between China and Indochina should be regulated by a commercial agreement on the basis of most favored-nation treatment. And, finally, provision was made for a restoration to China of the Indochina-Yunnan Railway. Following the conclusion of this agreement, the Chinese troops were withdrawn from their zone of military occupation, leaving to the French the remaining problem of adjustment of their relations with the Viet Nam Republic, which was still in control.

To pave the way for peaceful entry of French troops into the northern part of Indochina to replace the Chinese, the agreement referred to above was made between France and Viet Nam on March 6, 1946. By this Hanoi agreement, France not only recognized the Viet Nam as a free state, but agreed that its territorial extent (whether it would include Cochin China) should be determined by referendum. It was further stipulated that, a favorable atmosphere having been created, negotiations would be instituted to "deal particularly with the diplomatic relations between Viet Nam and foreign states, the future status of Indochina, and economic and cultural interests."

On the basis of this agreement, French troops were able to enter Hanoi without opposition. During the subsequent period of negotiations, consequently, France was in effective control of Hanoi in the north and of Saigon in the south, of the territories claimed by the Republic. It thus had ports of entry from which, as its military establishment was augmented, it could, if necessary, move to extend its control in the hinterland.

THE ISSUES BETWEEN FRANCE AND
THE VIET MINH DEFINED

It was quickly revealed that the agreement of March 6 did not carry the same meaning to the French that it did to the Vietnamese leadership. The fundamental points at issue were defined at conferences at Dalat, in the spring, and at Fontainbleau, in the summer of 1946. One of these concerned the nature of relationships between the Viet Nam, on the one side, and Cambodia and Laos, on the other. The Viet Nam conception was limited to "federation" of three independent states, with federation in turn construed to mean limited co-ordination of economic policies, such as customs arrangements and currency. Federation meant to the French, on the other hand, close co-ordination of policy through the French High Commissioner, who would not only represent France, and the French Union, but also the Indochinese Federation, of which he would be the President. In spite of this fundamental disagreement, however, a *modus vivendi* was signed at Fontainbleau on September 14, 1946. This provided for

> one legal currency throughout Indo-China. A mixed commission, including representatives of the different states in the Federation, was to study the creation of an issuing agency to replace the Bank of Indo-China, and

would also coordinate customs and foreign trade. There was also to be an Indo-Chinese customs union, and no internal customs barriers....Another committee was to study the re-establishment and improvement of communications between Viet Nam and other countries in the Indo-Chinese Federation and the French Union. And in response to Vietnamese insistence on their own diplomatic representative abroad, a Franco-Vietnamese commission was to arrange for Vietnamese consular representatives in neighboring countries and for Vietnamese relations with foreign consulates.[9]

The other fundamental difference between Viet Nam and France at this time was over the territorial question of inclusion of Cochin China in Viet Nam. In spite of the provision for a referendum in the March agreement, France set up an autonomous government in Cochin China which nevertheless could be expected to respond to French direction. Since the French had already effectively resumed control of Cambodia and Laos, three of the five prewar parts of Indochina could then be "federated" under the High Commissioner. These actions made it possible for the French to act in military support of an Annamite government of Cochin China, presented as an alternative in Viet Nam to that of the Viet Minh headed by Ho Chi-minh, who was not only a nationalist but also a Communist in his ideology.

The net effect of these unresolved differences was civil war, with actions on both sides which enabled each to accuse the other of bad faith. The Viet Minh government did not have sufficient military power to dislodge the French from the cities and the coastal area within its claimed territory, nor to force the French to accept its conception of a federation which would be close to independence. It did have the power, however, in spite of augmented French forces in the country, to prevent the restoration of peace and the establishment of French authority throughout Annam and Tongking. There was little enthusiasm for the French-controlled Cochin China government which the French sought to utilize against the Viet Minh-dominated republic of Viet Nam. Its utilization was viewed as an attempt to maintain French power by application of the principle of "divide and rule." Cambodia and Laos had apparently accepted a status in relation to France which made them useful in maintaining the French point of view with respect to, and within, the Indochinese federation. If Cochin China could be sustained as a separate component of the federation,

9 *Ibid.*, pp. 256-57.

and kept under French domination, three elements would be subject to manipulation by the French against Tongking and Annam.

Whether or not this was the idea held by the French, either in France or in Indochina, it defines one aspect of the problem. The situation was such that the French had to accept the necessity of acting through or in support of Indochinese regimes unless they could impose their ideas of a reasonable solution of the problem by military means, as they found they could not. Finding the Cochin China regime an unacceptable, and thus weak, instrument France had to develop an alternative capable of attracting support within Viet Nam partly by rallying to itself elements previously supporting the Viet Minh regime. The basis of this attraction had to be found in a nationalism which differentiated the nationalist as such from the revolutionary.

THE FRENCH-SPONSORED VIET NAM GOVERNMENT

It was along these lines that an attempt was made to organize an alternative regime around the former Emperor, Bao Dai. He was still nominally an adviser to Ho Chi Minh's government but he had not returned from China where he had been sent on a mission in early 1946. The French, in approaching him, hoped to use him to detach nationalists among the Vietnamese from support of the Ho regime, getting them to accept terms of settlement with France more satisfactory to it than those demanded by Ho. It was as a nationalist leader that Bao Dai could be useful to France but only if he could be kept restrained in his nationalism.

Protracted negotiations were required to attain the French objective. The negotiations were complicated by the necessity not merely of reaching agreement between Bao Dai and his supporters in Indochina and France but also between them and competitive groups in Indochina, including General Xuan, then head of the Cochin China government, and between Bao Dai, France, and the French in Indochina, to ensure that agreements acceptable in Paris would be effectuated by French officialdom in Viet Nam. The fate of the earlier agreements reached between France and the Vietnamese through the Viet Minh had revealed the latter necessity.

When established the regime headed by Bao Dai was termed the Provisional Government of Viet Nam (embracing the prewar protectorates of Annam and Tongking, and the crown colony, Cochin China).

It was supported by France as an "associated" state in the conflict with the Democratic Republic of Viet Nam, controlled by the Viet Minh party, and popularly referred to as Viet Minh.

The first stage of negotiations between the French High Commissioner, General Xuan, and Bao Dai (President of the Provisional Central Government of Viet Nam) was completed with the signature by the two former "in the presence of His Majesty Bao Dai," of the Agreement of the Bay of Along (of June 6, 1948). This read:

(1) France solemnly recognizes the independence of Viet Nam to which belongs the right freely to bring about its unity. On its part, Viet Nam proclaims its adherence to the French Union in the capacity of a State associated with France. The independence of Viet Nam is unlimited except for such restrictions as its membership in the French Union imposes upon it.

(2) Viet Nam undertakes to respect the rights and interests of French nationals, to give constitutional guarantees of its respect for democratic principles, and to give preference in the tasks of its internal organization and of its economy to French political and technical advisers.

(3) As soon as the provisional government has been established representatives of Viet Nam will confer with representatives of the French Republic concerning suitable methods of arranging the transfer of specific activities in the fields of educational, foreign, military, economic, financial, and technical services.[10]

Upon the signature of this agreement Bao Dai left for France where he remained until the necessary decisions and actions had been taken to make it clear that there was not only agreement in principle but that the principles would be made effective. The agreements reached in Paris almost a year later (March 8, 1949), known as the "Agreements of the Elysée," were designed to give formal confirmation to the new set of relationships. In general these agreements reaffirmed the stipulations of the Bay of Along Agreement. In certain respects, however, they extended that agreement and gave it greater precision. Thus as to the restrictions resulting from membership in the French Union:

Vietnamese diplomacy would come into play only in close accord with the diplomatic missions of France and within the frame of directives issued by the High Council. Viet Nam would from then on have its national army. The army of the French Union would be confined to the bases, the garrisons, and the communications facilities.[11]

[10] W. L. Holland (ed.), *Asian Nationalism and the West* (New York: Macmillan, 1953), p. 230. Quoted by permission.
[11] *Ibid.*, p. 239.

An additional provision was that Viet Nam would enter into a monetary and customs union with Cambodia and Laos; and joint institutions would be "created to harmonize the interests of the three states with each other and with France."

These agreements did not dispose of one important question. This was the position of the colony of Cochin China, claimed as part of its territory by Viet Nam. The 1946 agreement to settle the question by referendum had been disregarded by the French, with a resulting charge of bad faith. Its previous separate status brought Cochin China within the provision of the new French constitution requiring consultation with the people affected before there could be any cession of territory. Consequently the French government could only commit itself to accept the decision of the people and act to organize a referendum. Before Bao Dai would return to Indochina from France, however, he insisted that French good faith be demonstrated in relation to Cochin China. The necessary action was consequently taken with the organization of a "Mixed Territorial Assembly—one-fourth French, three-fourths Vietnamese" elected by "an electoral college of about six thousand persons." On April 23 this assembly passed a resolution to the effect that Cochin China was to be attached to Viet Nam and be one of the Associated States of Indochina, but was to be allowed a special status in that state. An act adopted on June 4th made the transfer final.

THE ASSOCIATED STATES OF INDOCHINA

Thus by 1950, upon acceptance of the agreements by the French Parliament (February 2), the conception of an Indochina Federation within the earlier formulation of the French Union had been replaced for Indochina by that of "independent" states (Viet Nam, Cambodia, and Laos), associated with one another and each in separate association with France. The government established in Viet Nam which came to have Bao Dai at its head as Chief of State, was thereafter considered as being assisted by France (1) to overcome the internal opposition presented by the Viet Minh and (2) to secure its independence within the limits determined externally by its membership in the French Union.

This consummation had the effect of focusing attention on the communist as distinguished from the nationalist aspects of the Viet Minh, and of bringing the struggle in Indochina out of the context of a purely colonial war into that of the larger international struggle. This might not have been so clearly the case if it had not coincided in point of time with the victory of the Chinese Communists over the National Government in mainland China. This brought the Viet Minh into territorial contact with a Communist power which could assist it against the non-Communist or anti-Communist Vietnam state. The new situation was crystallized by the recognition by Peiping and Moscow of the Ho government and by recognition of the Viet Nam Associated State by the United States and other Western states. India, Indonesia and other Asian states refused, however, to recognize the Bao Dai regime because they viewed it as being still too much within the framework of colonialism. Thus they applied the conception of neutralism to the contending regimes although inclining to the view that Ho Chi-minh was more expressive of the will of the people of Viet Nam than was Bao Dai.

While there was a real difference between "associated statehood" and independence, the new status was closer to independence than that of statehood within a federation within a Union. Had the associated-state conception been accepted earlier and put into effect so as to induce real confidence in French good faith the action might have transformed the colonial struggle into more of the appearance of a civil war, with the French assisting the Bao Dai regime to re-establish internal order in Viet Nam. But, at the time when taken, the Ho regime was strengthened for purposes of resistance by outside assistance so that it could undertake military operations on a sufficiently large scale to keep France and French power in the foreground of the struggle, as contrasted with the earlier period when Viet Minh power had been reduced to the point of conducting relatively small-scale guerrilla operations. The associated-state conception conformed sufficiently to the Ho interpretation of the meaning of federation, which he had accepted in the 1946 agreements, to have made it difficult for him to hold his following in 1947 and 1948 against the attractions of nationalism thus expressed within the French Union. It was the attempt of the French in Indochina to enforce their interpretation of the Union conception which had enabled Ho to charge them with bad faith and to hold and even enlarge his following among the nationalists during those years.

This question of ultimate intention of the French in Indochina remained to be answered after the signature of the new agreements on the basis of which the Bao Dai regime was constructed. Would the

French on the spot attempt to modify the concessions made to nationalism if and as resistance to the new regime was overcome? Unless the French moved rapidly and decisively to transfer power to the Bao Dai regime as the government of an associated state, doubts would be raised as to their ultimate intentions among those who were prepared to accept the status of independence within the limitation set by membership in the French Union. Such a question of good faith might bring about new demands for complete withdrawal of the French in order to enable the self-control sought to be attained. Such doubts, furthermore, might reflect back into relations established with the two other associated states.

In contrast to the Associated State of Vietnam, Laos and Cambodia had apparently reached a point of stability in their relations with France by 1950.

> Within the framework of the Postwar agreements signed by the French with Laos and Cambodia, considerable governmental changes took place. Both Countries became constitutional monarchies under constitutions adopted in 1947, with popularly elected assemblies and responsible cabinets. Although their kings retained considerable power, the change in political forms was marked, giving opposition elements for the first time a legal mechanism for the expression of their views. French control in both countries was still strong, however, and certain elements never accepted the agreements with France. The greater part of the Laotian guerrilla movement, which was based largely on personal rivalries within the royal family, seems to have collapsed in 1949 and made its peace with the Laotian government and with France. The Cambodian Issaraks, who have links with important members of the Democratic party, the countries largest political group, collaborate militarily with the Viet Minh.[12]

By 1953, however, the struggle in Viet Nam had so developed as to find the reflection referred to above in Cambodia and in Laos. The ruler of Cambodia not only expressed dissatisfaction with the results of application of French policy in Viet Nam but went beyond that in a demand for a redefinition of the status of Cambodia as an associated state. The situation in Laos was affected by its direct invasion by the forces of Ho Chi-minh. The result was a further attempt to strengthen the position of the government in Viet Nam against the now clearly Communist Viet Minh by renegotiation of the status within the French Union of all three associated states.

[12] L. K. Rosinger and Associates, *The State of Asia* (New York: Knopf, 1951) pp. 250-51.

THE UNITED STATES AND THE CONFLICT IN INDOCHINA

Doubts as to French purposes and intentions, as measured by colonialism, had complicated the relations of the United States with France as well as those of France with nationalist but non-Communist elements in Indochina. The France which had been seeking to regain and to retain as much as possible of its power in Asia and Africa was simultaneously attempting to bring about internal reconstruction and rehabilitation at home and the re-establishment of the French position in Europe. The solution of the European aspect of the problem was rendered more difficult on account of the necessary diversion of even limited amounts of French resources, both military and economic, to re-establish the French position in Indochina.[13]

To solve the European aspect of the problem France came within the system of American economic assistance and military aid. This was justified, from the United States standpoint, as necessary for the realization of common purposes in Europe. There seemed to be no common purpose, however, as far as Indochina was concerned until after the Communist victory in mainland China and the subsequent assistance given by the Mao regime to the Viet Minh in the struggle in Indochina. Consequently, until after 1950, the United States was inclined to question the direct or indirect use of American assistance to France to strengthen the French position in Indochina through waging what was understood to be a war to maintain colonialism against nationalism. Even though it was French matériel or French military manpower which was transferred to Indochina it was argued that this was an indirect use of American assistance given to France in Europe. In other words, if, to attain common purposes in Europe, France needed so many tons of steel, for each ton of French steel used for purposes of war in Indochina there would have to be replacement by a ton of American steel to meet the total requirement in France. It was, consequently, only when the Americans began to view the war in Indochina as one front in the general struggle against the Soviet Union that the United States became willing to view aid to France, translated into assistance to the French in Indochina, as different aspects of the same thing. In making this translation or transition a part of the frame of reference in American policy inevitably French policy tended away

[13] Between 1945 and 1950 the war [in Indo China] had cost France $1,800 million and more than 20,000 lives. Holland, *op. cit.*, p. 244.

from colonialism, at least until the problem of containment of communism submerged all other considerations in the development and application of United States' foreign policy.

Some of the contradictions in American thinking were both revealed and eliminated as a result of developments in the Korean War. There was considerable criticism of France as well as Britain and others because of the limitation of their direct participation in United Nations' operations in Korea. This criticism was met by the French and the British by calling attention to the efforts, comparable to the American effort in Korea, which the former was making in Indochina and the latter in Malaya. The validity of this comparison came to be accepted in the United States as the Chinese Communists became associated with the solution of the French problem in Indochina and the American problem in Korea. This association had become so fixed in 1952 that the new administration in Washington declared in effect that no solution in Korea would be acceptable which did not carry with it an assurance against Chinese Communist support of the Viet Minh in Indochina. At this same stage the United States committed itself to direct assistance to France and the Associated States of Indochina to the extent necessary to prevent successful Chinese intervention in that area, viewing the Associated State of Viet Nam as the "key to Southeast Asia" for international communism. When this conclusion had been reached it served to displace, as a factor in the development of American policy, the traditional enmity to "colonialism" in the United States. Up to that time, however, the attitude in the United States toward assistance to France for use in Indochina was determined in part at least by doubt as to the intention of France to translate into deeds the words used in the agreements establishing independence of states associated with one another and France within the French Union. This attitude had some effect in moving the French government further and further from the intentions revealed in the application of the 1946 agreement toward acceptance of actual independence, although the movement was slow and represented reaction to the pressures applied by nationalism rather than at the outset real conversion from colonialism.

As a French writer well puts it: [14]

By abruptly revealing the danger of aggression in Asia and the expansionist character of Asian communism, the Korean war contributed to speed-

[14] Philippe Devillers in Holland, *op. cit.*, p. 244.

ing American decisions. On June 27 President Truman announced that economic and military aid would be extended to Indo-China in order to enable it to resist aggression. Programs for the provision of arms and supplies were drawn up in the course of Franco-American conversations. The most delicate matter requiring a decision had to do with whether the direct beneficiaries of American aid should be the French army and administration in Indo-China or the still embryonic Vietnamese army. Although Vietnamese nationalist circles were most anxious to receive American aid directly, practical considerations of efficiency finally led to the adoption of a compromise solution: economic aid was given directly to the Associated States through the intermediary of an ECA mission, while military aid would be distributed through the agency of the experienced General Staff of the French army in Indo-China, assisted by an American military mission.

THE STRUGGLE FOR CONTROL OF VIET NAM

Even with augmented American economic and military assistance, however, the French found it difficult to come to grips with the Viet Minh forces and win a decision. Local successes were followed by local reverses. In some respects France faced the same situation as that which confronted the Chinese National Government in 1948. The French had to hold, govern and reconstruct areas against an enemy without fixed positions and responsibilities. The Ho Chi-Minh forces were able to combine the tactics of the guerrilla and of the armed force in proportions determined by them rather than by their enemy. Operating from the difficult hill country toward the settled coastal areas, they could maintain themselves by destructive activities in areas from which they were prepared to retire in the face of superior force. Thus the French were kept on the defensive and prevented from employing their total strength so as to meet and decisively overcome the enemy. In other words, circumstances related to the nature of the country and of the enemy made it difficult for the apparently superior power to win a decision.

The continuation of the war, furthermore, made it difficult or inadvisable for the French to show the reality or the insubstantiality of their intentions with respect to autonomy by the transfer of defense and other functions to the Bao Dai government. That government was itself not so constituted as to ensure confidence in its ability to govern, and it was difficult for the French to bring about its re-constitution without undue interference. And yet unless France could effectuate this transfer of authority the confidence of the people was weakened in the commitment to the measure of independence represented by the conception of the associated state. Popular support both of France and of the government of the Associated State of Viet Nam was dependent upon the ability of the new regime to bring about economic and social improvement. But the effective execution of plans for reconstruction depended upon the re-establishment of order. This, in turn, required concentration of effort and resources on the military effort.

For several reasons an emphasis in French military policy came to be on the organization, officering, and equipment of an Indochinese army capable of sustaining the defense of Vietnam against the Viet Minh Republic. One reason for this emphasis was growing dissatisfaction in France with the continued loss of French life, especially of officer personnel, and the depletion of French resources in the attempt to maintain an unsatisfactory position in the former colony. In this respect French opinion paralleled that expressed in the United States on the Korean War. A second reason was that only in some such way could the war be transformed from a colonial conflict into one in which the French could be viewed, and could view themselves, as primarily fulfilling their Union obligation to assist the government of an associated state to maintain itself against both internal and external attack. If more of that appearance could be given it might reasonably be anticipated that nationalists in Ho Chi-Minh's following would come over to Viet Nam, thus bringing about the collapse of the rebellion.

It would take time to create a military force, officered by Vietnamese, capable of assuming as much of the burden of defense as that which had come to be assumed, for example, by the army brought into being in Korea. The necessary time, however, was lacking, after the attempt began to be made, because the armistice in Korea enabled the Chinese to increase their assistance to the Viet Minh regime sufficiently so that the latter was able immediately to step up its military operations, moving armies into Laos in support of the guerrillas previously operating there and in Cambodia, while maintaining constant pressure on the French in Viet Nam. This confronted the French with a situation in which (1) they could not transfer defense responsibilities to Viet Nam since the latter was not prepared to assume them, and (2) they could maintain themselves and the Associated States against Viet Minh and China only by increasing their own military effort. This effort they might have been prepared to make if given assurance of extended support by the United States. Washington had come to the view that the defense of Viet Nam against the Communists was vital, but not to the point of committing the United States to all-out support of France in Indochina.

NEGOTIATION OF AN ARMISTICE AT GENEVA

It was under these circumstances that the French insisted on placing the question of an armistice in Indochina on the agenda of the Geneva Conference. The issue was dramatized on the eve of the conference by the siege of Dienbienphu, which was reported as if it were the decisive operation in the war. The final capitulation of the garrison, after a protracted and heroic defense, put Ho Chi-Minh and the Chinese in a strong position as negotiations were begun.

It was quickly made apparent at Geneva that an armistice agreement could be reached only on the basis of a division of the territory of Viet Nam between the contending forces. The Chinese sought an agreement which would facilitate establishment of political control of Viet Nam by the Viet Minh and would enable a position to be maintained by the Communists in Laos and Cambodia. The French government was initially prepared to accept a military agreement which would mean immediate loss of northern Viet Nam, except for the Red River delta area, provided it brought about the withdrawal of Viet Minh forces which had been infiltrated into southern Viet Nam, and termination of the threat to Laos and Cambodia. France was apparently not prepared to make a political settlement, as demanded by the Chinese for the Viet Minh leader, Ho Chi Minh, which would have given his party status within the government of Vietnam and a base of operations in Laos. In their unwillingness to negotiate a political settlement in advance of establishment of a military armistice reasonably satisfactory to them the French were vigorously supported by the United States but opposed openly by India and tacitly by the British.

The position of the French delegation was, however, weakened by French opinion which was in favor of termination of the struggle if that could be accomplished on any terms short of complete capitulation. This sentiment led to an overturn of the French Cabinet. The new French government, with M. Mendès-France as Premier, accepted the mandate to continue negotiations with the understanding that if no agreement had been reached by July 20 the Premier would tender his resignation. France resumed negotiations at Geneva, however, with the reiterated view that any agreement which was satisfactory must be "honorable" and thus fall short of capitulation.

Initial cause for optimism was found in a preliminary conversation at Geneva between M. Mendès-France and the Chinese Premier and Foreign Minister, Chou En-lai, following which the negotiation of an armistice line was transferred temporarily from Geneva and the diplomats to the military commands in Indochina. The slowness with which the negotiations in Indochina were put under way reduced the intial optimism as to an agreement by July 20—M. Mendès-France's deadline. Nevertheless an armistice agreement was concluded only a few hours after the date set.

Under the armistice agreement Viet Nam was partitioned at approximately the 17th parallel, the Viet Minh forces securing all of the northern territory, including the Red River delta and Hanoi and the port of Haiphong.[15] The Viet Nam territory south of the demarkation line remained under the control of the French-supported Viet Nam government. The governments of the associated states of Laos and Cambodia were to be left undisturbed. Those two states were, however, to be neutralized, with their armed forces limited to those necessary for self-defense. These provisions were reported from Geneva as preventing the United States from supplying military instructors or equipment. Laos and Cambodia would find real protection only through the realization by the Communists that an armed attack might precipitate intervention by the United States.[16] Furthermore Viet Minh forces were to be permitted to remain in Laos, "concentrated in two provinces near the frontier with Viet Minh territory." [17]

On the political side it was agreed that elections would be held throughout Vietnam within two years. These elections would be held under supervision of the committee agreed upon for supervision of the armistice. The committee was to be composed of Poland, India, and Canada, with each member having a veto on decisions.

These agreements were guaranteed, as insisted upon by the Chinese, by the states participating in the Geneva Conference, except for the

[15] Hanoi and Haiphong, however, were to remain in French hands for a time (possibly as long as a year) to enable the French to make an orderly evacuation of their forces and civilian evacuees.
[16] *New York Times*, July 21, 1954, p. 1. The dispatch was written by Thomas J. Hamilton.
[17] *Ibid.*

United States. Although not signing them, Washington accepted them in principle and committed the United States not to undertake military action to upset them.

These agreements represented a substantial Communist victory. The termination of hostilities put the Viet Minh and China in a position to employ the methods of conquest—propaganda, infiltration and subversion—at which they were most adept not merely in southern Viet Nam but also in Cambodia and Laos. The United States, in its attempt to contain communism was forced to define a new line of defense. This would necessarily have to be fixed at Thailand and Malaya since the establishment of a firm position in southern Viet Nam, Cambodia and Laos was made virtually impossible as a result of the agreements reached at Geneva. Additionally, the governments of Thailand, Burma, Malaya and Indonesia were made more vulnerable to assault through local Communist parties as a result of Chinese efforts in behalf of Ho Chi-Minh and the Viet Minh at the Geneva Conference of 1954.

THE DIEM REGIME

On the eve of the Geneva Conference on Korea and Indochina, and in the midst of the crisis situation which led to the demand that the Indochina war be put on the agenda of that Conference, a new personality was projected to the top position in Viet Nam with the appointment by Bao Dai on June 16, 1954, of Ngo Dinh Diem as Premier. Diem was new to the political scene only in the sense that he had steadily refused to hold office during the postwar years. This refusal was the expression of his uncompromising nationalism. Since he was also a devout Roman Catholic, his nationalism had not allowed him to give his support to the Communist-dominated Viet Minh regime of Ho Chi-Minh. With the French apparently on the way out, however, and with the prospect of Communist domination of the entire country unless a regime was constituted which could command the confidence of the non-Communist nationalist elements in the country, Diem accepted the premiership and undertook the task of holding the country together. Before assuming office he required that Bao Dai, the Chief of State, should give him full powers to govern. Shortly after his assumption of power, however, the drawing of the armistice line denied him authority in northern Viet Nam and the Geneva agreements, although without his signature to them, faced him with the requirement that elections should be held throughout the country in 1956 and with the immediately more pressing problem of evacuation and resettlement in southern Viet Nam of Catholic and other anti-Communist elements from northern Viet Nam. This immensely complicated the problem of government for a premier who was without any real administrative and governmental experience.

The refugee problem complicated the problem of government for Diem and not for Ho Chi-Minh because, just as had been the case in Korea, the great movement was from the north to the south and not from the non-Communist to the Communist area. This was the case despite the fact that there was a greater degree of order and stability in the north than in the south.

Lacking administrative experience, the Diem regime did not envisage in advance the difficulties of handling the refugees and take steps rapidly enough to overcome them. The flow from the north to the south presented the problem of housing and resettling close to 800,000 people, many of whom were suffering from beri-beri, malaria, enteritis, conjunctivitis, tropical ulcers, measles or other diseases. Thus the health problem was serious. It was made more so by a shortage of medical supplies and of doctors. The slowness with which resettlement was undertaken aggravated the problem through the inevitable overcrowding in camps and other temporary quarters. By the end of March, 1955, however, some 300,000 people had been successfully resettled and the indications were that the problem would be solved within a reasonable period of time. Such success as had been attained must be ascribed in part to the assistance given by the United States and by France, Australia and other countries.

It was not, however, exclusively or even primarily administrative inexperience which made it difficult to solve the refugee problem more expeditiously. It was only one of a series of problems confronting the Diem regime. In many respects the most pressing problem was that of establishing its authority in southern Viet Nam. From the time of its inception the Diem government was faced with internal factionalism and armed threats to its continued existence. This situation was fostered from France, since Bao Dai, as Chief of State, did not give Diem the complete support which the delegation of full powers of government implied; and since the French government was, not unnaturally, unsympathetic to him because of his unconcealed hostility to France as a colonial power. Thus Bao Dai, even if the charges made against him of intervention against the government were untrue, certainly did not use his continuing influence in unqualified support of the Diem regime nor did France press him to do so.

The first threat to the southern Viet Nam government came with the refusal of the Chief of Staff of the National Army to comply with an order to give up his command and take a six-month vacation in France. With the support of the Binh Xuyen, "a band of near gangsters of whom the Prime Minister strongly disapproved because of their unsavory connections with gambling and prostitution" [18] but who had come into control of the police and security services under preceding regimes, Diem weathered this crisis of some seven weeks.

Another threat to the authority of the government was presented in the attitude of the two major religious sects, the Caodaists and the Hao Haos. At first they gave their support to the Chief of Staff in his revolt against the government, but subsequently were persuaded by Diem to accept seats (six each) in the new Cabinet which he constituted when his situation had begun to seem hopeless.

It was, however, American support which enabled the Diem government to surmount the critical internal situation which confronted it in the fall of 1954. This support took the indirect form of pressure on Bao Dai in France to order the Chief of Staff, General Nguyen Van Hinh, to come to France, thus removing him from the local scene, and of direct asistance through the decision to send American aid direct to Viet Nam instead of channeling it through France.

The ending of the crisis through the removal of General Hinh to France gave the government its first real opportunity to execute any plans which it had for solving pressing local problems. With American encouragement, advice, and assistance, consequently, it instituted, during the winter of 1954-55, a program of land reform designed to bring fallow land under cultivation, to control rents, and to distribute land to needy peasants. It also was enabled to grapple more vigorously with the problem of resettlement of refugees, and to inaugurate a campaign against vice and corruption. All of this, and especially the moves undertaken against the more important beneficiaries of the existing system of control of vice and of the exploitation of public office for

[18] Brian Crozier, "The Diem regime in southern Vietnam," *Far Eastern Survey*, Vol. 24, No. 4, April, 1955, p. 51. The author goes on to say that the Binh Xuyen gave their support to Diem because of their loyalty to Bao Dai and because of their bitter rivalry with the army. It may be added that Diem accepted their support because of the fact that he lacked the power to do otherwise.

personal gain, brought again to the surface the latent opposition of important elements. To this was added the opposition, in the spring and summer of 1955, of the sects, who sought to maintain the power which they enjoyed because they controlled, as private armies, substantial military forces. Their forces had been theoretically incorporated in the National Army in 1952, but in fact those forces had retained their autonomy. This enabled each of the Sects, controlling its own private army, to exercise authority, even against the government, in a portion of the country.[19] After 1954 moves began to be undertaken by the government to change this situation by more effectively integrating the sects' armies into the National Army.

A formal break with the government was forecast with the formation of a "United Front of all Nationalist Forces" by the three major sects. This United Front then attempted to persuade Bao Dai either to dismiss the Premier or to return to Viet Nam and resume active direction of affairs of state. "The Emperor's reaction, as might have been expected, was ambiguous; he congratulated the sects on forming the United Front, but renewed his confidence in Premier Diem and declined to return." [20] This expression of confidence in Diem on the part of Bao Dai did not, even if so designated, discourage the sect leaders from attempting by direct local action to displace the Premier. With continued American support, however, Diem, by the end of the summer, had been able to rally sufficient military support in the National Army to establish his authority over the sectarian forces.

On the political side, Diem at the same time took steps to dispose of the influence of Bao Dai. On June 16, 1955, under Diem's persuasion, the "Council of the Imperial Family" dismissed the Emperor from his position as Chief of State and proposed Ngo Dinh Diem as President of the Republic. This decision was not accepted by Bao Dai, whose office in France issued a statement to the effect that the Council had been suppressed at the beginning of the war against the Viet Minh and that

[19] "During the Indochina war, the sectarian armies were armed and subsidized by the French, who found them useful as auxiliary forces against the Viet Minh. The Caodaists maintained order in Tay Ninh province in Cochin-China, and the Hao Haos in the Long Xuyen region, also in the South, while the Binh Xuyen gang held sway in a small area near Saigon. Each sect enjoyed a large measure of local autonomy and collected its own taxes. The matter was complicated by the existence of dissidents from the main bodies of the sectarian armies, such as General Trinh Minh The, the rebel Caodaist, and General Ba Cut, the rebel Hao Hao." *Ibid.*, pp. 52-53.
[20] *Ibid.*, p. 53.

consequently its decisions could have no validity. The statement issued further declared that the Emperor Bao Dai was committed to the principle of popular consultation concerning the nature of the regime. He could not, therefore, give up his powers, except to the people. "To hand them over to a single man would be contrary to democratic principles."

This statement did not, of course, change the situation. It did, however, leave Bao Dai free to exercise such influence as he could from abroad. This had been considerable in the confused postwar situation. What his influence would be, and in what direction it would be exerted, if he should return to Viet Nam in the immediate future remained a matter of speculation at the end of the summer of 1955. At that time, within southern Viet Nam, Diem had established himself as the strongest leader. There was, however, sufficient latent opposition to his government to make its future uncertain in the event that it should have to contest elections throughout the entire country against the northern Viet Minh regime, as provided in the Geneva agreements.

The holding of elections which would be really "free" and as a result of which the entire country could be united satisfactorily under a common government posed the same type of problem in Indochina as it had previously in Korea. Northern Viet Nam was unified under the control of a monolithic, authoritarian party, the Communist Party headed by Ho Chi-Minh. If that party should be able to determine the conditions of voting, the outcome, at least in its area, would be predictable. The elections would not be a free expression of the desires and will of the people according to Western democratic standards. One party would control the vote in the north without permitting serious competition from the parties existing in south Viet Nam, where, however, the Communist Viet Minh would be able to compete with relative freedom. In that event the probability was that the elections would result in Viet Minh control of the entire country. This probability was certainly an important consideration in causing Ngo Dinh Diem to go as far as he reasonably could in repudiating the provision for elections in the Geneva agreements, to which in any case he did not feel at all bound since his government had not accepted them.

Thus in a broadcast of July 16 Premier Diem stated that his government, even though not bound by the Geneva agreements, was prepared to accept the principle of general elections, provided there was assurance that the elections in the north would be really free. This, he said, required proof that "the Viet Minh government was putting the higher interests of the national community before those of Communism." The proof could be given in the renunciation of terrorist and totalitarian methods and by ceasing to violate the Geneva agreements by preventing the movement of refugees from the north to the south. Subsequently (August 9) apparently under some pressure from France, the United States, and Britain, Diem replied to a communication from the Viet Minh government asking for pre-electoral consultations. In its reply the southern government reaffirmed the view previously broadcast that elections were desirable in principle, but it took the position that nothing could properly be undertaken, even in the form of consultations, until democratic rights had been restored in the North. It characterized the Viet Minh proposal for negotiations as propaganda designed to represent the Viet Minh as defenders of national liberty.

This exchange did not represent any advance toward agreement on the conditions for holding elections and for unifying the country. It did, however, although in general terms, mark out the avenue of approach to agreement. This approach was similar to the one insisted upon by the United States in connection with proposals for negotiation with the Soviet Union prior to the "Summit Conference" at Geneva in midsummer of 1955. It was an avenue down which, however, the Viet Minh could not be expected to move unless Moscow and Peiping, following the lines set in the Summit Conference, were prepared to persuade Ho Chih-Minh to modify his regime in order to "lessen international tension." There is no evidence that any such persuasion was attempted while Ho was visiting Peiping and Moscow in the summer of 1955. His reception, nevertheless, indicated acceptance by them of Ho as the head of an important satellite regime.

Enough has been said, however, to make it clear that it was not alone the situation with respect to freedom in north Viet Nam which made the idea of elections in the near future one which Diem found unacceptable. Factional division in southern Viet Nam, until the authority of the government had been more fully established, gave reasonable assurance of Communist success in any elections, regardless of any democratic reforms undertaken in the northern part of the country. And in the measures taken against the factions, the Diem regime laid itself open to the charges that it had been making against the Ho regime in the North with respect to freedom and democracy.

From the international point of view, furthermore, Diem did not have, and could not readily be given, the same vigorous support by France, the United States, and Britain as that extended to the Viet Minh by China and the U.S.S.R. This showed itself, for example, in relation to the work of the International Armistice Commission which, as in Korea, was unable to perform its functions with respect to supervision of the transfer of refugees in a satisfactory manner. The Commission was undoubtedly correct in its view, expressed in its third interim report, that north Viet Nam and south Viet Nam had both obstructed the transfer of refugees. But the south Vietnamese were also justified in their criticism of the Commission because of its inability to bring about proper action in the North as well as in the South.

The feeling in the South that the Commission was either unwilling or unable to function impartially led to demonstrations in Saigon, apparently officially organized, against the Commission on the anniversary of the signing of the Geneva armistice agreements. These demonstrations led to rioting in which two persons were reported to have been killed and at least fifty injured. The Hotel Majestic, in which the principal members of the International Commission were housed, was sacked and the Indian President of the Commission was manhandled in the course of the riots. Similar attacks on personnel of the Commission occurred elsewhere in the city. These attacks led to representations by the French, American and British governments, in which they urged on the Diem government the fulfillment of the terms of the Geneva agreements. Although denying that pressure had been put on it by foreign powers to do so, the Diem government ordered an inquiry into the attacks on the headquarters of the Armistice Commission, took steps to prevent its repetition, and promised to make full reparation for all damage done. Similar violations of the letter and the spirit of the armistice agreements by the Viet Minh regime, although, to be sure, not involving attacks on the personnel of an international commission, did not lead to similar protests to Ho Chi-Minh by Soviet Russia or Communist China.

Thus the end of the first postwar decade found the problem of Indochina reformulated but not solved. It was clear that the French colonial regime had been destroyed. It was not yet apparent whether or not the future form of government would be freely decided as a result of decision taken exclusively within Indochina, or, if so, what the outcome would be. Internally, much would depend on the ability of the Diem regime to create satisfactory conditions in southern Viet

Nam. From the point of view of external forces, as they would affect the situation, the attitude of Peiping toward the Viet Minh and the general character of relationships developed on the part of the United States with the Soviet Union and Communist China would have major significance in determining the immediate political fortunes of the governing regimes in northern and southern Viet Nam.

BIBLIOGRAPHICAL REFERENCES

Bodard, L., "Quelle leçon tirerdes élections vietnamiennes" in *France Illustration* no. 383, 215-16, February 14, 1953.

――――, "Aspects of the Vietnamese Problem," *Pacific Affairs*, Vol. 25, no. 3.

Committee on Foreign Relations, U. S. Senate, *Indo-China* (Washington, 1953).

Devillers, Philippe, "Vietnamese Nationalism and French Policy," Pt. III of *Asian Nationalism and the West*, W. L. Holland (ed.), (New York: Macmillan, 1953).

Devillers, Philippe, *Vietnam and France* (New York: 1950).

Emerson, Rupert, Mills, Lennox A., and Thompson, Virginia, *Government and Nationalism in South East Asia* (New York: International Secretariat, Institute of Pacific Relations, 1942).

Gourou, Pierre, "For a French Indo-Chinese Federation," *Pacific Affairs*, Vol. 20, no. 1.

Hammer, Ellen, "Indo-China," in *The State of Asia*, by L. K. Rosinger and Associates (New York: Knopf, for the Institute of Pacific Relations, 1951).

Hammer, Ellen, "Blue-printing a New Indo-China," *Pacific Affairs*, Vol. 21, no. 3.

Isaacs, H., *New Cycle in Asia* (New York: Macmillan, 1947).

"Les États associes d'Indochine," Special edition of *France Illustration*, no. 350, 609-659, J. 28, 1952.

Sabattier, General G., *Le Destin de L'Indochine: Souvenirs et Documents, 1941-1951* (Paris: Librarie Plon, 1952).

Thompson, Virginia and Adloff, Richard, "Cambodia Moves Toward Independence," *Far Eastern Survey*, Vol. 22, no. 9.

11

War and
Postwar Thailand

❈❈❈❈❈❈❈❈❈❈❈❈❈❈❈❈❈❈❈❈❈❈❈❈❈❈

PREWAR THAILAND

THAILAND LIES to the west and southwest of Indochina.[1] Almost completely enclosed within the prewar colonial area, it was the only country of southeastern Asia which was able to retain its formal and actual independence of Western imperialism. This is to be explained in large part by its buffer position between British and French colonial territory, which enabled independence to be preserved by playing off the British against the French. While maintaining its independence, however, Thailand (then Siam) did lose some of its Malay provinces to Britain and provinces bordering Cambodia and Laos to France. Much of this territory was regained during the period of Japanese ascendancy, only to be lost again as a consequence of Japanese defeat. In its present-day form as an independent state, Thailand includes somewhat over 200,000 square miles of territory. It thus comprises less than a third of the peninsula projected southward from China and contains only one of its five major waterways, the Menam. Two others, the Mekong and the Salwin, are shared with Indochina and Burma. The Menam and its confluents, however, give Thailand a system of waterways that provides easy communication between its upland territory and the sea.

The total population of Thailand was estimated in 1954 at 19,192,000, an increase of some two million over the 1947 census figures. Of con-

[1] Originally known as Siam, it renamed itself Thailand in 1939, resumed the name Siam after liberation from the Japanese in 1945, and again took the name Thailand (land of the free) in 1949.

siderable political significance is the fact that more than two and a half million of this total were Chinese, and more than a half million were Malay. It should also be noted that the Thai themselves were not all included in Thailand, some living in Tongking and others in Laos, two of the Associated States of Indochina and some in southwestern China. The situation in Indochina and the relationship of Communist China to that situation tempted the Peiping regime to attempt to further the extension of Communist authority through the sponsorship of a "Free Thai" movement as well as to utilize the Chinese minority in Thailand as elsewhere in Southeast Asia for the same purpose.

The original external orientation of Thailand had been toward China. This was changed as China's weakness *vis-a-vis* the West was revealed during the nineteenth and early twentieth centuries. The Asiatic type of monarchy was consequently changed into an "enlightened despotism" and serious attempts at Westernization of the country were made after the middle of the nineteenth century. The rule was sufficiently enlightened, at any rate, to prevent the development of internal conditions such as frequently invite foreign intervention. Thus Thai statesmanship enabled the country to avoid colonial status and to transform Thailand (Siam) from a feudal country into a modern state. It was only with the revolution of 1932 that as a national state Thai policy began to show aggressive tendencies.

This revolution, or more accurately coup d'état, of 1932, was not ideological in character, nor were those of 1933 and 1947, each expressing primarily a struggle for power among individuals or groups.

> Briefly, the "revolution" of 1932 simply transferred power from a handful of princes to the only other educated group in the country—the intellectual and military bourgeoisie. The subsequent political history of Thailand has been chiefly a struggle for power between the latter two middle-class elements; the advocates of a restoration of monarchial privileges have sided alternately with the civilian liberals or the military conservatives. But none of those groups has ever wholly accepted the democratic principles enunciated by the civilian liberals in the constitution of 1932.[2]

The coup d'état of 1932 was engineered by civilian liberals led by Pridi Bhanomyong. Their assumption of control in 1932 was followed by the introduction of a constitutional system of government which was originally pointed toward democracy of the English type. Internal

[2] Virginia Thompson and Richard Adloff, "Thailand (Siam)" in L. Rosinger and Associates, *The State of Asia* (New York: Knopf, 1951), p. 271.

conflicts within the group in control, however, led quickly to the elimination of the liberal and radical elements in the government and to control by military elements. The seal was set on this military control with the assumption of the premiership by Pibul Songgram in 1938. Pibul began his rise to power, however, when he supported the government against a princely attempt to overthrow the constitution in 1933.

The coup d'état of 1933 was followed by the abdication of the King, Prajadhipok, in 1935, in favor of a minor, Ananda Mahidol, who was then being educated in Switzerland. Concurrently, freedom of speech and of the press were limited and authoritarian rather than democratic tendencies were clearly predominant by 1938. This did not mean, however, that a static internal policy of an illiberal sort was followed. Reform continued to be promoted from above after 1933, just as it had been during the period of absolute monarchy. There was substantial progress made in education, with a trebling of appropriations in the three-year period following the fiscal year 1933-34. Literacy subsequently rose to 30 per cent of the population. Similar progress was made in the field of public health. Communications were extended, particularly with the construction of motor roads; and the attempt was made to improve the condition of agriculture and of the peasantry.

The entire internal program of development was nationalistic in the sense that it was designed to strengthen the state, and so to put it in a stronger position to maintain its independence. But a new expression of nationalism marked the attempt to create a Thai economic middle class. The two million Chinese were the dominant commercial element in the country. Since the Thai interested themselves in agriculture, in government, and in the professions, the Chinese had come to fill an economic vacuum rather than to displace the Thai from commerce and from tin and rubber production. Performing a necessary function, they were viewed with tolerance as long as the control which they had over the economic life of the country was not fully perceived. It was only in 1911 that they were classed with other foreigners and were required to pay a capitation tax.

The tax produced a strike among the Chinese, which brought the economic life of the country to a standstill. This for the first time made the Siamese aware of the extent to which the Chinese controlled the trade of the country, and from this time onwards, not only did the Siamese seek to encourage their own people to enter increasingly into trade, industry and commerce, but they also sought by legislation to limit the flow of Chinese immigrants, to assimilate those Chinese who were already in the country, and to place obstacles in the way of further development of trade and industry.[3]

The natural inclinations of the Thai limited the scope and the success of this anti-Chinese movement until after 1932. In the following decade, however, it was accentuated because some of the new leaders felt that the poverty of the Thai peasant could be directly traced to the absence of a Thai commercial class and that the forcible ejection of the Chinese, particularly from commerce, would create a vacuum which the Thai would automatically fill. It was, however, only after 1939, when the military authoritarian government had consolidated its control of the country, that a vigorous program of exclusion of the Chinese from the economic life of Thailand was put into effect. The issue was important, however, before then in the development of nationalist sentiment and in putting that sentiment behind the government.

ORIENTATION TOWARDS JAPAN

This new, and more intolerant, nationalism of the 1930's coincided with an orientation of the foreign policy of Thailand toward Japan as the new strong power in the Far East. The failure of the Western states, through the League, to restrain Japan in Manchuria in 1931-32, threw Thailand back on its historic policy of either playing-off one power against another where that was possible or of conciliation of the predominant power. The government of Thailand evaluated the situation as one in which Japanese power was predominant. Consequently it abstained when the vote of censure of Japan was taken at Geneva in 1932. Thereafter its ties with Japan were steadily drawn closer. In relation to the internal program, the new relationship with Japan made it possible for Japanese to begin to displace Chinese in commerce and industry, thus paving the way for the more vigorous anti-Chinese policy followed after 1938. This was made possible under the terms of the commercial treaty of May, 1938 which placed Japanese in Thailand on the same footing as Thai for business purposes. Thus instead of Thai being sucked into the vacuum in trade and industry

[3] George W. Keeton, *China, the Far East and the Future* (London: Stevens, 1949), pp. 315-316.

created by the attempted elimination of the Chinese, the vacuum was partially filled by Japanese traders and by Japanese goods.

In foreign affairs the Japanese orientation was signalized by a new treaty of friendship with Japan which was concluded in 1940. This coincided with Japan's move into Indochina, following the defeat of France in Europe, and with the demand of Thailand for the retrocession of four provinces lost to France at the end of the nineteenth century. The people involved were Thai, as well as some Cambodians. The move, which came shortly after the change of name of the country from Siam to Thailand, was an expression of a nationalist desire to "redeem" the members of the nation by reincorporating them in the independent state.[4] At that time the weak spot was Indochina, and the new relationship with Japan gave Thailand the support of the then Far Eastern power in presenting its demands at a time when Japan was beginning to move southward. This move was ostensibly to strengthen its position against China, but, as it turned out, also to pave the way for the operations undertaken after December 7, 1941.[5]

In its new role as predominant power in the Far East, Japan offered its services as mediator between Thailand and French Indochina, "mediating" by compelling a settlement which gave Thailand the part of the territory in dispute in which it was most interested. This friendly action further strengthened the tie between Japan and Thailand, while at the same time underscoring Japan's new position in Indochina. This position of dominance in Indochina, of course, brought Japan's power, and the ability to exercise it, directly to the borders of Thailand. This paved the way for enforcement, if that had proved necessary, of the demand made on December 8, 1941 for the right to move Japanese troops across Thailand for the invasion of Malaya. This demand was ostensibly debated by the Thai government for some hours, during which time a token resistance was made to the Japanese. The military clique, headed by Pibul Songgram, then agreed to collaborate with the Japanese although it had insisted previously that Thailand would resist invasion to the last, and the National Assembly had voted to this effect on September 11, 1941.

[4] Rupert Emerson, Lennox Mills, and Virginia Thompson, *Government and Nationalism in Southeast Asia* (New York: International Secretariat, Institute of Pacific Relations, 1942), pp. 219-20; see also Thompson and Adloff, *op. cit.*, p. 217.
[5] Subsequently (in 1943) Thailand again extended its frontiers with the transfer to its administration by Japan of provinces in Burma and Malaya which had once been part of the Kingdom of Siam.

Acceptance of the immediate Japanese demands was followed by the signature (December 21, 1941) of a treaty of alliance with Japan, acceptance of a ten-year cultural-exchange pact with Japan, and declaration of war by Thailand on Britain and the United States.

EFFECT OF WORLD WAR II ON THAILAND

The declaration of war on the United States was not reciprocated, Washington refusing to consider the declaration of war as expressive of the will of the Thai people. Consequently, throughout the war the United States maintained diplomatic relations with those Thai officials, especially the Thai minister in Washington, who refused to concur in the decision of a government which those officials held to have acted under Japanese duress. Britain, however, with its larger interests in Thailand, found itself to be in a state of war with Thailand, a status which could only be changed with a treaty of peace.

For the period of the war Thailand was a Japanese puppet state under a government headed by Luang Pibul Songgram, one of its prewar military leaders. The leader of the civil faction, which called itself the People's Party, remained in office as a member of the government although he had urged against acceptance of the Japanese demands and had refused to vote for the declaration of war. Under his (Pridi Phanomyong, known previously by his title Luang Pradit Manudharm) leadership an internal resistance movement was organized which was able to render considerable service to the United Nations in military operations and internal sabotage toward the end of the war.

By the time of the Japanese surrender Thailand had been brought within the area of operations of the (British) Southeast Asia Command. It was consequently Britain which received the surrender of the Japanese forces in that country. There had been no prior agreement between the United States, Britain, and China concerning the treatment of Thailand at the end of the war so that their immediate military control made it possible for the British to act so as to establish a satisfactory position for themselves. They consequently presented

the Siamese authorities with a series of far-reaching demands. The British insisted that the whole of Siam's civil administration be placed under British authority, that all Siamese exports be regulated solely by the British government, and in general and until such time as Siam might eventually be received into the membership of the United Nations, that Siam become a British protectorate.... These demands not only were vigorously objected to by the leaders of the Siamese people but they were also vigorously denounced by the Chinese government and less openly but equally condemned by the Government of the United States.[6]

As a consequence of this internal and external reaction, British requirements of Thailand were modified to a point warranted by Thai war activities. This made it possible to negotiate a treaty with the new government which had come into power before the end of the war. By the treaty of January 1, 1946 the territorial status of December 7, 1941 was restored and Thailand agreed to pay compensation for losses or damage sustained by British subjects during the war. Thus the Malay provinces transferred to Thailand by Japan were restored to British control. The treaty also guaranteed Britain the air rights possessed before the war and renewed the obligation on the part of Thailand not to consent to the cutting of a canal across the Kra Isthmus except with Britain's approval. As a further concession, Thailand accepted provisional controls of its economy and promised to give Britain 1,500,000 tons of rice.

When it became evident that this amount would not be forthcoming, successive agreements were negotiated granting Thailand ever larger payments for smaller rice commitments, and the restrictions on other exports were either eased or lifted. In its dealings with Britain and the United States, Thailand soon learned that rice was its most useful instrument of national policy, the predominant Anglo-American concern being to maintain maximum stability in neighboring food-shortage areas.[7]

The British, on their side, together with India, agreed to sponsor the application of Thailand for admission into the United Nations. Thus the war ended for Thailand, as far as Britain was concerned, with the restoration of the pre-1932 British position but with Thai sovereignty safeguarded.

RE-ADJUSTMENT OF RELATIONS

In order to re-establish its international position and to secure admission into the United Nations, however, Thailand had to readjust its relations with France, China, and the Soviet Union, any one of which could veto its admission. The principal grievance of China concerned the post-1932 Thai treatment of resident Chinese. This griev-

[6] Sumner Welles, *Where Are We Heading?* (New York: Harpers, 1946), p. 309.
[7] Rosinger and Associates, *op. cit.*, pp. 273-74.

ance was only partially removed by the terms of the treaty of amity which was signed on January 23, 1946, but diplomatic relations were restored and, as the Kuomintang government became increasingly preoccupied with the maintenance of its internal position against the Chinese Communist Party, the issue came to be more and more resolved along lines satisfactory to Thai nationalism.

The re-establishment of satisfactory relations with France proved more difficult. Assisted by the United States, however, an agreement was reached in November, 1946 which provided for return to France of the territories which Japanese mediation had secured for Thailand under the terms of the Convention of May, 1941. This November agreement provided for the establishment of a conciliation commission to examine the ethnic, geographic, and economic arguments for the cession to determine whether or not the pre-1941 boundary between Indochina and Thailand should be re-established. Nevertheless this did not serve to change the situation since, in August, 1947 Thailand formally renounced all claim to Indochinese territory.

To avoid Soviet opposition to its application for membership in the United Nations, Thailand sought the establishment of the diplomatic relations with the Soviet Union which had been nonexistent since the revolution in Russia in 1917. The way was paved for this by the repeal of an anti-Communist law which had been enacted in 1933. These moves were designed to prevent opposition to Thai admission into the United Nations. The other state with a veto—the United States—had officially maintained relations with Thailand during the war. After the war the attitude of the United States had been consistently friendly to whatever government was in power. Washington thus was prepared to support the Thai application for United Nations' membership. As a result Thailand formally resumed its membership in the international community through admission to the United Nations in December, 1946.

After this initial adjustment of relations with China, Russia, and France during the postwar years Thailand generally developed its foreign policy in sympathetic alignment with the United States and Britain. With the American and British interest in the order and stability necessary to enable production to be maintained, Britain and the United States understandably accepted any changes in government which had the effect of strengthening authority. Maintaining Thai rice production and ensuring its availability for export to the disturbed food-shortage countries in the area was of great importance to both Britain and the United States. Rice primarily, but also the position of Thailand as the most important country in the southwest Asia area able, because of its stability, to supply tin, teakwood, and rubber, enabled Thailand to associate with Britain and the United States as much on its own terms as on theirs. It was thus able to receive necessary American economic assistance without the fear shown by Indonesia and Burma of so-called American imperialism. The fact, of course, that Thailand was not just emerging from the colonial status but had consistently maintained its independence in the prewar period, during which it had developed the technique of survival by playing-off one aggressive power against another, helps to explain the difference in its postwar reaction to Western policy from that of the new nationalist states in the area.

INTERNAL POLITICS

Thai nationalism in the 1930's, it will be recalled, had been a reaction against the dominant economic position in the country of the Chinese rather than against Western imperialism. The change in the situation in China which brought the Communist Party to power, consequently, produced a different reaction in Thailand from that of India, Burma, and Indonesia. The difference was shown in the failure to recognize the Central People's Government and in the continued maintenance of relations with the Kuomintang regime, although the Thai embassy in China was withdrawn in 1949. Thus, for its own reasons, Thailand's reaction to the Communist victory in China was similar to that of the United States and the resulting situation had the effect of confirming the alignment of Thailand with the United States in regional and general international relations. This difference in reaction from that of India was further shown in the affirmative support given to the United Nations' action in Korea, Thailand sending an expeditionary force of four thousand men as its contribution to the defense of South Korea.

In all of this, however, Thailand avoided the appearance of following a policy dictated by hostility to communism or to China. While clearly aligned with the United States and the recipient of American aid, the appearance as well as the reality of mutuality of interest as determining the alignment rather than dictation of policy from Washington was consistently maintained. This, together with its greater internal stability, made it possible for Bangkok, the Thai capital, to be accepted as the Far Eastern center of United Nations' activities in preference to Manila. Thus the country's international importance was signalized and enhanced through the establishment of the Far Eastern regional office of the Food and Agricultural Organization, of the Children's Emergency Fund, and of the headquarters of the Economic Commission for Asia and the Far East at Bangkok in or after 1949.

The references which have been made above to the stability of Thailand may appear to be somewhat at variance with the facts. There were recurrent overturns of the government, or attempts at its overturn, during the entire postwar period. But none of these had revolutionary implications either of a nationalist or of a Communist nature. On the whole they may be said to have represented the resumption of the struggle among the factions which had contended for power in the 1930's. This was encouraged by the removal of external threats to the independence of the country such as that presented in immediate postwar British policy.

The military element, headed by Pibul Songgram, which had established its dominance by the end of the 1930's, was temporarily discredited, both at home and abroad, because of its responsibility for the alignment of Thailand with Japan, an alignment which, during the war, carried with it a loss of real independence. As with collaborators in other countries, however, it did not take too long for the collaborator to re-establish himself as an active participant in politics. Pibul resumed his political activity by forming a political party (the Tharmathipat party) early in 1947; entered into a combination with the conservative wing of the so-called Democratic Party; carried through a coup d'état in November; and took over the headship of the government in April, 1948. Despite periodic attempts to overthrow it, this government of the military clique remained in power, with the acquiescence of the United States, Britain, and other interested states after 1948.

Pibul's re-entry into politics was facilitated by a split in the Free Thai camp group organized under Pridi's leadership. This split occurred only after the principal external threat to Thai sovereignty had been removed with the signature of the Anglo-Thai treaty of 1946. This made it less dangerous for the normal personal and factional rivalries to express themselves. Two groups followed the leadership of Pridi. While they had only vague programs, they may be said to have stood theoretically for the resumption of the movement toward democracy which had been inaugurated in 1932. Thus the constitution adopted in 1932 was revived and amended in 1946 so as to make the Lower House completely elective,[8] and to make provision for an elective Upper House. The executive State Council or Cabinet remained responsible to the Assembly, or Lower House. Following the election held August 5, 1946 a government dominated by the political groups following Pridi was constituted, under the premiership of Thawan Thamrong Nawasawa, a former judge advocate of the Thai navy and one of the leaders in the 1932 revolution. Although apparently firmly seated in power through control of the Assembly and the new Upper House, this immediate postwar regime soon found itself faced with mounting dissatisfaction. The unexplained death of the popular young King Ananda and the inability of the government satisfactorily to dispose of charges of complicity in it; the mounting indiscipline and corruption of Pridi's followers both in and out of Parliament; his growing intolerance of criticism of his own behavior and that of his followers; but above all the inability of the government to ameliorate the economic situation resulting from the war and the immediate postwar disorganization all contributed to this dissatisfaction which paved the way for the successful coup of November, 1947.

The economic problem was that of shortage of food as well as of other necessities. The method of solution imposed by the government was that of the rationing of rice in a country that had always been one of the major rice-producing areas of the world. Rationing was necessary (1) because of the agreement concurrently made with Britain and the United States to apportion and restrict domestic consumption so that rice might be exported at a fixed rate of $80 per ton and (2) to enable Thailand to meet even the decreasing quotas of rice which it had agreed to export.

The parliamentary opposition was able to capitalize on the dissatisfactions engendered by the economic situation and the disorders which it produced, to execute the coup of November, 1947. Although engineered by Pibul, this immediately brought back into power the conservative civilian leaders of the country rather than the military. The latter remained in the background until there was a greater assurance of foreign acquiescence in control by those who had been tainted by collaboration with the Japanese. The new government, con-

[8] Originally only half had been elected, half having been nominated.

sequently was headed by Khuang Aphaiwong, one of three leaders of the Free Thai group which, when the split occurred, organized itself into the Democratic Party or Club and constituted the parliamentary opposition to the first postwar government organized on the basis of a majority in the parliament.

Having gained power by the method of the coup d'état rather than by the process of parliamentary opposition, the Aphaiwong government reverted to constitutional and democratic methods of governing the country, promulgating a new constitution designed to re-establish the position of the Crown as it had been in 1932 under the then existing constitution. New elections to the Assembly were held in January, 1948. These gave the Democratic faction, rather than the Thermathipat party of the military clique, a majority. It being thus apparent that Pibul could resume power only by waiting for the time of new elections or by the violent method of the coup d'état, he chose not to wait and displaced the Aphaiwong government on April 8, 1948 with one headed by himself.

ECONOMIC RECOVERY

Improvement in economic conditions during this period caused the people to view these changes in government as of little direct concern to them. Their concern, as in agricultural countries generally, was with the processes of earning a livelihood. Government and politics was accepted as the business of those who chose to undertake it, and beyond the concern of the masses of the people; provided that the government maintained conditions which would enable the people to plant and cultivate in the customary manner and reap without undue disturbance or interference. The methods of democracy had not been sufficiently deeply implanted to make the maintenance of democracy a matter of primary concern to the people. Consequently, given good harvests, they were not apt to raise serious objections to shifts of power by nondemocratic methods among the groups or individuals who made up the governing elite. Disturbances, or threats of disturbances, at the top did not produce instability in the country as a whole. Thus, despite successful and unsuccessful coups, Thailand actually was one of the few relatively orderly and stable countries in the area after the initial postwar readjustments had been made.

Beginning with the 1946-47 harvests, rice production reached and sometimes surpassed the prewar level, making it possible for the country to make substantial exports, approximating the rice exports of prewar years, and at the higher postwar price. These exports produced dissatisfaction only when they did not represent a real surplus over the normal internal consumption. The government's emphasis on rice production enabled it simultaneously to conciliate Britain and the United States through exports and prevent internal unrest and disorder. The demand for rubber and tin, both for current consumption and for stockpiling by the United States, stimulated production of those commodities. Their export directly to the United States from Thai ports, rather than into the channels of world trade through Singapore, coupled with the amount of American economic and military assistance necessitated by the requirements of postwar reconstruction and rehabilitation, had the effect of increasing American influence over the economic life of the country, with a corresponding decrease of that of Britain. The foreign demand for the production of Thailand enabled the country to maintain fairly consistently, after 1946, a favorable foreign trade balance, and the restoration of production enabled the government to support increased expenditure out of current income.

This relative prosperity made Thailand somewhat unique among the countries of eastern Asia during the postwar period. Their prosperity made the Thai people less susceptible to the propaganda of the Communist. This enabled the government to go further in aligning itself definitely with the United States against the Soviet Union and Communist China than would otherwise have been viewed as expedient. This alignment was, to be sure, a natural one in the light of Thai nationalism which resulted in part from the earlier popular hostility to the large Chinese minority. Despite this, however, Thai policy might have developed along the lines of the same neutralism as that proclaimed by Indonesia and India if the country had not been relatively stable politically and prosperous economically, and if it had had the deep-rooted suspicion of the motives of the Western powers which a colonial past would have developed.

The sympathetic alignment with the United States caused the Thai government to follow the American lead in the United Nations at the time of the Korean crisis. Within the limits of its capacity Thailand made an active even though small contribution to the war in Korea, it and the Philippines being the only Far Eastern states contributing to the United Nations forces in Korea.

The factor of fear was introduced into Thai policy in 1953 and 1954 with the extension of the military operations of the Viet Minh, assisted by the Chinese Communists, into Laos and Cambodia. This led the Thai government, as it became apparent that a satisfactory settlement of the Indochina problem would not be reached at the Geneva Conference, to put the question of need for a peace observation commission on the agenda of the Security Council, and to express a real interest in the construction of a Pacific security system along the lines proposed by the American Secretary of State. Thus the situation in Indochina had the effect of confirming and strengthening the orientation of Thai foreign policy toward the United States.

RETURN OF PIBUL SONGGRAM TO POWER

The international situation, as well as interest in economic stability, made the United States, on its side, less doctrinaire in its reaction to internal political developments in Thailand than might otherwise have been the case. These developments, as stated, were in the direction of authoritarianism rather than democracy in government. This authoritarianism was a natural consequence of the return to power of Pibul Songgram in 1948.

Pibul came to power because of general dissatisfaction with the apparent inability of the government to bring about real economic improvement. He was fortunate in attaining power at a time when the harvests were good and when improvement had begun to set in. Following the same policies as their predecessors, the governments headed or dominated by Pibul were able to capitalize on improvements which were largely due to natural causes or to world conditions. Pibul was accepted abroad, in spite of his political antecedents, because he seemed to be able to produce the results which were immediately desired by the United States and Britain. He was accepted at home because economic conditions were tolerable. But he maintained himself in power through intolerance of organized opposition and by means of its drastic elimination when it appeared to threaten his position.

This authoritarian trend was partially written into the constitution finally adopted, after considerable delay due to parliamentary opposition, on January 28, 1949. The new constitution was objected to (1) by the Pridi elements because it provided for appointment of the Upper House by the King, and (2) by the Army clique because of the crown being given control over army appointments and troop movements. It was also opposed by the latter because of the safeguards constitutionally provided for civil liberties and free economic enterprise. A coup d'état attempted in February, 1949, was, however, unsupported by the military. In its failure the coup provided an excuse for the elimination of the liberal opposition and thus for the strengthening of the control of the military. The resulting order was maintained until another coup was attempted, in June, 1951, by navy elements who kidnapped Premier Pibul and managed to hold him prisoner for twenty-four hours on a navy gunboat. He was able to escape, however, and the revolt was put down. Subsequently, his government was overthrown by the military faction but the deposed premier was immediately named to succeed himself. The result was a reconstruction of the government, followed by the re-establishment of the constitution of 1932. Thus Pibul remained a constant factor in the construction and reconstruction of governments after his re-entry into politics in 1947.

This was possible because of his ability to eliminate, by degrees, oppositional elements. It was also possible, however, because of his ability to ride prevailing tides one after another. The country, including the opposition leaders, reacted as he did to the nationalist stimulus provided by fear of China after it became communist. For example, the organization of the Free Thai movement in China could be viewed by and in Thailand only as an attempt on part of Communist China to engage in imperialist and antinationalist activities. For reasons previously suggested the movement could not be exploited successfully in Thailand, as similar movements had been elsewhere, as an anti-imperialist, anticapitalist, and anti-Western movement. Thus Pibul's nationalism and anticommunism were a source of strength both internally and externally. His external acceptance by those in a position to aid Thailand economically and by military means, rather than merely to promise aid and support, enabled his governments to maintain the prosperity on which his rule was ultimately dependent, and to turn with some assurance to the United Nations for support in the prospective international crisis.

BIBLIOGRAPHICAL REFERENCES

Great Britain, *Papers by Command, Cmd.* 8163, "Exchange of Notes Between the Governments of the United Kingdom and Thailand *re* Settlement of Outstanding Commonwealth War Claims Against Thailand," Bangkok, May 4 and Nov. 8, 1950 and Jan. 3, 1951;

Cmd. 8140, "Agreement Between Britain and Thailand for the Termination of War," Jan. 1, 1946.
Cmd. 9090, "Exchange of Notes Regarding the Agreement of January 1, 1946 for the Termination of the State of War," Bangkok, Jan. 14, 1954.

Landon, K. P., "Siam" in *The World of Southeast Asia*, by Lennox A. Mills and others (Minneapolis: Minnesota University Press, 1949); *Siam in Transition* (Chicago: University of Chicago Press, 1940); *The Chinese in Thailand* (Chicago: University of Chicago Press, 1941).

Peterson, Alec, "Britain and Siam: The Latest Phase," *Pacific Affairs*, Vol. 19, No. 4.

Thayer, Philip W. (Ed.), *Southeast Asia in the Coming World* (Baltimore: Johns Hopkins Press, 1953).

Thompson, Virginia and Adloff, Richard, *The Left Wing in Southeast Asia* (New York: Sloane, 1950); "Thailand" in L. Rosinger and Associates *The State of Asia* (New York: Knopf, 1952).

12

Burma and Malaya
in the Postwar World

❋❋❋❋❋❋❋❋❋❋❋❋❋❋❋❋❋❋❋❋❋❋❋❋❋❋❋❋

I. BURMA

THE PREWAR ECONOMY OF BURMA

BURMA IS DISTINCTLY a peripheral country in the Far Eastern area from the standpoint of politics and political orientation. It has a frontier connection with India on the west, with China to the north, and with Thailand on the east. The Indian connection has, however, always been the one of major political and cultural importance. Politically, Burma had been actually attached to India by the British in 1897, remaining an Indian province until 1937. Under British-Indian auspices the country had been developed fairly typically as an exploitation colony (or dependent area) along lines of advantage to the metropolitan country. Its agricultural production was mainly rice, with 70 per cent of the total cropped area being in paddy. Of the total prewar production of some six million tons, approximately half was exported, principally to India, which was also the main market for petroleum, the most important nonagricultural commodity. The annual petroleum production in the decade 1929-39 averaged 250 million gallons. These as well as such other forms of production as that of teak (also primarily an export industry) were administered so as to give

a fat return to the fortunate shareholders, with a margin for new equipment foreshadowing still larger profits. All this was wholly the product of about a hundred years of British rule, based on law and individual freedom: freedom for everyone to make money within the limits of laws intended to protect the liberties of property and person. Not without reason those connected with the development of Burma under British rule could look on their handiwork with honest pride.[1]

The problem of government in Burma was complicated for the British because of the lack of homogeneity of the population. Of the total population (estimated in 1941 at between sixteen and seventeen million) only about 66 per cent was Burmese, the remainder being the "frontier" peoples—the Shans, Karens, Chins, Nagas, and others—together with a foreign population made up of over a million Indians, some two hundred thousand Chinese, nineteen thousand Anglo-Burmans, and upwards of eleven thousand Europeans. Some 80 per cent of the population were Buddhists, including all of the Burmese; the Indian population was Hindu; 4 per cent of the total were Moslem; and slightly more than 2 per cent, mostly Karens, were Christians.

Under British rule the lines of economic development had been set in terms of the interest of outsiders. The Burman was connected with this development only as a cultivator. The period of development had brought him into debt to the Indian moneylender, with the result that, by the time of the outbreak of World War II, 25 per cent of the rice-lands in the thirteen principal rice-growing districts had passed into Chettyar hands.[2] Like the Thai and the Annamite, the Burman was not attracted into industry or commerce, nor did he find himself particularly adapted to the new capitalistic type of agriculture. But, whereas in other countries of southeast Asia the industrious and businesslike Chinese supplemented the European in playing the role of capitalist, thereby ultimately incurring the hostility of the indigenous peoples, in Burma it was the Indian who played that role and whose unpopularity supplied one of the pillars of the nationalism which began to express itself after the First World War.

BURMESE NATIONALISM

Beginning to be driven off the land except as a laborer, the Burman found it necessary to attempt to earn a livelihood in commerce or industry, even though not attracted to or particularly fitted for such work. Here, as well as in capitalistic agriculture, he found himself in competition with imported Indian labor. And during the depression

[1] J. S. Furnivall, "Twilight in Burma: Reconquest and Crisis," *Pacific Affairs*, Vol. XXII, No. 1, pp. 3-4.
[2] The Chettyars were the hereditary banking caste of Hindus from the Madras Presidency.

years of the 1930's, the anti-Indian animus of the people was increased as they found themselves displaced in labor by Indians who could live on less and were consequently willing to work for a smaller wage. Thus by the end of the 1930's anti-Indian sentiment was rooted deeper than the normal antipathy to money-lenders who were Indian. A consequence of the operation of all these considerations was the prewar nationalist movement.[3]

A result of nationalism was the beginning of the association of Burmans with the processes of government through the introduction in 1923 of the scheme of dyarchy, applied first in the reforms of the Indian government instituted after World War I. Of greater importance was the decision taken by the British in 1935 to separate Burma from India. This reflected public opinion as well as financial and administrative difficulties resulting from Burma's status as a province of India. Under the Government of Burma Act (1935) which went into effect in 1937 a bicameral, largely elective, legislature was set up which

controlled all of the administration of Burma except defense, foreign affairs, ecclesiastical affairs (relating solely to the maintenance of fewer than a dozen Anglican Chaplains), the excluded areas, and monetary policy. The last related to actual coinage and the external debt, and not to the Budget.[4]

These important exceptions were powers reserved to the governor who also had extensive emergency powers.

In spite of the reservations, the Act put the Burmans a fairly long step ahead of the Indians in the move toward self-government and ultimate Dominion status or independence. In doing so, of course, it increased the desire and demand for complete self-government, and, in the legislature and the Council of Ministers, provided agencies for the expression of the desire. All of this, however, was in advance of the preparation of an essentially naïve and provincial people to assume and effectively to discharge responsibility for their own affairs. Prior to

[3] A somewhat different point of view was expressed as follows: "Though some observers trace the nationalist movement back to 1905, it may be said generally that the Burman showed no interest in politics until the World War. The great Hindu-Moslem and caste problems of India did not effect Burma, and the Congress movement found barren soil there." Rupert Emerson, Lennox A. Mills, and Virginia Thompson, *Government and Nationalism in Southeast Asia* (New York: International Secretariat, Institute of Pacific Relations, 1942), p. 160.
[4] John L. Christian, "Burma," *Annals of the American Academy of Social and Political Science,* Vol. CCXXVI, p. 122.

1923 their only association with government had been in the lower levels of administration. It was "in the routine of general administration" that Burmans were indispensable. At that level many found a subordinate place as clerks, magistrates, and judges. The educational system, in a country which had a tradition of education when the British first arrived, had been directed by the British toward "training for the market" in subordinate and mainly clerical capacities.

> As there was no employment for Burmans as engineers and doctors, the scientific branches of education were neglected. In 1936-1937, according to the last quinquennial report on education, only seven Burmans obtained a degree in natural science, four others in medicine and two in engineering. Similarly, as there was no opening for Burmans in industry and commerce, the study of economics was neglected. The new educational system did practically nothing to give Burmans an insight into the working of the modern world. From about 1920, on an average some half-dozen men were sent annually to England for various special studies, but most of them were absorbed into government service.... Apart from officials and lawyers, there were probably not more than a couple of dozen Burmans, if so many, who knew anything of the world outside Burma.
>
> And if Burmans knew little of the outer world, they knew perhaps even less of modern Burma.[5]

With the elections of 1936 for the new House of Representatives, it was revealed that the basis of democratic government would have to be party coalition. The parties which had sprung up were themselves essentially personal groupings within the general framework of nationalism. This insured multiplicity of parties and made it inevitable that cabinets formed under the constitution after 1937 would be coalitions. When the first legislature of 132 members was elected it was said to contain 132 parties. The resulting situation led the Governor from the outset to use his special powers of intervention. It also supported the conclusion of many, in 1942, that Burmese politicians could not be expected to operate an effective government without some measure of outside assistance during a period of transition. This conclusion, generally accepted by the British, shaped the thinking about the future of the exiled government of Burma established at Simla for the war period.

The war itself introduced some important changes in the situation which were not initially fully appreciated by the British. In the first place, the circumstances and the rapidity of the Japanese conquest of

5 Furnivall, *op. cit.*, p. 6.

Malaya and Burma so lessened British prestige that, in spite of Japanese conduct during the occupation, it was impossible for the English rulers to reclaim the position of 1937-41. In the second place, by the end of the war a new local leadership had emerged which had gained experience and assurance and a feeling of power through the organization and operation of an anti-Japanese movement within Burma.

The Japanese invasion had been assisted by anti-British extremist elements in the Thakin party who had previously been pressing for complete independence. They formed a relatively small (about 4,000) Burma Independence Army which set up "Free Burma Administrations" in the wake of the Japanese armies. "These, however, acted in such a violent and high-handed way that the Japanese soon suppressed them and governed the country under military rule." [6]

This Japanese military administration outwardly transferred governing power on August 1, 1942 to the Burma Executive headed by Ba Maw, a former Premier who at the time of the invasion was held in internment by the British after serving a sentence for sedition. In spite of the formal grant of independence a year later it became increasingly apparent that the collaborationist Ba Maw government actually enjoyed little freedom of action and that, under its auspices, Burma was being utilized to serve Japan's war purposes. As elsewhere, Japanese propaganda, which had met with considerable success before the invasion, was sufficiently contradicted by Japanese behavior to lose its effectiveness. Consequently, even many of those Burmans who had participated in the invasion went into the anti-Japanese opposition which was organized under the name of the Anti-Fascist Peoples Freedom League (AFPFL).

The Anti-Fascist Peoples Freedom League was quite unlike any Burmese political organization the British had experienced. It was new and different. The Japanese had scarcely overrun Burma before Aung San and the rest of the "thirty Heroes" who had helped them were organizing to drive them out. A number of groups seem to have been at work, but the most successful were the People's Revolutionary Front, the Communists, and the Burma Defense Army commanded by General Aung San. By August 1944 these revolutionary groups had united to form the AFPFL.[7]

[6] A conclusion presented in "Statement of Policy by H. M. Government," May, 1945, Great Britain, *Papers by Command, Cmd. 6635.* Hereafter cited by number as *Cmd. ——.*
[7] Clarence Hendershot, "Burma Compromise," *Far Eastern Survey,* Vol. XVI, No. 12, p. 134.

The fact that the AFPFL had an army as one of its component groups meant that the British, upon their return, were faced for the first time by a political group which had a measure of organized power behind it.

The conditions which the British found upon their return have been described by a former official as follows:

> There was a vast difference between the land to which they returned and that from which they had been driven three years earlier. Then it had been rich in things that measure the material wealth of a nation.... Now after little more than three years, the British came back to find their work in ruins. During those three years the country had been twice invaded; British and Japanese armies had fought stubbornly throughout the length and breadth of Burma, and each in turn had scorched the earth to cover its retreat. The mines, oil fields and plantations had been deliberately wrecked, and the management and technicians, wholly foreign, and most of the labour, very largely foreign, had fled to India. Agriculture had been unprofitable and rice, of which formerly more than three million tons had been exported annually, was worth so little that it was fed to pigs.... The productive capacity of the country had fallen by about two-thirds.... The moral damage was even more lamentable than the material damage. For three years the youth of Burma, which should have been learning in the towns and villages how to live as citizens, had been apprenticed to the more exciting and less laborious art of guerrilla warfare, without even the benefit of military discipline.[8]

British plans for meeting the requirements of the postwar situation in Burma were announced in May, 1945, concurrently with the re-occupation of Rangoon. Broadly stated, the plan [9] involved the restoration of substantially the prewar status as quickly as possible. At first there was to be direct rule by the governor, assisted as rapidly as they could be recruited by nonofficial Burmans. Elections were to be held and the government to be re-constituted, if possible within a three-year-period, on the basis of the 1935 Act. It was then planned that the parties in Burma should agree on a constitution, after which negotiations would be instituted designed to bring about agreement on the conditions of Dominion status for the country. On the economic side, the Simla government (which developed the plan) had prepared a number of projects designed both to stimulate production and to facilitate a return to the "normalities of competitive business as soon as possible."

[8] Furnivall, *op. cit.*, pp. 3-4.
[9] Published as *Cmd.* 6635.

The British army was welcomed by the Burmans when the country was liberated from the Japanese. The initial attitudes were, however, soon changed. During the period of military government, administration was in the hands of a Civil Affairs Service (Burma) composed exclusively of returned British residents and "official" Burmans who had been in exile during the three-year period of the Japanese occupation. This disregarded the authority exercised and the services rendered by those Burmans who had not left the country, especially the leaders of the AFPFL. The resulting situation was not improved materially when, upon the return of the Governor, it was realized that, under the terms of the White Paper, he was required to exercise exclusive powers for an indeterminate period, and that only after the restoration of the status of 1937 could the future position of Burma be brought under consideration.

POSTWAR INDEPENDENCE SOUGHT

The principal source of opposition to the government was the leadership of the AFPFL, which refused to co-operate with the British on the terms defined by them. The strength of this organized opposition lay, in the first place, in its unity and in the public support given it and, in the second place, it came from its capacity for obstructing the government. Its third source of strength, underlying the first two, was in its military support. The demonstrations of its ability to maintain its unity and direct the activity of its supporters, especially against the threat to its leadership presented by returned Burmese politicians who were anxious to regain their prewar positions of power, soon made it expedient for the new Governor to constitute an Executive Council of eleven members, six from the AFPFL and five from the other parties. The strength of the opposition was shown in its ability to secure this change within three months, in August, 1945, of the first policy statement. The negotiations which were thereafter instituted resulted in a conference in London between the British government and a delegation (headed by Aung San, leader of the AFPFL) from the Executive Council of the Governor of Burma. This conference was preceded by a statement of the British Prime Minister (Dec. 20, 1946) that Burma would be granted Commonwealth status or independence, as it desired, "by the quickest and most convenient way possible." This meant that for the British the conference really had as its purpose the working out of arrangements moving from the policy defined in May, 1945 toward the nationalist goal of independence.

The conclusions reached in January, 1947 were for the convocation of an elective constituent assembly instead of a legislature of the sort provided under the 1935 Act. Until the constituent assembly had met and had established a permanent framework of government, a transitional government was to be instituted, with an interim legislative council, as provided by the 1935 Act, of 180 members nominated by the government from those elected to the Constituent Assembly; an interim government, made up of the Executive Council of the Governor; and a High Commissioner for Burma to represent the Burmese government in London. The British government was to support an application to be made by Burma as soon as possible for membership in the United Nations, and to request of other governments an exchange of representatives with Burma, as desired by that country. The problem of relationship with the frontier areas was to be considered by a committee to be constituted, which committee, it may be noted at this point, proposed federation of those areas with Burma.

This agreement did not meet the extreme demands of the Burmese nationalists for immediate and unqualified independence. It did, however, indicate a noteworthy adjustability on the part of the British. It did also seem to Aung San to represent a sufficiently long step forward to warrant its acceptance. He was able to carry the country with him over the opposition of the Communist leaders and of leaders of some non-Communist elements.[10] Consequently elections were held in April, with the AFPFL securing an overwhelming majority of the seats in the Constituent Assembly and the Legislature. The new constitution was adopted on September 24, 1947, and the independence of Burma was recognized by Britain in the Treaty of October 17 which went into force in January, 1948.

The constitution of the new state provided it with a President, elected for a five-year term by secret vote of the combined Chambers of the Parliament; a Cabinet, responsible to a majority in the Chamber of Deputies which, with the President, exercises the executive power; a legislature, the upper House of which is a Chamber of Nationalities in which indigenous minorities controlled 72 of the 125 seats, while the lower House (Chamber of Deputies) represented the people of the

[10] Ba Maw, for example, one of the Burmese representatives at the London conference, refused to sign the agreement.

country and was the strongest organ of government; and an independent Supreme Court.

After the elections and before the completion of the new constitution, the political situation was changed by the assassination (July 19, 1947) of Aung San and six other members of the Executive Council by agents of opposition groups led by U Saw. "The objective was apparently to spread confusion preparatory to the overthrow of the government." [11] As indicated in the adoption of the constitution and the proclamation of independence, the action did not attain the desired result. What it did do, however, was to remove some of the ablest, most experienced and most disinterested AFPFL leaders. Nevertheless, Thakin Nu, in succession to Aung San as Premier, held both the government and the party to the agreed course.

POSTWAR POLITICS AND GOVERNMENT
AFTER INDEPENDENCE

The establishment of independence removed the central issue on which the unity of Burma's political leaders had been based. Consequently the new government was certain sooner or later to encounter opposition. One source of opposition had expressed itself at the All-Burma National Congress of 1946, when the Communist Party began to put itself in the position which led to the expulsion of the Burma Communist Party from the AFPFL in November, 1946. Before this, internal division in the Communist ranks had led to a split and the formation of the Communist Party of Burma as an opposition group both to the Burma Communist Party and the AFPFL. At the other extreme from the Communist opposition was that of the rightist parties which were opposed to the government's program of economic reconstruction along socialist lines. A third source of difficulty came to be presented in the attitude of the Karen people whose representatives had accepted federation but who did not seem prepared fully to accept the consequences of that decision, and who also were prepared to oppose any Communist influence in the government.

The postindependence opposition did not express itself through the

[11] John F. Cady, Patricia Barnett, and Shirley Jenkins, *The Development of Self-Rule and Independence in Burma, Malaya and the Philippines* (New York: Amer. Institute of Pacific Relations, 1948), Pt. 1, "Burma," p. 19. Hereafter cited as Cady and others.

use of parliamentary methods but used the methods of force and violence. Thus in its first years the new government had to develop sufficient power to enable it to exercise its authority against both Communist and non-Communist rebels, who were able to seize control of large sections of the country in 1948 and to hold their positions during 1949. By the end of 1950 the position of the government as against both the Communists and the Karens had been strengthened but the two civil wars were still in progress. The larger rebel groups had been broken up but had scattered in smaller groups throughout the country, and were not consequently completely eradicated. These smaller groups were harder to find and dispose of. They continued to ravage the teak forests, some of the best rice lands in the Irrawady Delta and the tin mines and rubber plantations in Tenasserim.

Nevertheless although rebels continued to have to be dealt with, by the end of 1954 the government had a much more secure hold on power than could have been anticipated at the end of the first year of independence. It was sufficiently sure of itself by 1952 to regard the period of transition, during which the Constituent Assembly had exercised legislative power, as terminable. Thus elections, as provided in the constitution, were held, beginning in the fall of 1951 and into February, 1952. The election results gave the AFPFL a strong majority (about 80 per cent of the 235 seats) in the Chamber of Deputies and thus renewed that party's mandate to rule.

The general lines of internal policy followed by the AFPFL as the governing party were those of moderate socialism. This involved nationalization of communications and of basic features of the national economy, with, however, compensation to the original owners. The application of the program was mainly at the expense of British and Indian interests. This naturally produced some friction but both countries accepted the policy as appropriate and, as a matter of fact, Britain, especially, assisted financially in its execution. This assistance, under the Colombo Plan, together with extensive United Nations and American financial and technical assistance, enabled the government to maintain itself and to bring about such recovery as the disturbed internal conditions permitted. This had the effect of bringing Burma into international relations without its politics being complicated by the question of imperialism or even that of colonialism. Those questions, however, as raised by the Communists especially in relation to China, caused Burma to orient its foreign policy in general somewhat along the lines of Indian neutralism, although without acceptance of Indian leadership in Asian affairs. This qualification as to leadership grew out of a fear held of possible Indian imperialism, a fear which, however, was not sufficiently great to overcome a latent hostility to the charge of American "imperialism" and consequently bring Burma to accept unequivocally American leadership in Far Eastern affairs.

Thus Burma recognized the Central People's Government of the People's Republic of China in December, 1949, and exchanged representatives with Peiping in June of the following year. Thereafter the government of Burma sought to maintain friendly relations with Communist China, although steadily showing an unwillingness to settle the question of the northern frontier on China's terms. The government, furthermore, refused to sign the Japanese Peace Treaty, among the grounds assigned being the occupation of Japanese territory by foreign (i.e., American) troops, and the refusal to allow the Chinese Communists to occupy Formosa. On the other hand Burma co-operated, short of military participation, in the United Nations effort in Korea and in the embargoing of trade in strategic materials with China, and, for a time, tolerated the presence within its territories not only of Chinese Nationalist refugees but of Nationalist troops driven across the frontier. This toleration of Chinese Nationalist troops was brought to an end when those troops began to overassert themselves in the territories in which they had been permitted to reside. Then Burma appealed to the United Nations for assistance in getting them out of the country. Its animus against the Formosa government was increased because it was felt that these troops were still under the command of the Generalissimo. After negotiations, the conditions of evacuation of these Chinese troops were agreed upon, and the evacuation was held to have been completed by the spring of 1954. These difficulties with the Nationalist Chinese, whose principal support was the United States, helped to keep Burma on the same line of relationship to Communist China as that followed consistently by India, and were among the considerations which caused Burma to join with India, Ceylon, Pakistan and Indonesia in the passage of a resolution at the conference held at Colombo on the eve of the Geneva Conference which by implication expressed equal condemnation of United States and Soviet policies.

II. MALAYA

BRITISH RULE IN MALAYA

British Malaya projects as a peninsula southward from Thailand and Burma toward what in prewar days was known as The Netherlands East Indies, now the Republic of Indonesia. Thus it is a link between the latter and the continental countries of southeast Asia. The geographical orientation is strengthened by cultural, racial and religious factors, since the peoples in both Malaya and Sumatra are Malay and the Malays and Indonesians are predominantly Moslem.

In the prolonged period of British rule before the Japanese occupation a pattern of both direct and indirect rule had been evolved, the former for the Crown colony (Singapore with Malacca and Penang forming the Straits Settlements) and the latter for the five Unfederated and, to a lesser extent, for the four Federated Malay States. The Unfederated Malay States had a predominantly Malay governmental system. Their governments were, however, under the necessity of following the advice of British advisers on all questions except those involving the Mohammedan religion and Malay customs. The Federated States also had a qualified autonomy with respect to such matters as education, forests, some aspects of public health, agriculture and Islamic law. On other questions the high commissioner, consulting with the Federal Council, had jurisdiction. The same individual represented British authority as governor of Singapore and as high commissioner in the "protected" states, but in the colony the machinery of government was similar to that in other Crown colonies, while in the protectorates authority was exercised, under the high commissioner, through the resident adviser in each of the states. The latter had his advice translated into policy through the Malay structure, working downward from the sultan.[12]

One of the peculiarities of the situation which developed in Malaya, giving some of its direction to political development under British auspices, was the racial composition of the peninsula. The Malays constituted at the end of 1937 only 42 per cent of the total population, with the Chinese having 41 per cent and the Indians 14.8 per cent of the total. The Chinese were a decisive numerical majority in the Straits Settlements, and predominant in Johore. It was only in the

[12] For a more detailed exposition see Cady and others, *Ibid.*, Pt. II, Malaya.

Unfederated States (other than Johore) that Malay predominance was beyond question. The same relative proportions of the population existed during the postwar period.

In the economy of the country the Malay found his place as a rice cultivator, as a small peasant proprietor, and as a fisherman. Plantation production of rubber, industry, including the mining and smelting of tin, and commerce were all financed and managed by Europeans or Chinese, with some Indian and a slight Japanese participation. The Japanese before, and of course during, World War II controlled the iron mines. Apart from the British, the Chinese had attained the strongest economic position in Malaya.

If, under these circumstances, there had been a strong nationalistic sentiment developed among the Malays before the war it would probably, as in Thailand, have taken an anti-Chinese direction because of the greater number of Chinese than British and their closer occupational contact with the people. The British, in spite of their predominant economic influence, were looked upon by the Malays (and also by the Chinese and Indians) in fact as well as in name as "protectors." It took the war, however, to bring into being anything like a vigorous nationalism. The Malay was essentially unpolitical in the Western meaning of the term, and the Chinese and Indians, before 1941, even though Malaya born, developed their political interests and affiliations in relation to China or India rather than to the country of their domicile. This, with the Chinese, resulted in some anti-British sentiment at times of Sino-British tension in China, but without changing their nonpolitical role in Malaya or causing them any the less to look to Britain for the fair and full protection of their interests. British rule, in other words, was considered useful by the Chinese.

The colony and protected states were financially self-supporting except for the outlays made necessary for Imperial defense. Even for that purpose, for which Singapore and the Straits Settlements were expected to bear a share of the cost, the states made only voluntary contributions. The conception of the problem of defense was based upon the probability of attack from the sea so that expenditure was concentrated upon the building of the great naval base at Singapore and on air bases, with only a small military establishment maintained. This helps to explain the ease with which the peninsula was overrun by the Japanese.

Release from the burden of defense made it possible for public income to be devoted to the development of public services. Communications facilities were developed, including hard-surfaced roads and a railway line running from Singapore to Bangkok in Siam. The public health and sanitation services were fairly highly developed. Elementary education, free for the Malays in the vernacular schools, and limited secondary and college education were provided for out of public funds. An excellent medical school was maintained, and Raffles College was established in 1928. A few selected students were sent each year to England for their higher education. The revenue to support these services and also the civil service was derived, in the Straits Settlements, from duties on tobacco, liquor, and petroleum; from an opium monopoly; and from fees for services of various sorts. Customs and excise taxes were principal sources of revenue in the Unfederated States. The Federated States had an additional source of revenue in an export tax on tin as well as on rubber. The latter, especially, yielded considerable sums. Thus it was possible to provide services from revenue which was not extracted directly from the Malay peasant or the smaller producers. This serves somewhat to explain the greater acceptance in Malaya than in some of their other colonies of British rule as beneficent, although it should be added that in Malaya, as in many other areas, British rule was synonomous with the introduction of the rule of law and its impartial administration.

Just as Burma, the Philippines, and Indonesia, as staple-crop exporting countries, found the measure of their prosperity in external conditions, so Malaya was dependent upon the outside world as a market, mainly for its tin and rubber. In both of these industries the major investment interest was British, although capital was also invested by Chinese, French, and Americans, while the mining of iron ore was in Japanese hands. The rubber estates were 75 per cent European owned, 16 per cent Chinese, 4 per cent Indian, and 5 per cent Japanese and other Asians. An additional 1,250,000 acres (almost the European-owned acreage) was in the possession of smallholders, principally Malay but also Chinese and Indian. The main market for tin and rubber was the United States but, in spite of the largely free-trade policy followed by Britain for Malaya until the inauguration of imperial preference, the main source of imports, until cheaper Japanese goods began to invade the market in the 1930's, was Britain. Some of the restrictions on free trade introduced in the decade before the war were designed to restrict Japanese imports.

CONSEQUENCES OF THE WAR FOR MALAYA

The war had, for Malaya, as for other southeastern Asian countries, important consequences. One of these was that of economic disruption and destruction. The fighting itself, coupled with some application of the "scorched earth" policy and with some guerrilla warfare after the Japanese occupation, accounts for much of the destruction. But the inability of the Japanese to replace the United States, Britain, and Europe in general, as a market for tin and rubber, and the inability of Japan to maintain necessary imports into Malaya had for a period of four years not only a disrupting but also a deteriorating effect on the economy of the country. Thus the end of the war saw Britain faced with a problem of economic rehabilitation of some considerable proportions. Because of the products involved, furthermore, the restoration of production in Malaya was of great importance to the rest of the world.

The cultural program of the Japanese also had postwar implications, as did native resistance to it. The conditions of the occupation had the consequence of developing political self-consciousness among the Malays especially, and of advancing their political maturity. The local barriers to the development of a Malay nationalism, represented by the existence of nine protected states and a colony, were at least somewhat diminished by the common resistance to Japanese rule on an essentially centralized basis. The Japanese attempts, toward the end of their occupation, to introduce or extend some of the institutions of self-rule also had significance in the development of political self-consciousness. Thus even in Malaya, because of local circumstances as effected by the war, the British did not have, as it proved, complete freedom of decision in planning and executing the postwar political reorganization of the country. Immediate postwar developments further limited their freedom of decision.

POSTWAR BRITISH POLICY FOR MALAYA

The British re-entered Malaya early in September, 1945, with the military force they had intended to use for invasion had the Japanese surrender not already occurred. Contact was made with the underground army and civil government was transferred to a British Military Administration (BMA).[13]

[13] For "Statement on Policy" see *Cmd.* 6724. For the orders in Council summarizing the proposed constitutional arrangements *Cmd.* 6749.

Malaya, it was contemplated, would continue under military administration until plans which had been matured for a change in the system of administration could be put into effect. The general plan was to establish a Malayan Union comprising the nine "protected" states and all of the former Crown colony except Singapore, which was to remain a colony. There was to be a common Malay citizenship within the union. Thus the plan was designed to break down the separatism of the Malay states rather than to destroy the Malay structure of government within the states. British authority was to be represented by a governor for the union and a different appointee serving as the governor of the Crown colony of Singapore. Both governors were to have fairly wide powers of legislation and appointment. Within limits, however, the plan extended the institutions of self-government, lessening official control of the legislative councils which were to be constituted and establishing a Council of Sultans to advise the governor on matters which he submitted to it and to enact legislation on religious questions, as recommended by Malay advisory councils.

A preliminary step to the institution of the union was taken with the revision of the prewar treaties between Britain and the sultans. It was on the foundation of these treaties that the protectorates rested. But within the short time which it took to elicit agreement of the Sultans considerable opposition to the Union idea developed in Malaya. A "United Malays National Organization" was formed among the Malays for purposes of opposition. The grounds of opposition were: (1) the inconsistency of the new treaties with Malay "sovereignty, custom and tradition; and (2) a contention that the integrity and independence of the Malay race would be undermined by the proposed conditions of union, especially those providing for Malayan citizenship."

After considerable discussion, the British plan for union was modified along lines proposed by a Malay-British Working Committee. The new proposals, while substituting for the Malayan Union a new constitution in federal form, appeared to His Majesty's Government to be calculated to achieve their own fundamental objectives of essential cohesion and a basis for common loyalty.[14]

---

[14] *Cmd.* 7171, p. 3. The principles which were regarded as fundamental by the British Government were:

(a) that there should be a strong central government to ensure the economical and effective administration of all matters of importance to the welfare and progress of the country as a whole;

These proposals also met with the approval of the sultans and the United Malays National Organization, and were consequently substantially embodied in the "constitution" which became effective in 1948.

The Federation thus constituted consisted of the nine Malay states and the Settlements of Penang and Malacca. Singapore was left out of the federation, it being the view of the British government that "the question of Singapore joining in a Federation should be considered on its merits and in the light of local opinion at an appropriate time." [15]

New State Agreements concluded in connection with the establishment of the Federation of Malaya provided for the enjoyment by the Sultans of "the prerogatives, power and jurisdiction which they enjoyed prior to the Japanese occupation." The British government, however, retained complete control of the defence of the States and of all external affairs. Each ruler, it was laid down "will undertake to govern his State subject to the provisions of a written constitution, which is to be in conformity with the State Agreement and the Federation Agreement . . . " It was also stipulated that

> The State Agreements will also provide that the Ruler desires, and His Majesty agrees, that it shall be a particular charge upon the Government of the State to provide for and encourage the education and training of the Malay inhabitants of the State so as to fit them to take a full share in the economic progress, social welfare and Government of the State and of the Federation.

The Federation Agreement provided for a British-appointed high commissioner, a Federal Executive Council "to aid and advise the high commissioner," and a Federal Legislative Council.[16] The Executive

---

(b) that the individuality of each of the Malay States and of the Settlements should be clearly expressed and maintained;

(c) that the new arrangements should, on the long view, offer the means and prospects of development in the direction of ultimate self-government;

(d) that, with a view to the establishment of broad-based institutions, necessary for principle (c) to become effective, a common form of citizenship should be introduced which would enable political rights to be extended to all those who regard Malaya as their real home and as the object of their loyalty;

(e) that, as these States are Malay States ruled by Your Highnesses (the Sultans), the subjects of Your Highnesses have no alternative allegience, or other country which they can regard as their homeland, and they occupy a special position and possess rights which must be safeguarded.

[15] *Ibid.*, p. 12.

[16] It should be noted here parenthetically that similar advisory bodies were to be established in each state.

Council was composed of three ex officio members, at least four official members, and not less than five or more than seven unofficial members, of whom not less than two in the former case and three in the latter were to be Malays. The Legislative Council was constituted with the high commissioner as president, three *ex officio* members, eleven official members, the nine presidents of the Councils of State in the Malay states, and fifty unofficial members selected to represent interests, groups, and activities. From the racial standpoint the Eurasian, Ceylonese, and Indian communities were given one member and the Chinese community two. Otherwise the basis of representation was, aside from that given the states and settlements, the economic interest group. It was estimated, however, that this would result in giving the Malays a total of twenty-two seats, the Chinese fourteen, the Indians five, Europeans seven, and the Ceylonese and Eurasians one each.

POSTWAR AREAS OF CONFLICT IN MALAYA

The Federation Agreement was supported by the United Malay Organization which had led the opposition to the original union plan, since its views, as well as those of the sultans, had been taken into account by the British. There was nevertheless opposition to the new governmental system. This was led by a newly formed organization called the Pan-Malayan Council of Joint Action, an amalgamation of Chinese, Indian, and Eurasian groups. Another opposition group—the Malay Nationalist Party—dropped out of the Council of Joint Action after its initial meeting. It thereupon formed a Malay Council of Joint Action which followed a course parallel to that of the Pan-Malayan Council. At about the same time the non-Communist Chinese organized themselves locally in the Malayan Chinese Association. The opposition groups demanded the inclusion of Singapore in the Federation, responsible self-government through a fully elected central legislature, and equal citizenship for all who were permanent residents of Malaya.

Aside from the problem of maintenance of public order growing out of the terroristic activities of the Communist party, the two major areas of internal conflict after 1948 were those concerned with: (1) the issue of citizenship,[17] and (2) the amount of self-government to be instituted. The question of complete union, including Singapore, was

[17] For the operative provisions with respect to citizenship under the Federal Agreement, *Cmd.* 7171, pp. 10-11.

to a considerable extent tied in with these two. The issue of citizenship obviously grew out of the external orientation of the large Chinese and Indian populations. Regardless of place of birth and continued domicile the Chinese and Indians, especially the former, initially regarded themselves as Chinese and Indian in allegiance rather than as in an exclusive and undivided allegiance to the country in which they permanently resided. They consequently tended to reproduce in Malaya, the party organizations and affiliations of India and China, although becoming more and more assertive in Malayan affairs. Thus the Indians, in August, 1946, formed the Malayan-Indian Congress, and the Chinese were divided between Kuomintang and Communist organizations as well as being organized in the Malayan Chinese Association. What each group wanted at this time was a dual citizenship. Neither wanted actually to confine its allegiance to a Malay state. Each wanted local security, however, and neither attempted to play a political role in Malaya until the protection of its interests against the new Malay nationalism required local political action.

Self-rule was a demand growing naturally out of war experience and out of the general climate of opinion at the end of the war. For some years it was a demand, however, of an advanced minority rather than of a majority of the Malays who were enrolled in the United Malays National Organization. That party supported the position of the sultans and the policy of federation under Britain, rather than self-government, whether or not coupled with independence. The opposition Nationalist Party, on the other hand, was said to be dominated by liberal Malays, mainly from the professional, student, and labor groups. As Malays, the nationalists had a strong Indonesian orientation. The party program aimed at an independent Malaya, composed of the Malay states, the settlements, and Singapore, which would co-operate with Indonesia. Because of its objectives the Nationalist Party was anti-British as well as anti-Sultan, the latter because it advocated greater local self-government, although with safeguards to ensure Malay control.

The other important party—the Communist Party—had primarily a Chinese membership. In general it followed the international Communist party line. Lacking any widespread popular support it sought by terrorist methods to prevent the re-establishment of order and the restoration of production. Since Britain especially needed Malayan production of rubber and tin to finance necessary purchases in the United States, successful restriction of production had consequences for Britain which were felt at home as well as in Malaya. The augmented forces which had to be used in Malaya in the attempt to preserve life and property against terrorist attacks, furthermore, constituted a serious drain on the military manpower and the resources of the United Kingdom.

As the authorities brought terrorism to some extent under control, the tactics of the Communist Party in Malaya were modified, as they had been in Indonesia after the failure of the attempt to seize power under imported leadership. The new tactics involved infiltration in the labor organizations of the country, work among students, attempted conciliation of the propertied elements among the Chinese and Indians, and the establishment of a working relationship with the more extreme Malay elements. In all of this the Communists made some progress.

Terrorism, however, continued, although General Sir Gerard Templer, upon his retirement as High Commissioner in May, 1954, expressed the opinion that

> the emergency could be ended in three months if everyone cooperated with the security forces and gave any information they had. Security forces were dropping 2 m. leaflets every week in pursuance of the propaganda campaign, and planes were broadcasting to about fifteen jungle targets each week.

The Communist strength he reported as being between 4,400 and 6,000 men, which was a decline of about 2,000 as a result of the campaign carried on over a three-year period. While this was not a great decline it represented more of a loss than the figures would indicate since it included a large proportion of the leaders.

> The terrorists, [according to a report of General Templer's comments], had withdrawn into the jungle to avoid attack and surrenders had become more difficult to obtain. The Communists' main objectives were: (1) to establish bases for their higher command; (2) to strengthen control of villages and towns on the jungle fringes so that they could get supplies; and (3) to penetrate political parties and trade unions and to build underground organizations in the town.[18]

While the struggle against the terrorists had been going on there had been consideration given to what were stated above to be the major areas of internal conflict—the questions of citizenship and self-

[18] General Templer's farewell press conference, as summarized in *Chronology of International Events* (London: [British] Royal Institute of International Affairs), Vol. 10, No. 11, p. 354.

government. The directive to General Templer as High Commissioner had required him to "go on with the work of building up a Malayan nation and to give the peoples of Malaya an increasing responsibility for the management of their own affairs." [19] This was held to require the establishment of some system of elections, and that in itself brought the two questions of citizenship and of self-government together. In the negotiations which went on the British dealt mainly with the two organizations, one of Malays and the other of Chinese, which sought development within the existing framework rather than independence or any other fundamental change in the system of federation. These two conservative organizations—the United Malayan National Organization and the Malayan Chinese Association—sent a joint delegation to London early in 1954 "authorized to raise certain points with the Secretary of State for the Colonies." [20]

One of their points was that native officials should not be debarred from standing for election to the Legislative Council, since that would reduce the number of really qualified candidates. A second point was that designated categories of noncitizens should be given the right to vote in addition to those who had federal citizenship and those who were subjects of the native rulers. On the first point, the Secretary of State for the Colonies took the position that the concessions already made had reached the upper limit of expediency.[21]

On the second point Mr. Lyttelton was unwilling to make a concession on the ground that the enfranchisement of noncitizens would "run counter to the practice of modern states."

The main point advanced was that the Legislative Council should be constituted with three-fifths of the members elected. The Committee on Constitutional Reform had recommended a balance of elected and nominated members. However upon recommendation of the high commissioner (in agreement with the sultans), the proportion of fifty-

[19] *A Monthly Survey of Commonwealth and Colonial Affairs,* issued by the Conservative Research Department in conjunction with the Conservatives Overseas Bureau, No. 18, p. 1.

[20] *Ibid.,* p. 2.

[21] The concessions were that government servants in junior grades might take a month's leave without pay in order to stand as candidates; while senior officials nearing retirement could retire on pension for the same purpose. "To go further than that," said Mr. Lyttelton, "would involve the risk of grave damage to the status and efficiency of the Civil Service upon which largely depended the success of the Federation's advance toward self-government and its stability when it had been achieved." *Ibid.,* p. 2.

MALAYSIA, THE PHILIPPINES,

AND SOUTHWEST PACIFIC

two elective to forty-six nominated had been accepted. The three-fifths majority proposed was a compromise with the extreme demand in Malaya for fully elective Councils.

The rejection of this proposal caused the United Malayan National Organization and the Malayan Chinese Association to decide "to withdraw all of their members from all administrative councils on which they serve, from the federal executive down to town council levels." [22] In doing so they rejected in effect Mr. Lyttelton's cogent argument presented in a letter to the delegations on May 8, 1954.[23]

[22] *Ibid.*, p. 2.

[23] In his letter the Colonial Secretary wrote: "You put it to me that the matter was one only of degree and not of principle, since you were not asking for so large a number of elected seats as to ensure that the party which won the elections would in all circumstances enjoy a clear majority in the council. You put forward two arguments in support of this contention. First, you said that if the majority of elected members were no more than was at present intended, the people would not think it worth while participating fully in the elections; and, second, you said that, as no party could hope to win more than 70 per cent of the seats, the present proposals would allow the victorious party too small a majority for it to function effectively in government, since it could not always be sure of the substantial support from non-elected members of the council upon which it would have to rely to secure approval of its policies.

"I fully appreciate the sincerity of these apprehensions, but I believe that... There is already convincing evidence of the readiness of the peoples of Malaya to play their part in elections without insisting upon an elected majority larger than that at present contemplated. . . .

"Moreover, there is in my view every likelihood that the victorious party in the federal elections will be able to rely on such stable support in the Legislative Council as will enable it to take part with real confidence in the government of the country. For one thing, in becoming the Government party, it will automatically secure the support of the three *ex-officio* members of the Legislative Council and also of the two other members charged with the duties of Secretary for Defense and Members for Economic Affairs. Again, it seems clear that if, for example, your party commanded a majority of the elected members of the council, they would be regularly supported by a number of the nominated members, since it is a reasonable expectation that these will include some councillors who are already members of the party.

"Finally, I am sure that, whatever party may win the elections, it will set itself with a high sense of purpose to pursue sober and progressive policies; and if it does I have no doubt that it will enjoy the dependable support of a large number of the other nominated members.

"At the same time, it must be recognized that that is a bold and adventurous step, a token not of timidity or distrust but of appreciation of past achievement and faith in future progress. But with the welfare of the Malayan peoples as our only touchstone in these matters, it would be wrong for us to pass beyond what is bold into what would be reckless; and I am bound to express my conviction that, at this important experimental stage in the advance toward self-government, the checks and balances provided by the proposed allocation of seats between elected and nominated members, and by the quality of the nominated members who are likely to sit in the council, are both necessary and desirable."

MALAYAN MOVES TOWARD SELF-GOVERNMENT

In the face of this threat to withhold co-operation in government the British authorities decided to go ahead with the holding of elections, in Singapore as well as in the Federation. Confronted with this decision, which represented a positive step forward toward self-government, the Malays National Organization, the Malayan Chinese Association, and the Malayan Indian Congress decided to participate in the Federation elections and formed an alliance for campaign purposes. Elections were held in the Federation during July, 1955. The Singapore elections were, however, held first (in April) and the results there may properly be summarized before turning to the later political developments in the Federation.

Of the five most important parties which contested the elections in Singapore, three could properly be viewed as conservative with respect to the issues presented and two as radical. The radical parties, riding the wind of anticolonialism, were unexpectedly successful. Twenty-five seats were contested, with the leftist Labor Front party winning ten and the even more extreme People's Action Party (led by Lee Kuan Yew, who had "entered Singapore politics with the avowed aim of arousing the political consciousness of the Chinese-educated Chinese") [24] seating three of its four candidates. The rightist Progressive Party won four seats, the Alliance (formed by the United Malays Nationalist Organization, the Malay Chinese Association, and the Malay Union) three, the Democrats two, and independents three.

The victory of the left in the elections was due to the campaign promises of the Labor Front and the Action Party to repeal the Emergency Regulations, establish immediate independence, and create a socialist society, in contrast with the "cautious and realistic" election program advanced by the rightist parties which caused them to be labeled the tools of British capitalism and imperialism. An additional consideration in bringing about the success of the Labor Front was the splitting of the conservative vote between the Democrats and the Progressives, to the advantage of the Labor Front.

If the leader of the Labor Front had seriously contemplated having to assume responsibility as Chief Minister as a result of success in the

[24] Francis G. Carnell, "Political Ferment in Singapore," *Far Eastern Survey*, July, 1955, Vol. 24, p. 98. This article presents a careful appraisal of the political situation at the time of and immediately after the elections.

elections, it is possible that he might not have overcommitted himself and his party in the campaign. It is also probable that if the Progressives had not fully expected to carry the elections their program would not have been as "cautious and realistic" as it was. However that may be Mr. David Marshall, the leader of the Labor Front, did have to assume the responsibilities of office and he did find that he had made promises during the campaign which were too advanced for ready fulfillment. He was, consequently, immediately faced with the problem of dealing, in his turn, with leftist pressures on the new government in the form of strikes and riots. The strikes were sponsored by the extremist labor unions and the riots were an expression of dissatisfaction on the part of the Chinese middle-school students.

There seems little reason to doubt that the Malay Communist Party agitated among the laboring masses and the Chinese students to set in motion the wave of strikes and riots of May and June, 1955, thus seeking to establish control of the Action Party, the trade unions, and the student movement. Existing social and economic conditions, however, provided an environment which the Communists could readily exploit against a government that had itself previously promised to make drastic changes. The Communist role was well put by an informed writer [25] who concluded that "the Labor Front itself, by its election campaign, played a prominent part in bringing these tensions into the open. The Communists are merely following their traditional policy of exploiting grievances before they can be remedied."

When faced with the responsibilities of government, the new Chief Minister in Singapore showed himself to be more moderate in action than he had previously been in words. In forming his government after the elections, the Labor Front leader entered into a coalition with the moderate (UMNO-MCA) Alliance rather than with the radical People's Action Party. The new government did attempt to put into effect some of its campaign proposals, such as the repeal of some of the Emergency Regulations. But when it was confronted with demands, implemented by strikes and riots, to institute even more drastic changes it moved backward by reimposing the revoked Regulations rather than forward along the lines demanded. The firm position taken, with the support of the Singapore Trade Union Congress as well as the rightist parties, enabled the government to maintain itself and to bring the disorders under control by July, 1955.

[25] Francis G. Carnell, *Ibid.*, p. 100.

It was essential for the Labor Front leader and new Chief Minister, Mr. Marshall, to take an advanced position with respect to colonialism in order to maintain himself against the nationalist extremists and the Communist-propagandized elements in Singapore. This led him to demand revision of the constitution looking toward immediate self-government and the union of Singapore and the Federation of Malay states. Again, however, his words proved to be stronger than his actions. He threatened to resign unless the British gave way but was persuaded to continue until the Colonial Secretary arrived on the scene. By that time the elections had been held in the Federation and the British were faced with comparable demands on the part of a new government there. Since Britain had committed itself to acceptance of leftist governments when invested with power through the democratic process, it proved possible for face-saving arrangements to be made with the Labor government in Singapore as well as with the new regime which came into power in the Federation.

The Federation elections were held as planned at the end of July, 1955. The returns showed that the alliance of the Malays National Organization, the Malayan Chinese Association, and the Malayan Indian Congress had won fifty-one of the fifty-two elective seats in the Legislative Council. The other seat was won by the Malayan Muslim Party rather than by Dato Sir Onn bin Ja'afar's Party Negara. 818,000 votes of the total vote of 1,027,211 were cast for candidates of the Alliance. The results seemed to give a clear popular endorsement of the Alliance program of self-government within two years and independence within four years. Self-government, in this program, was construed to mean abolition of the High Commissioner's veto and control of all internal government, including finance, defense, law, the army, and the economy. Independence, even within the Commonwealth, would add control of foreign affairs.

The principles uniting the parties in the Alliance thus were nationalist, in the sense of agreement on the necessity of eliminating, within a short period of time, all outside control of policy. There was no excessive popular hostility expressed to Britain, however, such as nationalist agitation had developed against the Dutch in Indonesia, especially during the postwar years, and against the French in Indochina. This difference may be ascribed to the British policy of gradual withdrawal and to the British willingness to move from one announced position to another as the political situation changed. The new constitution had, however, seemed to establish a reasonably defensible advanced position to be firmly maintained by the British government. Nevertheless the new Malayan leadership made it clear immediately that it was prepared to put pressure on Britain to attain the objectives of self-government and independence within the short time limits set if the British proved reluctant to grant their demands.

To the objection that immediate self-government would probably mean serious deterioration in the public services, as it had elsewhere in the area, the natural rejoinder for the nationalist there as elsewhere was that they were prepared to take that chance as one preferable to better government under foreign direction and control.

Following the elections the leader of the Alliance, Tengku Abdul Rahman, became the Chief Minister in the government as reconstituted. As Chief Minister he was given precedence, second only to the High Commissioner, in both the Federal Legislative and Executive Councils. The Executive Council, it was announced by the High Commissioner, would be composed of the Chief Minister, together with four European, six Malay, three Chinese, and one Indian, ministers. The Legislative Council, including elective and nominated members, was made up of fifty Malay members, twenty-five Chinese, seven Indians, two Ceylonese, five European officials, seven unofficial Europeans, and one member for Malacca. This represented a real move toward self-government, attaining the limits set and earlier generally agreed upon in the operative constitution. The sights of the Alliance had, however, been elevated beyond that point, as was indicated in their campaign platform and in postelection statements.

Tengku Abdul Rahman, in an interview on July 29, immediately following the elections, expressed the view, already advanced from Singapore, that the constitution needed immediate revision, particularly with respect to the High Commissioner's powers of veto. These powers had been accepted in the Federation of Malaya Agreement concluded before there were elected members of the Legislative Council. The elections had however, it was now urged, changed the previously accepted situation. As the new situation was put by Abdul Rahman: "Today, with support enjoyed by no other government in the world, the alliance represented people. If the High Commissioner vetoed Bills passed in the Council, the alliance would not be working for the people and might as well walk out." For that reason the Alliance leader held the constitution to be unworkable. Nevertheless he insisted only that the powers of the High Commissioner must be made purely advisory within a period of two years, "or one year if possible" rather than demanding their immediate abolition. This left the way open for discussion of the new situation. Coupled with the changed situation in Singapore, it forecast a Roundtable conference in London, probably in the spring of 1956, since Abdul Rahman expressed a willingness to participate in such a conference and it seemed clear that Mr. Marshall would also welcome it. But the prospects for realizing the aims of the Alliance in the Federation and of the Labor Front in Singapore with respect to self-government and independence through agreement at such a conference would depend upon internal developments in Malaya, especially with respect to control of Communist activities affecting public order.

It was fundamentally anticolonialism which united elements of otherwise dissimilar outlook both in the Federation and in Singapore. As has been pointed out, the new leadership was in agreement to bring pressure to bear on Britain to attain the objectives of self-government and independence. But there was no real indication that the groups in Alliance in the Federation were agreed on the uses which would be made of power if and when self-government and finally independence had been attained. That being the case it was uncertain whether the alliance would be able to extend itself into the period of independence.

The immediately pressing internal problem at the time the elections were held and thereafter was that of Communist terrorism, coupled with the tactics of subversion. With respect to that problem the new Federation leadership did have an agreed policy. This was that the olive branch in the form of amnesty should be offered concurrently with repressive policy measures to be undertaken against those who did not, in good faith, accept the conditions of amnesty. The existence of the problem, in one respect, gave the new regimes a leverage on Great Britain to grant immediate self-government, even though it could reasonably be argued that Communist terrorism would have to be completely wiped out before power could be safely turned over to a local regime. The argument, from the pressure side, was, as Abdul Rahman put it, that Great Britain must grant the request for immediate self-government because the British government had to realize that "unless it gives self-government it is inviting communism and we have had enough of that during the past seven years," since communism had been exploiting successfully the issue of colonialism. On the other hand, it would have to be accepted that if serious economic deterioration set in following the institution of self-government that would also create the conditions which breeds communism. Thus unless terrorism could be brought to an end by grant of amnesty, coupled with the exertion of sufficient power against those who refused to accept amnesty and continued to carry on terrorist guerrilla operations from their jungle bases, the problem would remain as a serious threat to the continued existence of an independent or completely self-governing democratic regime. That amnesty, coupled with rehabilitation measures for those accepting it and vigorous police measures against those rejecting it, offered possibilities of solution of the problem had been revealed in the success of the Magsaysay policy in the Philippines. The terrorist nature of Communist activities in Malaya, however, and the bitterness which terrorism and the countermeasures taken against the terrorists had engendered, together with environmental differences in the two countries, raised doubts as to whether what had been successful in the Philippines would be equally successful in the Malayan environment.

BIBLIOGRAPHICAL REFERENCES

BURMA

Bailey, Sydney D., *Parliamentary Government in Southern Asia* (New York: International Secretariat, Institute of Pacific Relations, 1952).

Cady, John F., "Burma," in John F. Cady, Patricia Barnett, Shirley Jenkins, *Development of Self-Rule and Independence in Burma, Malaya and the Philippines* (New York: American Institute of Pacific Relations, 1948).

The Constitution of the Union of Burma (Rangoon: Supt. Government Printing and Stationery, 1947).

Dennison, F. S. V., *Public Administration in Burma* (London: Royal Institute of International Affairs, 1953).

Economic Survey of Burma, 1952 (Rangoon: Supt. Government Printing and Stationery, 1952).

Furnivall, John S., *Colonial Policy and Practice: A Comparative Study of Burma and the Netherlands* (Cambridge: Cambridge University Press, 1948).

———, "Burma, Past and Present," *Far Eastern Survey*, Vol. 22, no. 3.

———, "Twilight in Burma," *Pacific Affairs*, March, June, 1949.

Great Britain, *Papers by Command*, Cmd. 6635 (1945); Cmd. 7029 (1947); Cmd. 7138 (1947); Cmd. 7240 (1947); Cmd. 7246 (1947); Cmd. 7360 (1948); Cmd. 7560 (1948).

Inlow, E. Burke, "The Constitution of Burma," *Far Eastern Survey*, Vol. 17, no. 22.

Thakin Nu, *From Peace to Stability* (Rangoon: Government Ministry of Information, 1951).

MALAYA

Barnett, Patricia, "Malaya," in John F. Cady, Patricia Barnett, and Shirley Jenkins, *The Development of Self-Rule in Burma, Malaya and the Philippines* (New York: American Institute of Pacific Relations, 1948).

Great Britain, *Papers by Command*, "Malayan Union and Singapore," 1945-46, *Cmd*. 6724, *Cmd*. 6749. "Federation of Malaya, Summary of Revised Constitutional Proposals," *Cmd*. 7171 (1947).

Kabcroy, Phyllis M., *British Colonial Policy in Southeast Asia and the Development of Self-government in Malaya* (London: British Royal Institute of International Affairs, 1944).

Lakeman, Enid, *Report on Malaya* (London: McDougall Press, 1952).

Purcell, Victor, "A Malayan Union," *Pacific Affairs*, Vol. 19, no. 1.

Rees-Williams, David R., and others, *Three Reports on the Malayan Problem* (New York: International Secretariat, Institute of Pacific Relations, 1949).

Silcock, T. H., and Ungku Abdul Aziz, "Nationalism in Malaya," Pt. III of W. L. Holland (ed.), *Asian Nationalism and the West* (New York: Macmillan, for the Institute of Pacific Relations, 1953).

13

The Republic of Indonesia

✻✻✻✻✻✻✻✻✻✻✻✻✻✻✻✻✻✻✻✻✻✻✻✻✻✻✻✻✻✻✻✻✻✻

THE NETHERLANDS EAST INDIES

WHAT THE POSTWAR world knows as Indonesia the prewar world knew as the Netherlands (or Dutch) East Indies. The territory involved consists of a chain of islands extending from Malaya in the west to New Guinea in the east, covering a distance of more than 3,200 miles and with a land area of between seven and eight hundred thousand square miles. Thus in prewar days Dutch territory reached from British colonies in Southeast Asia to Australia, with the United States to the north in the Philippines.

During the early colonial period the richness in natural resources of these tropical islands had made them a source of rivalry among the expanding European states. But with the withdrawal of the Dutch from active participation in European and world politics, no serious external threats of disturbance of the Dutch position in their eastern empire had been presented until the late 1930's. Aside from the explanation to be found in the concentration of the Dutch on trade rather than politics, their uncontested control of their East Indian colony was due to their successful maintenance of order in the islands. This deprived others of a suitable excuse for intervening to abate a nuisance. Since the major general interest had come to be in trade, the policy followed by the Dutch of allowing foreign traders relatively free access to the islands removed one of the incentives of economic imperialism. The status quo represented by Dutch colonialism was more satisfactory to all the Western powers than would have been a transfer of control to any one of the major powers except the immediate beneficiary. Thus it had come to be viewed as being to the British interest to support the Dutch in possession as against, for example, Japan or Germany. The

United States' position in the Philippines similarly supported rather than threatened the status quo, except in one respect. The American policy of ultimate and then dated independence for the Philippines, as its implications and justification came to be understood in adjacent areas, was utilized to support local nationalist demands for self-government and independence. Thus while the Dutch had no reason to fear American territorial aggrandizement at their expense, the example of United States policy toward the Philippines could not be viewed as favorable to the maintenance of colonialism.

In governing their colony the Dutch, as far as possible, ruled indirectly, maintaining local institutions and especially local (adat) law and custom. Nevertheless, after the Dutch East India Company was displaced by the Netherlands Government in 1798, the paramountcy of Dutch authority was kept clearly evident through a centralized and bureaucratic structure. The governors of the provinces were subordinated to the governor-general who was, in turn, subordinated to the government of the Netherlands. This excessive centralization, when "the Governor General at Batavia had minutely controlled the whole government of the Empire, and he in turn had been under the strict supervision of the Government of Holland," [1] began to be modified in the nineteen twenties. More autonomy was given to the colonial government, and the Volksraad (People's Council) created in 1918 gradually assumed more power. "Until 1927 it (the Volksraad) had only advisory powers, but in that year it was given co-legislative powers, which in practice meant that legislative measures normally required the approval of both the Volksraad and the Governor General." [2] Of the sixty members of the Volksraad, 30 were Indonesians, of whom 20 were elected; 25 were Europeans; and the remainder were selected from among the nonindigenous Asians, of whom the largest group was the Chinese. Thus that body did not necessarily reflect at all accurately the point of view of the majority of the people.

[1] Rupert Emerson, Lennox A. Mills, and Virginia Thompson, *Government and Nationalism in Southeast Asia* (New York: International Secretarial, Institute of Pacific Relations, 1942), Pt. II, "The Governments of Southeast Asia," p. 97.
[2] Amry Vandenbosch, "The Netherlands Indies," *Annals of the American Academy of Political and Social Science*, Vol. CCXXVI, p. 91.

PREWAR DEVELOPMENT OF INDONESIAN NATIONALISM

Concurrently with this loosening of centralization in the governmental system and with its counterpart in the form of what was called
the "ethical" policy of paying more attention to the social and economic interests and needs of the people, there came the prewar development of Indonesian nationalism. The first nationalist society held its
first congress in 1908. Its purpose initially was the economic and educational improvement of the position of the people. To realize its
purposes, however, the new Indonesian cultural organization necessarily turned more and more to political matters. It was followed, and
eclipsed, by the Sarekat Islam, founded in 1911 and first motivated by
a desire to secure economic independence of the increasingly dominant
Chinese. The new society grew considerably in the years between its
first congress, held in 1913, and its emergence as a "full-fledged political
party" in 1916 when the Sarekat Islam held its first National Congress
in Bandung. Its program was one of social and economic reform, to
be achieved in co-operation with and through the colonial government. Politically it began to seek association of Indonesians with the
Dutch in the working out of a policy for the colony looking toward
self-government. In this phase it could properly be called a "nonrevo-
lutionary, essentially middle-class organization" from the point of view
both of its program and its methods of action. On the economic and
social side its activities were somewhat co-ordinated with those of the
trade unions which came into being during and after the period of
the First World War.

Sarekat Islam had just begun to be a national political movement
of significance sufficient to claim some credit for the Dutch action in
establishing the Advisory People's Council when it began to be caught
up in the revolutionary currents flowing from Russia. The anti-imperialism and anticolonialism of Leninism, together with the revolutionary techniques of violence, were brought into Indonesia through
a newly organized Indonesian Communist Party. As economic conditions deteriorated in the years after 1918, the economic weapon of the
strike was utilized to bring about changes in Dutch policy. The measures taken by the authorities to maintain the established order stimulated demands for a less moderate kind of program than the one advanced in 1918. In order to maintain itself, the national movement
became a nationalist movement seeking independence, while at the

same time (in 1923) expelling the more radical members from the organization. These went into the Indonesian Communist Party. By 1927 what had once been an essentially moderate reform agitation had become the Indonesian fight for independence. An attempted Communist insurrection in 1927 was rigorously suppressed. Thereafter the repressive policy of the government was directed more vigorously against all nationalists, many of whom had the label of Communist attached to them to justify their suppression or internment.

An Indonesian National Party (Partai Nasional Indonesia, or PNI) led by Soekarno, was formed in 1927. There was not, however, brought into being before World War II, even among the class of intellectuals, one united nationalist organization of a disciplined sort, including in its membership all elements with nationalist aspirations, comparable to the Congress Party of India or the Kuomintang of China. Soekarno was able to bring into being a Federation of Indonesian National Political Parties but not to bring about a submergence of differences sufficient to give real unity against the Dutch. This was revealed in the ability of the latter to seize and hold him out of political activity in 1928 and again in 1933, after which time he remained interned in Sumatra until released by the Japanese.

One important reason for this was that Indonesian nationalism was not then a mass movement or a mass sentiment. In contrast to the Philippines, the masses in Indonesia were more readily moved by economic considerations than by political sentiment. Political awareness was largely confined to a small but growing class of intellectuals, many of whom were removed in experience, feeling, and understanding from the masses. But while this was true, there had been sufficient growth of nationalism to disturb the Dutch and cause them to proceed with some vigor against those who showed political inclinations or who did not formally agree to co-operate, by which was meant to accept the Dutch policy of gradual introduction of self-government, with the pace of development set by Holland. Numerous Indonesians, where qualified by training, did, however, show their willingness to co-operate by entering the bureaucracy in its lower ranges.

One of the retarding factors in the growth of a competent and experienced Indonesian political leadership was to be found in the comparative lack of emphasis by the Dutch on education. Only a small proportion of the adult Indonesians were literate and only about 400,000 could read Dutch. Those who achieved an education in the islands were not actively encouraged to go abroad, even to Holland, for advanced studies. Despite this, however, considerable numbers of Indonesians had studied in Holland. From this relatively small group of foreign-educated Indonesians came the ideas and much of the initiative which was found in the prewar nascent nationalist movement. Its ideas were drawn largely from foreign sources, which also provided a basis for ideological division among the educated leaders. To the extent to which the views seriously held by the leaders were foreign they could not readily be rapidly translated into terms widely understood and accepted. This consequently constituted a barrier between the leaders and the masses. And frequently, as in the case of Soetan Sjahrir, before the leader could carry forward the work of translation of concept into mass thinking, he found himself imprisoned or interned in one of the settlements utilized for political prisoners.

JAPAN IN INDONESIA

It was, consequently, not domestic nationalism but foreign invasion which initially destroyed Dutch power in Indonesia. It was Japanese power rather than Dutch weakness which forced changes in the Indonesian policy of the Netherlands government itself. The invasion of the Netherlands by Germany, which forced the Dutch government into exile in London, did not seem seriously to disturb conditions in Indonesia.

In so far as there was greater interest and concern for the seventy million brown subjects, it was expressed by a strengthened police force, an increase in political arrests, and further restriction of freedom of action. And finally, it was felt that the educated Indonesians could be mollified by pretending to pay attention to their political aspirations. The Visman Commission held hearings to ascertain the political views of the outstanding members of the Indonesian community, but this was the only liberalizing consequence of the occupation of Holland as far as Indonesia was concerned.... Experiments (in defense arrangements) with nationalists who might later be a source of disturbance, were considered unnecessary. The government (in Indonesia) maintained its supercilious attitude right up to the Japanese invasion.[3]

This was, of course, the appraisal of a nationalist leader. The Dutch were naturally more impressed with the purposes of the Visman Commission

---

[3] Soetan Sjahrir, *Out of Exile* (New York: John Day, 1949), p. 18.

and felt that a larger change of policy not only was forecast but was being made. Since Japan immediately utilized the new conditions in Europe to apply pressure on the Netherlands Indies government for economic concessions, Dutch repression of nationalists may have been due not so much to complacence as to fear and to a possibly shortsighted but real suspicion of the motives, *vis-a-vis* themselves, of the nationalist leaders who declared themselves antifascist and therefore willing to co-operate in the defense of Indonesia.

With its leadership suppressed by the Dutch,

> It would not have been surprising if the Indonesian Nationalist Movement had declared itself out of the war against fascism. But this was emphatically not the case. After Europe was overrun by the Nazi armies, the nationalist leaders denounced fascism . . . both of the European and Japanese variety . . . and asked that Indonesians be trained to defend their homeland against possible aggression. It was evident at this time that Japanese aggression would almost surely be extended to Southeast Asia. Yet the colonial administrators were apparently more afraid of the Indonesian people than the armies of Japan. Every suggestion that an Indonesian militia be set up was rebuffed. With the exception of Ambonese mercenaries, traditional soldiers of the crown—the Indonesian people were not entrusted with weapons to defend themselves.[1]

This, again, is a nationalist reading of the situation. The Dutch, as with the British in Malaya and Burma, read it somewhat differently. Their conclusion apparently was based upon the fear that arming nationalism against the Japanese might have the long run effect of giving weapons to those who would use them against themselves.

However that may be, the Dutch attitude changed with some rapidity after December, 1941. Unfortunately for them, however, by that time anti-Dutch feeling among the masses and part of the nationalist leadership had grown

> stronger and stronger. This was naturally reflected in the nationalist movement and its leadership, part of which expressed sympathy for the Axis openly.
> Essentially, the popularity of Japan increased as one aspect of the growing anti-Dutch animus and as projection of frustrated desire for freedom. . . . The idea grew that the liberation of Indonesia would begin with the expulsion of the Dutch by the Japanese.[5]

[4] Information Office of the Republic of Indonesia, *Seven Years of Indonesian Independence* (New York, Aug. 17, 1952), p. 5.
[5] Sjahrir, *op. cit.*, p. 219.

However, disillusionment with the Japanese as liberators was quite rapid in Indonesia. As in other Southeast Asian countries, the Japanese conquerors shipped to Japan, without exchange, as much of everything already produced as possible. They proved unsuccessful, furthermore in re-establishing production, in the field of exports, on a reoriented (to Japan) exchange basis. Thus the years of Japanese rule were years of increasing economic deterioration and impoverishment. And, until Japan's eventual defeat was in sight, military government was not ameliorated by moves toward greater self-government, or toward even as much self-government as had been introduced by the Dutch; nor by a proclamation of independence as the ultimate goal of Japanese policy, as in the case of the Philippines and Burma. The program of cultural assimilation to Japan, attempted in Indonesia as elsewhere, had little effect in modifying the anti-Japanese feeling which soon replaced that of welcoming the Japanese as liberators. There was little over-statement by Hatta in his *Political Manifesto* of November, 1945, when he declared that

> For a full three and one-half years, the Japanese worked their will on the population, subjecting the people to a type of pressure and oppression unknown in the last decades of Dutch rule here.
> The Japanese looked upon the Indonesians as mere chattels.... Forced labor was imposed on the common people; the peasants were intimidated into handing over to the Japanese the products of their toil.... the entire population was obliged to conform to Japanese military discipline....[6]

What was known of the adverse effects of, and the reaction to, Japanese rule led the Dutch until the end of the war, to base their post-war plans on the assumption that they would be able freely to establish the terms and the timing of future political development. In this the Dutch made the same mistake as the British did with respect to Burma. In neither case did anti-Japanese sentiment and action indicate an atti-tude favorable to colonialism even if it were modified in the direction of self-rule and oriented toward an ultimate complete autonomy, or even with independence "in due course" promised. Furthermore, in Indonesia, as in Burma, the effect of the period of Japanese occupation, and the resistance to it, in maturing politically the nationalist leader-

[6] This is the statement, after its termination, of one who collaborated with the Japanese during the occupation. Hatta, however, maintained contact at the same time with the resistance leaders, as was not so clearly the case with Soekarno who was the outstanding collaborator. The quotation is from *Seven Years*, p. 6.

ship was not fully appreciated by the metropolitan country. While the Dutch correctly concluded that the Indonesians realized that the Japanese were worse rulers than they, the Dutch, had ever been, they did not realize the extent to which the Japanese had been successful in denigrating the European. He had lost the prestige on which, as much as on power, his rule depended. Consequently, Indonesian nationalism was strengthened and its leadership made more self-confident as a result of the war.

DUTCH PLANS FOR THE POSTWAR PERIOD

Dutch postwar policy for Indonesia was first announced by Queen Wilhelmina on December 6, 1942. It envisaged at the end of the war a "Conference of the Netherlands Realm" at which there would be "joint consultation about the structure of the Kingdom and its parts in order to adapt it to the changed circumstances." "Ultimately the Queen envisioned a 'commonwealth in which the Netherlands, Indonesia, Surinam, and Curacao will participate with complete self-reliance and freedom of conduct for each part regarding its internal affairs, but with readiness to render mutual assistance.' " [7]

More significance was attached to this declaration in the Anti-Axis Western world than in the Indies where it was not widely publicized. It represented a move which would have met the desires and demands of prewar Indonesia nationalism. And it might have had greater effect in Indonesia if the general lines of application of the policy, from the Dutch point of view, had been amplified and given greater precision before the end of the war.

The march of events at the end of the war, however, presented the Dutch with a different situation from that which had been envisaged in 1943, and one which seriously modified their control of postwar developments. In and after 1943 the Japanese began to associate Indonesian leaders with the government of the country in an advisory capacity. Thus some Indonesian nationalist leaders were brought into collaboration with the Japanese. Others participated in an internal anti-Japanese resistance movement. The collaborators and the anti-Japanese leaders, however, maintained contact with one another. On

[7] H. Arthur Steiner, "Post-War Government of The Netherlands East Indies," in Taylor Cole and J. H. Hallowell (eds.) "Post-War Government and Politics of the Far East," *Journal of Politics*, Vol. IX, p. 631.

the eve of the Japanese surrender, the collaborationist group, apparently with Japanese approval, proclaimed the independence of the country, adopted a provisional constitution, and put the powers of government in the hands of Soekarno as President and Hatta as Vice President. Soekarno and Hatta proceeded to govern in concert with a committee (Komite Nasional Indonesia Peosat, or KNIP) of some 120 members.[8] The government was supported by forces equipped with Japanese arms seized or turned over to Indonesian forces after the surrender. By the time when, in late September, British forces of the Southeast Asia Command (of which war theater Indonesia had been made a part) arrived to receive the Japanese surrender, the new regime had been able to establish its authority in Java, Madura, and Sumatra. Thus it had to be reckoned with by the British as well as the Dutch. The latter initially re-entered their colony in the wake of the British in the form of the Netherlands' Indies Civil Administration.

If the Dutch had been authorized and had been able to send in military forces of their own large enough to receive the Japanese surrender and take over from the Japanese they might have been able to gain control of the situation. Allied troops arrived (September 29, 1945), however, only after a period of delay. The troops were British and under a British commander who initially limited his mission to effecting the Japanese surrender and evacuating Allied prisoners of war and civilian internees. He refused to undertake for the Dutch reconquest of the entire island (Java) against Indonesian resistance. The British attitude expressed a *de facto* recognition of the Indonesian Republic within the territories under its military control. The enforced delay in entrance of Dutch troops in sufficient strength to attempt the reconquest of republican territory not only made reconquest more difficult by enabling the government of the republic to perfect its organization and equip its forces, but it also created the necessity for prior negotiation with the republican regime by the Dutch, thereby giving it still further *de facto* standing as a government.

THE ESTABLISHMENT OF THE REPUBLIC

In the immediately resulting situation fighting and negotiation went on simultaneously. At first the Dutch refused to negotiate with Soe-

[8] All of this was apparently done in agreement with the leaders of the internal resistance movement. Sjahrir, *op. cit.*, pp. 253-54.

karno on the ground of his, and Hatta's, collaboration with the Japanese. A way around this difficulty was found by transferring, by tacit agreement, the president's powers to a cabinet headed by Sjahrir, with whom the Dutch were willing to deal. A year later the Dutch were prepared to deal directly with Soakarno. By that time, also, they gave up their insistence on acceptance by the Indonesians of the procedures defined in Queen Wilhelmina's declaration of 1942. Thus the way was finally cleared for the negotiation and ratification (March 25, 1947) of the Linggadjati Agreement on principles to be applied in settling outstanding differences. By that agreement the republic was recognized to have *de facto* authority over Java, Madura, and Sumatra, and it was agreed that Dutch and Allied forces would be gradually withdrawn from the occupied portions of those islands so that the republic would have them completely under its control by January 1, 1949. A United States of Indonesia, composed of three republics (Indonesia, Borneo, and the Great East) was to be established. A union was thereupon to be formed of the Kingdom of the Netherlands and the United States of Indonesia and the Dutch were to sponsor the United States of Indonesia for membership in the United Nations. On the economic side, of great importance to the Dutch, it was agreed that the government of the Republic of Indonesia would recognize the claims of all non-Indonesians to the restoration of their rights and the restitution of their goods as far as they were exercised or to be found in the territory over which it exercised *de facto* authority. This agreement on principles did not, however, include directions as to their application.

Criticised by conservatives in Holland and by nationalists in Indonesia, the necessary steps to make the Linggadjati Agreement effective were not taken. Consequently, when provisions which that agreement contained for dealing with the immediate situation, and which the United States in July, 1947, for example, held constituted a "reasonable basis of negotiation," were met with unacceptable counterproposals, the Dutch resorted to military action, declared to be a "police measure of a strictly limited sort." These operations were sufficiently extensive to compress the territory of the republic into a small district along the southern coast of Java in the neighborhood of Jakarta, the capital of the republic.

At this point of time (July, 1947), the Indonesian question was brought before the United Nations' Security Council by India and Australia. The Security Council, within forty-eight hours, adopted the "first cease-fire resolution of its career." [9] Both sides accepted the resolution, but the fighting continued. A consular commission was consequently set up (August, 25) to report on observance of the resolution. Concurrently a tender was made of good offices. This was accepted and a Three Power Committee of Good Offices was established. The three powers were: Belgium, selected by the Netherlands; Australia, selected by the Republic of Indonesia; and the United States, which was designated by the other two members.

The Good Offices Committee was able to bring the two parties to acceptance of an agreement (the Renville Agreement) on January 7, 1948. The Renville Agreement contained a detailed program for a truce and the principles for a future political settlement. The truce broke down, however, because of inability of the two sides to agree on the application of the "principles" for the political settlement. The truce itself was terminated on December, 18. The Dutch then again resorted to "police action" to resolve the situation along lines acceptable to them.

THE UNITED STATES OF INDONESIA

During the period of the truce (January to December, 1948) the Netherlands government had worked energetically at setting up separate "states" throughout the archipelago with governments each of which was dependent on Dutch military power. Each government was related to the others through the Dutch. This activity made it more and more difficult for the republican authorities to accept the principles in application of a future federated United States of Indonesia which would be created and become incorporated with the Kingdom of the Netherlands in an over-all Netherlands-Indonesian Union. The Dutch moves seemed designed to have the effect, as the nationalists subsequently put it

> of making the populous Republic, the center and mainspring of the independence movement, just one more state. It was obviously the intention to establish pro-colonial governments in these states to act in a bloc and nullify the Republic's strength in any future federation of Indonesia.[10]

[9] For comment on this see Rupert Emerson, "The Indonesian Case," *World Politics,* Vol. 1, no. 1, p. 70.
[10] *Seven Years,* p. 13. The idea of federation was acceptable at this time to the Republic Government, provided it and not the Dutch was in control of the federation.

The purpose and result of this Dutch activity during 1948 was put as follows by a sympathetic student of Indonesian-nationalism:

> What chiefly distinguished the new federal states from prewar colonial Indonesia was: (1) a new formula of indirect rule wherein ultimate Dutch control was more skillfully camouflaged than previously; (2) more Indonesians holding middle and upper administrative posts, and having in a few states a small measure of governmental initiative, subject to supervision and control from Batavia; (3) more Dutch military and policy power; (4) more Indonesian nationalists in jail.[11]

The resort to military action was undertaken by the Dutch when it was viewed as possible to compel the republic to accept the newly created situation and adjust itself to it. The Dutch forces were able rapidly to overrun the territories still under control of the government of the republic and to capture many of the members of the government. The immediate result was the acceptance by the republic (May, 1949) of the Roem-van Royen Agreement, wherein it was agreed that two-thirds of the representation in the future United States of Indonesia would be in the hands of the federal states. Republican sentiment was, however, opposed to the agreement, the opposition expressing itself in increased guerrilla activity against the Dutch and in an appeal to the United Nations Security Council.

The Dutch were then compelled to defend their action in an international forum, although consistently maintaining that the question was domestic and thus outside the jurisdiction of the United Nations and of the Security Council. Their position was weakened because the United States, which had supported the conclusion of the Roem-van Royen Agreement, shifted its position under the stimulus of nationalist activity, and urged the negotiation of a settlement. After protracted discussion, consequently, the Dutch accepted under international pressure the necessity for negotiating rather than imposing a settlement, and as the *sine qua non* of negotiation, the release of the captured members of the republican government. The result was that the government of the republic and that of the Netherlands again (August 3, 1949) entered into truce arrangements to go into effect on August 10, "but both sides made clear that only an armed truce existed for the present." [12] This agreement also provided for a Round Table Con-

[11] George McT. Kanin, "Indonesian Politics and Nationalism," in W. L. Holland (ed.), *Asian Nationalism and the West* (New York: Macmillan, 1953) Pt. I., p. 114.
[12] *New York Times*, August 4, 1949.

ference to be held in Holland to establish the final conditions of relationship.

The Round Table Conference was convened at the Hague in August and continued in session until an agreement was finally reached and signed on November 2. The issues that protracted the discussions were those over: (1) financial arrangements; (2) the character of the permanent organs of the union to be established between the Netherlands and Indonesia; (3) the status of the Crown as head of the Union; and (4) the territory to be included in the United States of Indonesia (i.e., whether or not Dutch New Guinea should be included). On the first issue, a compromise was reached which provided "that Indonesia would take over debts of 4,300,000,000 guilders.... This comprised the entire internal debt of the Netherlands East Indies Government of 3,000,000,000 guilders and its external obligations of 1,300,000,000 guilders." Decision on the fourth issue was to be reached by negotiation within a year. The others were debated to the conclusions embodied in the Hague Statute of Union of November 2, 1949. This established a co-operative union of the two parties "on the basis of voluntariness and equal status with equal rights" (Art. 1, Sec. 1).

It was further stipulated that: "The Union does not prejudice the status of each of the two partners as an independent and sovereign state" (Art 1, Sec. 2). The defined purposes of the union were to promote co-operation in the fields of foreign affairs and finance, and also "as regards matters of an economic and cultural nature" (Art 2). Separate agreements on foreign affairs, financial and economic relations, and cultural relations were attached to the statute. A third general article provided that the partners should "base their form of government on democracy"; that they should "aim at an independent judiciary"; and that they should "recognize the fundamental human rights and freedoms enumerated in the appendix to this statute."

Her Majesty Queen Juliana was designated as the head of the Union. Under the Queen, ministers from the two partners, duly designated for that purpose, were to meet in conference twice a year, and regular contact was to be established between the respective parliaments of Holland and Indonesia, their representatives to meet for the first time within eight months of the establishment of the Provisional Parliament of the United States of Indonesia. Disputes between the two partners over the meaning of the statute or growing out of any agreements between them or of joint regulations adopted by them were to be settled through arbtiration.

THE REPUBLIC OF INDONESIA

If the Dutch hoped to re-establish their political position in Indonesia as a consequence of the establishment of a federal structure around the states they had brought into being they were doomed to disappointment. The United States of Indonesia was replaced by the unitary Republic of Indonesia on August 15, 1950 as a result of (1) the merger of Dutch-established "states" with the Republic and then (2) an agreement between the federal government and the Republic of Indonesia state government. The recently created states in many cases were erected into provinces "with maximum autonomy" in the Republic but without separate governmental or state identities. The change, coupled with the Indonesian emphasis on the references to independence, equality, and sovereignty in the statute, had the effect, without revision of the statute, of putting the relations of the Netherlands and Indonesia essentially on the same basis as that of two independent states.[13]

The state which called itself the Republic of Indonesia after 1950 comprised all of the territory formerly known as the Netherlands East Indies except for West Irian (Western New Guinea) which remained under Dutch administration pending the conclusion of the agreement on its disposition. This agreement was supposed to have been, but was not, reached within a year after the signature of the Hague Round Table agreements. Viewing Western New Guinea as an integral part of the Dutch colony to which the new state had succeeded, nationalist Indonesia had not been willing to compromise its claim to that territory even to the extent of accepting the idea of determination of its status through a plebiscite. Thus there remained in 1955 one territorial source of contention between the Indonesia Republic and the Netherlands. Including Western New Guinea, the Republic has a total land area of 743,855 square miles. This land area, however is distributed among the large number of unequal islands which compose the archipelago which is the Republic of Indonesia. This dispersion of the territory of

[13] By the terms of the protocol signed by representatives of Holland and Indonesia on August 11, 1954, the union itself was dissolved.

the state in a chain of islands extending some 3,200 miles from the eastern to the western limits gives an element of uniqueness, although comparable to that of the Philippines, to the problem of government in the unitary state. The territorial aspect of the problem, is reshaped, however, by the great concentration of population on the island of Java and Java's position in relation to Sumatra, Borneo and the Celebes islands. Luzon, in the Philippines has a comparable demographic position to that of Java in relation to the other islands of the archipelago.

The lines of solution of the problem of government and the tone of politics have been set to a considerable extent by the nature of the population. The total population was estimated in 1952 at some eighty million. The people were, in overwhelming majority, indigenous, but subdivided into a large number of ethnic groups. Of the nonindigenous peoples the Chinese are at present the most numerous, with a total estimated in 1950 at upwards of two and a half million. A much smaller number of Europeans, Indo-Europeans (Eurasians), Arabs, and Indians make up the remainder of the nonindigenous population.

Before the war the Europeans, and to a lesser extent the Chinese and Arabs, played a role in the Indies' society out of all proportion to their numerical strength. Since the war, in consequence of the establishment of the new state, and especially because of the conditions of its establishment, the political role of the Europeans and the Indo-Europeans has been greatly lessened. Before the war the Chinese had been essentially nonpolitical in their behavior in Indonesia as elsewhere in Southeast Asia, although continuing to view themselves as overseas Chinese rather than exclusively as nationals of the place of their domicile. Their concern with politics was with China rather than Indonesia. The nature of the forces recently contending for power in China, however, has been such that they have affected the attitudes of the overseas Chinese toward the politics of the countries of their domicile. Thus the Chinese in Indonesia have been brought under pressures, partly from China, to play a more active political role than in prewar days. This has been shown in the support by Peiping of Communist parties in Indonesia, in the Philippines, and in other Southeast Asian countries, and support by Nanking and later Formosa of anti-Communist governments or parties through pressure applied in both cases on local Chinese.

External forces, however, have played a relatively minor part in the political life of the Republic of Indonesia. The determinative factors from the point of view of population have been: (1) its fundamentally Moslem character; (2) its concentration on agricultural pursuits, but without the division which landlordism created in other Asian countries; and (3) its low percentage of literacy. An overwhelming proportion of the people presented all three characteristics. To these factors must be added, as having importance in relation to government and politics, the existence of a small but growing educated class, the members of which have been accepted as entitled to exercise leadership in the nationalist movement of the postwar period as that movement has gained mass support.

The governmental apparatus of the Republic of Indonesia is relatively simple. As the central organ of government the Republic has a single-chambered parliament whose members, pending the holding of the elections which were planned first for 1953 but were postponed through 1954, were appointed by the political parties "under a system of proportional representation established by a presidential committee." The parliament has the function of selecting the president. The first Vice President (Hatta) was appointed by the President upon recommendation of the House of Representatives. Governing power was vested in a cabinet which was responsible to the Parliament but which is composed under the direction of the president "who forms the Ministries" and invites one or more party leaders to form a cabinet. They in turn appoint the other cabinet ministers, in conformity, of course, with the wishes of the majority of the House of Representatives. The president can, however, designate an individual as prime minister and thus, through him, determine the composition of the cabinet—subject to the approval of a majority of Parliament. The postwar governments, under these circumstances, have been constituted on the basis of interparty agreements, and, because of the absence of single-party majorities in the House, have been made up as coalitions from the party point of view, although invariably including ministers without party affiliations. Thus the Natsir Cabinet (September 6, 1950 to March 20, 1951) had as deputy prime minister a nonparty man, and nonparty ministers of internal affairs, defense, communications and transport, and education and culture. The new cabinet announced on July 31, 1953, from the point of view of party composition had, in addition to the prime minister, three members from the Nationalist Party; three from the Greater Indonesia Party; and thirteen from as many splinter parties, representing widely divergent points of view—from left to moderate right.[14]

As one writer put it:

> Indonesian politics, in spite of its facade of Western style organization and verbose statements of party principles, is carried on in an atmosphere often resembling that of a large, quarrelsome and neurotic family group. An acute Indonesian political observer once commented to the writer, "Really to understand our politics you would have to know the biography of every leader from before the war until now and every quarrel or disagreement they and their families have had with each other." Leaving aside imposing paper claims of party membership, Indonesian political life is a kind of poker game played by a few thousand people all of whom have known each other much too long and too well.[15]

Nevertheless it is essential for the student of Indonesia politics to have some appreciation of at least the paper differences between the parties.

INDONESIAN PARTIES

Almost all Indonesian parties, as presently organized, came into being as organized entities after 1945, although the names of some link them with previously existing organizations. Thus the Partai Nasional Indonesia (PNI) has the same name as the nationalist party originally organized in 1927. Its connection with the prewar party, however, aside from the name is personal rather than organic, some of the old leaders playing an active role in the postwar party. It has attracted much of its membership because of identification of the party name with Soekarno, although that leader has been dissociated from parties because of his occupancy of the presidential office. He had not only led the prewar nationalist party but

> he and (Vice President) Hatta had officially backed a shortlived official party of that name which had existed from August 22 to 31, 1945. Thus much of the initial mass backing of the P.N.I. rested on the fiction that it was "the party of Soekarna and Hatti." It took many Indonesians a year or more and several foreign correspondents much longer, to become disabused of this fiction.[16]

[14] For an analysis and description of the political situation at the end of 1953, see Amry Vandenbosch, "The Indonesian Political Scene," *Far Eastern Survey* Vol. 22, no. 11 (October, 1953), pp. 145-49.

[15] Mr. R. C. Bone, Jr., who served as senior political officer in the U. S. Embassy in Djakarta from July, 1951, to August, 1953. The quotation is from "The Future of Indonesian Political Parties," *Far Eastern Survey*, Vol. 23, no. 2 (February, 1954), pp. 17-28.

[16] Holland, *op. cit.*, p. 84.

Aside from this, the party had the attraction, in the early postwar years, of its firm stand for independence. This tends, however, to fix its eyes on the past now that the goal has been won. Its present position has been described in the following terms:

> The Indonesian Nationalist Party (P.N.I.), generally considered the second largest in the country, is a party with a proud past, a stormy present and a dubious future. Like Alice and the Red Queen, it has to run faster and faster in order to stay in the same place. It has been aptly said that the party is still fighting the Dutch for independence. The thinking of its leaders still seems to function in that frame of reference. Basing itself on its cloudy philosophy of "proletarian nationalism" (marhaenism), the party tries to be all things to all men.[17]

The real exception to the generalization just stated as to the postwar origin of parties, is to be found in the Partai Komunis Indonesia (PKI), a party which does represent the resumption openly of organization and activity of the prewar party of the same name. Many of its leaders, returning from Holland at the end of the war, however, first engaged in political activity within the Socialist or other parties, whether for purposes of conscious infiltration with a view to their transformation or for other reasons. Upon their return late in 1945 and early in 1946, they were found to be adhering to the international party line as interpreted by the Netherlands Communist Party. Their initial orientation was antirepublic, as was that of the Netherlands Communist Party. They viewed the republic sponsored by Japan as fascist, and their objective was to reunite the Netherlands and Indonesia. This objective was also that of the Netherlands government which consequently assisted their repatriation. As they moved into leadership of the PKI, they supplanted its initial leaders who had had "no connection with the prewar party nor with the wartime P.K.I. underground."[18] The returned leaders thus provided the link with the prewar party. By the time they had adjusted themselves to the existing situation they realized that the republic had general popular support. They thereupon took the nationalist-communist line. Even so, they sought to support those who were prepared to negotiate a settlement with the Dutch. As Moscow policy changed after 1947, however, there was a coincidental change in the PKI line of participation in Indonesian politics. Thus the observer quoted above found that:

[17] Bone, *op. cit.*, p. 22.
[18] Holland, *op. cit.*, p. 94.

During 1946 and most of 1947, the leaders of the P.K.I. as well as those proclaimed Communists who had joined the Socialist and Labor parties appeared to follow policies determined chiefly by what best served Indonesian interests rather than by what a conscientious Stalinist might have deemed best served the Kremlin. Beginning only at the end of 1947 did their attitudes commence to show any significantly increased conformity with Moscow policy, and not until late February did this increase become substantial. No approximation of real congruity was reached until August 1948.[19]

During this period there was a tendency in Indonesia to view the United States as supporting the Dutch, especially because it failed to take strong action against them (1) to prevent them from resorting successfully to military action and (2) particularly to enforce the terms of the Renville Agreement against the Dutch. The resulting situation caused those who felt that independence could not be won without outside assistance to consider the possibility of securing Russian support since the Russian propaganda line was anticolonial as well as anti-United States. The Communist Party as it inclined to this view had to accept with it the internationalist rather than the nationalist affiliation in the sense that it had to move in general over to acceptance of support of the Russian position in international politics, as defined by Russia, as against the American.

THE FOREIGN POLICIES OF THE REPUBLIC

The result of this movement was to align the party against the foreign policy of the Republic. That policy initially was officially stated as follows: [20]

> The Indonesian Government is of opinion that the position to be taken is that Indonesia should not be a *passive* party in the area of international politics but that it should be an *active* agent entitled to decide its own standpoint.... The policy of the Republic of Indonesia must be resolved in the light of its own interests and should be executed in consonance with the situations and facts it has to face.... The lines of Indonesia's policy cannot be determined by the bent of the policy of some other country which has *its* own interests to serve.

19 *Ibid.*, p. 95.
20 Mohammed Hatta, "Indonesia's Foreign Policy," *Report on Indonesia*, Vol. 4, no. 17, April 23, 1953 (special feature), p. 7. This is a reprint of Hatta's article in *Foreign Affairs*, April, 1953. Thus the policy followed has been that of independence and "neutralism."

This policy of determination of foreign policy in the light exclusively of Indonesia's direct interest has been accepted as the proper one to follow by all parties except the PKI, which would naturally prefer to have the Republic align itself with the U.S.S.R. on all questions. There has been difference of opinion, however, as to the application of the policy to specific issues, situations or problems. Because of the greater sensitivity to or suspiciousness of American motives and intentions among some groups than among others, this has shown itself particularly where the United States has been involved as, for example, in the reaction to the acceptance of American economic, technical, or military assistance. Any suggestion of the conditioning of aid by commitments of a continuing character has been viewed by the more sensitive nationalists in Indonesia, as in India, as being designed to qualify the freedom of judgment of the government and thus the independence of the country in the conduct of its foreign relations. Reaction in terms of this understandable, even though exaggerated, sensitivity has led to action on occasion possibly more exclusively determined by the desire to show independence than by a determination to approach a problem strictly and exclusively on the basis of Indonesian interest "in consonance with the situations and facts it has to face."

Thus it may be argued that Indonesian policy with respect to the recognition of the Communist regime in China, to the Chinese intervention in the Korean war, to the situation in Indochina, and to the Japanese Peace Treaty, was in part expressive of a determination to show independence of judgment in the form of reaction against American leadership. Since there has been a similar sensitivity shown by India, for somewhat the same reasons, there has been more of a correspondence between the Indian and Indonesian reactions in international politics than between Indonesian and United States or Indonesian and Russian policies. This correspondence between Indian and Indonesian foreign policy may also be explained by Indonesian admiration for the leadership which India has attempted to furnish in the Asian struggles for national independence. But a part of the explanation of Indonesian policy must also be sought in the strength in the Parliament of the leftist as well as the nationalist parties.

Partly because of the role played by the United Nations in the Republic's struggle against the Dutch, and partly because the United Nations affords the weaker states an opportunity to play an active independent role without commitment to the policies of the United

States against the Soviet Union or the reverse, the foreign policy of the
Republic, since admission to membership, has been developed as far as
possible along United Nations' lines. From this point of view Premier
Wilopo, who assumed office on May 22, 1952, redefined the government's independent policy in the following significant words:

> (a) its own conception of its aim and purpose as a sincere, loyal and
> serious member of the United Nations...
> (b) ...our Republic will rally or support every effort within the
> framework of the United Nations to do away with, or at least grind off,
> the sharpness of the controversy between the two trends or blocs, so as to
> ward off as much as possible the cropping up of a large-scale conflict that
> may set off a third world war....
> (But) First and foremost, we must see that the independence, sovereignty
> and territory of the state will not be infringed upon or threatened, and
> that the Republic of Indonesia does not become involved in any armed
> conflict except for the defense of its independence and sovereignty against
> a direct attack launched from without or within.[21]

In relation to the larger power struggle in the Far East this Indonesian
policy, as suggested above, has taken the country, on specific issues, in
much the same direction as India and Burma. While it cannot properly
be described as being conceived as anti-American or pro-Russian, it
has had much more of a modifying effect on United States policy than
on that of the Kremlin. This was the case especially as the United States
was forced and was able to act directly in relation to each country and
each situation, thus presenting the appearance of an outside power intervening in Far Eastern affairs. The Soviet Union for its part was
better able to present a surface appearance of nonintervention since it
was able to utilize China, a Far Eastern state, as its instrument of action.
Where that was not possible or necessary, the U.S.S.R. had at its disposal "national" Communist parties to serve as the instruments of its
power in the Far Eastern as in the European countries. China is not
sufficiently close territorially to Indonesia to cause it to be viewed as
a military threat. The Chinese Communist regime had not before 1954
been able to utilize the Chinese population of the islands sufficiently
for bringing political pressures to bear so as to cause China to be
viewed as a present danger to internal politics. And, since the failure
of the 1948 Communist Party attempt to overthrow the republic,
there seemed to be presented in the activities of the Indonesia Com-

[21] Quoted by Hatta, *Ibid.*, p. 8.

munist Party no serious revolutionary threat to internal peace. That party has greatly strengthened its position, however, since it changed its tactics after the Madiun revolt of 1948.

> Through a "popular front" technique, loud protestations of its stainless patriotism, continued consolidation of its control over organized labor, skilful exploitation of conflicts among the other parties (notably the Masjumi and Nationalists) and a worsening economic situation, the Communist Party, whether through the skill of its own leadership or (more likely) the guidance of an international advisory group, is today in the strongest position it has occupied since before the unsuccessful Madiun revolt of 1948. Memories of Madiun are the greatest handicap the Communists have to overcome....
>
> The Communist Party has been tireless in its organizational activity, is apparently well supplied with funds, probably via the Chinese Embassy, and is constantly on the alert to exploit any frictions.... Any detailed analysis of Communist activity is obviously impossible, but the time may well come, in the not too distant future, when those who have pointed to Indonesia's adherence to Islam as effective insurance against a Communist victory may find themselves sadly disillusioned. In its village propaganda, the party has apparently been very careful to avoid any offense to religious feeling and to present its program as merely the logical extension of Islam.[22]

These new tactics, looking toward the securing of power through elections, as stated, do not pose any apparent threat from communism of violent revolutionary action against the Republic. Thus the area of greatest sensitivity, in relation to foreign states, is to United States policy rather than to that of the U.S.S.R.

INTERNAL POLITICS

Since it is only the Communist Party which has ventured to question the wisdom of the general line of determination of foreign policy, it is not from the field of foreign relations but from domestic politics that multiplicity of parties has come. In this context, except for the Nationalist Party (PNI) the party name should indicate its general line of approach to the internal problems of the state or the basis of attraction to it of membership. This nevertheless, is only partly true, since one must again make an exception of the PKI which follows the

[22] Bone, *op. cit.*, pp. 22-23.

general Communist line with respect to the use which it would make
of power if it controlled the state.

The party which probably has the largest following is the Masjumi
or Moslem Party. Its importance is derived from the fact that it ties
together the Moslem religious community and the major Moslem social
organizations and their village leaders in a political organization. The
purpose of the party, however, is not to make coincidental the areas
of governmental and of religious authority. Rather it seeks to force
an approach to political decisions along lines harmonious with Islamic
religious teachings. Thus in its so-called Urgency Program, adopted
early in 1946, it set up as the first item: "Realization of the Islamic
ideology in matters concerning the state in order to be able to establish a state based upon popular sovereignty and justice in harmony with
teachings of Islam." This was held to require: (2) Enactment of laws
which guarantee workers minimum wages, maximum working hours,
accident and old-age allowances, protection as to security, health and
housing. (3) Enactment of laws guaranteeing the peasant private ownership of land sufficient to support him and his family, protection in
the sale of his products, and general improvement of his status.[23]

This is certainly not expressive of a reactionary point of view with
respect to social and economic problems. It is, however, expressive of
a point of view which is derived from perception of the nature of the
Indonesian environment and one designed to strengthen the position
of the village and the villager in the economy. It is thus conservative,
and has led to the characterization of the party as "the main conservative force in the Republic." Thus viewed, the Masjumi line of approach to questions of public policy would be set by the interest of
the individual and the village rather than of the national state. But the
program goes on to state that:

> The economy should be based upon collectivism in which individual
> initiative is not detrimental to the general interest and which is directed
> towards general prosperity. And while the right of private ownership is
> recognized, subject to limitations laid down in religion (taxes, charity,
> etc.) Capitalism that is obviously concerned with individual interest alone
> (i.e., socially harmful capitalism) must be opposed.

Since, following the premiership of Hatta, the first two prime ministers of Indonesia as a recognized state were from the Masjumi Party,

[23] Holland, *op. cit.*, p. 76.

the policies actually followed in an attempt to solve the pressing political, economic, and social problems of postwar reconstruction may be taken as indicative of the lines of application of Masjumi principles. This revealed no rigid control of policy by doctrine. The emphasis was put on collective action taken under the direction of government rather than on direct governmental intervention. There were elements of socialism as well as of capitalism in government planning and action. But socialistic developments were not expressive of hostility to capitalism nor were the safeguards erected around the capitalists properly viewable as based upon hostility to Marxist socialism. Thus the Masjumi would seem to be fundamentally indigenous in its ideology, but a party which, although nonsocialist, has arrived at a position which enables it to work closely with, for example, the Indonesian Socialist Party (PSI) of Soetan Sjahrir.

The PSI finds its chief support among the intellectuals rather than the masses. Although a Marxist party, its leader, Sjahrir

> espouses a socialism which is eclectic in its approach to Marxism and adapted to Indonesian conditions. It is not merely fortuitous that his party is called the *Indonesian* Socialist Party, for the socialism of Sjahrir and of the leaders associated with him has a distinctly Indonesian character.... The society that he does envisage as possible of development during the next two or three decades and which he advocates is based upon a mixed economy, with a substantial sector of economic life left to private enterprise. For a long time it will be physically impossible, he feels, for the state to direct more than a limited area of economic life, since there is not the administrative personnel available to do more.[24]

Thus Marxian socialism, a European-developed set of ideas, has been introduced into Indonesian politics by the Socialist Party as a body of doctrine to be first tested, examined, and modified in the light of the Indonesian environment before being applied. The result has been the reduction of the area of conflict between the Masjumi and the Socialist Party from that of principle to that of time and means.

There is no apparent fundamental cleavage between these two parties and the third which is of almost equal importance to the Masjumi from the point of view of parliamentary representation and direction or composition of government. The government headed by Wilopo, a leader of the Indonesian Nationalist Party (PNI), which succeeded those headed by two Masjumi premiers, did not take a line which was

[24] *Ibid.*, p. 91.

fundamentally different from that of its predecessors. This may, of course, be explained by the coalition nature of all three governments. But in the construction of party coalitions the difficulties to be overcome were not those resulting from fundamental differences over the nature and purposes of government. They grew out of specific issues. When leaders of the parties reached agreement, furthermore, the party memberships acquiesced. In other words, to a very considerable extent interparty negotiation was limited to a restricted group who had been previously working together and who were immediately concerned with the redistribution of power and work load.

The illiteracy [25] of the population ensured a degree of freedom to the party leaders (whether or not the party is as loosely organized as is the Masjumi or more completely and effectively organized as is the Socialist or the Communist Party), sufficient to enable them to act with reasonable independence in applying principle to specific situations and to agree in setting government policy. Thus, certainly until the electorate organized and began to function, the politics of the country was largely confined to competition for power among the members of the educated class. As long as the struggle for independence had to be waged the general acceptance of independence as the goal ensured agreement between parties because of the hazards to all of serious party conflict. It also brought about an approach to the problems of politics marked by concern for the general interest rather than special or self-interest. Consequently it put a brake on the development of a struggle for personal power within the government. The political position of President Soekarno and Vice President Hatta above, or dissociated from, party and individual rivalry was influential also in lessening the party and the personal struggle in the construction of government and in the development of public policy. Standards of party and personal behavior were consequently high during the first years of the Republic, as measured by elevation of the general interest of the new state and its people over that of the political, economic and social groups composing it.

With the winning of independence and after its initial consolidation, however, parliamentary politics began to assume the appearance of a struggle for power on both the party and the individual-leadership levels. Those in opposition (of whom the Communist have often been

[25] It was assertedly reduced to about 45 per cent of the population by the end of 1952. See *Report on Indonesia*, Vol. 4, No. 18, p. 7.

only a minority) soon began to try to discredit the government and to advance their own personal political fortunes. As a result they lessened the effectiveness of the government and stimulated disorder in the country. The effect on this deteriorated situation of an attempt to reconstitute government through general elections remains to be demonstrated in the future. It is probable that a multiparty system will continue after elections are held and that both government and opposition will be coalitions of two or more parties.

The political difficulties faced by the Republic of Indonesia, organized and attempting to operate as a parliamentary democracy, whether with or without elections, comes naturally out of past experience. The idea of democracy is an importation rather than a part of the traditional system, certainly above the village level. The tradition of the country is authoritarian. Colonial rule strengthened rather than weakened the native authoritarianism, except as provision began to be made for more general education by means of which new conceptions of the role and organization of government were introduced into the country. These conceptions had not, however, been widely enough disseminated by 1945 to change the authoritarian relationship of leaders and people. To this must be added the fact that the Indonesian parties and their leaders, until the Japanese occupation, had always acted mainly in opposition to what was proposed by the Dutch because of the sponsor, regardless of the nature of the proposal. They had never had the opportunity, until toward the end of the war period, to oppose responsibly through the presentation of alternative courses of action to those of the governing officials. Consequently the force of traditional ways and prior experience was bound to take the opposition parties into a course of criticism of the government of a negative sort and cause the leaders in the government to concern themselves primarily with the maintenance of their own power.

The government had the responsibility for maintaining order and re-establishing the productive life of the country. This was a large order which required sound planning. But the most soundly conceived plans could only yield results and the planners avoid dissatisfaction and criticism if the plans were put into effective operation. In this respect the conditions of administration of policy rather than the policy itself gave a lever for the opposition parties to use against the government and thus helped to determine the outcome of the struggle between parties and leaders. The successful execution of both the short-run and the long-run plans of the government depended upon trained and experienced administrators. Dutch colonial policy had not been, until shortly before the war, expressly directed toward the development of a civil service staffed with Indonesians, except in the lower ranges. Nevertheless, there did exist a body of Dutch-trained administrators. Many of these, especially of course the Dutch and the Indo-Europeans, aligned themselves against the Republic in the struggle for independence. From the dominant nationalist point of view, this tended to disqualify them for service in the new state, although the Hague Agreement stipulated for their retention for a two-year period. This period, however, many of them viewed as a sort of terminal leave rather than as an opportunity to establish their loyalty and competence with a view to future service. This reduced the number of available officials, experienced from the Dutch period, to execute the policies of the Republic. However, to that number there were additionally available those who had gained experience of one sort or another during the Japanese occupation. The total available, nevertheless, did not meet the need of the Republic for trained and relatively experienced civil servants. This forced the use of relatively untrained and inexperienced people in the public services, with a decline in the efficiency of the services. Even so, there were not enough people with any training at all to meet the need for expansion of the civil service. Those who had even minimum qualifications were indispensable. Because they felt themselves indispensable these tended to set their own standards of performance. Consequently, after the stimulus supplied by enthusiasm for the cause of independence had begun to diminish, corruption, laziness, and irresponsibility among public officials posed a serious problem for the government.

The long drawn-out (fifty-eight day) cabinet crisis of 1953, revealed in its inception and in its results, many elements of the problem of government in Indonesia.

The Wilopo Government resigned on June 3. It had maintained a precarious existence for 14 months. The immediate cause of its fall was an attack on the Minister for Home Affairs for his handling of the land-distribution problem in North Sumatra. It might, however, just as well have come over any one of a number of issues which divided the Nationalist and Masjumi parties, the two parties which formed the basis of the coalition upon which the Wilopo cabinet rested. The Nationalist members of Parliament frequently voted with the leftist opposition, thus putting the cabinet in a precarious position and finally making co-operation no longer possible.[26]

The land problem grew out of the Dutch policy of attracting Western agricultural enterprise by concessioning public lands in Sumatra for periods up to seventy-five years. During the Japanese occupation and immediately thereafter "squatters rights" were established on these plantations by indigenous laborers and peasants as well as by Chinese settlers. The original holders sought the return of their lands after the war and the establishment of the Republic. This caught the government between the Scylla of the foreign planters' demands for restoration of the land and its own desperate need for revenues and foreign exchange on the one hand,[27] and the Charybdis of the squatters unwillingness to move on the other. Under the pressure of existing conditions the foreign concessionaires had agreed to relinquish parts of their holdings with the understanding that the government would guarantee them full use of the remainder. The implementation of this guarantee made it necessary for the government to attempt resettlement of the squatters. From the nationalist standpoint this meant action against nationals in behalf of "imperialist" interests. The resettlement program had been carried to the halfway mark, with resettlement of about half of the 30,000 families which had to be moved, before violent resistance occurred. Some two months later the Nationalist parliamentarians joined the Communists and other leftist parties in voting a resolution demanding revision of the land-distribution policy. The defection of the Nationalists made necessary the resignation of the government.

An earlier controversy, the October 17 Incident, also had considerable significance for the Wilopo government. The incident itself was an anti-parliament demonstration, in the course of which the Parliament building was stormed. The demonstrators, however, disbanded after listening to a speech by the President. The demonstration had been staged with a view to bringing about the dissolution of Parliament and the holding of general elections. Its main accomplishment was the

[26] On the cause and immediate consequences of the crisis see Vandenbosch, *op. cit.*, p. 145.
[27] Before the war these plantations had been an important source of tax revenue. Since almost the total production had been exported it had also produced considerable foreign exchange. *Ibid.*, p. 146.

revelation of the currents moving under the relatively quiet surface of Indonesian politics.[28]

The demonstration grew out of opposition to the program of army reform undertaken by the Sultan of Jogjakarta who was the Minister of Defense. Within the army the opposition came from

> the group of former guerrilla officers, nationalist in political persuasion, who had received the somewhat sketchy military training they possessed from the Japanese. The Sultan's program involved modernizing the army into a strong and well-trained professional force. This might well have been done at the expense of the imperfectly trained revolutionary officer class. At any rate that group professed to see in it a plot, "master-minded by the professional army group (trained under the Dutch)" to oust them from their jobs. Thus in this incident, as well as in the resettlement difficulty, the issue of "nationalism" versus "imperialism" was raised.[29]

Since the President, apparently jealous and fearful of the Sultan as well as the Nationalist Party, supported the opposition to the Minister of Defense's program of army reform, the Sultan resigned. The Wilopo government, however, lost considerable prestige out of the incident and its aftermath, which included a series of local army revolts in which subordinate officers deposed area commanders. Nevertheless, the government continued to maintain an uneasy existence until it finally fell because of the resettlement issue.

The attempt to construct a new government, as stated above, took fifty-eight days. The initial attempts were again to construct a government on the basis of a coalition of the Masjumi and Nationalist parties. The split between them had, however, become too wide to make this possible. A new government was finally organized through the efforts of Wongsonegoro, the Chairman of the Greater Indonesia Party, the second strongest nationalist group in the temporary Parliament. Wongsonegoro became Vice Premier in the Cabinet headed by Ali Sastroamidjojo, who returned from the ambassadorship at Washington to take up the position of Premier.

The announcement of the new Cabinet was received "in most circles

---

[28] On this and other developments of 1953, see Robert Van Niel "Indonesian Political Developments," *Far Eastern Survey*, Vol. XXII (June, 1953), no. 7.

[29] *Ibid.* In this connection it may be pointed out that almost every issue which arose during 1953 and 1954 was utilized by the nationalists to increase hostility to foreigners, especially the Dutch. The failure of the Nationalist Party, and other nationalist groups to develop constructive and forward looking programs of internal development made it necessary for the Nationalists to develop and maintain support in politics by continuing to fight the battles of the past.

with shock and incredulity," according to one writer.[30] This was because the Cabinet did not seem sufficiently representative of what were viewed as the more important elements in Indonesian society to have a very long tenure. What it lacked in representative character was not compensated for in the distinction of its members. The new Prime Minister, Sastroamidjojo, and his Foreign Minister were, to be sure, political leaders of some distinction. The others given cabinet rank were, however, either generally unknown or viewed at Jakarta as secondary figures.

With all its limitations, nevertheless, the Sastroamidjojo government maintained itself through 1954 and into 1955 despite considerable disorder and confusion in the country. The explanation of its continued existence probably was the strong support given to the Premier and the Foreign Minister by President Soekarno. Both had long been Soekarno's supporters and trusted associates. Through them the President was able to shape policy without assuming responsibility in case of failures. In addition to presidential support, the new government did have a small parliamentary majority (114 out of 212) and thus fell within the framework of the existing system. Its membership was drawn from the left to the moderate right. It did not, however, contain any representatives from either Sjahrir's Socialist Party or the Communists. Nevertheless the Communist Party exercised considerable passive influence because, possessing so narrow a majority in Parliament, the Cabinet increasingly found itself dependent on Communist votes.[31]

This dependence upon the Communist Party may serve to explain one of the positive steps taken by the Sastroamidjojo government. This was the inauguration in 1954 of diplomatic relations with the Soviet Union. Another positive step was the conclusion of a treaty of friendship with Thailand on March 3, 1954. In this treaty the two countries agreed, among other things, to regulate questions of commerce, navigation, consular privileges, cultural relations and extradition. A positive achievement, also, was the signature in Djakarta on April 22 of a treaty with Communist China defining the conditions of retention or loss of Chinese nationality on the part of Chinese residing in Indonesia. The principle defined in the treaty, as stated in its first article, was: [32]

[30] Bone, *op. cit.*, pp. 19-20.
[31] Vandenbosch, *op. cit.*, p. 148.
[32] From the text as broadcast by the New China News Agency and published in the *Far Eastern Survey*, Vol. 24, no. 5 (May, 1955), pp. 75-6.

That all persons who hold simultaneously the nationality of the People's Republic of China and the nationality of the Republic of Indonesia shall choose, in accordance with their own will, between the nationality of the People's Republic of China and the nationality of the Republic of Indonesia. All married women who hold the above-mentioned two nationalities shall also choose, in accordance with their own will, between the two nationalities.

This nationality treaty may properly be considered an important by-product of the Bandung Conference since it was that conference which brought the Chinese Communist Premier and Foreign Minister, Chou En-lai, to Indonesia and gave him an incentive to reach an agreement on terms acceptable to the Indonesian government. The role played by Premier Sastroamidjojo in the calling and staging of the Bandung Conference, as well as this nationality treaty, represented positive achievement in the field of foreign relations to be credited to the Sastroamidjojo government.

Internally, the government put down a Moslem revolt organized by the extremist Moslem party, Dar ul Islam, in north Sumatra in September, 1953, promising that reforms would be instituted in the territory as it was recaptured. And, as a government supported in Parliament by the nationalist party and those of the left, it neither put impediments in the way of the liquidation of the Dutch Military Mission in Indonesia, which was officially terminated on December 16, 1953, nor did it respond sympathetically to protests made by the Dutch over the increasingly hostile treatment accorded to Dutch nationals and Dutch enterprises in Indonesia.

One thing which the Sastroamidjojo government failed to do, however, was to lessen the corruption which had shown itself in the Indonesian government. On the contrary, from this, as well as from the general economic, standpoint conditions in Indonesia seriously deteriorated during Sastroamidjojo's two year tenure of office. That tenure was ended on July 24, 1955, when the Premier tendered his resignation and that of his Cabinet. The immediate issue was the refusal of the leaders of the Indonesian Army to accept the appointment of Colonel Bambang Utyo as Army Chief of Staff. Their action, it was reported, was due to objection to the growing influence of the Communists within the government as well as to professional disapproval of the quality of the proposed appointment. Whether or not their reported objections were well grounded, their action represented an obvious attempt at intervention in politics on the part of the Army. It was undertaken at a time when President Soekarno, a principal supporter of Sastroamidjojo, was out of the country on a pilgrimage to Mecca. Consequently the resignation of his government was tendered to and accepted by Vice President Hatta, under whose auspices the successor government was constituted.

The new government, headed by Burhanudin Harahap, re-established the control of the Masjumi. Hatta sought to form an all-party government under himself as Premier but was unsuccessful because of insistence on the part of the Nationalist and Communist parties that he must resign as Vice President before they would accept him as Premier. Since he was not prepared to do this, he appointed the President of the Masjumi as Premier. The Harahap government included some eleven parties in addition to the Masjumi, including two Socialist ministers but excluding both the Nationalists and the Communists.

This reconstruction of the government raised a question as to whether or not the date set for the holding of elections would again be advanced. The new government, as had its predecessors, had a majority in the Parliament. But the extent to which the Parliament was actually a representative body had never been actually established through the election of its members. The promise of elections in January, 1954, had not been fulfilled, the Sastroamidjojo government having taken the position that considerable advance preparations would be necessary. The elections were, consequently, re-scheduled for January, 1955. The nominations, however, which were expected to take two months, were not even begun until January, 1954, and the date of the elections was necessarily advanced, first to August and then to the end of September, 1955. Since the new government was not constituted until August it could readily have found justification in its turn for postponing the elections. It did not do so, however, and the election process was begun on September 29. Since elections in such a country as Indonesia are necessarily long drawn out affairs the final official outcome, from the point of view of representation of the parties in the new Parliament, would not be known much before the end of 1955.

The unofficial returns, as reported on October 10,[33] gave the Nationalists 7,369,000 votes, the Masjumi 6,769,000, the Moslem Teachers party (Naldatul) 6,167,000, and the Communist party 5,785,000. The

[33] *New York Times*, October 11, 1955.

Masjumi leaders charged, and claimed to have evidence of, widespread intimidation and fraud in the conduct of the elections, especially in Central Java. If the charges should be sustained it would be necessary under the law to hold new elections in an area where the Nationalists had polled more than three million of their seven million votes and the Communist almost three million of their total. Re-polling might move the Masjumi total vote considerably ahead of that of the Nationalists and also reduce Communist representation in the elected Parliament.

The final returns in any case should give a clue as to the future lines of internal political development and also as to the lines of evolution of Indonesia's foreign relations. The existing lines of relationship, as revealed at the time of reconstruction of the government on the eve of the elections, presented two competitive coalitions—the group of parties of the right and left center under the leadership of the Masjumi, on the one side, and the coalition of the Nationalist and Communist parties and their affiliates, on the other. Success of the Nationalist-Communist coalition in the elections would strengthen the "neutralist"—pro-Communist orientation of foreign policy. Masjumi success, on the other hand, would move Indonesia in the contrary direction. Past tendencies, however, indicate a possibility that personal rivalries and relationships may, even after the elections, affect these groupings into two opposing coalitions, as might also a renewal of nationalist hostility to the Communists if the Communist Party should fail to maintain successfully its recently assumed appearance of being a national Communist party rather than being part of an international Communist system directed from Moscow or Peiping.

BIBLIOGRAPHICAL REFERENCES

Boeke, Julius H., *Economics and Economic Policy of Dual Societies as exemplified by Indonesia* (New York: International Secretariat, Institute of Pacific Relations, 1953).

Bone, Robert C., Jr., "The Future of Indonesian Political Parties," *Far Eastern Survey*, Vol. 23, no. 2.

Bro, Marguerita Harmon, Indonesia: Land of Challenge (New York: Harper and Brothers, 1954).

Collins, J. Foster, *The United Nations and Indonesia* (New York: International Conciliation, 1950), no. 459.

Diplomatic Correspondent, "Disillusion in Indonesia," *Eastern World* (Djakarta), January, 1954.

Emerson, Rupert, "Reflections on the Indonesian Case," *World Politics*, Vol. 1, no. 1.

Emerson, Rupert, Mills, Lennox A., and Thompson, Virginia, *Government and Nationalism in South East Asia* (New York: International Secretariat, Institute of Pacific Relations, 1942).

Furnivall, John S., *Colonial Policy and Practice* (Cambridge: Cambridge University Press, 1948).

Information Office of the Republic of Indonesia, *Seven Years of Indonesian Independence* (New York, 1952).

Ingber, Davis, "The Indonesian Political Scene," *Eastern World*, January, 1954.

Jaquet, L. G. M., "The Indonesian Federal Problem Reconsidered," *Pacific Affairs*, Vol. 25, no. 2.

Kahin, George McT., "Indonesian Politics and Nationalism," in Holland, W. L. (ed.), *Asian Nationalism and the West*, Pt. I (New York: Macmillan, for the Institute of Pacific Relations, 1953).

———, *Nationalism and Revolution in Indonesia* (Ithaca: Cornell University Press, for the Institute of Pacific Relations, 1953).

May, J. J., "Dutch Indonesian Trade," *Eastern World*, February, 1954.

Sjahrir, Soetan, *Out of Exile* (New York: John Day Co., 1949).

Steiner, H. Arthur, "Postwar Government and Politics of the Netherlands East Indies." In Cole, Taylor, and Hallowell, J. H. (eds.), "Postwar Governments of the Far East," *Journal of Politics*, November, 1947.

Van der Kroef, Justus M., "The Dutch Position in Indonesia Today," *Far Eastern Survey*, Vol. 23, no. 6.

———, "Conflicts of Religious Policy in Indonesia," *Far Eastern Survey*, Vol. 22, no. 10.

Vandenbosch, Amry, *The Dutch East Indies; Its Government, Problems, and Politics* (Berkeley: University of California Press, 1942).

———, "The Netherlands Indies," *Annals of the American Academy of Political and Social Science*, Vol. CCXXVI, p. 91.

———, "The Indonesian Political Scene," *Far Eastern Survey*, Vol. 22, no. 11.

Van Helsdingen, W. H., "The Netherlands-Indonesian Draft Agreement," *Pacific Affairs*, Vol. 22, no. 2.

Verdoorn, J. A., "Indonesia at the Crossroads," *Pacific Affairs*, Vol. 19, no. 4.

Vlekke, B. H. M., "Communism and Nationalism in Southeast Asia," *International Affairs*, Vol. 25, no. 2.

Westerling, Raymond, *Challenge to Terror*, tr. by Root, W. (London: Kimber, 1952).

Wolf, Charles, Jr., *The Indonesian Story: The Birth, Growth and Structure of the Indonesian Republic* (New York: John Day, 1948).

14

Postwar Politics in the Philippines

※✳※✳※✳※✳※✳※✳※✳※✳※✳※✳※✳※✳※✳※✳

THE UNITED STATES IN THE PHILIPPINES

THE PHILIPPINES entered the postwar period as an independent state. This was required to fulfill the terms of the Commonwealth Act of 1935 and the pledge made by President Roosevelt during World War II. Ultimate independence had been proclaimed as the American policy almost from the time of transfer of the Philippines by Spain to the United States. The Republican Party, in power for some time after the acquisition, conditioned this policy, however, by two considerations. The first was that independence would be granted only when the United States reached the conclusion that the Filipinos were capable of maintaining their independence. The second was that there should be a demonstrated desire for independence on the part of the Filipinos. The Democratic Party which was by declaration anti-imperialist at the time of acquisition of the Philippines, was for that reason also committed to independence. And in the islands themselves independence was consistently advocated by the political leaders and supported by a strong majority of the people.

Almost from the beginning Filipinos were associated with Americans in the government of the Islands. Thus the Organic Act of 1902 made provision for an elective assembly, and, as quickly as they were considered to be prepared, Filipinos were introduced into the executive and administrative services in subordinate capacities. The more important positions, and thus effective control, remained practically as well as theoretically with the American officials during the periods of Republican ascendancy in the United States. The first decisive advance toward the goal of the advocates of independence, consequently, was made under the auspices of the Democrats, with the enactment of the Jones Law in 1916. This law, and especially its administration under Governor-General Harrison, went a very considerable distance toward placing actual control of the government in the hands of the Filipinos. With the return to power of the Republicans after the election of 1920, however, steps were taken to restore effective American control, on the theory that as long as there was American responsibility there should be adequate authority retained to enable that responsibility to be discharged.

With the coming of the depression in the United States in the Hoover administration, political attitudes began to be modified in the light of new economic considerations. The advocates of Philippine independence on political and "moral" grounds found their cause being advocated on economic grounds, in terms of American rather than Philippine interest, by the representatives in the Congress of various farm interests, by groups of processors, and by organized labor groups.

Three decades of American control of the Islands, however, had resulted in the creation of very intimate ties between the economy of the United States and that of the Philippines. Especially after 1909, when virtually free-trade relations between the Islands and the United States and "closed door" relations between the Philippines and the non-American world had been inaugurated, the economic ties between the dependency and the metropolitan country had been drawn closer and closer. On the side of imports, the Philippines supplied an increasingly important market for American goods while the American market was of even greater importance to the Philippines: 79 per cent in 1930, 87 per cent in 1933, and 84 per cent in 1934 of the total volume of Philippine exports going to the United States.

While it might be concluded that the United States could get along without the Philippine market for its manufactured goods, the Islands had been brought into a condition of virtually complete dependence on reasonably free access to the American market. This condition had been the direct result of American policy. Because of this economic interrelationship, it had come to be considered questionable whether the United States would, or properly could, ever fulfill its promise to grant independence to the Islands; or whether it would actually be to the interest of the Filipino to gain independence if that meant that he would be placed beyond the American customs' frontier. The support in the United States for the fulfillment of that promise, up to 1930, lay in a point of view, essentially political, that the responsibility of the United States, sharing the "white man's burden," was to uplift the Filipino and train him in the art of self-government so that he could finally be entrusted with the responsibility for governing himself. Thus until after 1930 independence sentiment in the United States was founded upon asserted concern for the welfare of the Filipino. To retire from the Islands was conceived as an ultimate duty, an unusual act of self-denial, rather than as an action to be taken in the interest of the United States and its nationals. The Filipino, however, asserted his capacity to govern himself and was concerned with acquiring independence rather than with economic or other considerations which might be urged against it.

The first concrete evidence of a shift in point of view in the United States from concern with the Filipino to concern with the interest of the American producer of competitive products came when, in connection with the enactment of the Smoot-Hawley tariff measure in 1929, an amendment was offered providing for the levy of import duties upon Philippine products. Almost immediately, however, the issue was changed from that of tariff legislation to that of independence on the basis of a bill introduced in the Senate by Senators Hawes and Cutting. Discussion of this measure continued during the years 1930-33. From the viewpoint of economic-interest groups, the Hawes-Cutting bill was supported by representatives of the agricultural sections of the country and found its principal opposition among the manufacturers, who were interested both in the Philippine market and in the supply of raw materials essential to their production. To both sides were joined those who were principally concerned with the political implications of the proposed action. Thus the advocates of independence on grounds of economic interest were joined by those who believed in the right of the people to govern themselves. The opponents found support among those who held to the view (1) that the Filipino was not yet ready for self-government, and (2) that the international consequences of independence, under the disturbed conditions produced in the Far East by Japanese policy at the outset of the 1930's, would be unfortunate for the Philippines and also for states with colonies in the area. This latter consideration was especially emphasized by the executive branch of the American government.

The combination of those who wanted to protect themselves against asserted Philippine competition with the earlier advocates of independence, including the Philippine leaders themselves, resulted finally in the enactment of an independence measure, the Tydings-McDuffie Act, in March, 1934, after the Hare-Hawes-Cutting measure had been enacted over a veto by President Hoover in the last days of his administration. The Hare-Hawes Law provided for an immediate legislative vote on the question in the Philippines. This, when taken, was adverse to the measure, not so much on account of opposition to independence as because of objection to some of the conditions attached to its achievement. Reconsideration in the United States Congress resulted in the enactment of the Tydings-McDuffie measure, which was then put into effect.

THE COMMONWEALTH GOVERNMENT

This authorized the holding of a constitutional convention, after approval of independence either by the Philippine legislature or by a special convention called for that purpose. The constitution had to be drafted to conform to certain conditions defined in the Act, and it had to be approved by the American President. The constitution was successfully drafted and was given Presidential approval, and the new Commonwealth government was inaugurated before the end of 1935. The new regime was not that of an independent state, the final severance of American control having been postponed until the end of a ten-year period, during which economic relations were to be adjusted toward the realization of the status of complete independence and arrangements were to be made which would enable the new state to sustain an independent position.

The constitution of the Commonwealth of the Philippines, adopted in 1935, as amended in 1940, gave the islands a democratic government of the presidential rather than the parliamentary or cabinet form. The president and vice president were to be directly elected for a four-year term, with immediate re-election restricted to one additional term. The two houses of the legislature were also constituted by direct election. The senate was composed of twenty-four members elected at large for six-year terms, one-third being elected every two years. The membership of the House of Representatives was constitutionally fixed at "not more than 120 members," apportioned among the provinces on the basis of population.[1]

Given a status independent of the legislature, the executive had greater constitutional powers in relation to the definition of public policy than those even of the American President since the President of the Commonwealth had an item as well as a general veto over legislation. Also, he could have his views defended in the legislature through the personal appearance in either house of the appointive heads of the several departments of government. On the other hand, the constitutional provision for a Commission on Appointments, made up of twelve members elected from the Senate and twelve from the House, which had to approve all appointments to important offices, including that of head of an executive department, carried with it the possibility of enhancement of legislative influence in the event of a struggle for power between leaders in the legislature and the president.

For purposes of control of elections, provision was made, by amendment of the constitution in 1940, for a Commission on Elections. The provision made was for three commissioners, appointed by the president, confirmed by the Commission on Appointments, and serving nine-year terms. This Commission was designed to supervise the administration of the electoral process, previously a responsibility of the Department of the Interior. For purposes of deciding contests growing out of election returns to the House and the Senate, however, each body used an electoral tribunal composed of three justices of the Supreme Court, designated by the chief justice.

Under the Commonwealth Act and constitution, the Philippines were granted virtually complete powers of self-government. The limitations were set in terms of constitutional amendment, the American President having the right of disallowance of amendments, and of laws which, in the judgment of the President would

> result in a failure of the government of the Commonwealth of the Philippine Islands to fulfill its contracts, or to meet its bonded indebtedness and interest thereon or to provide for its sinking funds, or which seems likely to impair the reserves for the protection of the currency of the Philippine Islands, or which in his judgment will violate international obligations of the United States.[2]

[1] The original provision had been for a National Assembly. An amendment in 1940 provided for the bicameral legislature, as described. Up to the present, the House of Representatives has not been brought to the upper limit of 120, only 100 representatives having been given seats.

[2] Tydings-McDuffie Act, sec. 7.

The last stipulation was especially necessary since, under the Philippine constitution, during the Commonwealth period "Foreign Affairs shall be under the direct supervision and control of the United States." [3]

Since foreign affairs also involves defense, the constitution further gave to the United States the right "to maintain military and other reservations and armed forces in the Philippines, and, upon the order of the President of the United States, to call into the service of such armed forces all military forces organized by the Government of the Commonwealth of the Philippines." [4]

These provisions with respect to foreign affairs and the military made it impossible for the Philippine government to develop an independent, or neutralist, policy toward Japan in 1941, even if it had been so minded. Consequently, the Philippine people, when the country was attacked, regarded themselves in their resistance to Japan as acting in behalf of the United States as much as in defense of their country.

The new system of self-government was in full and, on the whole, satisfactory operation at the time of the Japanese invasion of the Islands. The political elements under the strong leadership of the elected President, Manuel Quezon, and the Vice President, Sergio Osmeña, Senator Manuel Roxas, and others, had been united, after an initial split, in the overwhelmingly predominant Nacionalista Party. Since the President was generally accepted as the leader of the party which controlled the legislature, there was substantial executive direction in the development of policy and its enactment into law by the legislature.

When it became apparent that formal military resistance to Japan could not be sustained successfully in the Islands, President Quezon and Vice President Osmeña were evacuated, as was General Douglas MacArthur, who had been brought to the Philippines to organize the military forces of the Commonwealth. Those forces, after the outbreak of war, were incorporated in the American forces of which General MacArthur had been designated as the Commander-in-Chief. This evacuation resulted in the establishment in Washington of what was in the nature of a Philippine "government-in-exile." Through General MacArthur's Headquarters, established in Brisbane, Australia, the Commonwealth government maintained such contact as was possible with the guerrilla movement which came into being in the Philippines after the cessation of formal military resistance. In this way the continuity of

[3] Constitution, Art. 17, sec. 10.
[4] Constitution, Art. 17, sec. 12.

Commonwealth constitutional government was preserved during the period of the Japanese occupation, even though the war situation made necessary some constitutionally irregular actions. Furthermore, President Roosevelt not only reiterated the pledge of independence within the period set in the Commonwealth Act but proclaimed a willingness to advance the date if war circumstances permitted. Congress, by Joint Resolution of June 29, 1944, pledged complete independence and authorized the President to proclaim it prior to July 4, 1946.

POSTWAR RESTORATION OF THE COMMONWEALTH REGIME

By the time the Islands were liberated from the Japanese, President Quezon had died in the United States and had been succeeded as President by Vice President Osmeña. It was to the latter, consequently, that the powers of government were transferred by the Americans on February 27, 1945. No military government was formally instituted even for interim purposes since Osmeña and the Commonwealth authorities with him began to exercise civil authority in the liberated provinces shortly after American forces landed on Leyte Island.

While American military government was not instituted in the Philippines, it was nevertheless the case that the American military had a fairly decisive influence over government at least up to the time of independence. The Commonwealth authorities were almost completely dependent on the Americans, and the Americans on the military, for all of the facilities essential to government. Either in the course of military operations or as a result of deliberate destruction by the Japanese much of the interisland shipping and the land transportation facilities had been wrecked. Planes, motor transport of all kinds, and ships, where available, were American military equipment usable by the Commonwealth authorities only at the discretion of General MacArthur's Headquarters. Such telephone, telegraph and radio facilities as existed were American, and under military disposition. Materials and technicians for the restoration of utilities, public and private buildings, newspapers, and radio, docks and wharves, roads and bridges, were similarly immediately available to the Commonwealth government only through release to it by the American military authorities. Beyond this immediate and local dependence of the Commonwealth government on the American authorities, there was the larger long-run dependence on the United States for assistance in rehabilitation and reconstruction of the national economy. As it appeared to the Filipino, the destruction of war had been visited upon him and his country because his government had been loyal to the United States rather than because pursuit of Philippine objectives had embroiled the country with Japan. Public statements had led him to believe that this view was accepted in the United States and that the American government accepted the obligation to compensate him for the damage resulting from the war and to restore the Philippine economy. With this was inevitably connected the question of defining economic relations between the United States and the Philippines after July 4, 1946, when the Commonwealth was to be terminated and the Republic proclaimed. The power of decision in all of these questions of fundamental importance was in the American Congress, and the undertaking of the needed reconstruction and rehabilitation work was necessarily delayed until, after some months of discussion, Congress enacted the Philippine Rehabilitation Act and the Philippine Trade Act, both of 1946. The two were connected through a provision in the latter that no payments in excess of $500 (for war damages) under the terms of the former should be made until after completion of an executive agreement by which the Philippine government accepted the stipulations of the Trade Act.

As stated above, the major problem posed at the time of enactment of the Commonwealth law came from the virtually complete economic dependence of the Islands on the United States. As succinctly put by High Commissioner Paul V. McNutt, testifying before a Congressional Committee on February 15, 1946:

> In the Philippines the national economy was geared before the war entirely and completely to export trade. And 95% of that export trade was with the United States. Except for fish and rice, which are locally consumed, 98% of all other production in the Philippines, amounting to $266,000,000 in 1941, is produced for export. . . . And I might and should say here and now that we, the United States, managed it that way. We are responsible for the sole dependency of the Philippines on the American market. Our businessmen and our statesmen in the past years allowed the Philippines to become a complete economic dependency of the United States to a greater degree than any single state of the Union is economically dependent on the rest of the United States.[5]

[5] Quoted in John F. Cady, and others, *The Development of Self-Rule and Independence in Burma, Malaya and the Philippines* (New York: American Institute of Pacific Relations, 1948), Pt. III, "The Philippines," pp. 97-98.

POSTWAR DEFINITIONS OF UNITED STATES
–PHILIPPINE RELATIONS

The Commonwealth Act made provision for a gradual readjustment of the conditions of Philippine access to the American market with a view to lessening the economic shock at the end of the ten-year period when independence would be attained and for a period thereafter. The war situation went much further than had American planning in severing completely, for a four-year period, all economic exchanges between the Philippines and the United States. This gave the latter an opportunity to assist financially in the reconstruction of the economy so as to begin and carry forward the diversification of production which would have made the Philippines as nearly as possible economically independent. Such reconstruction would have been slower as a method of restoration of economic activities and processes than the attempt to restore established and customary production for prewar markets, but to attempt it would have been more consistent with the declared purpose of establishing an independent state which would be viable because independent economically.

For a variety of reasons, however, the Trade Act was apparently constructed on the assumption that the relationships of 1941 should first be re-established with a view to their gradual modification according to a planned schedule. The Philippine Trade Act of 1946 was based upon the principle of a prolonged period of free and preferential trade. It actually perpetuated the economic dependence of the Philippine Republic on the United States. Exclusive preferential treatment for the United States was provided and in such extreme terms that the amendment of the Constitution of the Philippines was required, although the Constitution already gave protection to American rights. This so-called parity amendment of the Philippine Constitution was made necessary by the stipulation of the Trade Act that American citizens should be put on a footing of equality with Philippine citizens with respect to acquisition of title to land and the right to engage in exploitative and industrial activity. This gave the American citizen an economic position in the Republic denied other foreigners and one which was stronger than the United States had conceded to its ctiizens when the Philippines were a dependency of the United States. While there was considerable opposition, this provision was accepted and the constitutional amendment ratified.

Beyond these economic definitions of relationship, since the United States assumed responsibility for the future defense of the Islands against external aggression, Washington asked for bases in the Islands to enable the United States to discharge its responsibilities. After protracted negotiations an agreement was reached on the number and location of bases which was satisfactory to the United States and to the Philippine government, although there was criticism of some of the provisions of these agreements. The basic agreement was approved by the Philippine Congress on March 26, 1947. It should also be noted, in connection with these security arrangements, that the United States Congress by Act of June 26, 1946, authorized the President to give military assistance to the Philippine Republic "in establishing and maintaining national security, and to form a basis for participation by that government in such defensive military operations as the future may require." A military assistance agreement was consequently signed on March 21, 1947, by the United States Ambassador and President Roxas.

THE ISSUE OF COLLABORATION

While the conditions of reconstruction and of independence were being slowly defined in Washington political activity was being rapidly resumed in Manila. To restore the constitutional machinery of government required the reconstitution of the legislature. Although the terms of office of legislators had expired, no elections for Commonwealth officials having been possible during the war period, it was deemed more expedient to re-constitute the old legislature than to attempt to hold elections under the conditions existing at the time of liberation. Re-constitution, however, presented the complication that a large proportion of the members of both houses had collaborated with the Japanese. American policy, as stated by President Roosevelt in signing two resolutions dealing with the Philippines on June 29, 1944, was that "Those who have collaborated with the enemy must be removed from authority and influence over the political and economic life of the country." The first apparent breach in this policy came when General MacArthur separated Manuel Roxas from captured members of the collaborationist Laurel government and declared him "liberated" and thus freed without undergoing even the usual clearance procedure. This enabled Roxas to resume his participation in politics and government as the President of the Senate.

The Senate's reconstitution, together with that of the House of Representatives, without the holding of prior new elections, meant that legislation on which action against collaborators would be based would have to be enacted by a legislature many of whose members, except as they were held covered by legislative immunity, were liable to action because they had held positions under the Japanese sponsored "independent" government. Under these circumstances it was virtually impossible for President Osmeña to respond quickly and decisively to the initial pressures from Washington to proceed against those charged with collaboration, even though this was raised as a primary issue in Philippine politics during the year prior to, as well as immediately after, the establishment of the independent Republic.

The issue of collaboration in the Philippines, as elsewhere, was one complicated by the question of motive. Thus it had in it subjective as well as objective considerations. At the one extreme were those who had merely carried on their normal administrative activities as a method of earning a livelihood and of holding the local communities together. Their assistance to the Japanese was passive rather than active. At the other extreme were those who had actively assisted the Japanese in organizing the puppet government and in shaping policy along lines set in Tokyo. Some of these men had seized the opportunity presented by the Japanese invasion and occupation for personal aggrandizement. Others, it could be subjectively argued, had been initially forced into collaboration. Still others, as nationalists and patriots, had accepted Japanese promises and had served Japan as a means of ensuring the early independence of the country; or they had used collaboration as a cover for their anti-Japanese leadership.

Roxas, who came to symbolize the early collaborationist issue, was apparently put in the latter category by the Americans themselves, but without the categories having been clearly established and proclaimed. His position as President of the Senate, coupled with his unclarified status as a collaborator, put him in a position of leadership, with tacit American support at Manila, against the government in its attempt to establish machinery for dealing with collaboration in the simplified terms of black and white. A bill was finally enacted establishing People's Courts to try those in custody. But as time passed it became increasingly difficult to proceed effectively against those charged. The chief collaborators, Laurel, Aquino, Osias, and Vargas had been taken to Japan, whence they were returned by the American occupation authorities to stand trial in the People's Courts. Laurel, as well as others, was released on bail, ostensibly to prepare his defense. He used his freedom to campaign for political rehabilitation and power. His reception indicated that collaboration was no longer an issue which could be pressed with resulting political advantage.

As a matter of fact, under the then existing circumstances, collaboration could have been dealt with decisively only by the Americans themselves during the immediate postliberation period when their influence was dominant. It could then have been dealt with for what it actually was—action against the United States. Turning the problem back to the Philippine government and then pressing that government, although ever less strongly, to act decisively, merely had the effect of embarrassing the restored government and of making it more difficult for it to maintain itself against the opposition which quickly arose and which was led by Senator Roxas.

THE HUKBALAHAP MOVEMENT

While collaboration presented one issue in postliberation Philippine politics, the principal area of disturbance was in central Luzon where the Hukbalahap (People's Army against the Japanese) movement had its principal center. This area had long been one of agrarian unrest. Thus that the movement, while anti-Japanese in its inception, had strong overtones of social and economic reform is understandable. During the war it had operated as a guerrilla movement against both the Japanese and the landlords who, as a class, collaborated with the Japanese and organized "peace preservation" corps to maintain their own and Japan's position against the guerrillas. Because of a fear that their reforms would be lost and that they would not only lose their influence but possibly also their lives, the Huks refused to surrender their arms upon the liberation of Luzon. This refusal to surrender their arms as demanded by the American Command, meant that the Huk forces were not incorporated in the Philippine army, as were other guerrilla forces. Thus they immediately lost some of their standing as anti-Japanese guerrillas, and much of their respectability in the eyes of the Americans. Nevertheless their leaders were among the most insistent that the government bring the collaborators to trial and punishment. This subjected the Osmeña government to a double pressure, from the left represented by the Hukbalahaps, and from the right led by Senator

Roxas. The Huks' stand on collaboration gave them a respectable issue at first but it contributed to their loss of respectability as the collaborationists regained and solidified their position in Philippine political life.

Provision was made by the United States Congress in December, 1945, and by the Philippine Congress in January, 1946, for the holding of the first elections since 1941, so that the Republic after its inauguration on July 4, 1946, might have a government which did not represent a holdover from prewar days. The collaborationist issue, as well as personal rivalry, had split the old Nacionalista Party into two wings, one headed by the incumbent President, Osmeña, which retained the party name, and the other by Senator Roxas, calling itself the Liberal Party. The attempts which were made to bring Osmeña and Roxas together were unsuccessful since neither was willing to take second place to the other. This made it inevitable that they should compete in the 1946 presidential election. It was almost equally inevitable under the circumstances that a large part of the old party leadership should follow Roxas into his new Liberal Party since most of them had stayed in the Philippines during the war and were consequently in need of Roxas' protection against a possible charge of collaboration. They might have remained with Osmeña if he had not been impelled to push the threat against them.

The magnitude of this defection made it necessary for Osmeña to seek support from beyond the Nacionalista Party ranks if he were to have any prospect of success in the election. Largely for this reason he allied his Nacionalista following with the Huks and similar groups, drawn together in the Democratic Alliance, for election purposes. He was, however, unable to wage a very aggressive campaign because of a lack of both resources and facilities. Roxas was supported by the wealthy elements in the Islands as well as, tacitly, by the Americans. More vigorous and less handicapped by scruples than Osmeña, Roxas, in his campaign, was able to emphasize the failure, even though it was readily explainable, of the government to bring about more rapid reconstruction, as well as some of its less excusable mistakes; and, above all, to leave the impression that American assistance would be given more readily to a government which he headed than to Osmeña. Thus he secured election with 54 per cent of the total popular vote and his party gained 13 of the 24 seats in the Senate and 58 seats to the opposition's 40 in the House of Representatives.

The Osmeña government, during its short tenure at the end of the

Commonwealth period, had of necessity followed a policy of compromise and conciliation toward oppositional elements. Thus it had accepted the Huks' demand for a more liberal division of the crops between the landlord and his tenant, although not accepting their full program in this respect nor in connection with land redistribution. The attempts made to bring distinguished guerrilla leaders into high governmental position, partly of course, to ensure their political support, had had to be compromised because of the control of the legislative Commission on Appointments by Senator Roxas. Competition for the favors of the United States had led to compromises on independence and on aid conditions.

Roxas, as Senator and leader of the opposition, had been in a position to compel the government to compromise, without getting himself labelled a compromiser. As President, while taking an extremely conciliatory attitude toward the United States, Roxas immediately indicated a determination to rule with the strong hand of a Quezon. His first move was to prevent the seating of some of the opposition candidates in the legislature who had been certified by the Electoral Commission as having been elected. Seven of the eleven whose election was challenged were, however, finally seated after almost a year of delay. In this action, in the handling of the question of revision of the constitution to give Americans parity with Filipinos, and in the seating in the House of Representatives of a Spanish-born citizen, the Roxas administration showed a desire to bend the constitution to serve its own purposes.

The policy followed toward the Huks by Roxas was also a strong one directed toward the forcible suppression of the movement. With that were, however, joined periodic attempts at conciliation in the endeavor to draw the peasants away from the Huk leadership. President Roxas recognized that there existed a real social and economic problem and that the peasants were justified in demanding some ameliorative action. In conference with peasant leaders, he agreed to, and had placed on the statute books, the 70-30 crop-sharing law under which the peasant, if he furnished the farm implements and work animals and financed the planting and harvesting, was entitled to retain 70 per cent of the rice crop, giving 30 per cent to the landlord as rent. President Quirino's action in 1948 creating the President's Action Committee on Social Amelioration, and the program of resettlement on other islands of Luzon dissidents and rebels who were captured or surren-

dered, undertaken as an anti-Huk measure by Secretary of Defense
Magsaysay, also represented perception of the problem as something
which could only be solved in the long run by nonmilitary measures.
These were all indicative, however, of a willingness to compromise
rather than of an intention to accept Huk demands. If these reforms
had been executed vigorously and in complete good faith the followers
of the Huk Communist leaders, some of whom were Communists, might
have been detached from them and the movement conceivably might
have been brought under control in its early stage. But the execution
of the reforms was such that the leaders were able to persuade many of
their followers that nothing could be hoped for from government except as constant pressure was maintained on it. The concessions, it was
argued, were not made because of understanding of the problem and a
real desire to solve it in a manner acceptable to the peasants. They were
offered as temporary expedients designed to cause the Huks to lay down
their arms. In other words there was the possibility that if and when
Huk resistance ceased the reforms would be withdrawn.

The early attempts at forcible suppression were not only largely
unsuccessful but they had the effect of reducing rather than increasing peasant confidence in the good faith of the government. Pacification was made a responsibility of the reconstituted Philippine constabulary. As reconstituted it was recruited in part from the forces
maintained during the Japanese occupation by the landlords to protect
their estates against guerrillas and brigands, and in part from ex-guer-
rillas who, although they surrendered their arms at the time of liberation, were not accepted for incorporation in the army and found it
difficult to resume their prewar activities. In its re-constitution the
Philippine contabulary consequently, never attained its prewar efficiency. It was not able to cope with the Huks partly because some
politicians in Manila interfered in the pacification program and partly
because many peasants looked upon the constabulary as a greater
menace than the dissidents.[6] This peasant attitude was derived from
the essentially terroristic activities of the Constabulary. These activities were more in the nature of feudal vengeance than of attempts to
support disinterestedly the public order. They gave color to the charge
that the state was actually using its power against one private interest
in support of another. The Huks used the same methods against the

[6] On the Huk movement, see Russell H. Fifield, "The Hukbalahap Today," *Far
Eastern Survey*, January 24, 1951, p. 17.

Constabulary which it used against them. Thus terrorism gave rise to reprisals in kind, regardless of which side initiated it.

The general election of November, 1949 resulted in the victory of President Elpidio Quirino. This marked a definite turning-point in the Hukbalahap movement. The turn was from a movement seeking reform in the interest of the peasantry within the framework of existing constitutional and republican institutions to one seeking to bring about the subversion or forcible overthrow of those institutions. This had been the purpose of some of the leaders of the movement in the early postwar period. Some leaders (e.g. Jesus Lava and Louis Taruc) were unquestionably Marxist in their views and Communist in their party affiliation. A large proportion of their following, however, was initially not concerned with doctrine, about which many knew little or nothing, or with politics. Their concern was with the protection and promotion of their own essentially local interests. As they came to distrust the government as an agency of reform, and as they were pushed back into the hills by government forces, they came more and more under the doctrinal influence of their leadership.

And when the Communists established themselves in mainland China against the National Government, many Huks were persuaded that they might secure outside support through affiliation with the Communist Party. Such affiliation involved, in the Philippines as elsewhere, subordination of the views of the local party and leadership within the complex of international communism. Under these circumstances what was attempted was not agreement with the government on satisfactory conditions of reform but the creation of a state and an apparatus of government within the state with a view to the overthrow of the government and the constitutional republic. In this respect the strategy and tactics—the ends sought and the means employed—paralleled those of the Chinese Communists from at least the time of the failure of the Marshall Mission to China.

Confronted with this type of movement after the elections of 1949, the government changed its strategy and tactics. The Philippine army, reorganized and strengthened, was utilized in place of the constabulary as the proper instrument of action against the Huks. Guerrilla tactics were developed for penetration of Huk-controlled areas. Rewards were offered for the capture, or for information leading to the capture, of the principal Huk leaders. Amnesty and resettlement as well as protection were promised to those, other than the leaders, who surrendered. To emphasize the difference between the operations of a constabulary which was essentially a private army, as was also that of the Huks, and of the military forces of the state seeking to restore public authority and order, the army by its behavior was expected to win the confidence of the communities in which it was operating, bringing about a feeling, previously lacking, that its operations were protective rather than exploitive of the barrio people.

The new method of approach proved more successful than the old, although it took time to make it effective. By 1953 many of the leaders who had not been apprehended were at least on the run, unable even to maintain the appearance of operating a government within the state. As one observer pointed out:

> By such a combination of military and non-military measures Magsaysay was able to check the spread of the Huk movement in the Visayas and Mindanao and gradually to localize the conflict in certain areas of Luzon. When he became Defense Secretary the Huks were believed to have between 15,000 and 20,000 well-organized and well-armed troops. By 1953 their strength had been reduced to an estimated 4000 in scattered squads. In two years (April 1950 to April 1952) Huk casualties numbered 12,680 (including 4,397 killed), while those of the government forces were only 745.[7]

Thus it was a reasonable conclusion in 1953 that the Huk movement, although not destroyed, was no longer a major problem in Philippine politics, nor even a primary complication in the solution of the major problem.

THE ECONOMIC PROBLEM

The major problem was economic. The new republic had, in the early postwar years, with limited American aid in the form of a $70-million loan from the Reconstruction Finance Corporation, attained a reasonable financial stability. As reconstruction was carried forward both internal and foreign trade revived, and with it some measure of prosperity. Thus the short-run purposes of the Trade bill, supplemented by payments for war damages, began to be realized. That the revival and reconstruction which had occurred were products of American governmental assistance together with some American private in-

---

[7] Donn V. Hart, "Magsaysay: Philippine Candidate," *Far Eastern Survey*, May, 1953, p. 68. The figures are from *U. S. News and World Report*, Feb. 13, 1953.

vestment and not of sound planning and effective execution of plans within the resources of the Philippines became apparent and came to be recognized when deterioration began to set in. Appeals for further support from the United States caused Washington to make studies of conditions to establish a basis for response to these appeals. Such a study was made for the American government by the Bell Mission sent to the Islands in 1950. On the economic side the Mission reported that:

> While production in general has been restored to almost the prewar level, little of fundamental importance was done to increase productive efficiency and to diversify the economy. In agriculture, the area under cultivation was brought to the prewar level, and the livestock population was partially restored. But almost nothing was done to open new lands for the increased population, to improve the methods of cultivation, or to better the position of workers and tenants.
>
> The inequalities of income in the Philippines, always large, have become even greater during the past few years. While the standard of living of the mass of the people has not reached the prewar level the profits of businessmen and the incomes of large land-owners have risen very considerably.[8]

The Bell Mission, in summary, proposed that the United States aid the Philippines with loans and grants totalling $250 million, and that the dispersal of these sums be carefully planned and supervised. It urged the adoption of a 7-point plan, providing (1) sounder government finance measures, (2) introduction of methods aimed at higher agricultural production, (3) encouragement of industries, (4) emergency taxation, (5) a program of improved health and education, (6) reorganization of public administration, and (7) a U. S. financial assistance program.

Connecting aid with acceptance of a program of reform only in part directly economic in character, constituted in effect a disguised criticism of governmental and political conditions which existed in the independent Philippines. Charges were being made, at least the partial truth of which was generally accepted, of corruption in government as well as ineffectiveness in planning and inefficiency in the execution of plans. The political situation revealed in the election of 1949 was one marked by such widespread corruption, coercion, violence, and disorder as to make people despair of the healthy development of democracy in the

---

[8] Quoted by Shirley Jenkins, from the Bell Report, "Philippine White Paper," *Far Eastern Survey*, Jan. 10, 1951.

new state.[9] Whether cause or consequence, the methods employed to gain office and the attitude toward government and administration could not be expected to be too greatly at variance.

THE STATE OF POLITICS IN THE ISLANDS

Elections in the Philippines, prior at least to that of 1946, had been contests less between political parties than between individuals claiming preferment over other individuals within the party which enjoyed a virtual monopoly of such political power as could be exercised under colonial and later under Commonwealth conditions. The party gained and maintained this monopoly by pre-empting the nationalist side of the primary national issue which was that of independence. This issue was, of course, an issue between the United States and the Philippines, and consequently was one with respect to which there was among Filipinos little difference of opinion. Where there might and on occasion did develop difference of opinion was with respect to the acceptability of particular American proposals viewed in relation to the concept of independence. These were differences over means of influencing American policy and over ability to affect it rather than over the independence issue itself. Other than the issue between the United States and the Philippines, which the United States could not repress because of its own early commitment to the policy of ultimate independence, the issues presented were essentially local and did not establish a basis for national division.

Still other factors which contributed to the perpetuation of a one-party system were a low literacy rate; scarcity of newspapers, an agrarian economy, a highly developed family system, and a strong tendency toward sectionalism. To these must be added the consideration that the provincial and local governmental personnel was under the control of Manila and thus of the Nacionalista Party which, as the single party, controlled the central government.

The circumstances of the war and the liberation, coupled with the approach of independence, produced an issue which brought about a violent disruption of the one-party system. The death in exile of Quezon removed from the helm the leader who had finally come to dominate the party. Neither Roxas nor Osmeña was willing to accept

9 For discussion of the election, J. J. Dalton, "Ins and Outs in the Philippines," *Far Eastern Survey*, July 30, 1952, p. 117.

subordination to the other, and they were separated by the issue of collaboration, on which they could not find a basis for compromise. Consequently, when Roxas entered upon the campaign of 1946 he did it as the leader and candidate of a new party, called the Liberal Party, leaving to Osmeña the Nacionalista label.

The victory of the new Liberals and of Roxas made it more difficult to restore the one-party system than would have been the case if the Nacionalistas had been returned to office. While Roxas himself argued the need for continuation of a two-party system, his methods after election were directed toward the elimination of as many sources of opposition to the government as possible. The result was that in the 1947 provincial and local elections the Liberals won 78 per cent of the offices, while in 1949 they gained 68 of the 100 seats in the House of Representatives and all of the 8 vacant seats in the Senate, giving them in all 21 of the 24 Senators. In that election (1949) furthermore, the Liberal candidate for the Presidency, Elpidio Quirino, was re-elected to the presidential office. Nevertheless the older Nacionalista name continued to carry sufficient weight with the voters to keep the party alive, and the very methods employed by the Liberals to perpetuate themselves in power provided an issue to replace the division on the question of collaboration. The latter issue could not be pressed effectively by the opposition party in view of the record of José Laurel, its presidential candidate in the election of 1949. Laurel had been the head of the Japanese-sponsored government of the Philippines during the period of occupation.

There was, as a matter of fact, no fundamental difference between the two parties over questions of public policy nor between the interest groups which supported each party. On the perennial question of relationship with the United States, which still affected Philippine politics after independence, the attitudes of the parties differed in emphasis rather than in objective. There was similarly a difference of emphasis rather than of basic approach to the solution of the internal problems which required solution.

Corruption in government and in elections, however, presented the "outs" with an issue against the "ins." Within the Liberal party itself corruption became an issue in the personal and factional struggle against the dominance of the Quirino faction, leading to an alliance of some Liberals with the Nacionalistas as the elections of 1951 approached. This struggle for power had previously been shown when

José Avelino sought office in the presidential election of 1949 as the candidate of what he claimed to be the real Liberal Party.

In the 1951 campaign both parties declared themselves in favor of honest and efficient government

> Since 1946 the Liberal administration had been beset by a series of scandals, including the disposal of American surplus goods, a gift from the United States, with an original cost value of some $2 billion, which had brought in a net return of only $45 million; the sale of political influence in expediting and granting import quotas under the import controls established in 1949; failure to collect more than 25% of the tax revenues levied, owing to the bribery of officials and political influence; and costly execution of the government's limited land reform program. The Nacionalistas, however, offered few specific plans for improvement of the administration; they concentrated on attacking the corruption and administrative bungling of the Liberals, thus stimulating and exploiting the already rising tide of mass dissatisfaction.[10]

The Nacionalistas, however, as the party out of power, were naturally more successful in capitalizing on this issue than the Liberals in spite of the lack of a positive program of reform and in spite of their own record in office in 1945-46 which had also been marked by a number of scandals. This was indicated in the election returns which showed that they had won all of the Senate seats (9) to be filled in 1951 and 23 out of 45 contests for provincial governor.

This victory, which reversed the trend toward the single-party monopoly of power and gave the prospect of continued existence of the two-party system, was made possible because of the relatively disinterested administration of the elections. This resulted from the cooperation to that end of the President and the Secretary of Defense. In general the revised election code, the greater power over election procedures given the Commission on Elections, and the assumption of responsibility for the policing of the elections by the Philippine army in place of the constabulary, on the official side; and the educational and observational work of the National Movement for Free Elections, on the unofficial side, may be referred to as factors in making the election of 1951 the freest and fullest expression of the will of the electorate registered up to that time through voting in the Islands.

[10] *Ibid.*, pp. 120-21.

THE ELECTION OF 1953

Nevertheless, the issue of corruption and efficiency in government was not lost with these elections as was evidenced in the grounds assigned by Defense Secretary Ramon Magsaysay for leaving the government and accepting the nomination of the opposition Nacionalista Party for the presidency in the 1953 elections. It was also part of the explanation offered for the withdrawal of the Foreign Minister, General Carlos Romulo, and his followers from the government and from the Liberal Party when it re-nominated President Quirino in preference to Romulo as its candidate.

The immediate result of the withdrawal of General Romulo, together with Vice President Lopez and others, from the Liberal party, was the formation of the new Democratic Party, which proceeded to put in the field a ticket headed by Romolo and Lopez. This split in the Liberal party was partly the result of personal rivalry. There had, however, developed a conflict of interest between the sugar planters and the Centralista group especially in the western Visayan area. The Romulo faction represented the planters' interest in this conflict which had been growing since 1946, and the Democratic Party was designed to express this interest.

The three groups (the Nacionalistas, with Magsaysay and Garcia as their candidates for president and vice president; the Liberals, headed by Quirino and Yolo; and the Democrats, under Romulo and Lopez) carried on a vigorous three-cornered race from July 21 to August 22, when a coalition was formed between the Nacionalista Party and the Democratic Party. Negotiations looking toward coalition for election purposes had been instituted as it became apparent that competition between Magsaysay and Romulo would probably weaken both and thus facilitate the re-election of Quirino. Since Romulo was the weaker of the two as a candidate for the presidency, the formation of the coalition necessitated his withdrawal from the race in favor of Magsaysay.

The weakness of General Romulo as a candidate resulted from the nature of his services to his country which had kept him abroad much of the time and thus had militated against the building of a personal following at home. His public activities had not, as had those of Secretary Magsaysay, brought him and his reputation to the personal attention of the people in the barrios. His postwar service, before his appointment as Foreign Minister, had been in the United States, and at the United Nations, as the representative of the new Philippine Republic. He, more than any other individual, symbolized the important role which the independent Philippines began to play in the international relations of the Far East and in the world. This role, and General Romulo as the player, had been formally recognized with his election as President of the United Nations General Assembly at its 1949 meeting. He and other spokesmen had not hesitated to express the Philippine point of view on questions ranging from those involved in colonialism and trusteeship, through those of human rights, such as freedom of expression, to those involving economic policy at various United Nations' meetings.

The positions eloquently taken in the United Nations by such Philippine spokesmen as General Romulo with respect to these matters were far in advance of some of the internal policies followed by Philippine governments. Nevertheless they involved no greater inconsistency for the Philippines than for other countries, and in any case, this active participation in international politics as the representative of the Republic gave General Romulo the advantage of a reputation outside the Philippines greater even than that of the President. It had the further consequence of dis-associating him from commitment with respect to objectionable internal policies and procedures. This was of advantage to him as a presidential candidate. But his external services had also disassociated him from the processes of politics at home to an extent which raised a serious question concerning his political future, except in an administrative capacity in the field of foreign affairs. Even in this field he was much more widely known abroad than he was at home. Especially at home, his achievements could also be recognized as those of the government which he represented. This was particularly the case since President Quirino had been directly connected with some important developments in foreign policy, with Romulo not always utilized as his spokesman.

In the Far Eastern region, the Philippine government showed an awareness of some of the dangers to it, and to other Far Eastern countries at the existing stage of their economic advancement, of those aspects of the American policy of revival of the Japanese economy which involved the exchange of Philippine raw materials for the products of Japanese industry. The Republic participated in conferences designed to develop a common policy among the Far Eastern states with respect to such questions as that of the continuation of disorder in Indonesia. And President Quirino, in consultation with Chiang Kai-shek, in the summer of 1949 attempted to take the initiative in the bringing together of the anti-Communist elements in the Far East in a Pacific regional security pact.

These moves, ascribable to the government headed by President Quirino rather than to General Romulo, indicated a desire on the part of the Philippine government to play an active rather than a passive role in the politics of the Far East. Independence of action was also shown in the demand for a specific security pact with the United States in connection with the negotiation of the Japanese Peace Treaty; as it was also in the refusal to ratify the signed treaty because of dissatisfaction with the treatment given the reparations question. All of these were matters of more immediate knowledge in the Islands than was the work done at the United Nations, until the Korean issue was raised. In that connection, the Philippine government took a firm stand alongside the United States in support of the United Nations position, and made its contribution to the war in Korea while General Romulo served in Manila as Foreign Minister. This emphasized the fact that the policy followed was that of the Quirino government.

Magsaysay, on the other hand, was a well-known and popular figure in the Islands. In spite of his connection with the government, no charges of irregularities were made against him in the administration of his office as Defense Minister. He was generally conceded to be honest and thus was able to campaign vigorously on the issue of corruption pressed against the Quirino administration. He had become widely and favorably known throughout the Philippines for his successful reorganization of the army, and the method of its employment against the Huks. His reputation in the Philippines had been enhanced by the favorable reception given to him in the United States. In comparison with Romulo he had the advantage of use in the campaign of the machinery of an old and established party—the Nacionalista Party. But it had to be recognized that he had come over to the Nacionalistas from the Liberals, and had been nominated by them because they had no comparable candidate within the party heirarchy. His chance of election as the Nacionalista candidate depended on his ability to bring nonparty voters to the polls because of his personal popularity, and to carry with him additional personal followers from the Liberal Party sufficient to give what had become a minority party a majority vote.

In the conduct of his campaign Magsaysay did not rely exclusively on the machinery of the Nacionalista Party. A Magsaysay-for-President Movement was put under way which reached in its organization from Manila into the provinces. A Women's Magsaysay-for-President and a Student's Magsaysay-for-President organization served a useful purpose in carrying his candidacy to the people. Through these organizations as well as by personal campaigning throughout the Islands the Nacionalista candidate brought himself into close contact with the people.

The issue successfully posed by the Nacionalista-Democratic coalition was that of graft and corruption in government, with a side-issue of improper use of the machinery of government to coerce and control the voters at the polls. The Liberals were unsuccessful in their belated attempts to focus the attention of the voters on the positive achievements of the Quirino administration. In the face of the issue of corruption it proved difficult, for example, to interest the people in the long-range program of economic mobilization planned and undertaken by the government. As initiated, this program included: a large dam and hydroelectric facilities at Maria Cristina in Mindanao; a fertilizer plant at Maria Cristina; a steel rolling mill at Iligan Bay; improvements in the Cebu Portland Cement Company; and the Ambuklao Hydro-electric Dam. Whether ill-advised or not, these represented undertakings of a Philippine government planned and executed sometimes against the advice of American government officials. To focus the attention of the voters on undertakings which will have long-run benefits to them, however, it is necessary for campaign purposes to build up gradually a backlog of understanding. This Quirino had neglected to do. He was equally unsuccessful in pressing, again belatedly, a charge of American intervention in the elections. This charge was based upon the generally favorable treatment given to his opponents' campaign by American correspondents and by the role played by Americans in the "crusade" for honest and free elections.

In the voting of November 10, 1953, Magsaysay swept the country, receiving the largest number of votes of any presidential candidate in Philippine politics. Under the circumstances the result could properly be viewed as an overwhelming personal victory for Magsaysay rather than a Nacionalista triumph. This was the case because he ran well ahead of his ticket. Nevertheless the coalition itself won an impressive victory, essentially a victory of the Nacionalistas, winning the 8 Senate seats to be filled and gaining control of the House of Representatives. The new Senate had 12 Nacionalistas, 6 Democrats, 1 Citizens Party member, and only 4 Liberals. In the House of Representatives the former large Liberal majority was reduced to about one-third of the total membership of the House. On the majority side the Nacionalistas far outnumbered the Democrats. However the situation in the House, because of the possibility of shifting affiliations, was less stable than in the Senate.

This was the immediate result of the election. In general, from the point of view of its significance, the election, as one writer put it,

> demonstrated that by democratic processes an opposition coalition could overthrow a well-entrenched and long established administration. Here stress should be placed on the words "democratic processes," for a major consideration was the holding of an election generally free from fraud and terror. Although the campaign indicated that political morality was not at a high premium, the election itself revealed definite progress in political maturity. The use of soldiers to police the polls was necessary but a practice that should eventually be terminated. Democracy in the Philippines should be able to flourish without the presence of armed men near the voting places.[11]

The election was also significant in that it brought into play a more direct relationship between the voters and those aspiring to election to high office. New leaders, employing new (to the Philippines) campaign techniques, began to displace the older generation of politicians, many of whom were born in the Spanish period.

Still another important development was the more active part taken by the Catholic Church in Philippine politics. This activity took the form, in the first place, of a pastoral letter calling for free elections. The pastoral letter, however, was followed by a later statement by prominent figures in the church which "amounted in effect to a plea for votes for Catholic candidates." This type of intervention, if continued, would raise a number of difficult questions involving the relations of church and state.

Finally, in terms of international relations, the elections had considerable significance. If the charges of American intervention had been proved, the Philippines would have suffered in the eyes of the other newly independent and strongly nationalistic states in South-

[11] Russell H. Fifield, "The Challenge to Magsaysay," *Foreign Affairs*, Vol. 33, no. 1 (October, 1954), p. 153.

east Asia. Since the charges were not sustained, however, the election provided a good example, especially in Indonesia, which was in the planning stage with respect to elections. As for relations between the United States and the Philippines, those two states are sufficiently close not to have their relations too much affected as a result of political changes in Manila.

Regardless of the underlying considerations, the immediate problem which faced the new administration was that of so constructing a government, a program, and a policy as to enable the new leadership to retain the confidence of the country and ensure retention of the reins of power by the Nacionalista party and the coalition. The older Nacionalista leaders had accepted Magsaysay as the party candidate because they wanted to win the election. They had campaigned essentially on the slogan "turn the rascals out," rather than on the basis of an agreed program with respect to the use of power if it should be won. Thus real qualities of political leadership and administrative capacity had to be demonstrated by Magsaysay after his elevation to the presidential office.

Even after the President had constructed a cabinet which seemed to meet with general acceptance, the problem of solidification of leadership of the party remained to be solved since such of the older leaders as Claro M. Recto indicated opposition to Magsaysay's foreign policy and to his program of rural development. Their opposition forced a showdown in June, 1954. At that time President Magsaysay was able to secure from a caucus of the Nacionalista Party a pledge of all-out support for his foreign and domestic policies. This pledge was, however, given in the absence of Senator Recto who consequently did not feel bound by it. This was indicated in his statement: "I shall continue to criticize the administration whenever, in my judgment, it is in the public interest to do so." [12] Nevertheless, in a declaration of principles, the Nacionalista caucus "acknowledged the President as party spokesman for all major policies and empowered him to whip recalcitrant members into line. A party member may not publicly criticize the President's policy without first airing it within the party." [13] The immediate issue between the President and Mr. Recto was over foreign policy. It was reported that

[12] As reported in the *New York Times*, June 8, 1954.
[13] *Ibid.*

Mr. Magsaysay is for all-out collaboration with the United States in any collective security action to check Communist aggression in Asia, while Mr. Recto is opposed to any commitment to the United States unless it is with the United Nations sanction. This applies specifically to Indochina. Mr. Recto has vowed to oppose sending Filipinos to Indochina.[14]

The verdict of the caucus was, as stated, in favor of the President and signalized continued acceptance of him as the leader of the presently dominant party. The fact that it had to be called, however, was indicative of a continuing struggle between the old and the new leadership for control of the party. The rule adopted by the party with respect to criticism of the President's policy did not prevent continued opposition to his leadership. It was designed only to maintain party unity against the opposition by seeking to prevent too early a public airing of conflicting views held by leaders of the party. Thus in the initial test, Magsaysay was successful in maintaining his position as leader of the party. This enabled him, thereafter, to assert himself successfully as the directive head of the government.

BIBLIOGRAPHICAL REFERENCES

Abaya, Hernando J., *Betrayal in the Philippines* (New York: Wyn, 1946)

Aruego, Jose M., *Philippine Government in Action* (Manila: University Publishing Company, 1952).

Bernstein, David, *The Philippine Story* (New York: Farrar, Straus, 1947).

Dalisay, Amando M., *Economic Aspects of the Baguio Conference of 1950* (Manila: Philippine Council, Institute of Pacific Relations, 1950).

Department of State, *Military Bases in the Philippines*, Publication 4604; Treaty Series, 2406 (Washington, 1952).

Grunder, G. A., and Livizey, W. E., *The Philippines and the United States* (Norman: University of Oklahoma Press, 1951).

Jenkins, Shirley, *American Economic Policy toward the Philippines* (Stanford: Stanford University Press, 1954).

"The Philippines" in John C. Cady, Patricia Barnett, and Shirley Jenkins, *The Development of Self-Rule and Independence in Burma, Malaya and the Philippines* (New York: American Institute of Pacific Relations, 1948).

Martin, Ruperto G., *Philippine Constitutional Law* (Manila: Philaw Publishing Company, 1952).

[14] *Ibid.*

Porter, Catherine, *Crisis in the Philippines* (New York: Knopf, 1942).

Quezon, Manuel, *The Good Fight* (New York: D. Appleton-Century Co., 1946).

Renne, Ronald R., "Agrarian Problems and Foreign Aid in the Philippines," *Far Eastern Survey*, Vol. 22, no. 13.

Republic of the Philippines, *The Revised Election Code*, Republic Act No. 180, annotated and commented on by Vincente J. Francisco, 2nd ed., (Manila: East Publishing Company, 1953). *Reglamenta dee Senado* (Manila: Bureau of Printing, 1951).

Romani, John H., *The Office of the Philippine President* (Manila: University of the Philippines, Institute of Public Administration, 1954).

Storer, James A., "Philippine Economic Progress," *Far Eastern Survey*, Vol. 22, no. 8.

15

Japan: Through Occupation to Independence

✳✳✳✳✳✳✳✳✳✳✳✳✳✳✳✳✳✳✳✳✳✳✳✳✳✳✳✳✳✳✳✳✳✳

MEANING OF "UNCONDITIONAL SURRENDER" FOR JAPAN

"UNCONDITIONAL SURRENDER" meant for Japan acceptance in advance of such conditions for the ending of hostilities as were deemed consistent with their interests by the wartime United Nations. The war purposes of the Allies in the Pacific war *vis-a-vis* Japan were first affirmatively stated in the Cairo Declaration of November 26, 1943. It was there laid down that surrender would mean acceptance by Japan of the loss of all territories added to it, (thus making up the Japanese Empire), after 1894. These included Korea, Formosa, the Ryukyu Islands, Manchuria, and the islands in the Pacific brought under Japanese mandate at the end of World War I. The Yalta agreements ensured Anglo-American support for the transfer from Japan to the Soviet Union of the Kurile islands, the southern half of Saghalin Island, and the rights and interests in Manchuria acquired from Russia by Japan at the end of the Russo-Japanese war (which rights Russia had acquired from China before that war). These territorial terms were finally incorporated in the "Proclamation Defining Terms for Japanese Surrender" issued by Britain, China and the United States, on July 26, 1945, at the time of the Potsdam Conference. Paragraph 8 of the Proclamation stated that: "The terms of the Cairo Declaration shall be carried out and Japanese sovereignty shall be limited to the islands of Honshu, Hokkaido, Kyushu, Shikoku and such minor islands as we determine." [1] Thus, in effect, when Japan surrendered, it was on the

[1] From text printed in *A Decade of American Foreign Policy, 1941-1949*, 81st Cong., 1st session, Senate Doc. No. 123, p. 49. Hereafter cited as *Decade*.

basis of an acceptance of the territorial status of the time just a century earlier when that country emerged from its historic seclusion.[2]

The surrender terms laid down at Potsdam also involved: (1) acceptance of the elimination from power "for all time" of militarists "who have deceived and misled the people of Japan into embarking on world conquest, for we (the Allies) insist that a new order of peace, security and justice will be impossible until irresponsible militarism is driven from the world"; (2) the repatriation of Japanese military forces overseas "with the opportunity to lead peaceful and productive lives"; (3) the nonenslavement of the Japanese although "stern justice shall be meted out to all war criminals, including those who have visited cruelties upon our prisoners. The Japanese government shall remove all obstacles to the revival and strengthening of democratic tendencies among the Japanese people. Freedom of speech, of religion, and of thought, as well as respect for the fundamental human rights, shall be established; (4) Japan shall be permitted to maintain such industries as will sustain her economy and permit the exaction of just reparations in kind, but not those (industries) which would enable her to re-arm for war. . . ." (5) the military occupation of the country, subject to the understanding that "the occupying forces of the Allies shall be withdrawn from Japan as soon as these objectives have been accomplished and there has been established in accordance with the freely expressed will of the Japanese people a peacefully inclined and responsible government." [3]

INITIAL POST-SURRENDER POLICY FOR JAPAN

Implicit in the wording of the Potsdam Declaration and in the Instrument of Surrender which was signed on September 2, 1945, was the idea of maintenance in being of the Japanese government, headed by the Emperor, rather than that of its displacement by an Allied Occupation government. The Instrument of Surrender was signed for Japan by those "acting by command of and in behalf of the Emperor of Japan, the Japanese Government and the Japanese Imperial General

[2] Although actually in the midnineteenth century the Japanese viewed the Kuriles and the Ryukyus, at least, as an integral part of Japan. Thus the surrender terms went beyond the application of the principle announced at Cairo of depriving Japan of all territories which had been acquired by means of military aggression in the modern period of Japanese history.

[3] From text as printed in *Ibid.*, pp. 49-50.

Headquarters." With their signature Japan accepted "the provisions set forth in the declaration issued by the heads of the Governments of the United States, China and Great Britain on July 26, 1945 at Potsdam, and subsequently adhered to by the Union of Soviet Socialist Republics. . . ." In the same Instrument it was explicitly accepted that "The authority of the Emperor and the Japanese Government to rule the state shall be subject to the Supreme Commander for the Allied Powers who will take such steps as he deems proper to effectuate these terms of surrender." All Japanese forces and the Japanese people were instructed to "comply with the requirements which may be imposed by the Supreme Commander for the Allied Powers or by agencies of the Japanese Government at his direction. . . ." [4]

Thus Japan entered the postwar period with its own government, but with that government subordinated to the occupation authorities in relation to the effectuation of the surrender terms and for the period necessary to attain the defined Allied objectives, at which time "the occupying forces of the Allies" were to be withdrawn. What may be viewed as implicit in the Potsdam Declaration and in the Surrender Instrument was made completely explicit by the United States in the statement of "United States Initial Post-Surrender Policy for Japan" (September 6, 1945), which defined occupation policy. Under the head of "Relationship to the Japanese Government" it was stated that

> In view of the present character of Japanese society and the desire of the United States to attain its objectives with a minimum commitment of its forces and resources, the Supreme Commander will exercise his authority through Japanese governmental machinery and agencies, including the Emperor, to the extent that this satisfactorily furthers United States' objectives. The Japanese Government will be permitted, under his instructions, to exercise the normal powers of government in matters of domestic administration. [5]

INTERNATIONAL ASPECTS OF THE OCCUPATION

While this was an American definition of policy, it represented at the same time Allied policy since, in point of fact, the occupation of Japan was American, even though formally designated and organized

[4] The quotations are from the "Instrument of Surrender" as printed in *ibid.*, pp. 625-626.
[5] From "U. S. Initial Post-Surrender Policy for Japan." The full text is in *ibid.*, pp. 627-633.

as an Allied operation. An American, General of the Army Douglas MacArthur, was designated by the United States as the Supreme Commander for the Allied Powers (SCAP).[6] Aside from a small British Commonwealth contingent, which occupied a relatively small area in western Japan for several years, the occupying forces were from the United States Army which was under American command. And, as just suggested, the initial statement of post-surrender policy for Japan was formulated by the United States through a joint committee of the State, War, and Navy Departments. The policy therein defined was given operational form in a directive to the Supreme Commander on November 1, 1945. This "defines the authority which you will possess and the policies which will guide you in the occupation and control of Japan in the initial period after surrender." [7] This basic policy statement was substantially reaffirmed by the Far Eastern Commission on June 19, 1947, when the Commission issued the "Basic Post-Surrender Policy for Japan."

While being determined to maintain control of the occupation, the United States was not unwilling to have other states co-operate with it in an advisory relationship. Thus, before the Japanese surrender, "the United States suggested that there be created an international body to help formulate future policy in Japan and to assist in planning the organization which would be required to make sure that the Japanese fulfilled their obligation." [8]

The British objected and the Soviet Union refused to participate in the purely advisory commission which was in mind. It was thus after the occupation had been instituted and the initial policy decisions had been announced by the United States that, at the Moscow Conference of Foreign Ministers of December 27, 1945, an agreement was reached

---

[6] "His title, abbreviated to SCAP, is also popularly used to designate that part of general headquarters which is responsible for the direction of the occupation. A separate chain of command, also leading to General MacArthur, controls American tactical troops in Japan. Until 1949 Civil Affairs teams were responsible for the administration of Allied policy and for liaison with Japanese government officials on the prefectural level (roughly the equivalent of the state in the United States). In that year the teams were dissolved, and remaining military government affairs were transferred from the control of tactical forces to that of the general headquarters of the Supreme Commander." J. M. Maki, in L. K. Rosinger and Associates *The State of Asia* (New York: Knopf, 1951), p. 184.

[7] *Decade*, p. 635.

[8] Department of State, *Occupation of Japan: Policy and Progress*, Far Eastern Series No. 17, p. 7.

on the basis of which international organs for the occupation were established.

With General MacArthur as the Supreme Commander for the Allied Powers, as well as, concurrently, the Commander-in-Chief of the Far Eastern forces of the United States and thus of the American forces occupying Japan, the Allied organization of the occupation was established through the Far Eastern Commission, with its seat in Washington, and the Allied Council for Japan, located in Tokyo. The position of the Far Eastern Commission was described as follows by one writer:

> The Far Eastern Commission has (had) two main responsibilities: to "formulate the policies, principles and standards" by means of which Japan can fulfill its obligations under the surrender terms; and, at the request of any member, to review any directive or action of the Supreme Commander for the Allied Powers involving policy decisions. In fact, the Commission's role has been a minor one. The dominant position of the United States in Japan; the comprehensiveness and excellence of the initial and basic American policy for Japan; the distance of the Commission from the scene and its consequent lack of familiarity and contact with the problems of the occupation; and the general disagreement between the United States and the U.S.S.R. have made it impossible for the Commission to function effectively. Although it has made many policy decisions, all have fallen within the framework of previously announced American policy or have confirmed actions previously taken.[9]

While the Far Eastern Commission had usefulness, even though it was limited, in modifying American policy, or in establishing it as Allied policy, the Allied Council in Tokyo was, from the start, rendered "worse than impotent" by SCAP. General MacArthur's deputy as the American member served as the Chairman of the Council. At its initial meetings he made it clear for SCAP that the function of the Council was not to give advice or to discuss critically occupation policies or activities, but was to receive such information as he chose to have presented to it. Its meetings, consequently, resulted in "little more than a series of acrimonious and unedifying quarrels between the Amer-

[9] Maki, *op. cit.*, pp. 182-183. The American intention with respect to the position of its Allies in the occupation was made explicit in the Initial Post-Surrender policy paper which stated: "Although every effort will be made by consultation and by constitution of appropriate advisory bodies, to establish policies for the conduct of the occupation and control of Japan which will satisfy the principal Allied powers, in the event of any differences of opinion among them the policies of the United States will govern." *Decade*, p. 628.

ican and Soviet members." The Americans used it for purposes of attack on communism and on the Soviet failure to repatriate all Japanese nationals under its control; the Russians used it primarily to attack United States policy in Japan.[10]

Under these circumstances the real authority in Japan, as previously stated, was that of the United States, or more accurately, that of the Supreme Commander. His authority was erected over, but not in displacement of, that of the Japanese government. The latter was continued as the instrument through which, under SCAP direction or guidance, the purposes of the Allies as defined primarily by the United States were to be realized. Anticipating this relationship, the presurrender Japanese government established a Central Liaison Office through which contact between the Japanese government and the occupation authorities was channeled during the first phase of the occupation. Acceptance of this channel of communication meant in effect that occupation views, directives, and orders filtered to the Japanese government through an agency which represented a carry-over of traditional Japan into the new order, the creation of which SCAP was instructed to "encourage." There was this same carry-over through the Cabinet itself, since the personnel of the successive post-surrender governments was drawn largely from the prewar bureaucracy or party leadership. This had to be anticipated and accepted in the absence of an internal revolution initiated at the start by the Japanese themselves, something which conceivably might have but did not occur.

The policy announced of "encouraging" the Japanese people to form "democratic and representative organizations" indicated a willingness to do more than tolerate a change in the prewar political order. This was emphasized in relation to the use of the existing government in the statement that:

> This policy, moreover, does not commit the Supreme Commander to support the Emperor or any other Japanese governmental authority in opposition to evolutionary changes looking toward the attainment of United States objectives. The policy is to use the existing form of government in Japan, not to support it. Changes in the form of government initiated by the Japanese people or government in the direction of modifying its feudal and authoritarian tendencies are to be permitted and favored. In the event that the effectuation of such changes involves the use of force by

---

[10] Maki, *op. cit.*, p. 183. See also, Harry Emerson Wildes, *Typhoon in Tokyo* (New York: Macmillan, 1954) which is one of the most informed as well as most readable accounts of the occupation.

the Japanese people or government against persons opposed thereto, the Supreme Commander should intervene only where necessary to ensure the security of his forces and the attainment of all other objectives of the occupation.[11]

The question of intervention in a revolutionary situation to ensure the security of the occupation forces was not raised in the absence of any wide-spread sentiment for fundamental change. There was acquiescence among the Japanese people in the fact of occupation, and acceptance by the government of the necessity of making such changes as SCAP, by direction or advice, deemed justified and necessary. SCAP-sponsored reforms were certainly at the level of any popular demand for change, except from the point of view of the leadership of the extreme (Communist) left. Thus on the one hand, the reforms undertaken were sufficiently advanced to ensure against successful revolutionary agitation. On the other hand, the SCAP reform program, which actually went much beyond the policy-direction merely to "encourage" democratic tendencies among the Japanese, was not so extreme as to bring about resistance on the part of Japanese governments which did not themselves initiate any reform program. The principal interest of many Japanese was in bringing about an early termination of the occupation. Those uninterested in or opposed to fundamental change were acquiescent in the views of SCAP as to the necessity of change because they viewed its accomplishment as essential to the regaining of the independence of action which would enable the changes made to be re-examined.

THE DEMILITARIZATION OF JAPAN

Under the terms of the Potsdam Declaration, the forces of the occupation were to be withdrawn from Japan when Allied purposes had been realized. The primary mission of SCAP was to bring about the disarmament and demilitarization of Japan. A secondary objective was popularly labelled the "democratization" of Japan. This was related in certain respects to the primary objective of demilitarization in the broad construction of that term. No responsibility was assumed by or devolved on the occupation with respect to the Japanese economy beyond that of noninterference with measures taken by the Japanese

[11] *Decade*, p. 629.

government to restore the economy to the point where it would enable "the peacetime requirements of the population to be met." [12]

It was, however, part of the mission of SCAP, under the first two sets of responsibilities, to supervise the Japanese economy and "encourage" changes in it in relation where necessary to democratization and demilitarization of the political system, and to ensure against economic deterioration to the point where it might present dangers to the occupation forces.

By the end of the first quarter of 1947 the Supreme Commander was able to announce the completion of his mission and the readiness of Japan to move from occupation to independence. The desirability of an early peace treaty was immediately concurred in by the American government. The Japanese forces had been disarmed, repatriated (except for those still held in Russia), and demobilized. The Japanese navy and air force had been destroyed. The War and Marine departments of the government had been abolished. The Supreme Headquarters had been disbanded; the General Staff organization had been broken up; and the paramilitary organizations into which it was feared the military might readily retire and from which they might emerge to reestablish their position after the termination of the occupation, were prohibited. Thus the Allied objective of disarmament had been fully attained, as had that of demilitarization from the point of view of the military establishment and the structure of the government, although the War and Marine departments had been in fact temporarily continued during this period as civilian demobilization boards until the armed forces had been completely disbanded. These changes in structure seemed designed to solve, by elimination, the perplexing prewar political problem of military manipulation of domestic and foreign policy through the right of access to the Emperor which the chiefs-of-staffs and the ministers of War and Marine possessed. The changes were also designed to prevent the making and unmaking of cabinets through professional military control of the appointment of the ministers of War and Marine. In the new constitution of 1947, furthermore, provision was made against the revival of militarism through the constitutional renunciation of both war and force as a means of settling international disputes. In order to accomplish this it was laid down in Chapter III of the new constitution that "land, sea and air forces, as

[12] *Ibid.*, p. 628.

well as other military potential, will never be maintained." This, together with the elimination from the constitution of all references to a separate military prerogative of the Emperor, was designed to perpetuate the immediate solution of the problem of military control of policy.

The attainment of the objective of demilitarization also was taken to involve the elimination from positions of power and authority of those who had had responsibility, together with the military, for the development of the expansionist and war policies followed by Japan in the decade from 1931 to 1941. This went beyond the provision of the Potsdam Proclamation that "stern justice shall be meted out to all war criminals, including those who have visited cruelties upon our prisoners," being extended to include those who had helped to formulate aggressive war policies. The Emperor was exempted from trial as a war criminal since it had been decided to utilize him in the effectuation of Allied policy. But among those officers of government tried and punished under the authority of the International Tribunal set up in Tokyo to carry out the provisions of the Potsdam Proclamation were: the Premier at the outset of the Pacific War, General Hideki Tojo; Marquis Koichi Kido, Lord Keeper of the Privy Seal; former Foreign Minister Yosuke Matsuoka; Kiichiro Hiranuma, ex-President of the Privy Council; and Mamoru Shigemitsu, also a former Foreign Minister. Prince Fumimaro Konoye, listed as one to be tried as a war criminal, committed suicide before he could be brought to trial. The International Tribunal imposed the death sentence on some of those found guilty and a term of imprisonment on others, and the sentences had been executed by the end of 1948.

The war-crimes trials were supplemented by "purges" designed to take from directive positions first in government and subsequently in industry, those who had had any important relationship to the formulation of Japan's immediate prewar and war policies. To carry out SCAP directives, the Japanese government issued the first set of purge ordinances on January 4, 1946. A year later, by ordinances of January 4 and 14, 1947, the scope of the purge was substantially widened. Thus, even though in their application the purge ordinances were somewhat manipulated for purposes of domestic politics, and although the Japanese machinery set up for examination of those coming under the ordinances operated in the direction of leniency, many of the more experienced political and industrial leaders of prewar days were for the time made ineligible for post-surrender leadership except by in-direction.[13]

STRENGTHENING DEMOCRATIC TENDENCIES

Other actions taken or instigated by SCAP had a relationship to demilitarization but were more intimately connected with the "strengthening of democratic tendencies and processes in governmental, economic, and social institutions; and the encouragement and support of liberal political tendencies in Japan." [14] This required action to bring about the removal of all impediments to the expression of such tendencies. SCAP was therefore instructed to "require the Emperor to abrogate all laws, ordinances, decrees and regulations which would prejudice the achievement of the objectives set forth in the Potsdam Declaration" and in particular those

> which established and maintained restrictions on political and civil liberties and discriminations on grounds of race, nationality, creed or political opinion. Agencies or parts of agencies charged specifically with the execution of legislation abrogated or to be abrogated shall be abolished immediately.[15]

The fulfillment of these instructions enabled the Japanese political parties, including the Communist, to reorganize and resume the political competitions which had been suspended with their formal disbandment and consolidation in the Imperial Rule Assistance Association and the Imperial Rule Assistance Political Society in 1940. As part of the process of restoration of party activity, leaders who had been either in retirement or in prison during the war because of their political opinions, were able again to assert themselves. The time which had elapsed since the suspension of party competitions had not been long enough to eliminate or bring about forgetfulness of prewar political associations and relationships. Consequently the revival of parties took

[13] By mid-1947 some 2,000 persons, all outstanding wartime business leaders, according to Professor Cohen, had been purged under this program. (Jerome Cohen, *Japan's Economy in War and Reconstruction* (Minneapolis: Univ. of Minn. Press, 1949, p. 432). This was in addition to the much larger number of political purgees. Measured against the million and a half who came under the purge ordinances it is a relatively small number. Measured against the total top managerial group, however, it bulks large. On the purges see Harold Quigley, "The Great Purge in Japan," *Pacific Affairs* Vol. 20 (Sept., 1949), pp. 299-308.
[14] From "Initial Post-Surrender Policy," *Ibid.*, p. 634.
[15] *Ibid.*, p. 636.

place along lines which somewhat reproduced the old parties (the Seiyukai and the Minseito) under the misleading new names of Liberal and Progressive Parties, with a leadership of party and bureaucratic politicians carried over from prewar days. A third party, the Social Democratic Party, under the leadership of a prewar labor lawyer and politician, completed the list of major political parties, unless the Communist Party be included in that category.

In addition to action designed to remove the legal obstacles to the free expression of opinion and to voluntary association for political, economic and social activity pointed toward institutional change, SCAP not only encouraged the Japanese government to undertake a revision of the Meiji constitution but insisted upon it.

> He [MacArthur] clearly recognized at the outset that no political reform that did not encompass revision of the constitution would be worth serious consideration. The problem was whether to permit and encourage the slow growth of local democratic institutions and political maturity and at some later time to advise the development of an organic law that would merge and reflect the new institutions, or to promote the early and drastic overhaul of the basic law and then build on that new foundation.[16]

The choice was made for an "early and drastic overhaul of the basic law" since that

> would give to the Japanese people a goal at which to shoot, as well as a solid foundation on which to build. Under conditions existing in September, 1945 there could be no assurance that a reactionary cabinet, privy council or Emperor would not, overnight, wipe out all the gains that might be achieved. Precisely this had been done in the early thirties, bringing to a sharp and bitter close the nearest approach Japan had made to political liberalism. This compelling reason alone made the decision of General MacArthur an eminently wise one.[17]

Of course the same reasoning would support the conclusion that, unless debarred by enforcible treaty provisions, an independent Japan under a "reactionary cabinet, privy council or Emperor," might similarly wipe out the gains achieved by revision of the new constitution.

Viewing a drastic overhaul of Japan's constitutional structure as essential, the Supreme Commander informed "Prince Higashi-Kuni,

---

[16] *Political Reorientation of Japan, September 1945 to September 1948*, Report of Government Section, Supreme Commander for the Allied Powers (Washington, 1948), 2 vols., Vol. 1, p. 90. Hereafter cited as *Pol. Reorientation.*
[17] *Ibid.*, p. 90.

Prime Minister of the so-called Surrender Cabinet in September, 1945, that he regarded revision of the constitution as a matter of first importance." [18]

The Political Adviser to General MacArthur thereupon outlined twelve points which SCAP regarded as basic in any revision. These were: (1) Extension of the authority of the House of Representatives; (2) Removal of the veto power of the House of Peers; (3) Establishment of the principle of parliamentary responsibility; (4) Democratization of the House of Peers; (5) Abolition of the veto power of the Emperor; (6) Curtailment of the Emperor's authority to legislate by means of rescript and ordinance; (7) Provision for an effective bill of rights; (8) Establishment of an independent judiciary; (9) Provision for impeachment and recall of public officials; (10) Abolition of the influence of the military in government; (11) Abolition of the Privy Council; (12) Provision for amendment by popular initiative and referendum.[19]

A reminder of the importance of constitutional revision was given to Baron Shidehara, who succeeded Prince Hidegashi-Kuni as Prime Minister in October, 1945. This stimulated the government to appoint a committee, headed by Dr. Joji Matsumoto, "charged with the express responsibility for drafting a revised constitution." [20] While other bodies, and individuals engaged in discussion of, or prepared drafts of what should be embodied in, a new constitution, the attention of SCAP was naturally focused on the work of the Matsumoto committee and on the proposals for revision which it finally made, although the Government Section of SCAP meanwhile made its own studies of the problem.

With respect to the fundamental question whether national sovereignty should be lodged in the Imperial Institution or be transferred to the people, the general climate of opinion was conservative and the government and the Matsumoto committee were more conservative even than the parties. Consequently the "Gist of the Revision of the Constitution" and the "General Explanation of the Constitutional Revision drafted by the Government" which embodied the views of the committee as submitted to SCAP proved unacceptable since they did not "go beyond the most moderate of modifications in the language of

[18] *Ibid.*, p. 91.
[19] *Ibid.*, p. 91.
[20] *Ibid.*, p. 91.

the Meiji Constitution." [21] This brought about direct SCAP intervention in the drafting of what was actually a new constitution, promulgated as a revision of the Meiji constitution.

THE CONSTITUTION OF 1947

The draft which was prepared in the Government Section of SCAP
was designed to develop and apply three major points laid down by
General MacArthur. These were:

I

The Emperor is at the head of the State.

His succession is dynastic.

His duties and powers will be exercised in accordance with the Constitution and responsible to the basic will of the people as provided therein.

II

War as a sovereign right of the nation is abolished. Japan renounces it
as an instrumentality for settling its disputes and even for preserving its
own security. It relies upon the higher ideals which are now stirring the
world for its defense and its protection.

No Japanese Army, Navy, or Air Force will ever be authorized and no
rights of belligerency will ever be conferred on any Japanese force.

III

The feudal system of Japan will cease.

No rights of peerage except those of the Imperial family will extend
beyond the lives of those now existent.

No patent of nobility will from this time forth embody within itself
any National or Civic power of Government.

Pattern budget after the British system.[22]

The draft or working paper presented to the Japanese government
by the Government Section of SCAP was "received with a distinct
sense of shock," [23] but became the basis for a draft prepared by the
Japanese Cabinet in consultation with members of the Government
Section. The draft was presented in Japanese. It was then translated
into English and put into "acceptable English phraseology and re-
translated (it) into Japanese that would fairly and satisfactorily convey
the intent of the English translation." [24]

[21] *Ibid.*, p. 98.
[22] *Ibid.*, p. 102.
[23] *Ibid.*, p. 106.
[24] *Ibid.*, p. 107.

In the view subsequently cultivated by SCAP the new constitution, made public in March, 1946, and put into effect a year later after its adoption with minor changes by the Diet, was an instrument "drawn up by the Japanese government" even though "with considerable advice and presssure from the occupation authorities." [25] Another way of putting it is that it was an instrument which embodied occupation views as to the nature and form of government best suited to Japan in the light of its past development and existing situation and one which was accepted by the Japanese people and government as immediately workable and ultimately adaptable to the requirements of the times. Certain of its provisions were clearly "foreign" to Japanese experience and tradition. Others, equally clearly, represented a projection of or a building on earlier tendencies to change the political environment, tendencies which had been reversed in whole or in part during the decade and a half before 1946.

The most far-reaching and fundamental theoretical change made in the Japanese state and governmental system under the 1947 constitution was the one which was most strongly resisted by the Japanese drafters of the new constitution but which had been put as the first of his major points for revision by General MacArthur. This was the change made in the position of the Emperor and the Imperial Institution. Under the Meiji constitution the foundation principle had been that of Imperial supremacy.[26] For this principle of Imperial supremacy the new constitution substituted that of the supremacy of the Diet as "the highest organ of state power" and "the sole law-making organ of the State." (Art. 41). The position of the Emperor was characterized constitutionally as being one of symbolic importance, he being "the symbol of the State and of the unity of the people, deriving his position from the will of the people with whom resides sovereign power." (Art. 1)

The earlier foundation of Imperial supremacy lay in the accepted conception of the Imperial family as being of divine descent. Thus the source of the Emperor's power was spiritual as well as temporal. During the long periods of Japanese history when the Emperor was unable to exercise temporal authority the Imperial Institution had been pre-

[25] Edwin O. Reischauer, *Japan, Past and Present*, rev. ed. (New York: Knopf, 1953), p. 229.
[26] This was clearly revealed in the generalization as well as in the itemization of the Emperor's powers in the first chapter of the Meiji constitution, especially Art. IV-XVI.

served as the spiritual head of the state. Thus the Restoration of Meiji meant the restoration of temporal power to the Throne, with the support to it that came from a concurrent revival of State Shinto. In accepting Imperial rule for purposes of implementation of the surrender terms and to facilitate government through occupation, the Allies accepted the Imperial Institution in its temporal but not in its supporting spiritual aspects. Considerable importance was attached in Allied policy, consequently, to the elimination of the spiritual supports for the exercise of temporal authority. This was understood by the Japanese who, probably in anticipation of a SCAP instruction, took the action which prepared the way for the constitutional provisions with respect to the Imperial Institution.

On January 1, 1946, an Imperial Rescript was issued by which the Emperor formally divested the Imperial Institution of its divine, or spiritual, origin and attributes and placed his right to rule on the basis of leadership of the nation. SCAP itself directed the abolition of State Shinto, placing responsibility for the voluntary maintenance of State as well as Sect Shinto Shrines on the people. These actions taken by Imperial, rather than by popular, decision or by that of SCAP put the Imperial Institution on an exclusively temporal foundation, thus making it more nearly possible to deal with it on a constitutional and democratic basis, as was later done. This reform was re-enforced by numerous public appearances of the Emperor designed to strengthen his position by bringing the head of the state into a more direct relationship with the people composing it.

The erection of the Diet into "the highest organ of state power" established the new Japanese governmental system as parliamentary in nature, subordinating the Cabinet to it. It was constituted as a bicameral legislature, with both houses elected by popular vote. Thus the members of the upper chamber, called the House of Councillors, which replaced the pre-occupation House of Peers, were elected by universal suffrage, for six year terms, one half being elected every three years. The members of the House of Representatives, also elected by universal suffrage, had four-year terms. The constitution provided that "The qualifications of members of both houses and their electors shall be fixed by law. However, there shall be no discrimination because of race, creed, sex, social status, family origin, education, property or income." (Chap. IV, Art. 44) This provision ensured, as far as it could be done constitutionally, against the Diet's writing the election laws in any other terms than those of universal suffrage and fixing qualifications for office in other than broadly democratic social and economic terms. Since universal male suffrage had been the accepted basis of the electorate since 1925, the principal innovation made by the new constitution in this respect was in the enfranchisement of women and in the application of the principle of elections to the upper house of the legislature. The former change was more completely foreign to the Japanese social tradition than was the latter. It was, however consistent with the underlying purpose of the occupation. This was to establish the equality of the sexes and to put the individual in place of the family as the political, economic, and social unit. To that end, Chapter III of the constitution of 1947 dealt in considerable detail with the rights and duties of the people as individuals, with the principle laid down that "All of the people shall be respected as individuals." (Art. 13) In respect to these rights and duties the supremacy of the Diet was more qualified than the legislative power had been under the Meiji constitution. By the latter, the several provisions of a comparable character had been qualified by the phrase "subject to law."

The subordination of the Cabinet to the Diet was accomplished constitutionally through provision that the Prime Minister should be a civilian designated "from among the members of the Diet by a resolution of the Diet." (Art. 67) The Prime Minister, however, was given the right to select and to dismiss other members of the Cabinet, subject to the requirement that they must be civilians and that "a majority of their number must be chosen from among the members of the Diet." (Art. 68) However, as was subsequently revealed, the Diet was in a position to influence the judgment of the Prime Minister in selecting and retaining his colleagues, since the question of Cabinet personnel had a bearing on the confidence which the Diet might have in the government. A resolution of nonconfidence in the government, if passed by the House of Representatives, or the rejection by it of a confidence resolution (Art. 69), necessitated the mass resignation of the Cabinet unless the alternative courses open to the Prime Minister, of a dissolution of the House of Representatives and an appeal to the country for support was taken through new elections to be held within forty days.

In respect to composition and control of the government as well as in relation to its other powers and functions, the House of Representatives was given the predominant position. Thus in the enactment of the resolution designating the Prime Minister, if no agreement could be reached between the two Houses through a constitutionally designated procedure, "the decision of the House of Representatives shall be the decision of the Diet." Resolution of differences between the Cabinet and the Diet through elections was accomplished through dissolution of the House of Representatives rather than the House of Councillors. The latter was "closed" during the period between dissolution and the convocation of the new Diet, except in case of national emergency when the Cabinet could "convoke the House of Councillors in emergency session." (Art. 54) And, in case of difference of opinion over the budget, "the decision of the House of Representatives shall be the decision of the Diet," (Art. 60) while, with respect to general legislation, "a bill which is passed by the House of Representatives, and upon which the House of Councillors makes a decision different from that of the House of Representatives, becomes a law when passed a second time by the House of Representatives by a majority of two-thirds or more of the members present." (Art. 59) Thus in effect the House of Councillors had only a suspensive veto on legislation (and also over the adoption of treaties). Diet supremacy, in the last analysis, was thus planned as the supremacy of the House of Representatives, with the Cabinet serving, in relation to legislation, as the chief committee of the House in the construction of legislation, in addition to its executive functions of "control and supervision over various administrative branches," management of foreign affairs and conclusion of treaties, which however were to receive either prior or subsequent approval of the Diet.

An important qualification of the principle of Diet Supremacy is to be found in the provision made (in the chapter on the judiciary of the 1947 constitution) for the judicial review of any law, order, regulation, or official act claimed to be unconstitutional. This introduced a relationship of courts to law drawn from American practice and without precedent in Japanese experience. It was also an innovation to give the Supreme Court the supervisory powers over judicial administration, including the procurators office, which was provided for in the constitution. Other innovations with respect to the judicial branch of the government were: the provision for review of appointments made initially by the Cabinet to the Supreme Court "by the people at the first general election of members of the House of Representatives following their appointment, and shall be reviewed again at the first general election of members of the House of Representatives after a lapse of ten (10) years, and in the same manner thereafter" (Art. 79); for the dismissal of a judge when called for by a majority of the voters; and the provision for nomination by the Supreme Court to the Cabinet of persons to be appointed to the inferior courts.

RENUNCIATION OF WAR

While most of the innovations in the constitution could be defended as part of a program of "encouragement" of democratic tendencies, Chapter II, "Renunciation of War," had a much closer relation to demilitarization than to democratization. In this chapter of one article

> Aspiring sincerely to an international peace based upon justice and order, the Japanese people forever renounce war as a sovereign right of the nation and the threat or use of force as means of settling international disputes.
> In order to accomplish the aim of the preceding paragraph, land, sea, and air forces, as well as other war potential, will never be maintained. The right of belligerency of the state will not be recognized.

These provisions had been defined by General MacArthur as the second of the three major points which he laid down for incorporation in the new constitution. The renunciation by Japan of the right to use force, and of the right to maintain the instruments of power, fitted perfectly into the war objective of elimination of Japan as a power factor in the politics of the Far East and of ending militarism—to which was ascribed Japan's aggressive policies—in Japan itself. On the assumption then made that it was Japanese militarism which threatened the peace and security of other Far Eastern states and also the vested interests of the Western states in the Far East, the permanent disarmament of Japan lessened the probability of war, even though it left Japan vulnerable to attack since, it was also assumed, no other Far Eastern state would have the power or the incentive to launch an attack on Japan. If such an attack should be made the defense of Japan would be a collective responsibility under the provisions of the Charter of the United Nations. Such defense would be possible if there were agreement on its terms and conditions among the great powers.

By the time the new constitutional renunciation of force as an instrument of policy had gone into effect it had become quite clear that the great powers were not going to be able to agree on the conditions of peace for Japan. As relations between the United States and the Soviet Union steadily deteriorated after 1947, the position of Japan had to be re-examined by the United States in relation to the possibility of war. The inability of the United States and the Soviet Union to agree on the conditions of termination of occupation in Korea, and the refusal of Russia to accept the United Nations' decisions on the constitution of a unified Korean government, brought the issue of United States-Russian relations close to the borders of Japan. It was brought into Japan itself in connection with the ending of the war.

But it was the Communist victory in mainland China which had most to do with American re-examination of the advantages of maintenance of a weak and disarmed Japan. This situation brought about reconsideration of the ultimate meaning of Japan's renunciation of the right to maintain "land, sea and air forces, as well as other military potential" by General MacArthur in his New Year (1950) message to the Japanese people. He then stated that the Japanese had not renounced the right to arm for purposes of national defense. This statement was interpreted by General Whitney, Head of the Government Section of SCAP, as including the right of alliance for defensive purposes. Premier Yoshida subsequently (January 24) accepted this view of the right to maintain defensive armament as a proper interpretation of the constitution. Moves toward defensive rearmament were soon initiated and they were accelerated after the outbreak of war in Korea.

The moral and material advantage of disarmament had, however, been so emphasized in Japan by the occupation authorities that there was considerable opposition to moves which were held to be in violation of the terms of the constitution and which carried the possibility of re-emergence of the military as a factor in Japanese politics. There was even stronger objection to rearmament, even in purely defensive terms, under conditions which would align Japan with one group of powers against another in circumstances which would make the country an advanced military position and thus a battleground in the struggle between the United States and the Soviet Union and Communist China. Defensive rearmament might enable Japan to maintain itself as a neutral in the event of the outbreak of war but alliance in connection with defensive rearmament would make that impossible. Thus by the time of signature of the Japanese Peace Treaty, the question of interpretation of this chapter of the new constitution had become a real issue in Japanese politics.

ECONOMIC REFORMS

The changes in the international situation which brought about a change in the emphasis on demilitarization had a similar effect on the economic aspects of the SCAP reform program. Some of these reforms were related to demilitarization and some to democratization. Labor and land reforms, for example, in addition to their strictly economic significance, were thought of as underlying supports for a democratic system of government and politics. The revival and great expansion of labor organization from the prewar peak of less than half a million members to the new peak of around six million could readily be viewed as having this significance. The local unions which came into being with rapidity after the old laws were repealed came to be organized nationally along American lines into two major organizations, a Japanese Federation of Labor and a Congress of Industrial Unions. SCAP policy originally encouraged this organization since the conception of union activities initially was along the lines developed in the American labor movement of utilization of organization to improve the economic position of labor. The policy began to change, however, when political significance was perceived in a general strike which was threatened at the end of 1946 and the beginning of 1947. SCAP intervened to prevent such a general strike with alleged political rather than strictly economic purposes, after having tolerated strikes on a fairly wide scale during the first year of the occupation.

By 1948, a general shift in policy from reform to revival of the Japanese economy made SCAP less tolerant of strikes with strictly economic objectives since they had a bad effect on production. The fact that the strike threats in 1948 came largely from organizations of public employees gave a political tinge, in any case, to strikes for wage increases which the existing inflation justified, except as the government, without pressure through strikes, acted to keep wages adjusted to living costs. The railways and other utilities, and many of the industries, were or had become, partly as a result of occupation policy, government-controlled enterprises. This established the dilemma of political as well as economic motivation for both organized workers and SCAP—one not clearly perceived at the time when labor organization was undertaken as a projection into Japan of American conceptions. Communist leadership in some of the unions served to create the presumption, furthermore, that strikes with which the Communists were connected had political purposes.

This conception of labor organization divorced from political activity and objectives not only created a dilemma because of economic conditions in postsurrender Japan, but it also made it difficult for any new leadership developed through the unions immediately to play an important role in politics, and thus in the development of public policy. The fact, however, that labor was given the right of organization and advantage was immediately taken of that right, brought into being an important force to be reckoned with, perhaps even more in the future than in the immediate postwar situation.

The labor reforms, viewed in relation to the total problem of demilitarization and democratization, were designed to help produce a balance in the control of the Japanese economy which was lacking in prewar days. Then control rested in the hands of the great industrial-financial combinations (the Zaibatsu) which had close working relations with the government. Without other changes, their power might have been modified, within a democratic political framework, through the development of strong labor and peasant organizations. But initial SCAP policy with respect to these combinations went beyond this type of neutralization of their economic-political power. Many of these (Zaibatsu) combines were linked directly with militarism and the so-called militarists. Consequently "SCAP's directives ordering the Japanese Government to stop the manufacture of arms, munitions, and aviation struck at the Zaibatsu specifically as well as war industry generally." [27]

Beyond this, on November 6, 1945, a directive was issued ordering the break-up of all of the great economic combines. The method had already been tentatively suggested by the Zaibatsu itself, in anticipation of SCAP action. A Holding Company Liquidation Commission was created to take over the assets of the Zaibatsu holding companies for administration, pending their resale to investors, so as to give a wider distribution of industrial power. This move, essentially one against monopoly, was subsequently extended beyond the holding company type of financial control of industry into an attempt to break the economic system down into its component, essentially small but special-

[27] Department of State, *Occupation of Japan: Policy and Progress,* p. 42.

ized, production units on the basis of the independence of each. Thus the movement against the Zaibatsu, which was essentially a pyramiding system of holding companies organized on a family basis, was extended into a movement to bring about industrial as well as financial deconcentration of control. In an attempt to avoid manipulation within this reform program, as well as to remove from directive and managerial positions those who had been associated with Japan's war program, the purge was extended in 1947 to include those who had been managing the Japanese economy, even though they had not held government office.

The immediate effect of these economic reforms was to lessen production and thus to put a brake on Japan's economic recovery even to the level of 1930-34, which was established by the Far Eastern Commission as the ceiling for industrial production. By September, 1948, for example, over-all industrial production had reached only about 58 per cent of the 1930-34 level. Consequently when, after midsummer of 1947, the emphasis in occupation policy began to be put on economic recovery the current of economic reform began to flow much less swiftly, if not to be entirely reversed. Reforms which had been directed, but which remained in the paper stage from the point of view of Japanese execution, were suspended as SCAP's pressure on the government was relaxed and the emphasis in its "guidance" was shifted.

The Land Reform Act, which was directed especially against the existing system of absentee landlordism, was also designed to strengthen the foundations of a more democratic system of political economy, in addition to its purpose of lessening or removing a chronic source of unrest. The implementation of its terms was made possible because of the unusual prosperity which the peasants, as compared with other classes in Japanese society, enjoyed during the immediate postwar years. Under the Act some two million *cho* [28] of land were set aside for redistribution through a financed system of sales to tenants.

It was the accomplishment, under SCAP direction, of these reforms which led General MacArthur, on March 19, 1947, to conclude that "the time is now approaching when we must talk peace with Japan" and to advocate a peace treaty "as soon as possible." He felt that the first two phases of the occupation had been accomplished: (1) The

[28] A cho is 2.45 acres.

military purpose, which was "to ensure Japan will follow the ways of peace, and never again be a menace," had been realized since

We have demobilized the troops, demilitarized the country, torn down military installations. (2) The political phase is approaching such completion as is possible under the occupation.... I don't, by that, mean to say that this thing called Democracy has been accomplished.... But insofar as you can lay down the framework, it has already been accomplished. There is little more, except to watch, control and guide.[29]

[29] From "Interview with Press Correspondents, Primarily Concerning Plan for United Nations Administration of Japan," *Pol. Reorientation*, Vol. 2, Appendix F, pp. 765-66.

16

Post-Treaty Japan

✳✳✳✳✳✳✳✳✳✳✳✳✳✳✳✳✳✳✳✳✳✳✳✳✳✳✳✳✳✳✳✳✳✳✳✳✳

CONSEQUENCES OF FAILURE TO CONCLUDE AN EARLY PEACE TREATY

ACCEPTANCE OF THE VIEW advanced by General MacArthur of the need for and the advantages of an early peace treaty led the United States in the summer of 1947 to initiate moves toward a peace settlement. The American proposals for a conference to negotiate the conditions for a permanent peace settlement proved unacceptable to the Soviet Union and, because of Soviet objections, to China. The Chinese (National) government attempted to secure agreement on compromise proposals, but without success. Consequently the conclusion of a treaty was deferred until 1951.

The failure to negotiate a peace treaty in 1947 had important consequences. If it had been concluded then

its terms would have been based upon the view then held in the United States as well as elsewhere that the existing condition of disarmament of Japan should be perpetuated through treaty terms as well as by constitutional provisions. Since this would have left Japan defenseless against external aggression, responsibility for Japan's security would either have had to be accepted by other states or devolved on the United Nations. Furthermore, the government of a disarmed Japan would, under existing conditions, have lacked the power to maintain itself against internal subversion. In addition, an independent Japan might have had to face unaided the problem of revival and reconstruction of its economic life for, as of 1947, little progress had been made toward the restoration of production to the level of the years 1930-1934.... In other words, the movement toward a peace treaty was initiated at a time when it was assumed to be consistent with American interests to withdraw from a Japan which could not be expected to maintain its own security, much less to play any other role, from the point of view of power, in the politics of the Far East than that of a problem country.

Since Soviet action prevented the realization of the American objective with respect to the termination of the occupation, American (and SCAP) policy toward Japan began to change from reforms which had at least a short-run weakening effect on the country especially economically, to an emphasis on economic recovery and reconstruction.[1]

The growing tension in the relations of the United States and the Soviet Union, the deterioration in the position of the Kuomintang in China and the success of the Chinese Communist Party in achieving power over mainland China in 1949, together with the cost of supporting the steadily deteriorating Japanese economy, were all factors in bringing about this shift in emphasis in American policy toward Japan; a shift which had in it the appearance of a view of Japan as a potential ally rather than an ex-enemy power. As an ally, or even as a base of operations for the United States in the Far East, Japan would be a liability rather than an asset unless it could be made at least self-supporting. From this point of view the problem was economic rather than political, except as political considerations must be viewed as a most important factor in the re-establishment of Japan's foreign trade. Without imports of essential raw materials Japan's industry could not be revived. Without the reopening of foreign markets Japan could not finance the necessary imports, except as the United States was prepared to finance Japanese economic recovery. And without a measure of recovery of production, at least to the level set by the Far Eastern Commission, the more than 83 million people (according to the 1950 census) living on the four main islands could not live except at a substandard level, which would invite instability and disorder.

EMPHASIS ON ECONOMIC RECOVERY AFTER 1947

Under these circumstances, at the beginning of 1948 the United States representative on the Far Eastern Commission, on the basis of a review of developments, made it clear that the United States had come to the conclusion that more direct and energetic measures should be taken by SCAP to bring about the industrial recovery of Japan since that had not been accomplished by the Japanese themselves dur-

[1] Harold M. Vinacke, *The United States and the Far East* (Stanford, Stanford University Press, 1951), pp. 73-74.

ing the period of reform when the defined Allied policy had not included responsibility for economic recovery. To that end steps had been taken during the second half of 1947 to bring about the revival of foreign trade, with an increasing amount of private participation. Previously imports and exports had been handled entirely on a governmental basis through SCAP. In 1946 this had meant a United States expenditure of $187 million to finance necessary imports to meet the food deficiency. This type of aid was necessarily continued and, in addition, import of raw cotton was begun through arrangements with the U. S. Commodity Credit Corporation. Under the SCAP controls, imports of necessary raw materials increased in value in 1947 over 1946 by upwards of $200 million. This increase in the value of imports continued during 1948 and 1949 with a total reached in 1949 of almost $1 billion, which doubled the 1947 figure. Exports also were steadily increased, although not reaching a foreign trade balance by the time of independence. This latter was made possible initially through the negotiation, under SCAP auspices, of essentially barter arrangements such as those made in 1948 between Japan and Pakistan and Japan and Australia. These represented moves, subsequently continued and extended, toward the re-entry of Japan into the international community as an independent state.

Moves toward the revival of the Japanese economy were not regarded with universal satisfaction. Those who had suffered from Japanese imperialism were still close enough to that experience to recall that, as of 1930-34, Japan was economically the most powerful Far Eastern state, and that it had been able to exercise by economic means considerable influence beyond its own territories in the countries of eastern and southeastern Asia and the Pacific area. There was, consequently, a latent fear of a Japan which had recovered its economic strength even though it had renounced war as an instrument of national policy. This made it more difficult for the United States to put a policy into effect which involved the re-establishment of the prewar channels of trade. Such action was also complicated by the success of the Communists in China. That country had been an important source of raw materials' imports for Japan's industry as well as its principal prewar Asiatic market. The restoration of trade with China was accepted by Japan as essential to its recovery.

Until the outbreak of the Korean war, and for a time thereafter, SCAP was tolerant of Japanese attempts to find ways and means of resuming direct trade with China. But with the United States in control of Japan, the Communist International, of which Chinese communism was a part, had no interest in action designed to strengthen Japan. Likewise the tactics of Japanese Communists were directed internally toward making economic recovery more difficult. The United States itself was hesitant to approve any agreements with Communist China which would have the effect, through trade, of drawing Japan into the Soviet orbit *via* China. Thus the trade with China which developed with the tolerance of SCAP was on a *de facto* basis, with all of the uncertainties which that involved. Apart from China, a planned approach was made to a system of exchanges with the non-Communist countries in the area, and with the plan supported financially by the United States. This underwriting of Japanese recovery by the United States remained necessary even after the war had been formally ended and the occupation terminated by the ratification of a peace treaty. This was so because of the general conditions of area politics as those conditions affected the problem of trade relations.

Nevertheless, as recovery occurred under American auspices, the Japanese government and people became more rather than less restive under conditions of occupation. "The despair and confusion of the early postwar years was wearing off, and many Japanese began to realize that not all that was distinctively Japanese was bad and not all that the Americans were attempting was wise." [2]

INTERNAL POLITICS

The governments which were constituted on the basis of elections held after the adoption of the new constitution were as essentially conservative as those which had carried Japan through the initial postsurrender period. The first postsurrender elections gave a Diet majority to the conservative Liberal and Progressive parties, and led to the installation of a Cabinet headed by Shigeru Yoshida, who succeeded to the Liberal party leadership when, shortly after the elections, its first President Ichiro Hatoyama, was purged under SCAP orders. This government continued until after the elections of 1947. Those elections gave a party composition in the House of Representatives of: 143 Social Democrats; 133 Liberals; and 126 Democrats; with the remainder

[2] E. O. Reischauer, *Japan, Past and Present*, rev. ed. (New York: Knopf, 1953), p. 215.

of the 466 members classified as independents or distributed among minor parties. On this basis, the House designated Katayama (Social Democratic leader) as Premier. His Cabinet was based upon a coalition of the Social Democratic, the Democratic, and the People's Co-operative, parties.

The failure or inability of the Katayama government to develop and carry vigorously into effect a program of economic adjustment produced sufficient dissatisfaction with it so that it resigned (February, 1948) and was replaced by a Cabinet headed by the Democratic party leader, Hitoshi Ashida. Scandals involving his government, leading finally to Ashida's indictment for perjury, brought about its overthrow (October, 1948) and his replacement as Premier by Yoshida, even though at the time the first Yoshida government was being investigated on the charge of improper use of and accounting for party funds. Even under these circumstances, the elections of January, 1949 gave the Liberals (then calling themselves Liberal Democrats) an absolute majority in the Diet. This enabled the government for the first time to be based on a firm party majority in the House of Representatives. As head of the majority party, Yoshida was enabled to remain as Premier during the remainder of the occupation period and during the first posttreaty years.[3] The 1949 election confirmed the view that the state of Japanese opinion was conservative, even though, at the same time, Communist representation in the House increased from 3 to 35. Both the Liberals and the Communists made gains in representation at the expense of the Democrats and the Social Democrats as well as the smaller parties.

The Communists attracted support from non-Communist voters who were affected adversely by the inflation and the generally bad economic conditions, and who did not feel that the government would or could develop a program which would bring about improvement in their situation. The Communist Party also capitalized on its outright opposition to the continuation of the occupation and to American policy. The sentiment for a peace treaty had become strong and many failed to place the responsibility for the failure to terminate the occupa-

[3] Virtually through 1954, when, after he had been "depurged," Hatoyama's maneuvers succeeded in forcing Yoshida out, Hatoyama himself becoming, at the end of 1954, head of an essentially "care-taker" government, authorized to carry on until elections were held in the spring of 1955.

tion where it properly belonged—on the Soviet Union rather than on the United States or SCAP. Consequently a vote for the Communist Party was viewed as a vote against the occupation even more than as one for Communist Party control of the country.

The Communist Party of Japan had been able to resume political activity with the repeal under SCAP direction of the prewar "dangerous thoughts" laws, and with the release from prison in Japan of some of its leaders and the repatriation from China of others. Its toleration by SCAP did not prevent it from engaging in clandestine opposition to the occupation during the first postwar years. This opposition expressed itself through the part of the labor movement which came under the domination of the Communist Party. Overtly, however, it did not engage in extreme manifestations of hostility to the occupation or to occupation policy until it felt that anti-American sentiment (or more accurately hostility to the continuation of the occupation) had reached a point in connection with the failure of the first moves toward a peace treaty which would enable the party to enlist popular support through agitation against SCAP. At this point in time the party was being subjected to criticism from abroad for not following the international party line and giving support to the Soviet Union and Communist China against the United States.

The principal Japanese issue in the relations of the United States and the Soviet Union was over the failure of the Russians to repatriate the Japanese prisoners of war in their custody. This was the one item recurrently placed by SCAP on the agenda of the Advisory Council. It was in connection with this question that the Soviet representative on the Council walked out of its meetings. And it was in connection with it that clear evidence was presented to the Japanese that the Japanese Communist Party was not strictly national in its outlook. Mr. Tokuda, one of its principal leaders, was reported to have sent a message in 1949 which indicated a lack of desire on the part of the party to have any prisoners repatriated except those with a thorough Communist indoctrination. He was further reported, on April 27, 1950, to have told a Diet committee investigating communism in Japan that the Soviet and not the Japanese figures on repatriation should be accepted. These and other revelations, as well as the general nature of party activity and its growing Diet strength as revealed in the elections, stimulated a demand among the conservatives for action against the

Communist Party and made communism a principal issue in domestic politics during 1950.

As the party, following Cominform criticism of the failure of Sanzo Nosaka and other party leaders to take it into active operations against the occupation, became more militant in its activities, General Mac-Arthur, on May 3, 1950, made it clear that SCAP would view the banning of the party by the Japanese government with approval. In the ensuing months SCAP itself took action, ordering the Japanese government to bar the twenty-four members of the Central Committee from holding office and to suspend the principal Communist Party paper. On July 2 the government banned all Communist publications and then issued warrants for the arrest of nine of the principal Communist Party leaders, following the failure of Tokuda to obey an order to report to the Investigation Bureau which had been established. These actions drove the party underground. By the end of 1950 it had been put in substantially the same position as that of the years 1937-45, after a five-year period of activity as a parliamentary party.

These actions lessened the possibility that internal subversion would readily bring Japan into the Soviet orbit when independence had been regained. And the state of American-Soviet relations made it evident that there could be no agreement between Washington and the Kremlin on the terms of a peace treaty with Japan. Since, therefore, the United States felt it desirable to terminate the occupation before Japanese sentiment toward the United States as the occupant became too unfriendly, the Truman administration decided to conclude a peace satisfactory to it and to as many states as were willing to participate in the negotiation and conclusion of such a treaty.

NEGOTIATING THE PEACE TREATY

Fortunately, United States policy toward Japan had not been made an issue in American domestic politics as China policy had been during the postwar years. Possibly, however, to avoid partisanship in the approach to the conclusion of a treaty of peace with Japan, President Truman gave a leading Republican, Mr. John Foster Dulles (who subsequently became Secretary of State in the Eisenhower administration), responsibility for conducting bipartite negotiations with the World War II allies of the United States. From the outset the Soviet Union was invited to participate in negotiations which were designed to bring about agreement on, or agreed modifications of, a draft prepared by the American Department of State.[4]

While modifications were made in the American draft, leading to a final Anglo-American draft, as a result of negotiations with Australia, New Zealand, Britain, the Philippines, Burma, France, and other states, the terms of the treaty signed at the San Francisco Conference were essentially those originally set forth. The main objective sought by other states in the Pacific—assurance against renewed aggression by an independent Japan—was gained collaterally through the negotiation of security pacts, by the terms of which Australia, New Zealand and the Philippines were pledged American assistance in the event of aggression. A similar security pact was negotiated between the United States and Japan. It was designed to enable the United States to maintain military forces and installations in Japan after the termination of the occupation so as to enable the United States to discharge the responsibility which it had to assume for Japanese security against external aggression. This would also enable the United States to utilize Japan as a base of operations in the event of war, as it was doing by the time of signature of the treaty, in September 1951, in connection with the military operations in Korea.

Since a final text had been agreed upon in bilateral negotiations, the conference convened on September 5, 1951 at San Francisco was restricted, under the rules of procedure adopted, to the hearing of "public and official statements" regarding the treaty and to the signature of the text which had been circulated on August 13, described in the invitations to the conference as final. The provision for public and official statements enabled various governments to register dissent to provisions of the final draft, but not to propose amendments to it. Thus, for example, the Philippine delegation was able to put on the record its dissatisfaction with the provisions made for reparation. Three of the invited states (Burma, India, and Yugoslavia) refused to attend the conference. The U.S.S.R., Czechoslovakia, and Poland attended but did not sign the treaty. There were, however, forty-nine signatures, including that of Japan.

India subsequently made a separate treaty of peace with Japan. It

---

[4] According to Mr. Dulles: "Throughout the period (September 1950-September 1951) the Soviet Union took an active, though reluctant, part. We had several conferences with Yakov Malik and our governments have exchanged ten memoranda and drafts."

refused to attend the conference because of the failure of the United States to provide for representation of China, especially of the Communist government which India recognized; and also because of dissatisfaction with the treaty terms, which the Indian government felt left Japan too dependent on the United States. These dissatisfactions did not, however, preclude the conclusion subsequently of a separate treaty of amity and friendship.

A separate treaty was also negotiated between Japan and the National Government of China. A principal difficulty in the conclusion of such a treaty was over the extent of territorial application of its terms. The Formosan government sought in it Japanese recognition of its claim to be the government of all China. The Japanese sought to restrict its operation to Formosa. A compromise formula was reached, however, and embodied in the treaty of April 28, 1952 which made it applicable to Formosa, the Pescadores Islands, and territories that might in the future come under the control of the National Government. Subsequently the Japanese government defined its policy as that of nonrecognition of the Peking regime, the chief of the Asia Bureau of the Foreign Office stating further that "the treaty with the Nationalist Government applies to all China. There no longer is a state of war that calls for any further treaty with any Chinese government." [5]

Japan was the first state to ratify the peace treaty. Ratification had been concluded by a sufficient number of states by the middle of 1952 so that it could be proclaimed as in force. The principal obstacle to ratification by Japan was the attitude taken by some of the Japanese political parties toward the security pact with the United States rather than objection to the terms of the treaty itself. This reaction was due to the desire of many Japanese to avoid being drawn into war. The Yoshida government, however, strongly supported the security pact and at the same time moved toward a firm alignment of Japan with the United States against the Soviet Union.

The repatriation question provided a serious obstacle to ratification of the treaty by the Philippines, Indonesia, and Burma. Philippine opinion was especially vigorous in denunciation of the terms of a treaty which avoided the obligation of the aggressor, and the defeated, state to fulfill the surrender terms requiring the making of adequate reparation for the extensive damage done in the Islands. Inability to bring Japan to a satisfactory agreement on reparation caused the Philippine legislature

[5] *New York Times,* June 19, 1952.

to withhold its consent to ratification of the peace treaty until 1954.[6]

In anticipation of the early conclusion of a peace treaty SCAP had encouraged and assisted the Japanese government in moves toward the re-establishment of its external contacts. Thus Japan had applied successfully for admission into a number of specialized international organizations such as UNESCO; and trade missions, which could be readily transformed into consular and diplomatic establishments, had been sent to a number of countries. This latter was an extension of the activity of SCAP in acting for Japan in the negotiation of the necessary trade agreements on the basis of which foreign exchanges could be resumed.

POST-TREATY INTERNAL READJUSTMENTS

Internally, it had become the policy of SCAP to transfer as much responsibility as possible from its civilian sections to the Japanese government. This policy was continued after the relief of General Mac-Arthur from his position as Supreme Commander in Japan as well as from his other command positions. In this connection it may be noted that the recall of General MacArthur, after the initial shock to the Japanese, had the effect of an object lesson on the American conception of the proper relations of the military and the civilian authorities which the United States and SCAP had written into the Japanese constitutional structure. Beyond this, after the recall it was made evident that it continued to be American policy to permit the greatest possible exercise of authority within Japan by the Japanese government consistent with the pretreaty situation.

The transfer of responsibility had proceeded so far, and there was sufficient anticipation of the actual conclusion of a treaty, that the Yoshida government was able, as early as January of 1951, to announce to the Diet its intention to abolish all laws "which had been enacted for the attainment of occupation aims" although keeping within any limits set by the peace treaties. Following this line, in May, 1951 General Ridgway, who had replaced General MacArthur, authorized the government to review and modify existing laws and ordinances issued in implementation of Headquarters' directives.

[6] An agreement on reparation was reached by the Magsaysay government. It represented a modification of the earlier Philippine demands but came closer to meeting them than had previous Japanese proposals. Indonesia, however, remained unwilling to make a settlement of the issue along similar lines.

In undertaking this review the Japanese government emphasized first of all the re-examination of the purge ordinances and scrutiny of their application. A second emphasis was on review of SCAP's decartilization and antimonopoly directives. And a third, which met with considerable internal opposition, seemed to indicate a move, justified on the score of Communist activities, toward the reinstitution of the "dangerous thought" controls through revision of the occupation-sponsored press laws.

The depurging which had been started in 1951 in anticipation of the termination of the occupation was continued in 1952, being completed with the granting of amnesty to 1,303,000 persons on April 28, when the peace treaty officially came into force. This action involved pardons, reductions of sentences, and restoration of civil rights. The government had previously cleared the name of General Homma who had been tried by the Manila War Crimes Tribunal, convicted, and executed in 1946. Clemency and repatriation were also sought for some 230 war criminals serving sentences in the Philippines, Australia, and elsewhere.

INTERNAL POLITICS AFTER INDEPENDENCE

One of the consequences of the restoration of civil and political rights to those who had been purged was that such prominent prewar leaders as Mamoru Shigemitsu and Ichiron Hatoyama were able to compete again for political leadership.[7] Shigemitsu was immediately elected to the Presidency of the Progressive Party (Kaishinto). Hatoyama, who had been head of the Liberal Party (Jiyuto) at the time when SCAP ordered him purged, sought to gather together his followers within the party with a view to displacing Premier Yoshida, who had been able to take over the leadership when Hatoyama had been debarred from political activity.

The strengthening of the Progressives through their acquisition of a "name" leader and the struggle for power within the Liberal Party, together with expressed Diet dissatisfaction with some aspects of government policy, caused Premier Yoshida to dissolve the House of Representatives in August, 1952 and appeal to the country while he was still in a position to command a majority support. In the elections held

[7] The former was not one of those purged. He had been tried and found guilty as a war criminal, re-entering politics after serving his term of imprisonment. He was generally felt to have been improperly convicted. Before the war his service had been as a diplomat rather than as a politician.

in October, 1952 the Liberal Party returned 240 of its candidates, thus remaining in control of the Diet, although with a majority reduced by 45 seats. This majority was, of course, less stable than in the preceding Diet because of the dispute of Yoshida's leadership of the party by the Hatoyama faction. The Progressives

> captured 85 seats, a gain of 18, but far below its pre-election expectations. The Right-wing Socialist party gained 57 seats, an increase of 27; the Left-wing Socialist party won 54 seats, a gain of 38. The Communist Party failed to seat a single candidate, although it had captured 35 seats in the 1949 elections and held 22 at the time of the dissolution of the Diet. Its total vote of 894,823 comprised 2.6% of the ballots cast, compared with its 1949 total of 2,984,771, which was 9.8% of the votes cast. The Co-operative party with 2 seats compared with the 5 it held in August; and the Labor-Farm party with 4 seats, the same as in August, remained unimportant. The various other small parties had 4 seats as against six in August. The unaffiliated successful candidates numbered 19 as against 2 in August.[8]

From the point of view of principle the division in the country which was revealed in this first election after termination of occupation controls was between the conservatives, comprising the Liberals, Progressives, and the Right-wing Socialists, together with some of the minor groups and unaffiliated Diet members, and the radicals, including the Left-wing Socialists and the Labor-Farm party, as well as the Communist party. The issues which produced immediate division, were (1) that of rearmament and (2) that of the position of the United States in Japan under the security pact and the Administrative Agreement which defined the status of American troops. Thus the government took a firm pro-American position. The left-wing Socialist party

> opposed not only re-armament, but also those parts of the Peace Treaty that provided for American garrisons in Japan. It opposed the Security Pact and the Administrative Agreement between the United States and Japan. Many of its candidates were openly hostile to the United States. On the other hand, the party advocated opening of trade relations with China and Russia and the negotiation of an overall treaty that would include those two countries. Domestically, while not going so far as to endorse all-out government ownership of property, Left-wing Socialists were in favor of a greater degree of government control of the nations economy than were Right-wing Socialists.[9]

[8] Paul S. Dull, "The Japanese General Election of 1952," *The American Political Science Review*, Vol. XLVII, no. 1, p. 202.
[9] *Ibid.*

While in basic agreement, however, the conservatives differed in the degree of their advocacy of rearmament and support of the United States as against the Soviet Union. Thus the Liberals, while in favor of eventual rearmament, "advocated for the present a program of strengthening the national power, materially and spiritually, before rearming," while the Progressives advocated "rearmament without the Liberal party restriction. In essence, they said they were for the Liberal program, but said they could carry it out better. The Right-wing Socialists placed their faith in the United Nations to protect Japan and were against rearmament. They were not anti-American." [10]

It was, consequently, not a difference in principle or even in policy between the conservative parties which threatened the life of the Yoshida government. The threat came from factionalism within the majority party resulting from the grouping of party members around individuals, and from the desire of the leaders of the Progressive party to replace the Yoshida government with one of their own. Yoshida's attempt to discipline Hatoyama's supporters after the election accentuated the rift and led Hatoyama to plan and undertake countermeasures even though he gave his support to Yoshida to enable the latter to form a new government.

A vigorous attack was launched on the government early in 1953. The attack centered on two controversial measures that the Liberal Party government prepared for introduction into Diet. One was a police law revision bill which was designed to eliminate the existing system of national rural police in rural areas, and the autonomous police in municipalities, replacing them with completely national police headed by a cabinet minister. The second bill would have made all Japanese primary and secondary school teachers national public servants under the administration of the Education Ministry instead of local school boards, as at present. "The two measures were described as part of Premier Yoshida's program to wipe out those laws and programs evolved under the Allied occupation of Japan which, he declared were "inappropriate in the light of objective circumstances here." [11] These measures were thus directed against two important aspects of the administrative decentralization program of the occupation, both of which were viewed by SCAP as significant in relation to the demili-

[10] *Ibid.*, pp. 200–01.
[11] William J. Jordan in *New York Times*, Feb. 22, 1953.

tarization of Japan. They were characterized by the opposition as part of a plan to restore the "police" state.

The government could probably have maintained itself against this attack on its program had it not been for the opportunity presented to Yoshida's opponents by his unparliamentary language in calling an opponent in the Diet a "stupid idiot." Although he immediately apologized a motion of censure was introduced and, due to the abstention from voting of one-fourth of the members of his own party, was passed. In the face of this vote of censure, Yoshida refused to resign and, furthermore, took steps to strengthen himself for a struggle with the opposition by reshuffling his Cabinet, putting two of his personal followers into it.

Faced with the threat of a no-confidence motion in the Diet, the Premier announced in March that passage of such a vote would not bring about his resignation. The implicit threat of elections following so closely on the October elections was not sufficient to prevent passage of the no-confidence measure. Yoshida immediately dissolved the House of Representatives and announced that new elections would be held in April. In the elections, held April 19, the Yoshida Liberals returned the most candidates (199 instead of the 205 in the dissolved House) but failed to secure a majority, except as they were assured of the support of the Hatoyama splinter group (35, reduced from the 40 members in the preceding Diet). Altogether the Liberals had a majority of only 2. The Progressives remained the second party, with, however, a reduction in representation from 88 to 76. The Right-wing Socialists also had their voting strength reduced from 80 to 66. The Left-wing Socialists, on the other hand, increased their vote from 56 members to 72, and the Communists returned 1 candidate.

These developments during the first two years of independence were significant in indicating a tendency to return to the early conception of the party as a personal following rather than a body of voters supporting a clear-cut body of doctrine. They did not indicate a serious swing in opinion from the right to the left, notwithstanding the gains made by the Left-wing Socialists and Communists. These gains were not sufficient to put the parties of the left within reaching distance of the premiership, which Yoshida was able to resume. His control of the House, however, was dependent upon the support of either Hatoyama or Shigemitsu, as was revealed in the elections of the Speaker and the Vice-Speaker. Given the support of one or the other in critical votes, a relatively long tenure could be predicted for the new Yoshida government. If, however, in their search for power those leaders combined their followings in opposition to him, the position of the Yoshida Liberals would become untenable.

The latter quickly proved to be the case. In November, 1954, the conservative elements seeking to displace Premier Yoshida formed a new political party which took the name of the Japan Democratic Party. The Democratic party was formed through a merger of the Progressives with the Japan Liberals (who had splintered off from the Liberty party in 1953), anti-Yoshida defectors from the Liberals, and a few independents. This merger was made possible because of acceptance by Mamoru Shigemitsu, head of the Progressives, of Ichiro Hatoyama as the President of the new party.

The Democratic Party controlled 121 seats in the House of Representatives as against 185 Liberals. Thus it had enough strength to launch a vigorous attack on the Yoshida government but it could not, by itself, force its resignation. To that end Hatoyama sought and secured the support of the right-wing Socialists. In this situation, in anticipation of a no-confidence vote in the Diet, Yoshida resigned on December 7, 1954, having previously given up the presidency of the Liberal party.

In order to secure the majority support necessary to enable him to form a government, Hatoyama promised his Socialist allies of the moment that elections for a new House of Representatives would be held early in 1955. This pledge, in effect, meant that the new government immediately had only care-taker functions and thus was not in a position to make any important changes in policy. Shigemitsu, who became Foreign Minister in the Hatoyama Cabinet, nevertheless did (December 11) indicate one line of policy development which was undertaken during 1955. The policy of the new government was stated to be that of rendering assistance,

technical and otherwise, to sister nations in Asia in collaboration with the free nations. We shall exhaustively explore all means available in restoring close and cordial relations with our friends in Asia...We are, therefore, willing to restore normal relations with Russia and China on mutually acceptable terms without prejudice, however, to our basic collaboration with the free nations. As for trade with the Soviet Union and China, we do not necessarily expect much from it at the present juncture, but, all the same, we shall welcome opportunities of expanding the volume which is now rather small.

The promised elections for the House of Representatives were held in February, 1955. In the new House the Democratic party replaced the Liberals as the party with the largest number of votes (185 as against 112). The right-wing Socialists secured 67 seats, taking fourth place, behind the left-wing Socialists with 89: the Labor-Farmer party elected four representatives; the Communist two. Thus the elections gave the two conservative parties in combination control of the House of Representatives, neither, however, having a majority. The Socialists, if they should combine, would take second place to the Democratic party in voting strength in the present House of Representatives, displacing the Liberals as the second party. Hatoyama in any case was faced with the necessity of securing support for his government from either the Liberals or the right-wing Socialists if he retained power.

The election also revealed a slight decline in the total popular vote for the two conservative parties and a corresponding gain of about 2 per cent for the four leftist parties. This gain was actually registered by the left-wing Socialists rather than by the right-wing Socialists.

During the postwar period the conservatives acted on the assumption that the struggle for control of the government would be carried on between two essentially conservative parties, conservative, that is, in point of view as to the uses to be made of power. The gains registered in the 1955 elections by the parties of the left, as well as the balance of power role previously played by a wing of the Socialist Party, raised a question as to the long-run validity of this assumption. The movement toward union of the left and right wings of the Socialist Party after the 1955 elections raised this question even more sharply. The possible strengthening of the parties of the left through union or coalition might well reopen the question of coalition or amalgamation of the two conservative parties. They are at present held apart, as one writer put it,[12] by "minor differences over policy and major differences over personality." These differences may serve to prevent coalition or merger until further gains are made by the Socialists to the point where the conservatives are faced with the possibility of a Socialist government. A merger of the two wings of the Socialist movement into one party would make that party the second in point of voting strength in the Diet. It could, consequently, claim the right to form a government if the Hatoyama government should fall. Such a Socialist government

[12] Kenneth E. Colton, "Conservative Leadership in Japan," *Far Eastern Survey*, Vol. 24, no. 6 (June, 1955), pp. 90-96.

would present the Democratic or the Liberal party with the dilemma of either supporting it or uniting with the other conservative party against it. Such union of the Socialists would thus have the effect of forcing the issue of union with the existing conservative parties. The issue for the conservatives was not, however, forced to this point by the end of the first postwar decade since the Hatoyama government remained in power with the somewhat reluctant support in the Diet of the Liberals.

Aside from this slight political movement toward the left, the general tendency in Japanese government and politics after the termination of the occupation was away from the innovations of the 1930's and 40's and back to a situation approximating that of the 1920's, when Japan attempted to adapt itself, within the limits of its own traditions, to the democratic currents then running in the world.

In seeking an answer to the question of future political development in Japan, aside from the tendencies discussed above, and to the question of the role to be played by an independent Japan in the politics of the Far East, it is essential to keep in mind two distinct but interrelated aspects of the problem facing any Japanese government. One is to be found in the essentially political field of security. The other is in the economic area.

THE PROBLEM OF SECURITY

The assumption made by the Japanese in accepting the principle of permanent disarmament was that national security against external aggression could be found through membership in the United Nations and through passive reliance on the assistance of the United States in the maintenance by Japan of an essentially neutral position in the event of world conflict. By the time of the peace treaty, however, the United States itself was encouraging the Japanese to undertake a limited rearmament and a revival of their economic strength so that their national power would at least be sufficient to enable them to defend themselves against overt attack.

Under the security pact Japan became in effect an ally of the United States and a base of operations in the event of war between the United States and the Soviet Union or Communist China. The war in Korea came to be waged by United Nations' forces, with the command headquarters in Tokyo. Thus from the start of the period of independence under treaty, Japan found itself under the pressure of circumstances which required an emphasis on rearmament for purposes of national security even though Japanese were carefully excluded from participation as belligerents in the war in Korea. The circumstances of relationship between Japan, the United States, and the Soviet Union were such, furthermore, as to ensure unfavorable action on any Japanese application for membership in the United Nations itself. This accentuated the relationship of Japan to the struggle in Korea as a base for American operations rather than as a state engaged in fulfillment of its own international obligations.

The general situation, then, as well as the traditional suspicion and fear in Japan of the Russians, made more acceptable than might otherwise have been the case an orientation of Japan's policy and relationships in conformity with American desires and interests. To this was added the possibility that some ground lost by reason of World War II decisions might be regained. The developments of the cold war produced a willingness on the part of the United States to reconsider its promise to support Russian claims to the Kurile Islands. Re-establishment of Japan in the Kuriles would be an important step toward more effective national self-defense. This would also be the case with respect at least to the southern part of Saghalin. Those losses, or at least the Kuriles, the Japanese might recoup as part of a general settlement in the Pacific between the United States and the Soviet Union, but only with vigorous American support of Japan's claims. A third territorial readjustment sought by the Japanese, also related intimately to the national security, was the restoration to Japan of the Ryukyu Islands, including Okinawa. Faithful support by the Japanese government of the United States in the Far East might cause the United States to propose the return of the Ryukyus, either directly or through a Japanese trusteeship under the United Nations. This concession might be made to an ally, since it could be held not to weaken the American strategic position in the area.

One way of ensuring American economic assistance and support for the international readjustments desired by Japan, then, was to take a firm position as an ally of the United States in the struggle against Communist China and the U.S.S.R., subordinating on occasion Japanese judgment as to policy to that of Washington. In relation to security this immediately involved acceptance of the views of the United States with respect to rearmament.

This question of rearmament, with all of its political and economic implications, was a principal issue in Japanese politics in the second half of the decade under review. As might be anticipated, the opposition based itself in part on the constitutional obstacle to rearmament which the American occupation authorities themselves had helped to erect. But the Socialists, who presented the most formidable opposition, also argued against rearmament on American terms because it could only mean taking sides in the international struggle. This argument was not expressive of anti-Americanism, although that animus existed on the part of some who opposed rearmament. It was rather based on acceptance of the neutralist view that the government should maintain and exercise independence of judgment in the formulation of foreign policy.

The Yoshida government, after independence, accepted the necessity for "defensive" rearmament, which it viewed as consistent with the letter and spirit of the constitution. What it assertedly sought to avoid was too much rearmament at too rapid a pace. Thus it sought to resist American pressure to rearm Japan rapidly and extensively, but not to the point of unduly offending the United States. Thus the Yoshida government was prepared to view Japan as in effect an ally of the United States in the international struggle, while seeking to retain as large a measure of control of policy *vis a vis* the United States as possible.

The Hatoyama government's foreign policy had been stated in the broad terms quoted above in December, 1954. The implication was that the government would seek to establish friendly relations beneficial to Japan with China and the Soviet Union as well as maintaining friendly and beneficial relations with the United States. On the one hand, the policy enunciated and subsequently followed could be viewed as being intended as a means of exerting pressure on the United States to secure greater support through presentation as an alternative to such support movement by Japan over toward the Soviet side in the international struggle. It could also be viewed on the other hand as a declaration of intention to follow a completely independent foreign policy designed exclusively to promote Japanese interests. In either case it represented modification of, rather than fundamental change in, the Yoshida policy. In either interpretation, it caused the Hatoyama government to take a more advanced position than that of its predecessor in favor of rearmanent since, under the circumstances of the times, the more organized power Japan developed the greater would be its ability to act independently *vis a vis* either the United States or the Soviet or to put pressure on either. In respect to re-armament Hatoyama's policy was better designed than Yoshida's to meet American specifications, but it was also more apt to encounter serious opposition in Japan. Any moves toward re-establishment of friendly relations with China and Russia would not encounter opposition from the same (although it did from other) domestic sources but it would meet with objection from Washington. Lacking power, furthermore, Japan might find itself unable to re-establish relations with China and Russia, except on terms defined by them. This was revealed as the attempt was made to re-open and enlarge trade relations during 1955. Thus the end of the decade found Japan again concerned with the development of state power but having to operate within a different political framework, both at home and abroad.

JAPAN'S ECONOMIC PROBLEM

But while rearmament might immediately assist the Japanese toward a greater measure of national security based upon national power, ultimately the problem of security for Japan is economic. As has been suggested above, this was perceived during the period of the occupation. During the first years of the occupation Japan had been sustained economically by the United States. As recovery set in, it was made possible by American assistance as well as by the trade agreements which began to give Japan access again to foreign markets and sources of supply of raw materials. But, at the time of the peace treaty, particularly because of attitudes towards the Japanese resulting from the war and on account of disturbed political and economic conditions in other countries of eastern Asia, Japan remained dependent economically on the United States. This relationship was an important consideration in bringing about acceptance by the Japanese government of a close political relationship to the United States. This dependence was obscured at the time of signature of the treaty and immediately thereafter by reason of the partial change from direct aid to its equivalent in the form of procurement in Japan for the United Nations' forces in Korea. These procurement orders enabled the Japanese to pay for necessary imports and helped to keep Japanese industrial establishments operative. In this way Japan benefited materially from the Korean War. But this was a short-run method of paying for imports out of exports and it left the fact of dependence unchanged.

In the long-run, the upwards of 83 million people living on the four islands to which Japan had been reduced could gain a livelihood only through a reopening of the channels of international trade and by open competition for markets and sources of necessary raw materials. Japan could continue to import from the United States, without financial assistance from the latter, only if the American market was opened more widely and freely to the products of Japanese industry. Alternatively, it could maintain the livelihood of the people through resumption and enlargement of trade with the countries of eastern Asia, including China, thus reducing Japanese purchases in the American market or securing the necessary foreign exchange to continue their purchases in the United States through selling their industrial and agricultural production elsewhere. But if they followed the lead of the United States and refused to trade with such Communist countries as China, and if the United States did not buy from Japan as much in value as it sold to it, then the United States would have to continue to support Japan financially if the Japanese economy was to become and remain viable.

Release of Japan from economic dependence on the United States through the re-establishment of prewar trade relations in eastern and southeastern Asia in and after 1950, in addition to the obstacle presented in the American attitude toward trade with Communist China, was seriously handicapped by the strong currents of nationalism which, in the postwar period, swept the countries of eastern and southern Asia. Nationalist economic policies followed by the countries in the area inevitably created difficulties for Japan in any attempt to re-establish relationships on the basis of exchange of processed goods for industrial raw materials. Each country in the area, including China, hoped to establish its own national industry with a view to making itself as independent of other countries as possible through the creation of balanced economies. Thus instead of the prospect of freer international exchanges throughout the Far East, to the benefit of Japan, the tendency was toward the erection of more barriers to trade in the interest of the new national economies. This tendency toward planning the establishment of balanced economies was shown, for example, in the interest of the Philippines, Indonesia, Burma, and China in the making of reparation by Japan through the export of industrial plant on reparations account. It was anticipated that this would facilitate industrialization in the recipient countries and lead to the processing of raw materials at home rather than their export to Japan. Confronted by this determination on the part of the new regimes in Asia to industrialize, and released in large part from the free supply, as reparation, of machines, tools, and other industrial facilities, Japan began to attempt to solve its economic problems by the export of capital goods instead of consumer goods, such as textiles, which had been one of its staple exports before 1931.

Unless, however, it can solve the problem of surmounting trade barriers by a readjustment of its production for export and, by that means or as a result of voluntary changes in the nationalist economic policies of other states, solve the problem of maintenance of more than eighty-three million people on a land area which a hundred years ago yielded a meager livelihood for some thirty-three million, the Japanese government may find itself under pressure to develop economic and military power sufficient to enable it to compel its neighbors to make changes in their policies. Thus it is partly in the policies of other states that the answer may have to be found to the question of the ultimate expression of Japan's foreign policy, and to the concurrent question of the soundness and permanence of Japan's commitment constitutionally never to use military power to realize national purposes.

BIBLIOGRAPHICAL REFERENCES

Ackerman, Edward A., *Japan's Natural Resources and their Relation to Japan's Economic Future* (Chicago: University of Chicago Press, 1953).

Ashido, Hitoshi, "The Role of Japan Today," *World Affairs Interpreter*, Spring, 1954.

Ball, W. MacMahon, *Japan, Enemy or Ally?* (New York: John Day, for the Institute of Pacific Relations, 1949).

Bisson, T. A., *Prospects for Democracy in Japan* (New York: Macmillan, for the International Secretariat, Institute of Pacific Relations, 1949).

Borton, Hugh, ed., *Japan* (Ithaca: Cornell University Press, 1950).

Bovenkerk, Henry G., "A Century of Protestantism in Japan," *Far Eastern Survey*, Vol. 22, no. 13.

Dangerfield, Royden J., *The New Japan* (New York: Foreign Policy Association, 1953).

Department of State, Office of Northeast Asian Affairs, *United States Relations with Japan, 1945-1952* (Washington, 1953).

Deverall, Richard Laurence-Grace, *Red Star Over Japan* (Calcutta: 1952).

Durgen, R. L., "Christianity in Postwar Japan," *Far Eastern Survey*, Vol. 22, no. 2.

Farley, Mirriam S., *Aspects of Japan's Labor Problems* (New York: John Day, for the International Secretariat, Institute of Pacific Relations, 1950).

Fearey, R. A., *Occupation of Japan: Second Phase, 1948-50* (New York: Macmillan, 1950).

Fine, Sherwood M., *Japan's Postwar Industrial Recovery* (Tokyo: Foreign Affairs Association of Japan, 1953).

Haring, Douglas G., "Speculations on Japanese Communism," *Far Eastern Survey*, Vol. 23, no. 1.

Higachuichi, Yoshio, *Literature on Contemporary Japan* (Tokyo: Tokyo Office, Hoover Institute and Library, 1951).

"Japan Looks Back on Occupation: A Symposium of Japanese Views," *Far Eastern Survey*, Vol. 22, no. 3.

Kawai, Kazuo, "The New Anti-Americanism in Japan," *Far Eastern Survey*, Vol. 22, no. 12.

Okocki, Kazuo, "Life and Labour in Post-war Japan," *Eastern World*, March, 1954.

Quigley, Harold S., "American Policy and Japanese Politics," *Political Quarterly*, January, 1950.

———, "Democracy Occupies Japan," *Virginia Quarterly Review*, Vol. 23, no. 4.

———, "The Great Purge in Japan," *Pacific Affairs*, September, 1947.

———, "Japan's Constitutions: 1890 and 1947," *American Political Science Review*, October, 1947.

Reischauer, Edwin, *Japan, Past and Present*, 2nd ed. (New York: Knopf, 1953).

———, *Japan and America Today* (Palo Alto: Stanford University Press, 1953).

Sansom, Sir George B., *The Western World and Japan: A Study in the Interaction of European and Asiatic Cultures* (New York: Knopf, 1950).

Scalapino, Robert A., *Democracy and the Party Movement in Prewar Japan* (Berkeley: University of California Press, 1953).

Shawantes, Robert S., "Perspective on Point IV: The Case of Japan," *Far Eastern Survey*, Vol. 22, no. 10.

Stewart, Kermit G., "The 1953 Japanese Elections," *Far Eastern Survey*, Vol. 22, no. 9.

Supreme Commander for the Allied Powers, Government Section, Report, *Political Reorientation of Japan, September, 1945-September, 1948*, 2 vols. (Washington: 1949). *Scapins* (Tokyo, 1952).

Swearingen, Rodger, and Langer, Paul F., *Red Flag in Japan* (Cambridge: Harvard University Press, 1952).

Textor, Robert B., *Failure in Japan* (New York: John Day, 1951).

Wildes, Harry Emerson, *Typhoon in Tokyo* (New York: Macmillan, 1954).

Yoshida, Shigeru, "Fair and Generous Peace," *Vital Speeches*, October 15, 1951.

17

At the End of the First
Postwar Decade

✳✳✳✳✳✳✳✳✳✳✳✳✳✳✳✳✳✳✳✳✳✳✳✳✳✳✳✳✳

END OF WESTERN COLONIALISM IN THE FAR EAST

AN IMPORTANT CONCLUSION which must be drawn from the foregoing analysis of Far Eastern politics during the first postwar decade is that Western capitalistic colonialism and imperialism had been destroyed. The French, whose revolutionary ideas of liberty, equality, and fraternity had shaken up Europe during the nineteenth century, made the last stand against the application of those ideas in the Far East in their colony of Indochina. The terms and conditions of the armistice agreement signed at Geneva in 1954 may be said to have terminated French rule in Indochina. Britain to be sure, remained in Malaya, but more as an organizer of relationships among the Malays, the Chinese, and the Indians, and as their protector against the Communist terrorists than as a colonial overlord.

The foundations of western colonialism had begun to be undermined as the colonial powers began to lose their belief in their right to govern others because of their mastery of the art of self-government. The withholding of self-government from the people in the colonies came more and more to be viewed as inconsistent with liberty within the nation-state as the West began to emphasize the growth and spread of democratic and representative government. This put a brake on action designed to extend the area of imperial control, and it lessened the self-assurance of the established colonial powers with respect to their right to govern others. The result was gradual acceptance of the idea of responsibility which was applied through the mandates' system of the League of Nations to the former German colonies and to parts of the Turkish state.

One of the factors serving specifically to undermine the colonial system in Southeast Asia was the course followed by the United States in the Philippines. From the time of establishment of the first Philippine Commission (1900) the United States declared that its right to rule was tempered by responsibility to prepare the people to govern themselves. While profession and practice frequently diverged, the profession of responsibility made it impossible to view a colony as a territory to be exploited exclusively to the advantage of the controlling country. This idea of responsibility, as well as its own tradition, led the United States to put emphasis on education of the people, on public health, and, in general, on developmental activities. This was a new emphasis in colonial policy. All of this assisted the Filipinos, who had previously revolted against Spain, to maintain their interest in and emphasis on independence.

The American example in the Philippines had a double effect elsewhere in the area. The emphasis on self-government and independence as a popular goal helped to stimulate similar nationalist aspirations in the neighboring colonies. It also helped to bring about modifications of policy on the part of the Dutch and the British, especially with respect to education. This, in turn, opened the way among the colonials to a greater understanding of the modern idea of self-government. The slowness of introduction of self-government within the colonial framework brought about an emphasis on independence as the ultimate means to that end.

Another factor in bringing about modification of European colonial policy was the gradual acceptance of the view that the national costs of colonial government were greater than the material advantages derived from the colony. The costs were borne by the state. The profits were taken by individuals or groups with exploitive rights which they were able to exercise under the safeguards of state power. With the acceptance of an enlarged measure of responsibility for service to and protection of the people of the colony the costs tended to increase and the profits to decrease. Under these circumstances, by 1941 several of the colonial powers had begun to plan their political retirement. Nationalism was voicing a demand for self-government, if not for independence, but the pressure which nationalists were able to exert was not great enough by itself to force the pace of change. Power of decision continued to rest with the colonial powers, and it was in terms of their judgment that modifications of the colonial order were being undertaken.

It was the temporarily successful Japanese military imperialism, consequently, not local nationalism, which immediately liquidated Western colonial imperialism. It was Western armed force, in turn, and not local nationalism, which liquidated Japanese imperialism. But it was local nationalism, strengthened by experience during the war years and armed by the Japanese, which gained control, either wholly or largely, in each colonial country during the postwar years. Burma, the Philippines, and Indonesia had had their independence recognized by the end of the first postwar decade. Singapore and Malaya had been brought close to the point of self-government, looking toward independence or Dominion status, by Britain. The French position in Indochina had been lost to the Viet Minh Communist party supported by China in the north and to nationalist regimes supported by the United States in southern Viet Nam, Cambodia, and Laos. The final triumph of nationalism in southern Viet Nam was registered in the plebiscite, in October, 1955, when the people chose Diem and rejected Bao Dai as head of the state.

When won, independence did not, however, end all relationships with the Western states or solve all problems of relationship. The new governments had to assume responsibility to the people for relief, rehabilitation, and economic reconstruction following the war. They could discharge their responsibilities only with outside assistance, both technical and financial. At the outset the one state in a position to give the necessary assistance was the United States. But in granting or withholding aid Washington quickly found that it had to tread warily because of the natural sensibilities of peoples who had just emerged from the colonial status and who were fearful lest their independence be unduly restricted by the acceptance of aid. Past experience had indicated that the reality of independence might be lost through the creation of an economic dependence. This caused some of the new governments of southeast Asia to consider American tenders of assistance with caution—not to say suspicion. This attitude of suspicion, where it existed, resulted also from the friendly relations maintained by the United States with the former colonial countries. In this respect it was, in the main, a carry-over from the colonial past rather than a reaction in terms of the newly won status of independence. Where the attitude existed, nevertheless, it made it difficult for the United States to attach conditions with respect to the use of economic aid which the American government felt obliged or was willing to give in order to increase production or to develop economic and political stability. And yet, from the American point of view, both past experience, especially with China, and existing conditions of government in the area indicated the necessity of conditioning aid as to its use so as to ensure a reasonable return in relation to the purposes of both the granting and the receiving state.

In this latter connection it must be said that the attainment of the nationalist's objective of self-government and independence had not always resulted in the improvement of the quality of government. To a varying degree the reverse frequently proved to be the case. Standards of public morality may not have seriously declined in such countries as Burma, Indonesia, and the Philippines but certainly the charges of corruption, terrorism, favoritism, and so forth, in relation to elections and also the operations of government on the administrative as well as the political side did not indicate improvement. Administrative efficiency certainly declined in the immediate postwar years. Beyond all of this there was a deteriorated situation with respect to the maintenance of public order in many of the countries. There was, to be sure, variation in degree of deterioration of administrative efficiency and in the success or failure in the establishment and maintenance of public order among the new states, but initial deterioration was common to all. Much of this was predictable at the outset, was understandable, and may be viewed as excusable under existing circumstances. Nevertheless this condition did raise a question as to the justification for granting the assistance called for without qualifying conditions. But where the conditions proposed were apparently designed to establish control by the lending state of important aspects of public policy, as in relation to the development and use of the armed forces of the state, rather than being exclusively directed toward securing a dollar of value for a dollar of expenditure for an agreed purpose, the ensuing attitude of suspicion would seem to be, under the circumstances of the times, quite understandable.

THE ROLES OF THE UNITED STATES AND
THE SOVIET UNION

While it is true that local nationalisms were the beneficiaries of the direction of allied power against the Japanese, in the first postwar decade the relations of Far Eastern states with one another and with the other states of the world were nevertheless determined more by outside forces than by those developed as a result of the creation of new states within the area. The second conclusion to be drawn, therefore, is that the world-wide struggle between the United States and its allies, on the one side, and the Soviet Union and its satellites, on the other, was of major significance in channeling the currents of politics in the Far East. At the same time, it must be recognized that developments and alignments in the Far East were of the utmost importance in shaping the course of events elsewhere. Europe and the Far East both were regional battlefields on which the contending forces were arrayed against one another. In both areas it proved impossible to define local problems and find solutions for them in local or regional terms because of the effect of decision on the relative power positions of the United States and its allies, on the one hand, and the Soviet Union and its satellites and supporters, on the other. This was clearly revealed in China, in Korea, and in Indochina; as well as in Greece and Turkey, Austria, and Germany. While not so directly apparent, the struggle between the United States and the Soviet Union also affected politics in the Philippines, Indonesia, Burma, Malaya, and Japan; as it did in Italy, France, and Jugoslavia.

As of 1945, the power of decision in the Far East seemed to rest with the United States. It was assumed that Russia's requirements had been met with the concessions made to Stalin at the Yalta Conference as these were confirmed and somewhat extended in the Sino-Soviet treaty of 1945. The introduction of Soviet power into Korea was viewed as a temporary war measure. Since, under the 1945 treaty with the Republic of China, the Soviet Union had formally committed itself exclusively to the National Government with respect to China, and since Stalin had indicated a willingness and the intention to let the United States assume the burden and the responsibility for bringing about the internal unification of China, the prospect seemed good for the reconstruction of China as a power under American auspices and in friendly association with the United States.

Between 1945 and 1947, however, it was revealed that Soviet policy in Manchuria, Mongolia, Sinkiang province, and Korea was just as imperialist as the policy followed by the Russian Tsarist government in the decade from 1895-1905. The agreements of 1945 were not, it became apparent, accepted by the Stalin government as a stable basis of relationship; they were rather viewed by the Kremlin as a springboard for future expansion. This was evident in the use made by the Russians of their newly acquired rights in Dairen, at Port Arthur, and in the Manchurian railways; in their looting of the Manchurian industrial plant; as well as in the conditions of control which they established in their zone of occupation in Korea.

Soviet policy and actions in Manchuria facilitated the Communist movement toward power in China. The Chinese Communists, however, derived more benefit in their conflict with the Kuomintang from the limited economic and military support given by the United States to a party government which the Chinese had come to believe was an ineffective instrument of rule than they did from any direct Soviet assistance. Successful labelling of the American policy of support of the National Government as "imperialist" helped to obscure the reality which was that of Soviet imperialism. It thus enabled the Chinese Communists to present themselves to the Chinese people and intellectuals as a nationalist party contending against American imperialism without real consideration of the threat presented to China in the imperialism of their Soviet supporter.

After 1947, with the proclamation of the Truman Doctrine of containment of Soviet expansion, the United States met with success in Europe and failure in China. The failure might not have been so complete if the Chinese Communists had not committed themselves in advance so strongly to an anti-American policy. This precluded their acceptance of American economic assistance in the reconstruction of China even if the United States had been disposed to offer it. American domestic hostility to communism made it hazardous for the administration at Washington to propose economic assistance as a possible means of enabling the new Central People's Government to free itself from exclusive dependence on the Soviet Union. It also forced the erection of the barrier of nonrecognition against any reversal of the Communist line of hostility to the United States. It cannot be asserted that a different policy would have met with success in changing the pro-Soviet orientation of Communist China's policy. If it had been attempted, however, and if it had met with failure, the full responsibility would have been squarely placed where it properly belonged— on the Soviet Union and on the Chinese Communist Party leadership. That would certainly have lessened the impact in India and elsewhere in Asia of the charge that the purpose of the United States in refusing recognition was to prevent the Chinese from exercising the right of national self-determination of their form of government. It would also have publicized the fact that the Chinese Communist Party was not in fact national but was an instrument of international communism which, in turn, was an instrument of Soviet Russia's foreign policy.

The anti-American emphasis in Communist China's policy was strengthened with the conclusion of the alliance between Moscow and Peiping in January, 1950. Although not so stated, the circumstances of the times made it clear that this alliance was directed against the United States. Such an emphasis, and the terms of its expression, made it virtually impossible for the United States to shift from a policy of non-recognition to one of recognition. It also made inevitable commitment of the United States to support of the National Government on Formosa, since overthrow of that government would have brought that strategically important island under the control of a power hostile to the United States.

From 1945 to 1947 the United States had officially viewed the struggle in China as civil war. Thus it had failed to relate its support of the National Government in China clearly to the international conflict until the outbreak of war in Korea, even though it had not recognized the Communist regime after that regime had driven the National Government from mainland China. When Britain, India, and other non-Communist states extended recognition to the new Central People's Government they thereby declared themselves to be accepting the outcome of a civil war. They did not view themselves as siding with the Soviet Union against the United States in the international struggle for power. With respect to that international conflict, Britain had definitely aligned itself with the United States, although refusing to accept a position of subordination to the United States which would deny the United Kingdom the right to take an equal part in the development of policy. Differences of opinion naturally arose between Washington and London as to strategy and tactics. But these differences were resolved through agreement, and they did not arise out of any determination on the part of Britain to play the role of an independent make-weight in a balance of power between the United States and the Soviet Union.

INDIA, THE UNITED STATES, AND COMMUNISM IN THE FAR EAST

India, Burma, and Indonesia, on the other hand—and especially India —sought to keep clear of commitments to either the United States or the Soviet Union. Thus India's policy of neutralism in the international struggle was markedly different from that of Britain. It did not involve an attempt to help shape the policy of a coalition of independent states organized and directed against a common enemy. Rather, it was an attempt to maintain equally friendly relations with both sides. In the process India sought to establish leadership of an independent bloc capable of weighting the balance between Washington and the Kremlin. Thus in effect after 1950 India became an active competitor for power in the Far East. Assertedly India did so on the premise that Far Eastern problems should be solved by Asian states without Western (and thus outside) intervention. Mr. Nehru refused to recognize that India, although Asian, is culturally about as alien to the Far Eastern countries as is the United States, Britain, or European Russia.

India had, however, just thrown off the colonial yoke, with which it exclusively identified imperialism, and all of the countries of the Far East had been exposed at one time or another to Western imperialism. Thus they had with India the common bond of fear and suspicion of Western states. In terms of the conflict between the United States and the U.S.S.R. there was the background of suspicion of the colonial powers with whom, after the war, the United States continued in friendly association. This background and this association, as far as India was concerned, produced a reaction against the United States rather than the Soviet Union. It thus caused India to suspect American motives where there was no real ground for suspicion.

An early instance of open divergence of Indian and American policy was presented with the Indian recognition of the Communist regime in China. The failure of the United States to do likewise was asserted in India to be evidence of the unwillingness of the United States to allow the Chinese people to have the form of government which they wanted if it did not meet with American approval. This view was strengthened as the United States continued to insist on the right of the Formosan government to speak as the voice of a China which Nehru contended had repudiated that government. With representation at Peiping, the Indian government received at first hand the views of the Central People's Government on questions at issue in the Far East. Because of this direct contact, which was permitted to it but not to some of the other governments which also had recognized the Communist regime, and because of its hostility to the Chiang regime, New Delhi tended to accept as its own the Chinese Communist point of view on many Far Eastern questions. This could only serve to accentuate existing disagreements between India and the United States. Thus it was the China problem, more than other question, which not only kept India from aligning itself with the United States but also gave a pro-Communist leaning to India's neutralism.

Another consideration in determining the Indian government's attitude was its desire to be treated as an equal, even if not as a superior power, in the reaching of decisions on Asian questions. Although weak and badly in need of economic and technical assistance which it could apparently secure only from the United States, India (and also Burma and Indonesia) were sensitive to the appearance of being supplicants for American aid. As newly independent states, furthermore, they were unduly sensitive to any conditioning of aid which seemed to be directed toward limitation of their freedom to determine their own policies. Preoccupied with its new position of power and its new responsibilities in world affairs, the United States failed on occasion to take this sensitiveness sufficiently into account. For too long in the postwar period of conflict, the United States seemed to act on the assumption that leadership meant that Washington would decide upon the policy and then negotiate regarding the conditions of joint action to implement the announced decision. This caused India (and others) on occasion to assert its independence by failing or refusing to follow the American lead.

This was clearly revealed in the negotiation of the peace treaty with Japan. The United States formulated the terms of a draft treaty which was then somewhat modified as a result of negotiations with Australia, New Zealand, Britain, France, and the Philippines. India's views were not particularly sought. From the point of view of interests involved there was no apparent reason why India should have been given an important or principal place in the negotiations, except for the fact that India thought of itself as a principal spokesman for Asia on Asian questions. Here certainly was one important Asian question which was being dealt with in the main by non-Asian states. Not sufficiently taken into account through prior consultation, India refused to take part in the ratifying conference on the Japanese peace treaty at San Francisco and subsequently negotiated a separate treaty with Japan. The reason given, of course, was not that of prestige but that of the failure of the treaty to establish Japan as a truly independent state. By this the Indian government meant a state free of American influence.

Regardless of intent, in such instances as that of recognition of Communist China and of refusal to accept the Japanese peace treaty, the Indian policy of independence or neutralism put New Delhi on the same side of such questions as the Soviet Union. It did not, however, materially affect the issue itself, nor give India a position of recognized Asian leadership. Nor, if that was the Indian aim, was the latter purpose realized through early attempts which were made to draw together the new states of Southeast Asia in the development of a common policy through conference among their governments.

The Korean war had a different consequence. In connection with the negotiations for an armistice, and in the implementing of the armistice terms, India was able to play an important mediatory role. The influence of the Nehru government was also felt at the Geneva Conference, which gave India a role also in the supervision of the application of the terms of the Indochinese armistice.

This, and the courting of the Indian government by the Chinese Premier and Foreign Minister, Chou En-lai, who made a point of stopping at New Delhi (and also Rangoon) on his return to China from Geneva, and who saw to it that Mr. Nehru was warmly received upon his return visit to Peiping, gave India a prestige position in Far Eastern and world politics much beyond that which it had previously enjoyed. Thus by 1955 a third conclusion to be drawn with respect to politics in the area was that India had become an important new outside factor in the Far Eastern equation. It remained to be demonstrated, however, that India had successfully taken over the role previously played by Japan as an Asian state, or that New Delhi would be able to compete successfully with China for leadership in the Far East. The People's Government had had its case argued for it in such international forums as the United Nations by Indian representatives, but that government had not given any real indication of acceptance of Indian leadership. On the contrary there were indications that China felt itself to be the natural leader of Asia.

RISE TO POWER IN THE FAR EAST
OF COMMUNIST CHINA

A fourth conclusion to be drawn from a survey of the last decade of Far Eastern politics, consequently, is that China, under the Communist regime, was more of an independent power-factor in politics than it had been at any time in the modern period of its history. While a member of the Soviet bloc, and following policies *vis-a-vis* the United States and its supporters identical with those of the Soviet Union, China demonstrated sufficient strength and independence in questions of concern to it to fully warrant its being characterized as an ally or partner of the U.S.S.R. rather than a satellite. This was shown in such readjustments of the conditions of relationship as were made after the initial agreements entered into in January of 1950. Soviet Russia's interests in Manchuria, for example, were contracted rather than expanded. There was, to be sure, no indication of a possible breach of relationship such as occurred in the case of Yugoslavia. One reason was that the Soviet government avoided making the mistakes in its China policy which were made in its treatment of Yugoslavia. Mao was accepted as one of the major prophets of communism. His views as to the applicability of Communist doctrine in Asian countries were not disputed. Tito had not been accorded that status by the Russians. Furthermore, while Russian support and assistance were important for the Chinese Communists, China was at least of equal importance to the Soviet Union as an ally in the Far East. Both were interested in the extension of the area of Communist influence and each wanted to overcome the barriers to expansion which American policy had sought to erect. Thus they had a common enemy and that gave them as strong an incentive to maintain their alliance as that of ideological affinity, perhaps an even stronger one.

Aside from the struggle for power in China itself, the disturbance of the peace which involved China came with the failure of the North Korean regime to conquer South Korea. While the evidence available at present is largely circumstantial, it supports the conclusion that the North Koreans did not launch their attack in 1950 without prior understandings with the Soviet Union and the Chinese Central People's

Government. There is, however, no satisfactory evidence of an advance understanding that, if the need for it developed, China would actively intervene in behalf of North Korea. The evidence indicates rather that the anticipation was that no such military intervention by either Peiping or Moscow would be necessary. The decision to intervene would seem to have been taken by the Chinese on their own initiative rather than under Russian pressure.

In any case, the intervention had the consequence of bringing China back into Korea as an active competitor for power, giving assistance to and exercising more authority over the North Korean regime than the U.S.S.R. If that position of dominance is maintained it can certainly be viewed as a move in the direction of re-establishment of the historic Chinese Empire from which Korea had been detached by the exercise of Japanese power. Since North Korea had already passed under Communist control it was Chinese Communist imperialism rather than the Communist world revolution which registered a victory with the signature of the Korean armistice. The Communist system itself was contained, as far as Korea was concerned, at the point of expansion of Soviet Russian power which had been reached when containment was proclaimed as the central objective of United States policy.

Another step toward the reconstitution of the Chinese empire was taken when the authority of the Peiping regime was established over Tibet. This was undertaken and carried through against the protests of New Delhi. In spite of assurances of friendship, this action brought China into direct territorial contact with India and Nepal, putting Peiping in a position to exert direct pressure on India, if that became necessary. That position will be further strengthened if the program of military and economic development of Tibet, announced by the People's Government in 1955, should be successfully put into effect. These developments advanced the strategic position of China in eastern Asia even though it could be argued that it would be exceedingly difficult to stage a large-scale invasion of India from Tibet.

Still another advance in imperial power was made by Communist China as a result of the 1954 Geneva Conference at which an armistice in Indochina was concluded. By the armistice terms the Communist Viet Minh was assured of control of the northern part of the country and was given an opportunity to acquire control of the remainder as a result of the provisions made for elections. It was Communist China's support before, at, and after the Geneva Conference which produced this victory for Ho Chi-Minh. The existing relationship between Communist China and Indochinese communism at the time of victory was comparable to that between the Soviet Union and one of its satellites. Thus it is reasonable to conclude that the forced withdrawal of the French from the northern part of Vietnam was in effect in favor of China, which gained at least as much direct authority in its old suzerainty of Tongking as that exercised by the Imperial China of the Manchu period. It was France which, in 1884-85, had compelled the retirement of China from Indochina. It was, in the last analysis, Chinese Communist which replaced French imperialism in the Far East, in the process extending China's own power into Southeast Asia.

It was against the threat of Chinese Communist rather than Russian expansion, furthermore, that the United States sought to erect barriers after the conclusion of the Indochinese armistice. The postarmistice situation brought Chinese communism to a point of direct contact with Thailand and Malaya as well as with Cambodia and Laos. Under Chinese auspices and in China a "Free Thai" organization was erected as a nationalist instrument of penetration of Laos, Cambodia, and Thailand. Thai nationalists could not, of course, make the same anti-imperialist appeal against the government as had the Viet Minh in Indochina, and as had nationalist parties in the other countries of the area. They could, however, take the same line against the existing government as that which had been exploited by the Chinese Communist Party against the Kuomintang in China, labelling it (1) as an instrument of American imperialism because supported by the United States, and (2) a feudalistic, bureaucratic, and capitalistic "remnant" because of its internal support. The division of the Thai people, some of whom lived in China, Laos, and Cambodia, as well as in Thailand itself, could also be exploited by means of nationalistic agitation.

A different instrument of penetration was presented in the large Chinese populations of Thailand, Malaya, Burma, Indonesia, and the Philippines. The Chinese Communists, as had their predecessors, insisted on considering all overseas Chinese to have Chinese nationality even though many such had had no contact with China for many years, even generations. Thus the census of 1954 listed 11,748,320 overseas Chinese as part of the population of China, in addition to the seven and a half millions living in Formosa. This listing occurred after Mr. Nehru had discussed their dual status with Chou En-lai and had received assurances that the Peiping government was studying the question and was considering the adoption of a policy under which the overseas Chinese would be required to choose either Chinese nationality or that of the country of their residence. Mr. Nehru was reported to have described as "rather frightening" a situation in which the Chinese populations of Thailand, Burma, Indonesia, and Malaya could not divest themselves of Chinese nationality.

Similar concern over this question had previously been expressed by the Premier of Burma and by the government of Indonesia. Inconclusive negotiations over the question, as a matter of fact, were conducted with China by Indonesia during 1954. In November of 1954 the Indonesian Minister of Information announced that negotiations at Peiping were running smoothly and that both parties were agreed that it was not good to retain double citizenship. Meanwhile the Indonesian government submitted a bill to Parliament under which a citizen of Indonesia, living in Indonesia would be considered as not possessing another citizenship. Without a redefinition of China's policy, nevertheless, the issue remained unresolved and the possibility remained that Communist China would seek to utilize overseas Chinese as instruments of political penetration and subversion. This redefinition was apparently made and for Indonesia incorporated in the 1955 nationality treaty previously referred to.

ORGANIZING SECURITY IN SOUTHEAST ASIA

All of the indications at the end of 1954 were that the immediate problem of Far Eastern politics was not that of finding security against an overt Chinese attack on the countries or areas threatened, except in the case of Formosa and islands nearer to the mainland. It was rather the one more difficult to solve of preventing an extension of the Chinese Communist position by means of stimulation and support of internal disruptive forces. This was recognized by the United States as it undertook to establish new and more effective barriers to the outward thrust of Communist power.

The United States, in connection with the negotiation of the Japanese peace treaty, had concluded bilateral security pacts with Australia and New Zealand, the Philippines, and Japan. It was also committed to the defense of South Korea. After the Geneva Conference Washington sought to extend this security system into a multipartite arrangement for the defense of Southeast Asia. It called a conference at Manila in September, 1954, which brought into being the Southeast Asia Treaty Organization (SEATO). Only three Asian states (Thailand, the Philippines, and Pakistan), however, were willing or able to participate. The terms of the Indochina armistice raised a barrier against participation by Cambodia and Laos. Japan was unwilling to accept obligations which might necessitate overseas military action for Japanese. The National Government on Formosa could not be invited to participate because of the position taken toward it by Great Britain and other states. India, Burma, Ceylon, and Indonesia took the position that international tensions would be increased rather than lessened by such a defense organization because it would be viewed by China as threatening it unless Peiping, and perhaps also Moscow, were invited to join. The Indian and Indonesian governments viewed as acceptable the post-Geneva assurance given to Mr. Nehru by Chou En-lai that the Chinese policy was that of peaceful coexistence and noninterference as elaborated in the joint declaration issued at the end of Mr. Nehru's visit to Peiping. The five principles therein set forth were: (1) respect for each other's territorial integrity and sovereignty; (2) nonaggression; (3) noninterference in each other's internal affairs; (4) equality and mutual benefit; (5) and peaceful coexistence. Acceptance of these principles, it was held, would make unnecessary and dangerous from the point of view of peace and security such military pacts, themselves menacing, as the one sought by the United States.

SEATO, as established, consequently, had as participants five Western states—the United States, Australia, New Zealand, Britain, and France; and three Asian countries—Thailand, the Philippines, and Pakistan. The purposes of the organization were to co-operate to strengthen defense against external aggression, to counter subversion from within, and to develop economic measures for social well-being. These purposes were to be realized through action taken in accordance with constitutional processes of the signatory states in the event of armed attack or aggression in the treaty area, and by consultation on measures to be taken if a threat other than armed attack was presented. It was agreed that no action would be taken on the territory of any state without the consent of its government; that the Security Council would be immediately informed of any action taken; that the treaty would not affect obligations under the Charter of the United Nations; and that no international engagements would be entered into in conflict with the terms of the treaty. It was also provided that the number of participating states might be enlarged by the unanimous agreement of the eight signatory states.

The treaty area was defined as the "general area of Southeast Asia, including also the entire territories of the Asian parties and the general area of the southwest Pacific, not including the Pacific area north of twenty-one degrees of latitude," thus excluding Formosa. The United States, however, subsequently entered into a security pact with the National Government under which Washington undertook to support that government in the event of an attack on Formosa and the Pescadores Islands. Cambodia, Laos, and the free territory under the jurisdiction of Viet Nam were also defined as within the scope of the treaty provisions concerning armed attack. They were also viewed as being eligible for economic assistance. The treaty further provided for the establishment of a Council to plan measures for the execution of its terms.

Experience had revealed the difficulty of containing communism by military means, especially where Communist parties were in a position to exploit the upsurge of nationalist feelings and of conditions of economic distress and governmental weakness. These were the conditions which were to be found in the countries of Southeast Asia, including South Viet Nam. Under the circumstances, the probabilities at the end of 1954, consequently, were that no immediate attempts at military intervention would be made by Communist China, but that Communist efforts would be directed toward the exploitation of internal weaknesses in the treaty area.

This meant that SEATO, if its purposes were to be realized, would have to put its major emphasis on measures designed to create economic strength and prosperity in Southeast Asia. Perception of this fact was shown in the United States with the replanning of the foreign aid and technical assistance program for purposes of stimulating economic development in southern Asia and the Far East, while at the same time giving advice and assistance when called upon in the strengthening of internal security forces. The shift in emphasis was even more strikingly shown in the proposals to contract rather than to expand the military forces in South Viet Nam as the United States replaced France in the field of military training and assistance, and as Washington channeled its economic assistance so as to emphasize the fact of independence of Viet Nam and thus the end of colonialism in that country.

What this meant was that the struggle in Southeast Asia would probably not involve military operations in the immediate future unless war should be precipitated elsewhere. It would, however, be carried on by diplomatic, economic, and propagandistic methods rather than being terminated unless and until a real basis of accommodation should be reached in the relations of the United States and Communist China.

In undertaking a political and economic offensive against China and the Soviet Union in Southeast Asia, the United States had obvious advantages but it also labored under severe handicaps. The advantages came principally from its ability to meet the needs of the countries concerned with respect to their economic and military development. The ability to furnish economic and technical assistance, however, might readily prove a political liability unless aid was given in terms of specifications set by the country in need of assistance. Otherwise, American aid might be viewed as a form of intervention and thus be fitted into the Chinese propaganda charge of American imperialism. American intentions have been and continue to be appraised in Asia not in terms of their significance for the United States but from the point of view of their estimated Asian consequences. An example of this (although not of the charge of imperialism) is to be found in the reaction in Burma to a plan to combat communism in Asia by lending surplus grain to needy countries. With a rice export surplus, the American plan would, said a Burmese Cabinet Minister, "force (Burma) to go to (Communist) China on our knees. . . . We will have to depend upon China for our rice market and this will naturally tie our economy to Red China. . . . Until our rice problem is solved . . . the Seato pact is just a 'keep off the grass' agreement." Other countries had similar special problems of economic development which could not be solved satisfactorily by a projection of American conceptions of need into the solution. Where that was attempted it was exploited as evidence of American interference and thus imperialism.

It was this weakness in American policy-making which strengthened the tendency in Indian and Indonesian foreign policy previously referred to. This tendency initially expressed itself adversely in relation to the American conditioning of aid on an expression of the recipient's willingness to participate in the struggle against Soviet communist expansionism. From this initial reaction to American policy, India entered the international scene as a mediator in the Korean war and as a participant in the Indochina settlement suspicious of the intentions of the United States and pro-Chinese in tendency. Following the conclusion of the Indochinese armistice agreements, India and Indonesia not only expressed disapproval of SEATO as a means of preserving peace and maintaining security but also moved to bring into being, formally, a bloc of Asian and African states through conferences planned at a meeting of the Colombo powers held at Jokarta in December, 1954. These developments followed a conference of India, Burma, Pakistan, and Ceylon, called by the Premier of Ceylon at Colombo just prior to the Geneva Conference. The Colombo Conference had little effect on international decisions, but it did suggest a means of enlarging the participation of "neutralist" Asian states in world and Far Eastern politics under the Indian leadership which had been successfully exercised first in United Nations discussions of the Korean question.

The conference of Asian and African states planned at the December meeting of the Colombo powers was duly held in April, 1955 at Bandung in Indonesia. From the start it was revealed that there was no real unanimity of view among the participants except with respect to general principles. There was a general hostility to colonialism but an insistence on the part of such states as Turkey, the Philippines, Thailand, and Ceylon that any resolution against colonialism and imperialism should condemn equally the old colonialism and the new communist imperialism. This attitude made it essential for Chou En-lai, representing the Central People's Government (neither the National Government nor that of the Republic of Korea were invited to send representatives), to take a much more defensive and conciliatory position than had originally been anticipated. The vigor of participation in the conference on the part of those who were or felt themselves to be threatened by communist expansionism, furthermore, made it difficult for the Indian and Indonesian governments to guide the conference along the lines originally projected. In this respect the conference exploded the view projected from India of an Asia and Africa with a completely unified attitude in international politics which could be expressed with one voice. In a sense this revived and expressed the original conception of "neutralism" as that of the independence of each state in the formulation of its foreign policy. This was completely consistent with the acceptance of the five principles upon which India and Communist China had previously agreed.[1]

[1] These principles were, it will be recalled, (1) respect for each other's territorial integrity and sovereignty; (2) nonaggression; (3) noninterference in each other's

What was at issue in Far Eastern politics was not the principles to govern the behavior of states but their effective implementation against the state (or states) which failed to govern its conduct in accordance with them. Neutralism, in the sense of independence of the state in the development of its foreign policy, left the Philippines, Thailand, Pakistan, and Turkey, for example, free to commit themselves to participate in the American-organized security system if their governments concluded that American assistance was essential to the maintenance of their security against the Soviet Union or China. It left the same freedom in the exercise of judgment to India, Burma, and Indonesia.

THE QUESTION OF FORMOSA

These moves and countermoves in Southeast Asia established the conditions of a precarious peace in that part of the Far East. However they left untouched the issue which carried the most immediate threat to international peace and security. This was the question of Formosa and the future of the National Government of the Republic of China. It was this question which had lessened the unity of the anti-Communist world as it was being forged under American leadership. Fundamentally the objection in many quarters to United States policy was Washington's support of the Formosa regime as the recognized government of China rather than American unwillingness to see Formosa itself come under the control of an unfriendly government. It was viewed as unrealistic to act upon the assumption that the National Government would be able, in the foreseeable future, to re-establish its position on the mainland through military operations. Such military operations could only be contemplated if the United States was prepared to embark on large-scale war in China itself in support of the Nationalists, whose objective would be that of overthrowing the Central People's Government. This the United States steadily refused to accept as a commitment, but without being willing to accept as an accomplished fact the reality of control of China by the Chinese Communist Party. Its continued support of the National Government on Formosa as the government of China consequently introduced an ele-

---

internal affairs; (4) equality and mutual benefit; and (5) peaceful coexistence. These are, of course, the generally accepted principles governing the relations of states, to which all states pay at least lip-service.

ment of uncertainty as to the nature and extent of the support which would be given to Formosa in the event of an attempt on the part of the Communists to conquer the island or to the National Government if it should hazard its existence in an attempt to regain power on the mainland.

Up to the time of the conclusion of the peace treaty with Japan United States policy had clearly envisaged Formosa as a part of China on the basis of the *de facto* restoration of that island to China in 1945. By the terms of the Japan treaty, however, Japan relinquished its title but the decision as to Formosa's future status, except as to its being no longer a part of the Japanese Empire, was left open. In other words, the objective set forth in the Cairo Declaration was construed negatively with respect to Japan but not positively with respect to China. When Japan re-established its relations with China, negotiations were conducted with the National Government on Formosa, and the treaty terms covered such territory as was under the control of the latter. These and other actions seemed designed to separate consideration of the status of Formosa from that of China, making an attack on Formosa something other than a completion of the struggle for power in China itself. And yet the United States seemed to view Formosa in relation to China, since, when the Eisenhower administration took office, it removed the prohibition imposed on the National Government with respect to operations directed against the mainland while maintaining the patrol of the Formosan Straits against Communist activity directed against Formosa.

This was the situation when, following the settlement in Indochina, the Peiping government reiterated its intention of completing the civil war by bringing Formosa under its control. This shifted the focal point of conflict from Southeast Asia to the place where it had been made clear that the United States might have to act without support from other members of the coalition which that country had been organizing against communism. The latest evidence of this was presented in the necessity of excluding Formosa from the area of operations of SEATO. American intentions were, however, underscored with the conclusion of the bilateral defense pact between the United States and the National Government. That pact, however, removed some apprehensions because of the restriction of the commitment of the United States to the defense of Formosa and the Pescadores and not to the general support of the National Government. Apprehensions as to the scope of American policy were further reduced when the United States obtained a diplomatic pledge from the National Government not to undertake operations against the mainland without having first secured the consent of the United States. These were all indications of a modification of American policy in the direction of divorce of the Formosan question from that of authority in China.

These definitions, however, left out of account various off-shore islands, such as the Tachens, Quemoy, and Matsu, which had remained in the hands of the National Government after its evacuation of the mainland. It was from them, rather than Formosa, that the Chiang Kai-shek government had launched guerrilla-type attacks on the mainland and on shipping in coastal waters. Used in that way they had a considerable nuisance value to the National Government. They could also be viewed as having strategic value in any attempt to reopen the struggle for power on the mainland. In effect, from that point of view and in pre-1945 terms, they were the only strictly Chinese territory remaining under the effective authority of the National Government. It was primarily in relation to attack on the mainland, however, rather than for purposes of defense of Formosa that they had importance. They differed in this respect from the Pescadores in that the latter had always been connected geopolitically with Formosa, just as the geographic and historic connection of the off-shore islands was with the mainland.

The questions raised early in 1955, when the People's Government renewed its attacks on these off-shore islands, was whether the American commitment to the National Government would be construed to include defense of the Tachens and the others. Support of the National Government in their defense could readily be construed as involving the United States in the struggle for power in China rather than involving it solely in the defense of Formosa against Communist attack in spite of the commitment secured from Chiang's government not to attack the mainland without securing the prior approval of the United States. The threat of attack on the Tachens, Quemoy, and Matsu, consequently, could be viewed as the inevitable preliminary to an attack on Formosa or as an attempt to find out finally where the precise limitations lay within which the United States would act in support of the Nationalists.

As the threat of attack increased, Washington took the position that the prospect of peace would be increased rather than lessened if the administration made clear the intention of the United States to use its military power in defense of Formosa and the Pescadores. This was done through augmentation of naval and air forces in the area and the territories involved, and through the enactment of a joint resolution presented to the Congress by the administration authorizing the President to take any steps necessary for the defense of Formosa, including the Pescadores. At the same time, naval forces were deployed for the purpose of facilitating the evacuation of the Tachens if the decision should be taken by the National Government to withdraw from them.

This decision was taken and the United States stood guard over the evacuation. A similar decision, however, was not taken with respect to Quemoy and Matsu, which have a more important relationship than the Tachens both to the mainland and to Formosa. Those islands the National Government apparently proposed to defend, a decision in which the United States appeared to have acquiesced. If attacked, it was apparently American policy not to assist in their defense unless the attack was staged in such force as to indicate an intention to extend the operation to Formosa. In that case the indication at the end of May, 1955 was that the United States would assist the National Government in their defense as part of the defense of Formosa. President Eisenhower accepted the responsibility for exercising personal judgment as to whether the attack on these off-shore islands was actually directed against Formosa.

While this question of the off-shore islands was being raised, the United States at the same time made it clear that it would not oppose an attempt on the part of the United Nations to bring about a cease-fire between the Communists and the Nationalists. Under the circumstances, it seemed apparent that this could be accomplished only through acquiescence in the Communist claim to control of the off-shore islands. If accomplished, even "without prejudice" to the claims of the National Government and the Communists with respect to the government of China, a cease-fire would presumably remove a principal threat to international peace and security for the immediate future.

Without agreement on the conditions of a cease-fire—which would maintain the two China's—the prospect of war between the United States and China remained, since, in the defense of Formosa in the event of attack, the United States might readily find it expedient to attack concentrations of shipping and of troops on the mainland if these were clearly made for the purpose of subjugation of Formosa. If the attack were launched, the United States forces would presumably operate against military installations on the mainland. Judging by the reaction to the experience of the Korean war, such action would, if undertaken, find widespread support in the United States. If this had occurred, rather than the defense of Formosa being confined to the actual re-pelling of an assault, a general war might well have been the outcome. At the moment, the possibility of such action being taken against main-land China in the event of an attack on Formosa was advanced as a threat or a method of adding to the assurance that peace would be pre-served by Communist China itself because of the probable consequences of an attempt to establish Communist control over a territory which had not been part of China between 1895 and 1945.

This particular issue was only one in the complex of issues in the relations of the Communist and the anti-Communist states which pre-sented a serious threat to world peace in the spring of 1955. Wrapped around the whole was the threat and the possibility of atomic war and resulting general destruction. To lessen this possibility through a lessen-ing of international tensions, the heads of state of the United States, the Soviet Union, Britain, and France met at Geneva in midsummer of 1955.

While this "conference at the Summit" failed to solve any of the problems which produced the tensions it did sufficiently change the international climate of opinion so that it became possible to undertake new explorations of old world problems such as that of disarmament with some prospect of agreement. In the new atmosphere, also, it was possible to institute diplomatic conversations between the United States and the Communist People's Government of the People's Republic of China over the question of release of Americans still held prisoner in China. These conversations were designed as a preliminary to negotia-tions over other larger political questions at issue between the United States and Communist China. The protraction of negotiations over a question which, as China itself showed initially, could have been given a quick answer, prevented an enlargement of the area of discussion and movement toward agreement on some of the other issues which pre-vented the consideration of normalization of the relations of the two countries. Consequently, while agreement was reached, and the agree-ment was gradually implemented, on the release of Americans, both military and civilian, held prisoner in China, the end of 1955 left inter-national relations in the Far East substantially unchanged after the conference at "the Summit." The general atmosphere was somewhat less tense but the positions of the United States and of Communist China remained substantially unchanged, as did also the interests and policies of other participants in the politics of the Far East.

Index

477